CONTRASTS IN BEHAVIOR

About the editors

ERNST S. REESE is Professor of Zoology at the University of Hawaii as well as Senior Researcher at the university's Institute of Marine Biology. Dr. Reese is also the Director of the Mid-Pacific Marine Laboratory. He received his Ph.D. degree in zoology from the University of California, Los Angeles. Dr. Reese is Past President, and currently a Fellow of, the Animal Behavior Society. He was also a U.S. Delegate to the International Ethological Conference Committee, 1971-77.

FREDERICK J. LIGHTER is a Lecturer at the University of Hawaii as well as the Volunteer Coordinator for the Honolulu Zoo. Dr. Lighter received his Ph.D. degree in zoology from the University of Hawaii. He is a member of the American Association for the Advancement of Science, the American Society of Zoologists, the Animal Behavior Society, and the Ecological Society of America. Dr. Lighter was a delegate to the International Ethological Conference in 1973.

CONTRASTS IN BEHAVIOR
Adaptations in the Aquatic and Terrestrial Environments

Edited by

ERNST S. REESE

FREDERICK J. LIGHTER

University of Hawaii
Honolulu, Hawaii

A Wiley-Interscience Publication
JOHN WILEY & SONS
New York • Chichester • Brisbane • Toronto

Library of Congress Cataloging in Publication Data:

Main entry under title:

Contrasts in behavior.

 "A Wiley-Interscience publication."
 Includes indexes.
 1. Animals, Habits and behavior of. 2. Fishes
—Behavior. I. Reese, Ernst S., 1931–
II. Lighter, Frederick J.

QL751.C67   596'.05   78-8284
ISBN 0-471-71390-2

Printed in the United States of America

10 9 8 7 6 5 4 3 2 1

PREFACE

The purpose of this collection of papers is to instill in the reader an appreciation of the insights that a broad comparative perspective can provide in his own area of research interest. Indeed, the starting premise of the book is the thesis that the comparative method is one of the most fruitful approaches in biology.

All organisms are confronted with problems related to survival and reproduction. In the living animal, the adaptive solutions to these problems—solutions that usually synthesize behavioral, morphological, and physiological adaptations—may occur together in space and time. In scientific research however, reasons of practicality often dictate separate treatment of the different problem areas and their solutions.

So it is in this volume. As the table of contents indicates, the book is organized around four broad problem areas. First, the problem of reproductive behavior is examined from three points of view: parental care, lekking behavior, and the evolution of hermaphroditism and unisexuality. Next, communicative and regulatory behavior are explored in chapters dealing with the origin of lateral displays, temporal patterning in acoustical signals, and the maintenance of stability in body temperature. The third problem area is feeding behavior. Aggregation is discussed as a solution to predation, and a broad comparison is made of feeding behavior in two tropical environments. In the final section, four chapters are addressed to aspects of social behavior. In the first of these, the implications of carnivorous behavior for social organization are explored. Next, agonistic behavior and its potential influence on social systems are discussed. The last two chapters involve an analysis of the social behavior of coral reef fish in comparison with other vertebrates. Although these subjects are arbitrary, based as they are on the authors' research interests, they do represent a wide spectrum of behavioral adaptive processes.

There are four unifying themes to the book. First, all the authors are actively engaged in research on aquatic vertebrates, especially fish. Only Chapter 9 deals with marine mammals. Thus, the material in each chapter dealing with aquatic animals is based on the author's own research and on his or her extensive knowledge of the related primary literature.

The second unifying theme follows from the first and is based on the following question: Is it possible to make valid and meaningful comparisons using largely the secondary, review literature? This is an important question because the primary literature in many fields is now so overwhelming that it is extremely difficult and time consuming for an active researcher to stay abreast of it in fields of endeavour other than his own. For example, a biologist interested in the social behavior and community structure of fish should be aware of what is known about birds. Yet the literature dealing with birds is very extensive. The question is: Will a secondary source such as Cody's (1974) book entitled *Bird Communities* provide sufficient details to allow the fish biologist to make perceptive comparisons, or will the book serve only to introduce him to what Cody sees as the key papers in the primary literature, papers to which he must then turn? Each author has attempted to answer this question operationally by contrasting and comparing his own research with information found in the literature on other animals.

The third unifying theme in this volume is the tenet of the contributors, reflected in each chapter, that the comparative method, combined with experimentation, is the most effective tool in biology. Accurate descriptions and predictions of behavior based on precise and meticulous attention to critical details provide insights into a range of behavioral phenomena and promote the formulation of hypotheses that can be tested experimentally. In this way science advances progressively, in a series of steps.

In seeking to emphasize the importance and fruitfulness of the comparative approach, we have made our comparisons between the aquatic and terrestrial environments. This is a juxtaposition of the two most extreme situations, but insights into adaptive behavioral processes can be gained equally well if comparisons are made across intermediate environmental settings. The initial premise is that all animals share a common set of problems: where to live, how to get enough to eat, how to avoid predators and overcome competitors, how to select the best mate, where to reproduce most successfully, and so forth. What we are interested in comparing are the adaptive solutions to these common problems in different species in similar environments, and in the same or closely related species in different environments.

What are the "principles" of animal behavior? One way to seek answers to this question is to compare the adaptive behavioral responses of a wide variety of animals in different environmental settings but under similar selection pressures. Where multiple solutions have evolved in responses to the same common problem, hence the same selection pressure, no unifying behavioral principle is involved. In contrast, however, is the situation where the same behavioral adaptation has evolved time and again in different species, in different as well as in similar environments, in response to the same selection pressure. Then one has a valid criterion for asserting that the particular solution is, indeed, a principle of animal behavior. For example, territoriality occurs repeatedly as a solution to the problems of determining how to get sufficient food and of where and how to reproduce most successfully. It may be concluded that territoriality is a principle of behavior related to the use of space.

The fourth and final unifying theme to the book is the ambitious hope that it will stimulate careful and critical application of the comparative method to a wide spectrum of behavioral phenomena across broad phyletic and environmental lines, and thereby provide insights into a better understanding of the principles of animal behavior.

We acknowledge with gratitude the interest and competent assistance of Ms. Lori Yamamura and the encouragement of Ms. Ilze Reese.

ERNST S. REESE
FREDERICK J. LIGHTER

Honolulu, Hawaii
July 1978

CONTENTS

CONTENTS

CONTENTS

CONTRASTS IN BEHAVIOR

Part I

REPRODUCTIVE BEHAVIOR

1

PARENTAL CARE BEHAVIOR IN FISHES AND BIRDS

MILES H. A. KEENLEYSIDE

Department of Zoology
University of Western Ontario
London, Ontario, Canada

1   INTRODUCTION

Parental care behavior is any behavior, performed after breeding, by one or both parents, that contributes to the survival of their offspring. For this Chapter, I exclude from the definition cases in which newly fertilized eggs are covered by the parents and then deserted. Such egg-covering behavior, which is found among some salmonids, lampreys, and cyprinids, for example, clearly protects the offspring from some environmental hazards and thus promotes their survival; but for the following discussion I shall restrict the term parental behavior to the *active care and protection of the offspring* by one or both parents. Also excluded by this definition are viviparous species (e.g., many cyprinodontoids) in which fertilization is internal and the females give birth to mobile young.

Parental behavior among vertebrates ranges from little or no care in most poikilotherms to intensive and prolonged care of the young in many birds and mammals. In this chapter as a contribution to the main theme of the volume, I shall first decribe some recent work from our laboratory on parental behavior in fishes and then compare the phenomenon of parental care as it occurs among fishes and birds. I hope that such a comparison will contribute to a greater understanding of the origin and phylogenetic development of a type of social interaction that plays a critical role in the early life of many animals.

Parental behavior is by no means universal among fishes. Of some 250 families described in Breder and Rosen's (1966) encyclopedic treatise on fish reproduction, about 77% show no parental care, another 17% include species that care for the eggs only, and less than 6% contain species that are known to care for both eggs and newly hatched young. However, within this latter group are some large and diverse families, including the Cichlidae, that are a major component of the freshwater fish fauna of Central and South America and of Africa.

Two general types of variation in parental behavior exist among cichlids. First, either both parents, or one alone cares for the offspring. Thus there are paternal, maternal and biparental species (Fryer and Iles, 1972). Second, the eggs and newly hatched young are either maintained on the substrate—that is, on plants, under stones, in excavated pits, and so on (these are usually called substrate-brooders or guarders)—or carried about in the parent's mouth (the mouth-brooders or oral incubators). Wickler (1966) has suggested that "open brooders" and "concealed brooders" are more accurate labels for the two main cichlid parental strategies, because some substrate-brooding species guard their eggs and fry in caves or burrows ("concealed" broods), where the degree of protection afforded the young is closer to that of mouth-brooders than to the substrate-brooders that guard their young in the open. In fact, as will be discussed below, some cichlid species use both strategies, first guarding their eggs on the substrate, then carrying the newly hatched offspring in the mouth. Certain difficulties in applying Wickler's terminology are discussed by Barlow (1974), and I shall continue to use the traditional labels—that is, substrate- and mouth-brooders.

2 MALE-FEMALE PARENTAL ROLES

In some biparental cichlid species there appears to be an unequal division of parental duties between male and female. Most of these species are substrate-brooders, and the differentiation between maternal and paternal roles is most pronounced when their offspring are at the egg stage. Typically, the female performs more of the direct egg-care behavior, and the male is the more active defender of the brood against potential predators (Baerends and Baerends-van Roon, 1950; Fryer and Iles, 1972; Barlow, 1974). Quantitative data related to these generalizations are, however, available for only a few species. Some examples follow.

Chien and Salmon (1972) found some differences in parental activities between male and female *Pterophyllum scalare*. The number of bouts of egg-fanning and the total time spent fanning were both greater in females than males on the first day postspawning, but these differences disappeared on days two and three. Egg-nipping and several activities directed at wrigglers (the developmental phase between hatching and free-swimming) and at fry (free-swimming juveniles) did not differ between parents.

In a study of parental behavior in *Tilapia mariae*, the females performed more egg-aerating bouts than did the males, but males did more "calling-the-young," an activity in which the pelvic, anal, caudal, and dorsal fins are repeatedly snapped open and shut, stimulating the fry to congregate below the signaling parent (Baldaccini, 1973). On the other hand, parental *Etroplus maculatus* also signal their young by pelvic fin-flickering, and Cole and Ward (1969) found that males and females did not differ in their fin-flickering rates, nor in the time spent with the school of young up to 12 days posthatching.

Female convict cichlids (*Cichlasoma nigrofasciatum*) performed more "fin-digging" than males did while guarding 12 to 30 day old fry (Krischik and Weber, 1974).In this behavior the adult fish settles to the bottom and, with vigorous undulations of the body and fins, stirs up loose substrate materials that stimulate the fry to congregate around the parent and feed on the loosened particles. These authors also found that male and female parents were equally aggressive in defense of their broods.

Two studies of cichlid behavior recently completed in our laboratory yielded quantitative data comparing male and female parental roles. These data are briefly reviewed here.

2.1   Male-Female Roles in *Herotilapia multispinosa*

Patricia Smith-Grayton studied the Central American, biparental, substrate-brooding cichlid *Herotilapia multispinosa* (Smith-Grayton and Keenleyside, 1978). In this work she made a detailed quantitative comparison of the behavior of males and females while guarding their young. Data were collected during 15 breeding cycles, from spawning until 11 days postspawning. The following results are pertinent to the question of male-female parental roles.

2.1.1   Fanning, Rocking, and Hovering

These are three types of behavior performed while the adult fish remains close to the offpsring. Fanning is the well-known aeration activity in which the adult maintains position 2 to 3 cm from the eggs or wrigglers and with large-amplitude, low-frequency beats of the pectoral fins moves water over the young. Simultaneous lateral undulations of the caudal fin prevent backward movement of the fish while fanning. This motor pattern is found among many egg-tending species and probably serves to ventilate and clean the eggs and young by providing oxygen-rich water and removing metabolic wastes and silt (Baerends and Baerends-van Roon, 1950; van Iersel, 1953). Female *H. multispinosa* performed more frequent bouts of fanning of the eggs than males did, but both sexes fanned the wrigglers equally often (Fig. 1.1). When measured as total duration of time spent fanning (Fig. 1.2), the mean value for females was higher than for males during the egg stage, but the difference was not statistically significant; the duration of fanning the wrigglers was almost identical in the two sexes.

Rocking is a parental activity directed only at the eggs and presumably serves ventilating and cleaning functions. In this pattern the adult fish remains close to the eggs and rhythmically pitches in the vertical plane while moving slowly about over the spawn. Brief contact is often made

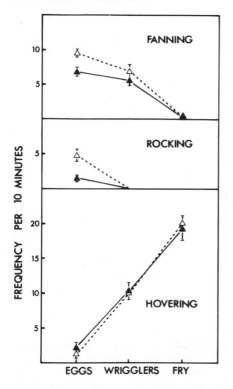

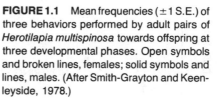

FIGURE 1.1   Mean frequencies (±1 S.E.) of three behaviors performed by adult pairs of *Herotilapia multispinosa* towards offspring at three developmental phases. Open symbols and broken lines, females; solid symbols and lines, males. (After Smith-Grayton and Keenleyside, 1978.)

with the eggs. The pectoral fins flutter with higher speed and smaller amplitude than in fanning. Females performed more bouts of rocking than males did (Fig. 1.1), but, as with fanning, the total time spent in rocking by the two sexes was not different (Fig. 1.2).

Hovering is a pattern in which the adult fish stations itself virtually motionless 3 to 4 cm above or beside the eggs, wrigglers, or fry, and with the longitudinal body axis parallel to the aquarium substrate. Fin and body movements are slight, and they apparently serve only to maintain position. Hovering is often performed when the fish is resting between bouts of other activities. Both male and female parents showed increased hovering behavior as their progeny developed from eggs to fry, and the only consistent difference between the sexes was at the egg stage, when males spent more total time hovering than females did (Figs. 1.1 and 1.2).

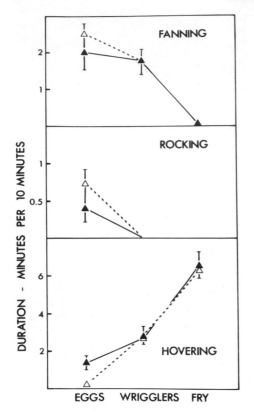

FIGURE 1.2 Mean duration (± 1 S.E.) of bouts of three behaviors performed by parental *H. multispinosa*. Symbols as in Fig. 1.1. (After Smith-Grayton and Keenleyside, 1978.)

2.1.2 Mouth-Contact Behavior

Three activities in which the parents contact their young with the mouth were also quantified.

MOUTHING THE YOUNG.   This includes gentle sucking at the eggs and picking up of wrigglers and immediately spitting them back onto the substrate. It appears to be primarily a cleaning action. Fungused or opaque (and presumably dead) eggs are removed from the substrate and eaten, and silt or debris is removed from eggs and wrigglers. Mouthing may also aid in the hatching process. The only consistent difference between sexes in this activity was that females mouthed the wrigglers more often than males did, although the eggs also tended to be mouthed more often by females than by males (Fig. 1.3).

SPITTING WRIGGLERS. This occurs when one or more wrigglers becomes separated from the others in a pit or when it drops from a plant (where newly hatched wrigglers are often placed, and from which they hang suspended by mucous threads from the head). The adult fish gently picks up the stray wriggler in its mouth and spits it back with the others. Both parents performed it equally often (Fig. 1.3).

RETRIEVING FRY. This was recorded when one or more fry had moved a short distance (usually more than 10 cm) from the main school

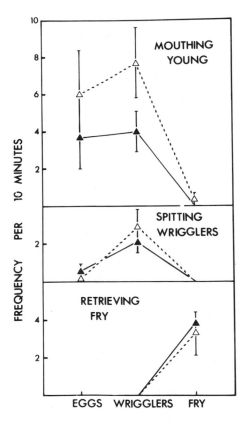

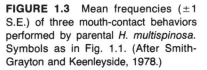

FIGURE 1.3 Mean frequencies (±1 S.E.) of three mouth-contact behaviors performed by parental *H. multispinosa*. Symbols as in Fig. 1.1. (After Smith-Grayton and Keenleyside, 1978.)

of fry, and then was snapped up in the mouth by one of the parents and spit back into the school. There was no difference between parents in the frequency of retrieving fry (Fig. 1.3).

2.1.3 Digging

This is the behavior by which adult *H. multispinosa* excavate pits for the retention of wrigglers. The fish thrusts its snout into the substrate, takes up a mouthful of gravel, moves up to 10 cm away and spits it out. Digging occurs frequently as the eggs approach hatching, but continues after hatching, since the wrigglers are usually moved about from one pit to another. The only sex difference in digging was that females performed it more often than males did when their progeny were at the wriggler stage (Fig. 1.4).

2.1.4 Chasing

This was recorded whenever one parent pursued a fish other than its partner away from the vicinity of the offspring. Duration of chasing was highly variable, because the pursued fish could not escape from the aquarium and the number of hiding locations was limited. A chase of any duration was recorded as one event. Figure 1.4 shows that both parents chased other fish away from their brood, and the only quantitative difference between sexes was at the egg stage, when males chased more often than females did.

2.1.5 Feeding

Feeding movements were recorded, not because these are forms of parental behaviors, but because they are a clearly functional activity that can be performed only when the adult fish is not engaged in one of the parental care actions. As Fig. 1.4 shows, feeding was relatively infrequent during the egg stage and increased as the progeny developed. This coincided with declines in several of the parental behaviors, such as fanning, rocking, mouthing young, and digging, and it presumably indicated that as the progeny developed, the parents were able to spend more time with their own maintenance activities, of which feeding must be of prime importance. No clear sex difference in feeding frequency was recorded.

In summarizing the main results of this study, both male and female *H. multispinosa* performed all of the species-typical parental activities;

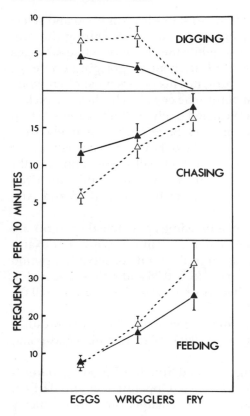

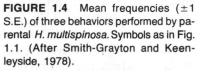

FIGURE 1.4 Mean frequencies (±1 S.E.) of three behaviors performed by parental *H. multispinosa.* Symbols as in Fig. 1.1. (After Smith-Grayton and Keenleyside, 1978).

that is, none was sex-specific. And yet quantitative differences between the sexes were found for some forms of parental behavior. These differences support the generalization of other workers that among biparental, substrate-brooding cichlid fishes, there is some separation of parental roles, with the female being more involved in direct care-of-the-young activities and the male more concerned with defense of the brood. The differences between the parents were most pronounced when the young were at the egg stage, and they disappeared as the young became free-swimming fry.

2.2 Male-Female Roles in *Aequidens paraguayensis*

A second study of parental behavior concerned the biparental South American cichlid *Aequidens paraguayensis* (Timms and Keenleyside, 1975).

In this species, a mature male and female establish a pair bond and select as a spawning site a loose leaf lying on the substrate. During the pre-spawning courtship period, and also while the clutch of 200 to 400 eggs is being guarded, the pair move the leaf about by grasping one edge with the mouth and pulling or pushing it. This occurs most often when the fish have been disturbed. Just before the eggs hatch, they are picked off the leaf, and the young fish are carried orally by both parents for up to several weeks, although once the fry have become actively free-swimming, they enter the parents' mouths only when disturbed and at night. Thus *A. paraguayensis* adults use both substrate- and mouth-brooding as parental care strategies. Only a few other South American cichlids are known to practise both types of brooding (Reid and Atz, 1958; Breder and Rosen, 1966).

During the egg-guarding phase of a breeding cycle, female parents are more involved with direct egg-care activities than males are. For example, the mean time spent *fanning eggs* per 10 minute observation period was 7.15 min for ♀♀ and 3.34 min for ♂♂ (S.D. 0.28 and 0.40 respectively). In 9 of 10 pairs the difference between sexes was significant ($p < 0.05$; paired-sample t-test).

Also, females *mouthed the eggs* more frequently than males did: ♀ mean, 19.0/min; ♂ mean, 1.7/min; ($p < 0.05$; Wilcoxon matched-pairs, signed-ranks test).

During oral incubation of wrigglers and fry, the brooding parents regularly perform an activity called *churning* (Oppenheimer and Barlow, 1968), in which the entire buccal cavity is enlarged and then quickly decreased in size. This is performed in bouts of from one to several distinct churns, and, although several functions have been ascribed to this activity in other mouth-brooding cichlids, it appears that ventilation of the young is the most likely function in *A. paraguayensis* (Timms and Keenleyside, 1975). Our observations, based on 10 pairs, showed that incubating males churned the brood more often than females did: (a) churns/min: ♂ mean, 26.2; ♀ mean, 17.4; (b) churns/bout: ♂ mean, 5.58; ♀ mean 3.57 ($p < 0.05$ in both cases; Wilcoxon matched-pairs, signed-ranks tests).

A more detailed examination of our churning records showed that churning activity by both sexes declined as the progeny developed, but the decline was steeper for males than for females (Fig. 1.5). The data fit two linear regression lines with negative slopes that are significantly different from each other (Timms and Keenleyside, 1975).

Thus, *A. paraguayensis* is another biparental cichlid showing some division of labor between the parents. The greater egg-care activity by the

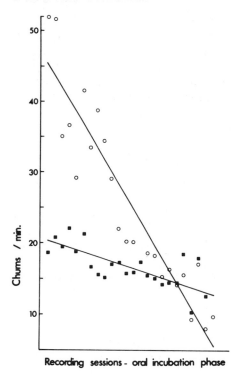

Recording sessions - oral incubation phase

FIGURE 1.5 Churning rates for male (open symbols) and female (solid symbols) *Aequidens paraguayensis.* Data from 10 pairs, adjusted so that each point represents pooled data for same elapsed time since eggs were picked off substrate. (After Timms and Keenleyside, 1975.)

female corresponds with results from the substrate-brooding *H. multispinosa.* The differential churning behavior is not yet clearly understood. Among our breeding pairs, males were slightly larger than females, and possibly this resulted in the males carrying a larger proportion of the brood, which in turn may have stimulated more frequent churning activity on the part of the males.

Oral transport of the progeny is common among African cichlids, where many of the Great Lakes species are maternal mouth-brooders, the female carrying the brood from immediately after spawning until they are several weeks old (Fryer and Iles, 1972). Among New World cichlids, only a few species within the genera *Aequidens* and *Geophagus* are known to carry their young orally. The others are either typical substrate-brooders, or their parental care strategies are unknown (Breder and Rosen, 1966). Little has been published about the ecological conditions associated with oral brooding in New World cichlids, although several mouth-brooding *Geophagus* species are said to occur in the main channels of streams over sandy substrate, sometimes littered with detritus, through which they forage for food (P. Loiselle, personal communication). *A. paraguayensis* occurs in the Rio Paraguay watershed, much of which is shallow, swampy, and subject to rapid changes in water level (Pearson, 1937). Many South American fish breed under such conditions (Lowe-McConnell, 1964), and it is possible that the choice of a movable leaf as spawning substrate and the oral brooding of recently hatched young are adaptations functioning not only to reduce predation on the offspring, but also to reduce mortality associated with rapid rising or falling water levels (Barlow, 1974; Timms and Keenleyside, 1975).

3 ONE-PARENT REMOVAL STUDIES

The studies on *H. multispinosa* and *A. paraguayensis* described above showed that all of the species-typical parental behavior patterns were performed by both members of breeding pairs. Some quantitative differences existed between the sexes, but none of the parental patterns was specific to one sex. This lack of pattern specificity suggested that the parental roles of males and females in these two species are virtually interchangeable, and led me to an investigation of the ability of a single parent to rear a brood of young successfully after the loss of the other parent.

Two questions formed the basis of this study. First, is one parent more successful than the other in raising a brood alone? Second, does the developmental stage of the progeny at which one parent is lost influence their subsequent survival? These are not likely to be trivial problems. The fish fauna of much of Latin America is rich and varied. Potential predators of smaller, biparental cichlid species are numerous, and the ability of one parent to defend its brood even if its mate has been lost would appear to be a real advantage.

H. multispinosa was chosen as the test species because it breeds readily in captivity, and its small size at maturity increases the probability that in nature an adult fish may occasionally be lost to predation while raising a brood. Adult males used in the study ranged from 7.7 to 11.5 cm total length (mean, 8.98 cm). Females ranged from 6.5 to 10.0 cm total length (mean, 7.87 cm; *n* for each sex, 132).

The experimental technique was to allow a pair of *H. multispinosa* to spawn, next to place potential predators in the same aquarium, and then to remove either the male or the female parent when the young had reached one of the following developmental periods: the beginning of the embryonic period as soon as spawning was complete; the beginning of the wriggler phase, when all eggs had hatched; and the point at which all wrigglers had first become free-swimming fry. The experimental variables—that is, the sex of parent removed, and the developmental phase of young when one parent was removed—were randomized among experimental pairs. Five replications of each treatment and of control tests were run in each of four separate experiments. The species and number of predators present, and other detailed features of the experimental designs, are described below for each of the four experiments. The number of different pairs of fish used in Experiments 1 to 4 was 8, 6, 10, and 10 respectively.

The data collected were the *number of fry surviving* at the end of the experimental period (15 or 12 days after spawning), and the *termination day* for each replicate. The termination day was either 15 or 12 days after spawning (if any fry at all were still alive at the end of the experimental period), or the day by which all progeny had disappeared.

The physical arrangement of the test apparatus was the same for all four experiments. Aquaria were 90 × 35 × 30 cm high, with a 3 to 4 cm deep layer of gravel, several plastic plants, and one flower pot. Photoperiod was from 0800 to 2000 hours, with a half hour of "dawn" and "dusk" provided by a 100 W bulb in the room before and after the photoperiod. Water temperature was 28° ± 1°C. Under these conditions the eggs hatched approximately 48 hours after spawning, and the wrigglers became free-swimming fry about 72 hours after hatching.

Two male and two female adult *H. multispinosa* were placed in each aquarium to provide some choice of breeding partners. When a pair was clearly preparing to spawn, the other two fish were removed. After spawning, the eggs were photographed and counted on enlarged prints. Separate tests were made of the accuracy of this method: eggs were photographed in the standard manner, then the flower pot was removed and the eggs were counted directly. The mean error, based on 10 such tests, was 3.5%; this was ignored in the later determination of fry survival. Estimated spawn size for the four experiments together ranged from 284 to 1612 eggs (mean, 787.3; $n = 145$).

3.1 Experiment 1

In this experiment eight treatments were applied: either the male or the female parent removed, at each of the three developmental phases; plus two controls, one with and one without predators present. Two male

Cichlasoma nigrofasciatum were used as predators. The predators ranged in total length from 5.8 to 10.0 cm (mean, 8.20 cm; *n,* 64). In captivity this is an omnivorous species that feeds readily on juvenile cichlids. Its natural range overlaps with that of *H. multispinosa* (Miller, 1966), although the two species do not appear to be sympatric when breeding (Baylis, 1974).

The mean percent survival of fry under all experimental treatments was low, and no clear differences were found among treatments (Fig. 1.6). The two control treatments resulted in high survival, and the control without predators had the highest survival of all, although there was great variability in both control series.

When the data are presented as mean number of days to termination (Fig. 1.7), the differences between treatments were more pronounced, although the small sample sizes and high variability within treatments resulted in a lack of statistical significance in these differences. In all cases, some of the progeny survived longer when the male parent was removed than when the female parent was removed. That is, the female parent alone appeared to be somewhat better able to protect the progeny from predation than did the male parent alone. This sex difference was most pronounced when parental removal occurred at the beginning of the egg and the fry phases. Also, the termination time tended to increase as the one-parent removal occurred later in the development of the young. This increase was not simply a function of increased duration of protection of the brood by two parents. In several replicates of the

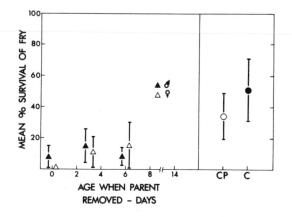

FIGURE 1.6   Mean percent survival (±1 S.E.) of *H. multispinosa* fry by 15 days of age in Experiment 1. Either male or female parent was removed at beginning of egg, wriggler, or fry stage. CP, control series with predators present; C, control with no predators. Predator species, *Cichlasoma nigrofasciatum.*

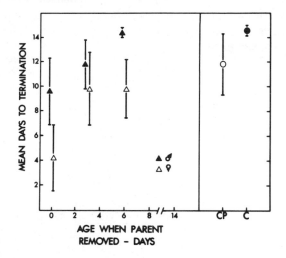

FIGURE 1.7 Mean number of days (±1 S.E.) to termination of trials in Experiment 1. Symbols as in Fig. 1.6.

removal-after-spawning treatment, all eggs were eaten within one day of parental removal. That is, predation did not generally occur at a uniform rate throughout the tests, but it was most pronounced at certain stages. This observation led to the design of Experiment 3 (see below).

3.2 Experiment 2

The object of this experiment was to measure the survival of uniparental broods in the presence of two different predator densities. The treatment consisted of removing one parent immediately after spawning was completed and then introducing either two or four predators. Controls consisted of leaving both parents with their brood in the presence of two or four predators. The predator was *C. managuense*, a cichlid whose range is the Great Lakes of Nicaragua and the Atlantic slopes of Costa Rica (Miller, 1966); it is thus sympatric with *H. multispinosa* (Baylis, 1974). It is mainly carnivorous and is a likely natural predator of our study species. *C. managuense* used as predators were juveniles that ranged in total length from 2.3 to 6.8 cm (mean, 4.30; $n = 90$).

The effects of this experimental treatment were clear. The percent survival of progeny on the terminaton date (15 days postspawning) was zero in 18 of 20 trials in which one parent was removed. Survival was

TABLE 1.1 Mean percent survival of *H. multispinosa* offspring 15 days post-spawning, with juvenile *C. managuense* as predators. Single parent was removed after completion of spawning

Treatment	Mean Percent Fry Survival	Standard Error
2 predators		
♂ removal	2.40	2.40
♀ removal	0	0
4 predators		
♂ removal	0.46	0.46
♀ removal	0	0
Control		
2 predators	28.58	8.92
4 predators	10.20	6.25

somewhat higher in the controls, and highest in the control with two predators (Table 1.1).

When the data are presented as mean days to termination (Fig. 1.8), broods with the male parent removed survived longer than those with the female parent removed, especially when only two predators were present. Thus, female *H. multispinosa* again appeared to be more successful than males as single parents. Both control treatments had longer

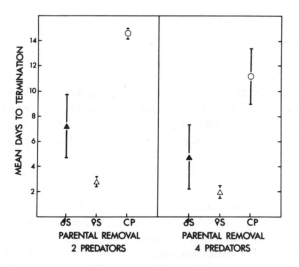

FIGURE 1.8 Mean number of days (±1 S.E.) to termination of trials in Experiment 2. Symbols as in Fig. 1.6. Predator species *C. managuense*.

survival times, and survival was longest and least variable in the presence of two predators.

3.3 Experiment 3

Under the conditions of Experiments 1 and 2, adult *H. multispinosa* were occasionally seen eating their own progeny. This occurred primarily in two situations. First, when one parent was removed immediately after spawning, the remaining parent occasionally began eating the eggs rather than caring for them in the usual way. Usually the predators joined in when parental egg predation began. Second, as the fry developed, they became more active, and the tight school formation that is typical of newly free-swimming fry became looser. The parents typically retrieved individual fry that strayed from the school and spit them back into the group. Toward the end of the 15-day experimental period, one or both parents occasionally ate, rather than retrieved, the dispersed fry. The first of the two observations suggested that removal of one parent was in some cases so disturbing to the remaining parent that its normal parental activities were seriously disrupted. In addition, the presence of potential predators of another species may have increased the level of disturbance of the single parent.

Experiment 3 was designed to test these possibilities. The treatment schedule was identical to that of Experiment 1, except that no potential predators were present. In only one of 35 trials were all progeny eaten

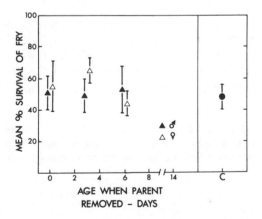

FIGURE 1.9 Mean percent survival (±1 S.E.) of *H. multispinosa* fry by 15 days of age in Experiment 3. Symbols as in Fig. 1.6. No predators present in any treatments.

before reaching the age of 15 days. The mean percent survival of fry across treatments is shown in Fig. 1.9. It is clear that one-parent removal, without the presence of other potential predators, did not result in lowered survival of the progeny. This strongly suggests that the cannibalism occasionally seen in the earlier experiments was related to disturbance caused by the combination of one-parent removal and the presence of predators.

3.4 Experiment 4

H. multispinosa are known to breed in shallow, weedy ponds close to the Rio Frio, Costa Rica. These ponds are flooded during the rainy season, but become separated from the river as water levels decline in the dry season. Breeding occurs during the dry season, at the end of which the ponds contain large numbers of adult and juvenile *H. multispinosa* (Baylis, 1974). Thus, it is possible that juveniles are important predators of the eggs, wrigglers, and fry of their own species in this habitat. Experiment 4 was designed to measure the ability of single-brooding *H. multispinosa* to protect their offspring against predation by juvenile conspecifics.

The experimental design was identical to that of Experiment 1, except that two young *H. multispinosa* were present as predators, and the maximum time allowed for each trial was reduced from 15 to 12 days, because the fry schools began to disperse by age 10 to 12 days, and the aim was to measure predation before this dispersion was pronounced. Potential predators ranged in total length from 4.3 to 6.8 cm (mean, 5.56; $n = 80$).

Under all experimental treatments, the survival of fry was below 20%; under the two control conditions survival was higher, and especially so in the control without predators (Fig. 1.10). In the latter case, mean percent survival from egg to termination was similar to that in the two comparable controls from Experiments 1 and 3 (Table 1.2). Although

TABLE 1.2 Comparison of percent survival of progeny (number of fry surviving at end of experiment as a proportion of number of eggs laid) in the control series of three experiments. In each case both parents and no predators were present

Experiment No.	Duration of Experiment (days)	Mean Percent Fry Survival	Standard Error
1	15	51.36	20.04
3	15	48.26	7.71
4	12	54.44	11.57

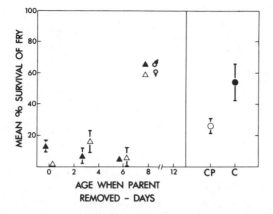

FIGURE 1.10   Mean percent survival (±1 S.E.) of *H. multispinosa* fry by 12 days of age in Experiment 4. Symbols as in Fig. 1.6. Predators were juvenile *H. multispinosa.*

there was considerable variation among replicates within each of these three control treatments, it appears that in the absence of other potential predators, approximately one half the eggs laid by *H. multispinosa* pairs survive until 12 or 15 days of age under these aquarium conditions.

Survival, measured as mean number of days to termination, varied considerably among the treatments of Experiment 4 (Fig. 1.11). It was greater following male-parent removal than female-parent removal for the postspawning and post-free-swimming removal treatments. This corresponds to the result of Experiment 1 (Fig. 1.7). But unlike Experi-

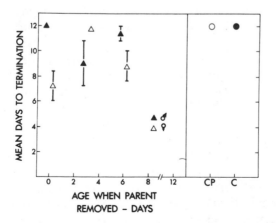

FIGURE 1.11   Mean number of days (±1 S.E.) to termination of trials in Experiment 4. Symbols as in Fig. 1.6.

ment 1, mean termination time in this experiment was greater following female-parent removal for the posthatching removal treatment.

3.5 Conclusions

The results of these four experiments suggest several inferences about the success of a single parent *H. multispinosa* in raising offspring to about 15 days of age.

First, a mated pair is more successful than either parent alone in the presence of potential predators. If no predators are present, however, either parent alone is just as successful as the pair together, and this holds true regardless of the developmental phase of the young at which one parent is removed (Fig. 1.9).

Second, in the presence of predators, loss of the male parent has somewhat less drastic effects on offspring survival than loss of the female parent. In spite of the fact that in an intact family unit the male performs more antipredator aggressive acts than the female does, at least when their offspring are at the egg stage (Fig. 1.4), if one member of the brooding pair is lost, the female seems better able than the male to combine the roles of direct care of the young (aerating, cleaning, moving) with defense against predators.

Third, in the presence of juveniles of a natural predator, *C. managuense*, the single *H. multispinosa* parent, whether male or female, is not a highly effective protector of its offspring (Fig. 1.8). Thus the success of a single parent in rearing a brood depends to some degree on the identity and number of predators present.

During these experiments, it became clear that the pair bond between mated male and female *H. multispinosa* was often unstable. In particular, the female was usually aggressive toward the male during the first day after spawning. This was also observed by Baylis (1974), although only when other *H. multispinosa* were present in the tank with a breeding pair. We observed some female aggression toward males during all our experiments. Figures 1.1, 1.2, and 1.3 clearly show that males were not prevented by female aggression from performing parental activities toward their eggs. However, it may be that postspawning aggression toward the male by his mate played a role in determining the ability of the single male parent to protect its young against predators. We noticed that when the treatment consisted of removal of the female directly after spawning, a male which had been prevented from approaching the eggs by a highly aggressive mate did not take over the full role of caring for and protecting the eggs for some time after female removal. Attacks on the eggs by the predators often occurred during that period.

The relationship between pair bond stability, intrapair aggression and effective defense of the young in *H. multispinosa* is currently under study in our laboratory.

4   COMPARISONS BETWEEN FISHES AND BIRDS

Parental care behavior is clearly more advanced among birds than among fishes. In general, the association between parent and offspring among birds is of longer duration and of a more direct and intimate nature. Despite the transport by some fishes of eggs in pouches, stalks, or skin folds, and by others of eggs and young held in the mouth (Marshall, 1965), the parent-offspring links in most of the fish species showing any parental behavior at all are generally looser and briefer than those of most birds. However, comparison of some particular aspects of parental behavior in these two large vertebrate classes indicates some interesting similarities as well as differences.

Four major functional aspects of avian parental behavior are: nest construction, incubation of eggs, feeding of the young, and protection of the young (Kendeigh, 1952; Kear, 1970). These features, and their counterparts in fishes, will be briefly discussed.

4.1   General Features of Parental Behavior

4.1.1   Nest Construction

Most bird species build nests—that is, structures in which the eggs are laid and then incubated. Some lay their eggs directly on sections of narrow rocky ledges or on patches of bare ground that have been scraped clean of vegetation and debris. Others make excavations in the ground or in trees, posts, and the like, while still others use existing excavations. In either case, the birds may or may not build nests inside such holes. A majority of species builds true nests, which range in complexity from simple collections of sticks to those requiring varying degrees of care and precision in the formation of the completed nest cup. Among the most elaborate are the nests of the weaverbirds (Ploceidae), which carefully weave plant materials together into nests of various shapes and sizes. An extreme form is the large colonial nest of the social weaver (*Philetairus socius*), which builds first a roof of coarse straws in a large tree and under this accumulates a large mass of woven plant materials with many individual nest chambers in it (Landsborough Thomson, 1964).

Among fishes, the extent and variation in nest-building is much more restricted. First of all, external fertilization, with simultaneous release of male and female gametes into the water, is the rule among fishes, and many species produce buoyant, pelagic eggs that are carried by the prevailing currents; these species do not make nests or provide any form of parental care. Among those with demersal eggs, some species (e.g., salmonids, lampreys, some cyprinids) dig excavations in gravel substrate, lay their eggs in the pits, cover them with gravel, and desert them. Other species (e.g., centrarchids, blenniids, some cichlids and pomacentrids) spawn in excavations they have made in the substrate, often under stones, sunken logs, and debris, or inside empty mollusc shells. At least the eggs, and sometimes also the newly hatched fish, are guarded in these locations.

Only a few fishes construct nests that are comparable in complexity to those of passerine birds. The best-known of these nest-building fish are the sticklebacks (Gasterosteidae). The male builds a spherical or elongate nest by collecting plant fragments, rootlets, and the like, and then binding them together with adhesive kidney secretions. The various probing, boring, sucking, and "glueing" activities of the male result in the formation of a compact nest with an internal chamber to receive the eggs. The most elaborate nest is made by *Apeltes quadracus*. With this species, a cup-shaped nest is attached to rooted plants close to the bottom. After a clutch of eggs is laid, the male builds an extension of the nest up and over the eggs, with a concave upper surface to the extension. A second clutch of eggs is laid on the new nest floor, and this procedure may be repeated several times, until the male has several clutches of eggs stacked vertically within a single multitiered nest (Rowland, 1974).

A number of other species build less complex nests of collected materials (Breder and Rosen, 1966). These are less tightly bound together than the stickleback nests and are usually placed under rocks or in dense vegetation. Presumably, in these locations they are protected against turbulent wave action, and the capacities of the parents to guard against predation are enhanced.

4.1.2 Incubation of Eggs

Incubation is defined as "the process by which the heat necessary for embryonic development is applied to an egg after it has been laid" (Landsborough Thomson, 1964). It is universal among birds, although some species do not incubate their own eggs directly. For example, some members of the Megapodiidae (such as the mallee-fowl of Australia) bury their eggs in mounds of vegetation, within which the heat from decaying plant material provides the incubation energy (Frith, 1956). Others, such as cuckoos (Cuculidae) and cowbirds (Icteridae), are brood-parasites, in that their eggs are laid in the nests of other species and are incubated by the foster parents.

Fish eggs are not maintained at temperatures above ambient, either by the parents or by surrounding substrate or nest materials, and hence no true incubation occurs. Even though some species maintain contact with their eggs by oral brooding (e.g., some cichlids), by wrapping the body around the eggs (some stichaeids and pholids, Marliave and De Martini, 1977), and of course by carrying them internally after copulation and internal fertilization (many cyprinodontoids), there is no evidence that these egg-tending behaviors influence the temperature of the eggs.

4.1.3   Feeding the Young

The chief avian methods of parental feeding of the young are: carrying food to the nest in the bill and placing it in the open mouth of the nestling; regurgitating food, which the juvenile picks up from the ground or from the parent's mouth and throat; and uncovering food items on the ground (by pecking or scratching), after which the juveniles pick it up for themselves.

Among fishes, there are no known direct counterparts to the first two of these methods, but there are two parental activities that appear to be analogous to the third. One of those is "fin-digging," described above in Section 2. The other is a form of plunge-feeding found among *Geophagus* species, in which the fish thrusts its snout vigorously into the substrate, withdraws it and expels the mouth contents. Loose particles may then be ingested, and if an adult *Geophagus* is foraging in this manner with a school of its progeny, the young fish also gather and feed on the expelled material (P. Loiselle, personal communication).

Another form of "feeding the young" also occurs among cichlids (e.g., *Symphysodon discus*, Hildemann, 1959; *Etroplus maculatus*, Ward and Barlow, 1967; *Cichlasoma citrinellum*, Noakes and Barlow, 1973). As the young reach the free-swimming fry stage of development, they begin to graze on the mucus on their parents' sides. Mucus-producing cells in the adults' epidermis are most numerous at this stage of the reproductive cycle, and it is clear that mucus is being ingested by the young fish. In fact, feeding from the parent's body can be induced in a number of cichlid species by depriving the fry of other food sources (Barlow, 1974). Similar parent-contacting behavior by juveniles occurs in the coral reef pomacentrid *Acanthochromis polyacanthus*, although no direct proof of mucus ingestion has been obtained (Robertson, 1973).

4.1.4 Protection of the Young

Here there are many similarities between birds and fishes, particularly in the use of overt aggression toward potential predators, and in the use of signals to stimulate the young to take evasive action. Visual displays, such as fin-flickering and body-jerking, performed by adults while guarding free-swimming fry, are often followed by the young fish settling and clumping more closely on the substrate. Acoustic warning signals may be produced by some species, although there is little supporting evidence for this as yet.

The specialized form of parental protective behavior known as "injury feigning" is common among shorebirds and waterfowl, where its chief function is probably to distract predators from eggs or juvenile birds (Kear, 1970). It does not appear to have a counter-part among fishes.

Probably the most efficient protective device used by fishes while guarding their young is oral brooding. This is common among cichlids (especially species of the African Great Lakes, Fryer and Iles, 1972), but it also occurs in other groups (Breder and Rosen, 1966; Oppenheimer, 1970). The only way a predator can capture young fish that are being carried in their parent's mouth is to injure or kill the parent, force it to jettison its brood, or wait until the parent releases its young voluntarily, then dash in and capture them. The best available evidence for this type of predation comes from several species of *Haplochromis* in Lake Victoria, which feed either exclusively or principally on the eggs and yolk-sac larvae of other cichlid fishes (Greenwood, 1974). The method these fish use to capture their food is uncertain because of the difficulty of observing them in the turbid waters of Lake Victoria.

4.2 More Specialized Features of Parental Behavior

There are several more specialized forms of avian parent-young interaction which according to present knowledge have no direct counterpart among fishes. These include long-term social bonding based on imprinting of the young on their parents, feeding of the female on the nest by the male, and communal nesting and rearing of the young.

On the other hand, brood-parasitism, which is paractised regularly by some birds of the families Cuculidae, Icteridae, and Ploceidae, is found in modified form in some fishes. The best-known examples occur among the North American freshwater Cyprinidae, where some species frequently spawn in the gravel mound nests built by other cyprinids or by centrarchids (Hunter and Hasler, 1965; Breder and Rosen, 1966). Since some of the "host" species practise parental care of the eggs, whereas the "brood-parasites" do not, the latter presumably benefit from this association, although there is little direct evidence of the type available for birds.

4.3 Conclusion

In general, it is clear that parental behavior is further advanced and diversified among birds than among fishes. This greater elaboration is associated with much smaller clutches of larger eggs, a more prolonged and intimate association between parents and offspring, and above all with homeothermy (Kendeigh, 1952). Homeothermy means that with suitable parental care behaviors, the avian embryo can develop rapidly at high temperatures outside the body. The young of altricial species are totally dependent on their parents for food and protection for some time after hatching, while the young of many precocial species stay with their parents and are either directed to food sources or are fed, often by regurgitation.

Among fishes, embryonic developmental rates depend on ambient temperatures, and clutches usually consist of large numbers of small eggs. Most species have no parental care at all, and among those that care for the eggs only, the young after hatching either join the plankton and drift away from the hatching site, or settle close to the substrate and remain near hiding places. In either case the parent-offspring association is quickly lost. Most fishes with posthatching parental care breed in shallow, fresh, or brackish waters, where turbulence and rapid change in water levels are common. Associated with these conditions one finds the furthest development of parental care, including what must surely be the most efficient and safest way to move freely swimming young away from danger—that is, in the parent's mouth.

5 ACKNOWLEDGMENTS

I wish to thank Patricia Smith-Grayton and Arthur Timms for their contributions to the work on which this paper is based. Betsy Baldwin provided invaluable assistance in the cichlid fish behavior work of our laboratory. I thank George W. Barlow and Paul V. Loiselle for helpful comments on the manuscript. This research has been supported by operating grants from the National Research Council of Canada.

For permission to use previously published illustrations I am grateful to Baillière Tindall (Figures 1.1 to 1.4) and to Paul Parey (Figure 1.5).

REFERENCES

Baerends, G. P. and J. M. Baerends-van Roon. 1950. An introduction to the study of the ethology of cichlid fishes. Behav. Suppl. **1**: 1–242.

Baldaccini, N. E. 1973. An ethological study of reproductive behaviour including the colour patterns of the cichlid fish *Tilapia mariae*. Monit. Zool. Ital. **7**: 247–290.

Barlow, G. W. 1974. Contrasts in social behavior between Central American cichlid fishes and coral-reef surgeon fishes. Am. Zool. **14**: 9–34.

Baylis, J. R. 1974. The behavior and ecology of *Herotilapia multispinosa* (Teleostei, Cichlidae). Z. Tierpsychol. **34**: 115–146.

Breder, C. M. and D. E. Rosen. 1966. *Modes of Reproduction in Fishes*. Natural History Press, New York. 941p.

Chien, A. K. and M. S. Salmon. 1972. Reproductive behavior of the angelfish *Pterophyllum scalare*. I. A quantitative analysis of spawning and parental behavior. Forma et Functio **5**: 45–74.

Cole, J. E. and J. A. Ward. 1969. The communicative function of pelvic fin-flickering in *Etroplus maculatus* (Pisces, Cichlidae). Behaviour **35**: 179–199.

Frith, H. J. 1956. Temperature regulation in the nesting mounds of the Mallee-fowl, *Leiopa ocellata* Gould. C.S.I.R.O. Wildl. Res. **1**: 79–95.

Fryer, G. and T. D. Iles. 1972. *The Cichlid Fishes of the Great Lakes of Africa*. T.F.H. Publications, Neptune City, N.J. 641p.

Greenwood, P.H. 1974. The cichlid fishes of Lake Victoria, East Africa: the biology and evolution of a species flock. Bull. Br. Mus. (Nat. Hist.) Zool., Suppl. **6**: 1–134.

Hildemann, W. H. 1959. A cichlid fish, *Symphysodon discus*, with unique nurture habits. Am. Nat. **93**: 27–34.

Hunter, J. R. and A. D. Hasler. 1965. Spawning association of the redfin shiner, *Notropis umbratilis*, and the green sunfish, *Lepomis cyanellus*. Copeia **1965**: 265–281.

Iersel, J. A. A. van. 1953. An analysis of the parental behaviour of the male three-spined stickleback (*Gasterosteus aculeatus* L.). Behav. Suppl. **3**: 1–159.

Kear, J. 1970. The adaptive radiation of parental care in waterfowl. *In:* J. H. Crook, Ed., *Social Behaviour in Birds and Mammals*. Academic Press, London–New York, p. 357–392.

Kendeigh, S. C. 1952. Parental care and its evolution in birds. Ill. Biol. Monogr. **22**: 1–356.

Krischik, V. A. and P. G. Weber. 1974. Induced parental care in male convict cichlid fish. Dev. Psychobiol. **8**: 1–11.

Landsborough Thomson, A., Ed. 1964. *A New Dictionary of Birds*. Nelson, London. 928p.

Lowe-McConnell, R. H. 1964. The fishes of the Rupununi savanna district of British Guiana. I. Ecological groupings of fish species and effects of the seasonal cycle on the fish. J. Linn. Soc. Zool. **45**: 103–144.

Marliave, J. B. and E. E. De Martini. 1977. Parental behavior of intertidal fishes of the stichaeid genus *Xiphister*. Can. J. Zool, **55**: 60–63.

Marshall, N. B. 1965. *The Life of Fishes*. Weidenfeld and Nicolson, London, 402p.

Miller, R. R. 1966. Geographical distribution of Central American freshwater fishes. Copeia **1966**: 773–802.

Noakes, D. L. G. and G. W. Barlow. 1973. Ontogeny of parent-contacting in young *Cichlasoma citrinellum* (Pisces, Cichlidae). Behaviour **46**: 221–255.

Oppenheimer, J. R. 1970. Mouthbreeding in fishes. Anim. Behav. **18:** 493–503.

Oppenheimer, J. R. and G. W. Barlow. 1968. Dynamics of parental behavior in the black-chinned mouthbreeder, *Tilapia melanotheron* (Pisces: Cichlidae). Z. Tierpsychol. **25:** 889–914.

Pearson, N. E. 1937. The fishes of the Beni-Mamoré and Paraguay basins, and a discussion of the origin of the Paraguayan fauna. Proc. Calif. Acad. Sci. **23:** 99–114.

Reid, M. J. and J. W. Atz. 1958. Oral incubation in the cichlid fish *Geophagus jurupari* Heckel. Zoologica **43:** 77–88.

Robertson, D. R. 1973. Field observations on the reproductive behaviour of a Pomacentrid fish, *Acanthochromis polyacanthus*. Z. Tierpsychol. **32:** 319–324.

Rowland, W. J. 1974. Reproductive behavior of the fourspine stickleback, *Apeltes quadracus*. Copeia **1974:** 183–194.

Smith-Grayton, P. K. and M. H. A. Keenleyside. 1978. Male-female parental roles in *Herotilapia multispinosa*. Anim. Behav. **26:** 520–526.

Timms, A. M. and M. H. A. Keenleyside. 1975. The reproductive behaviour of *Aequidens paraguayensis* (Pisces, Cichlidae). Z. Tierpsychol. **39:** 8–23.

Ward, J. A. and G. W. Barlow. 1967. The maturation and regulation of glancing off the parents by young orange chromides (*Etroplus maculatus:* Pisces-Cichlidae). Behaviour **29:** 1–56.

Wickler, W. 1966. Sexualdimorphismus, Paarbildung und Versteckbrüten bei Cichliden (Pisces: Perciformes). Zool. Jahrb. Syst. **93:** 129–138.

2

DO FISHES
LEK LIKE BIRDS?

PAUL V. LOISELLE
GEORGE W. BARLOW
Department of Zoology and Museum of
Vertebrate Zoology
University of California, Berkeley

1   INTRODUCTION

More than one biologist has been struck by the similarity between birds
and teleost fishes (Lorenz, 1962; Marshall, 1960). One may wonder

31

whether the impression of similarity is superficial or profound, or whether it holds for some comparisons but not for others.

The resemblances are most likely the result of convergent evolution. If so, an analysis of the similarities and differences between fishes and birds in an important aspect of their biology can reveal something about the principles involved. For example, the principles underlying sexual selection may explain the recurrence of the brilliant color patterns for which both groups are noted. In many instances, such conspicuous coloration is sexually dimorphic. And pronounced dimorphism is often a consequence of sexual selection in a polygynous mating system (Bartholomew, 1970; Selander, 1972; Sibley, 1957).

One of the most extreme examples of sexual competition is lekking, or arena behavior. Since it has become increasingly apparent that this type of behavior is common among teleost fishes (Table 2.1), we decided to compare lekking in the two groups.

In making the comparison we have purposely stressed major features and have not attempted a complete review of the literature. That would be difficult for fishes. Accounts of lekking behavior in fishes are often fragmentary and buried in papers with misleading titles, apparently in large part because of earlier workers' insensitivity to this phenomenon in fishes. It is therefore possible that some of our judgments with regard to the occurrence of lekking in a particular species may be proved premature by subsequent research. We nevertheless feel that our conclusions about the widespread occurrence of lek systems in teleosts are justified and will bear up under future scrutiny.

2   THE NATURE OF LEKKING

Lekking is the temporary aggregation of sexually active males for reproduction. In the typical case, males gather on a lekking ground or arena. There each male occupies a territory, or court, from which he displays to females and interacts with other males. The aggregation of males on the lek is visited by females, singly or *en masse,* who select the males with whom they mate. Once mating is accomplished, the females leave the lek.

Clusters of males holding permanent, all-purpose territories, even if visited there by females for reproductive purposes, are not considered by us to constitute a lek. In a more comprehensive treatment of reproductive adaptations, their relationship to lek systems would have to considered. In the context of this paper, such consideration would be too great a digression.

TABLE 2.1 Incidence of lekking among teleost fishes

Order: Cypriniformes	Order: Perciformes
Characidae *a*	Centrarchidae
Cyprinidae	Percidae
Catostomidae	Sparidae
	Embiotocidae *a*
Order: Atherinomorpha	Cichlidae
Atherinidae	Pomacentridae
Melanotaenidae	Labridae
Cyprinodontidae	Scaridae
Poeciliidae	Acanthuridae *a*
	Callionymidae
Order: Gasterosteiformes	Belontiidae
Gasteroteidae	

a Included on the basis of anecdotal accounts describing probable lek systems.

Some colleagues have suggested to us that the use of the term "colonial breeding" would be more appropriate in such a review. We disagree, insofar as our aim is to make explicit comparisons between lek systems in birds and fishes. That term has two significantly different applications in the avian literature. The first is exemplified by oceanic birds that nest as monogamous pairs in closely packed colonies. In our consideration of fishes, we are not dealing with aggregations of monogamous pairs, although colonial breeding of this sort has been reported for cichlids of the genus *Tilapia* (Loiselle, 1977). The second is exemplified by passerines such as weaverbirds and some blackbirds, in which a number of females mate with and nest within the territory of a single male. Such polygynous systems are closer to lekking as we define it and may even grade into it in fishes. But they suggest more appropriate comparisons with the harem societies of some mammals, such as occur in some pinnipeds and bovids, and, among teleosts, of some cichlids of the genera *Lamprologus, Nanochromis, Teleogramma, Apistogramma,* and *Nannacara*.

Reproductive adaptations based on lekking were first described in birds (Gadamer, 1858). Because it is an extreme departure from the usual avian pattern of monogamy and joint care of the brood, lekking has long attracted the attention of behaviorally oriented ornithologists, from the pioneer studies of Selous (1906–7, 1909–10) to recent papers by Robel and Ballard (1974), Rippin and Boag (1974), and Pitelka, Holmes, and MacLean (1974).

Concise descriptions of what appears to be lekking in teleost fishes were first published by Reeves (1907) and Newman (1907), and have appeared consistently in the ichthyological literature up to the present (Penrith, 1972; Brichard, 1975). However, no explicit analogy was made between lekking behavior in fishes and birds until Fryer and Iles (1972) pointed out the correspondence in the reproductive adaptations of ma ny species of the cichlid genera *Sarotherodon* (formerly *Tilapia*) and *Haplochromis*.

Lekking, or what seems to be lekking, has been described in a variety of other kinds of animals. It has been reported in a number of African antelopes living in open country, and most notably in the Uganda kob (Beuchner and Roth, 1974; Jarman, 1974), in a variety of other ungulates (Geist and Walther, 1974), in hammerhead bats (Bradbury, 1972), in one reptile (Brattstrom, 1974), in one anuran amphibian (Emlen, 1968; Weiwandt, 1969), and among insects in drosophilid flies (Spieth, 1968), fireflies (Buck, 1938; Lloyd, 1973), dragonflies (Campanella and Wolf, 1974), and cicadas (Alexander and Moore, 1962). One species of harvester ant also appears to engage in lekking (Hölldobler, in Wilson, 1975). Although lekking may prove more prevalent among some of these groups than the literature would indicate, fruitful comparisons of lekking in different environments must draw at present upon the ornithological and ichthyological literature.

To aid the reader, we enumerate at the outset the prerequisites to lekking in any species.

1. *Synchrony.* The reproductive activities of a substantial proportion of the males and females of a given population must be in phase.
2. *Lekking Ground.* The males must congregate at a given place, and the females must also proceed to that place.
3. *Mobility.* The species must be sufficiently mobile to travel to the mating ground.
4. *Parental Care.* If parental caretaking exists, it requires only one parent, not a pair.
5. *Feeding.* Either no feeding occurs on the lek, or only incidental feeding that is insufficient to meet energetic needs.

Further on we provide some tables that outline the major points in our central arguments. Although they are redundant to the text, we thought they would be useful in keeping the main themes obvious. In preparing the tables, we were motivated to provide testable propositions in the hope that these would stimulate observations to refute them. The reader will discover that the propositions are a pragmatic mixture of inductive conclusions, though often based on scanty evidence, and deductions that seem to us to flow from what we have learned.

We now summarize the main features of teleost and avian reproductive biology. Next we compare lekking as practiced by members of these two groups. In closing, we speculate on the ecological factors that may have led to the evolution of lek systems in both and attempt to account for its prevalence in teleost fishes.

2.1 A Comparison of Teleost and Avian Reproductive Biology

Teleosts are characterized by a wide range of reproductive modalities. Oviparity with external fertilization, ovoviviparity, and true viviparity have been reported for the group (Breder and Rosen, 1966). With the exception of the viviparous surfperches (Embiotocidae), for which we have only circumstantial evidence of lekking (Rechnitzer and Limbaugh, 1952; Wiebe 1968), and a single viviparous poeciliid, *Poeciliopsis occidentalis* (Constantz, 1975), all lek fishes known to us are oviparous. We will therefore concentrate on the pertinent features of oviparity with external fertilization.

In most cases, the female performs a number of spawning acts, releasing some portion of the total spawn each time. In a lekking species this means that the female may move from one male to another, leaving some eggs with each one. Alternately, she may perform all the spawning acts with one male.

The numerous eggs are large and full of yolk. After spawning, the female may not spawn again for several weeks, or until the next season, because it takes time to obtain enough food to lay down such a generous energetic larder. Alternatively, as appears to be the case in cyprinodont, melanotaeniid, and some atherine fishes, the female lays just a few eggs each day over a protracted period. Males, in contrast, need to commit only a small amount of energy to produce vast numbers of tiny sperm. They can spawn repeatedly during a day and for several days. Females therefore make a large initial investment per gamete, the males a small one.

A male may fertilize the eggs of a number of females, regardless of whether the spawning pattern involves production of demersal or pelagic eggs. Thus a male often accumulates a clutch that may number up into hundreds or thousands of eggs, if he is the custodian. Such a number is huge compared to the clutches of birds.

The eggs of teleost fishes are surrounded by a permeable membrane of variable strength. Substances necessary for the development of the embryo, such as water and oxygen, cross this membrane from the external environment while metabolites move in the opposite direction. Teleost eggs are susceptible to attack by bacteria and fungi because their dependence on a steady exchange with their surroundings has in most instances precluded the evolution of effective morphological barriers against such infections. Reproductive success among those teleosts that put their eggs on the substratum therefore depends critically on the accessibility of hygienic spawning sites.

Typically, such sites are characterized by a disturbed or inherently depauperate microbial community as well as adequate dissolved oxygen to allow normal embryonic development. Many fishes exploit recurrent natural phenomena, such as the scouring effect of the spates resulting from the spring melt in the temperate zone, or the monsoons in the tropics, to deposit demersal eggs upon the favorable substrata thus produced. Most nest-building species themselves create a substratum with a disturbed microbial ecology through their nest-building activities.

A different set of adaptations accompanies the releasing of pelagic eggs into the plankton. In reef-dwelling species that do so, it becomes important to expel and fertilize the eggs at the best place to assure that the zygotes are swept into the most favorable water mass. This often means spawning at the outer edge of the reef when the tides and currents are propitious (Randall and Randall, 1963; Warner et al., 1975).

Teleosts are poikilothermic. The normal development of their eggs therefore depends on the ambient temperature. This imposes a marked seasonality on the reproductive cycle of temperate zone fishes. Seasonal change in water temperature does not seem to play an important role in regulating the spawning of many tropical fishes. Instead the periodicity of rainfall appears to impose seasonality on most tropical freshwater fishes, for whom the arrival of the rainy season often provides the proximal stimulus for spawning (Blanche, 1964; Daget, 1954; Loiselle, 1970). Seasonality seems less pronounced in tropical marine habitats (e.g., Munroe et al., 1973; Sale and Dybdahl, 1975), but the intraseasonal cyclicity of spawning of some fishes in such habitats may be linked to lunar cycles (Randall, 1961; but see Reinboth, 1973, for contrary evidence). Taken together, these environmental factors often impose a degree of synchrony of sexual activity, from modest to great, even among coral reef fishes with prolonged breeding seasons.

Many fishes, especially freshwater species, practice parental care of their spawn. The caretaker is almost always the male. When the female is involved, the course of evolution appears to have gone from exclusively male care to joint care, then to exclusively female care (Barlow, 1963, 1964). That the male is the usual caretaker in fishes stands in contrast to the situation within the Vertebrata, with the exception of the Amphibia. A further contrast is that there is no reversal of sex roles when the male fish is the caretaker, contrary to Wilson (1975). The courtship behavior of the male fish is masculine by the accepted standards.

A key factor in the evolution of such a pattern is that in species that fertilize the eggs externally, the male can be certain that the zygotes left in his care were fertilized by him (Barlow, 1976c). Chances of cuckolding are slight compared to species that fertilize internally, the usual case in most of the other Vertebrata and in some fish groups. Thus an externally fertilizing male can significantly promote his genetic investment by protecting his offspring.

Dawkins and Carlisle (1976) have proposed a different explanation for why, among fishes, the male is the usual custodian. Their thinking also turns on external fertilization and is therefore applicable as well to aquatic amphibians with parental care. When fertilization is internal, "After copulation, the female is left physically in possession of the zygote, and while it is still in her body, she cannot desert it, but the male can. However fast she lays it, the male is still offered the first opportunity to desert, thereby closing the female's options and forcing her into Triver's cruel bind." The bind, as modified by Dawkins and Carlisle, is that the partner that deserts first does not necessarily condemn the progeny to death. Instead, it simply sloughs the decision off onto the parent left with the zygotes.

In fishes and many amphibians that fertilize externally, the sperm are lighter than the eggs and are hence more readily dissipated or swept away. From this, Dawkins and Carlisle reasoned that males have more to lose by spawning too quickly, on the chance that the partner delays, than do females. Thus a female can afford to go first in spawning, leaving the male with the zygotes after he has fertilized them.

In our collective experience, though synchronous ejaculation of gametes seems the general case, whenever one sex spawns first, as in gobies, blennies, and damselfishes, but not in cichlids, there is usually paternal care of the spawn. This explanation, nevertheless, has some problems in wide application.

First, one would expect males to evolve sperm that would not wash away, comparable to the spematophores of some salamanders. In fact, this solution appears to have been evolved by two maternal mouthbrooding cichlids, *Sarotherodon macrochir* and the Tanganyikan endemic *Opthalmochromis ventrailis* (Wickler, 1962; Brichard, 1975), although it does not appear to be inflexibly linked to prior ejaculation by the male.

Second, in many maternal mouth-brooding cichlids, the female takes the eggs into her mouth before the male fertilizes them, immediately after she has expelled them. Fertilization occurs intrabuccally (Wickler, 1962). This suggests that she is eager to possess the eggs, probably in order to minimize the time they are exposed to egg predators, not that she is eager to desert them. Recall, too, that maternal mouth-brooding has probably evolved from joint male-female parental care of the spawn. Finally, it overlooks the general case in seahorses and pipefishes, in which the female "inseminates" the male by leaving her eggs in his brood pouch.

The explanation proposed by Dawkins and Carlisle provides part of the answer to the prevalence of paternal care of the spawn in fishes. But we suspect that the necessity of sequestering a suitable spawning site (prerequisite to reproductive success in any species with demersal eggs), the energetic differences between the sexes in the production of gametes, and the certainty of paternity that follows external fertilization, are of equal or greater importance in its evolution. We shall return to this point.

Yet another general feature of teleost reproduction needs mentioning. When the male is the exclusive guardian of the zygotes, the female is driven away from the breeding site as soon as the spawning act has been accomplished. Females are notorious egg predators, as seen in cyprinodont fish (Loiselle, in prep.) and gouramies (Wright, 1976). Excluding all females save those immediately ready to spawn, thus increases the survivorship of the male's offspring. In addition, spawned-out females might interfere with subsequent matings by the male with other females. Chasing away the spent female is so universal among teleosts that it is remarkable that some groups have been able to evolve joint parental care of the spawn.

Parental care in fishes appears in most instances to have been derived directly from the defense of a territory for reproductive or other purposes (Barlow, 1963, 1964; Baylis, in prep.). It provides a suitable environment for the development of the zygotes, for their defense, and, less commonly, for defense of the mobile fry from predators. The eggs and newly hatched fry are fanned and/or mouthed, while predators are driven away by the guardian's attacks. In most teleosts the period of parental care is brief, extending only to the eggs and larvae. In the few instances where parental care of the mobile fry is practiced, a behavior whose occurrence is limited almost entirely to fresh water fishes, such a commitment rarely lasts more than six weeks.

Defense of the eggs or young differs to a degree from that seen in birds and mammals. By comparison, the eggs and fry of fishes are tiny relative to the size of the adult, and number at times into the thousands. Their predators are therefore relatively small, seldom larger than the parent and usually much smaller. Consequently, the parent can readily drive away individual spawn predators at little risk to himself, although his defense may sometimes be overwhelmed by sheer numbers of them (Meral, 1973). Adult fish are themselves subject to a different type of much larger predator. Thus when considering the effects of predation upon teleost reproductive patterns, one must keep in mind that it operates upon two different levels, the spawn and the parent, and in ways that elicit radically different responses by the breeding adults.

An additional important factor is that much predation on the eggs, and particularly upon the fry, may be by conspecifics. This is true of cichlids and of other freshwater fishes such as sticklebacks and pupfish. Such intense predation upon the eggs and young by conspecifics is less prevalent in birds and mammals. As a consequence, there is sometimes a semantic difficulty in talking about territorial defense because driving away conspecific intruders may actually represent defense of the spawn against such predators.

Although there are too few data available at this time to permit detailed comparisons, it is worth mentioning that territorial defense in lekking fishes may be more ritualized than in nonlekking species. Apfelbach and Leong (1970) compared reproductive aggressive behavior in three species of *Tilapia*. These were *Tilapia zilli*, a monogamous substrate breeding species; *T. galilaea* (= *Sarotherodon galilaeus*), a pair-forming species in which both sexes engage in mouth-brooding; and *T. macrochir* = *S. macrochir*), a lekking species with maternal mouth-brooding. Aggression was the most damaging in *zilli* and the most ritualized in the lekking species *macrochir*; *galilaea* was intermediate. Future studies should be alert to the possibility that a concomitant of the evolution of lekking is a shift from damaging aggressive behavior to ritualized threats.

There is no trophic component in the parental behavior of the majority of teleosts practicing defense of their spawn. In some species, e.g. substratum-spawning members of the family Cichlidae, the parents may protect the young as they forage (Barlow, 1976a; Burchard, 1967; McKaye and Hallacher, 1973; Loiselle, unpublished data). In cichlids of the genera *Symphysodon* (Hildemann, 1959) and *Etroplus* (Ward and Barlow, 1967), however, and in two species of bagrid catfishes (Sundara Raj, 1962), the fry depend on parental mucus for some of their nourishment. Nonobligatory feeding on parental mucus occurs in a number of other cichlid species (Noakes and Barlow, 1973; Ward and Barlow, 1967). In no instances known to us does parental care include a thermoregulatory component.

All birds are oviparous, with internal fertilization of a cleidocal (shelled and self-sufficient) egg. The shell of the avian egg encloses a milieu in which all of the raw materials of embryonic development are present save oxygen, and within which provision is made for isolating nongaseous metabolites from the developing embryo. The shell is permeable only to gases and provides a virtually impregnable barrier to bacterial invasion. However, because birds are homeothermic, their eggs require a reasonably constant temperature for development. Care of the developing eggs, predominantly thermoregulatory in nature, is consequently universal among birds. With the unique exception of the Australasian family Megapodidae, birds accomplish this end by brooding the eggs.

During this period, the eggs and one or both parents are vulnerable to predation. Security for the clutch and the incubating parent or parents is consequently a major factor influencing the evolution of avian reproductive adaptations during the incubation period (Ricklefs, 1969). That period may last as long as the entire interval of parental care in most teleosts. Lack (1968) has concisely summarized the nesting adaptations adopted by birds to maximize reproductive success. His account underlines the importance of a secure nest site and various adaptations favoring crypticity for the nest, clutch and parents. Nest site selection is therefore important in birds, but for reasons different than those dictating such behavior in teleost fishes.

Posthatching roles vary considerably between nidifugous and nidicolous birds. A thermoregulatory component of variable intensity, nonetheless, is characteristic of virtually all birds. It is most pronounced in nidicolous species, whose young are not feathered at hatching. The precocial young of nidifugous species, in contrast, have a coat of insulating down from the time they hatch. That lessens the need for heat from the parent and is therefore less restrictive of the caretaker's activities.

The major difference between these types of birds, however, is the way the young get food. Nidifugous birds do not usually bring food to their active young, but rather guide them to food sources and provide them with some protection against predators as they forage (Lack, 1968). The parents or parent of nidicolous young must forage for food, which is then brought to the young at the nest. The trophic dependence of the young persists until they are fledged and, in some species, even for a short time thereafter. Regardless of how they are discharged, the trophic responsibilities of breeding birds are of central importance in their overall reproductive strategy. The seasonality so clearly evident in avian reproduction is imposed in large measure by the necessity of having sufficient food at hand both to support the parents and to feed the young during a protracted period of growth, considerations that also limit the choice of nesting site.

2.2 Parental Role of Male and Female in Lekking Birds and Teleosts

In all lek birds the male has no parental role (Armstrong, 1947; Lack, 1968). To many ornithologists this is a *sine qua non* for lekking. Once the female has mated and completed her clutch, she avoids the lek, incubates her eggs, and rears her hatchlings alone. The ability of the female to discharge all parental functions unaided is therefore a precondition for the evolution of lekking in birds.

Among lekking teleosts, four possibilities exist with regard to parental care:

1. *Noncustodial Lekking.* Demersal eggs are deposited by one or more females within the male's territory on the lek with no prior preparation of a nest, as in most cyprinodonts (Barlow, 1961; Breder, 1934; Loiselle, 1969; Newman, 1907; Raney *et al.*, 1953) and in the atherine families Melanotaeniidae and Atherinidae (Baker, 1933; Smith, 1956; Loiselle, unpublished data). Alternatively, pelagic eggs are shed into the plankton in a "nuptial dash" launched from the reef, as in the lekking species of the marine families Labridae and Scaridae (Barlow, 1976b; Randall and Randall, 1963; Reinboth, 1973), and possibly surgeonfishes of the genus *Naso* (Barlow, 1974a). There is no overt defense of the spawn, either because of the brevity of the lek's persistence, of siting the lek where there are no predators, or because of the dispersal of the eggs and larvae.

2. *Lekking with Maternal Care of the Spawn.* This mode of lekking is known to occur only in one poeciliid (Constantz, 1975) and in the maternal mouth-brooding species of the family *Cichlidae* (Brichard, 1975; Coe, 1966, 1969; Fryer, 1956; Kirchshofer, 1953; Iles, 1960; Lowe, 1952; Lowe-McConnell, 1956; Ruwet, 1962a, b, 1963; Welcomme, 1970). In the poeciliid, the female visits the male and is inseminated on his court. In the cichlids, the female visits the male on his territory, where spawning occurs. The eggs are taken into the female's mouth, wherein they are fertilized if they have not already been fertilized (Wickler, 1962). The egg-laden female leaves the lek while the male remains, awaiting further mates. The female swims to spatially separate nursery grounds, where she remains until the fry become independent. Or both sexes may abandon the lek and re-

constitute the original school, as in several Lake Tanganyika open-water cichlid species (Brichard, 1975). In some instances the fry are shepherded and protected by the female for a while after they have emerged from her mouth. In others, the young are simply released and abandoned by the female.

3. *Protocustodial Lekking.* The male constructs a nest that is the focal point of his territory. Then females approach individually and deposit their eggs there. The spawn, of one to several females, are neither cleaned or aerated by the male. Whatever protection from predation the eggs and larvae receive derives incidentally from the male's defense of his territory from conspecific intruders. The fry depart as soon as they are mobile and thus are not protected. In the examples known to us, the males abandon their territories after completing the process of reproducing. This mode of lekking occurs in many cyprinids (Adams and Hankinson, 1928; Greely, 1929; Hankinson, 1920; Hubbs and Cooper, 1936; Langlois, 1929; Raney, 1940, 1947; Reighard, 1910; Stout and Winn, 1958), in the pupfishes of the genus *Cyprinodon* (Loiselle, in prep.), and in some darter perches of the subfamily *Etheostomatinae* (Petravicz, 1936; Reighard, 1913). It may also occur in the cod *Gadus callarias* (Brawn, 1961).

4. *Paternal Custodial Lekking.* The eggs of one or more females are deposited within the male's territory in a nest prepared for that purpose. The eggs are usually aerated and cleaned by the male, who vigorously repels all intruders. Some defense of the mobile fry is possible. This mode of lekking is practiced by some cyprinids (Greely, 1927; Raney, 1939), by one cyprinodont, Jordanella floridae (Mertz and Barlow, 1966; Barlow, unpublished data), by many darter perches (Petravicz, 1938; Raney and Lachner, 1939; Reeves, 1907; Winn, 1958), and by all lekking centrarchids (Barney and Anson, 1923; Beeman, 1924; Breder, 1936; Hubbs and Cooper, 1935; Larimore, 1957; Lydell, 1926; Breder and Rosen, 1966). There is some question, however, about the male parental role of one centrarchid fish, the Sacramento perch, *Archoplites interruptus* (Matthews, 1965; Murphy, 1948).

Further examples of paternal custodial lekking are provided by sticklebacks (Leiner, 1930; Iersel, 1953, 1958), by some lekking wrasses that produce demersal eggs (Fiedler, 1964; Soljan, 1930a, b), and by lekking species of the marine families *Sparidae* (Bruggen, 1965; Penrith, 1972) and Pomacentridae (Abel, 1961; Albrecht, 1969; Fishelson, 1970; Myrberg *et al.*, 1967; Barlow, personal observation). In Thailand, groups of male gouramies of the genus *Trichogaster* form discrete arenas under their bubble nests where they are visited by females ready to spawn (Wright, 1976).

The thermoregulatory and trophic components of avian parental care preclude the evolution of noncustodial, protocustodial, and strictly paternal custodial lekking in birds. These two considerations, taken with the practice of internal fertilization, produce the sharpest difference between lekking birds and fishes. They contribute importantly to the greater diversity in forms of lekking in teleost fishes.

That so few internally fertilizing fishes have been unequivocally reported to lek may be an accident of insufficient observation or of observations unguided by hypotheses about reproductive strategies. We expect additional examples of lekking to be found among internally fertilizing fishes, as we have suggested for the Embiotocidae. An obvious group to examine is the Goodeidae. They are in the same suborder as the Cyprinodontidae, which has so many examples of lekking species; the two families also resemble one another in ecological adaptations and in morphology. We also anticipate that field studies will reveal lek systems to be more prevalent among poeciliids than present evidence would suggest.

2.3 Occurrence of Polygamy among Lekking Birds and Teleosts

The absence of monogamous pair-bonding and the corollary occurrence of sequential polygyny are taken as defining elements of avian lekking (Lack, 1968). The extent of polygyny is precisely known only in the ruff (Hogan-Warburg, 1966; Rhijn, 1973) and in various grouse species (Hjorth, 1970; Rippin and Boag, 1974; Robel and Ballard, 1974; Wiley, 1973). The occurrence of polyandry is also possible in all lek birds but improbable in the galliformes because their females practice sperm storage and hence need visit the lek only once in a season to produce a clutch of fertile eggs. However, there are no data on polyandry in lekking birds. It seems a probable corollary of the attenuation of the pair bond (Pitelka, personal communication).

Lekking teleosts are likewise characterized by polygamy. Sequential polygyny is found in all lekking species, and sporadic instances of simultaneous polygyny have been reported among the Centrarchidae (Breder, 1936) and the Labridae (Reinboth, 1973). External fertilization of the eggs makes this departure from the typical pattern possible. Resident males, however, are normally receptive to but a single female at a time. In some instances, the male may actually repel females that attempt to enter his territory while he is engaged in the terminal phases of courtship or actual spawning (Ruwet, 1963).

The occurrence of polyandry among lekking teleosts is better documented than is the case among lekking birds. Polyandry has been reported among cyprinodonts (Barlow, 1961; Loiselle, 1969; Newman, 1907), and occurs among melanotaenids under aquarium conditions (Loiselle, unpublished observation). Females of four darter perches (Petravicz, 1938; Reeves, 1907; Winn, 1958) practice polyandry. Such behavior has been reported as normal in one cichlid, *Sarotherodon macrochir* and in one pomacentrid, *Chromis multilineata* (Myrberg *et al.*, 1967; Ruwet, 1963). Breder (1936) considered it typical of the reproductive behavior of most centrarchids. Subsequent investigations have revealed polyandry in one sunfish not cited by Breder, the Sacramento perch (Murphy, 1948).

Less information is available on the extent to which individual females of a given species indulge in polyandry. Ruwet reported female *S. macrochir* carrying a clutch of eggs fertilized by five or six males. Breder (1936) regarded centrarchid breeding systems as essentially nonassortative, citing an instance in which a female *Lepomis gibbosus* visited every male on a small lek of indeterminate size.

2.4   Topological Position of the Male, Female Choice, and Predictability of the Environment

The disproportionate reproductive success enjoyed by centrally located males of the ruff and many grouse species (Bendell and Elliot, 1967; Hogan-Warburg, 1966; Rhijn, 1973; Robel and Ballard, 1974; Wiley, 1973), with its overtones of Darwinian sexual selection, has attracted the attention of many workers (see review by Selander, 1972). The occurrence of such a position effect within the lek has not been documented in other lekking birds, however. This lack of information is particularly marked for forest-dwelling lek birds. Until these species have been more extensively studied, it would be premature to regard such position effects as being a universal feature of avian lekking.

In those avian species for which position effects have been determined, the classical cases of lekking among tetraonids, central males may enjoy in excess of 80% of the copulations that occur during the breeding season. Succession to central sites within the lek follows a clear protocol. If vacancies occur through mortality, they are filled by peripheral males, who are in turn replaced by marginal males. Direct competition for such sites is ritualized (Rippin and Boag, 1974). The protocol of succession resembles the seniority system of the American Congress. The chairmanships of powerful committees come almost automatically to those who succeed in assuring their regular reelection and avoid antagonizing their colleagues by displays of nontraditional behavior. To the best of our knowledge, hovever, the analogy breaks down in all but a few cases upon consideration of the rewards accruing to persistent males.

There is little information, in studies of fish lekking, on the mechanisms determining access to favored territories. The evidence suggests that in some centrarchids and cichlids overt competition exists and can be intense (Beeman, 1924; Coe, 1966, 1969; Lydell, 1926). There is no indication of a protocol of succession to favored sites.

There are only fragmentary indications that position effects characterize lekking in teleosts. The existence of discrete classes of central and peripheral males may be inferred for two lekking cyprinids (Adams and Hankinson, 1928; Langlois, 1929), one cyprinodont (Barlow, 1961), two darter perches (Petravicz, 1938; Reeves, 1907), two centrarchids (Hunter, 1963; Keenleyside, 1972), gouramies of the genus Trichogaster (Wright, 1976), and one cichlid (Coe, 1969). Hunter (1963) reported that leks developed around the first male green sunfish to spawn, and Wright (1976) observed that male gouramies place their nests around that of the most aggressive male. In Mediterranian wrasses of the genus *Crenilabrus,* a central male is surrounded by smaller nonterritoriäl satellite males who only occasionally fertilize eggs in the nest when the large male is temporarily away (Fielder, 1964); however, it is not clear whether there is a position effect among the territory-holding males.

The extent to which highly dimorphic dominant males enjoy augmented success in mating has been demonstrated well in only one teleost species, the bluehead wrasse (*Thalassoma bifasciatum*), by Warner et al. (1975). (These males are central in the sense that they are often surrounded by smaller nondimorphic males.) The females move across the reef from shallow to deeper water to reach the lek. There the large station-holding males are sought out. As the females approach the lek, they are solicited by the small drab males who are not territorial. Sometimes females spawn with groups of these smaller males. Still other drab males, "streakers," join the female when she spawns with the gaudy "central" male, and yet others, "sneakers," try to steal a spawn on the lek. Nonetheless, the "central" dominant male enjoys an enormous reproductive advantage over the small drab ones, regularly spawning about 40 and occasionally 100 times/day. In contrast, the nondimorphic peripheral males, spawning predominantly in groups, only achieve the equivalent of about one to two pair-spawnings/day.

The situation is less complex in gouramies of the genus *Trichogaster*. Among Thai populations of *Trichogaster trichopterus*, up to 20 to 30 males nest together. The nests are most closely placed around the central male, and each nest territory there is only about 20 cm in diameter. The female swims directly to and butts the male of her choice. In all 88 spawnings observed by Wright (1976), the central male was chosen by the female.

The example of the bluehead wrasse draws attention to another important difference in teleost lekking made possible by external fertilization. It is the possibility of neighboring resident males, or nonterritorial marginal males, joining the consorting couple at the moment of oviposition and participating in the fertilization of eggs. Such behavior has been documented in one cyprinid (Adams and Hankinson, 1928), one darter perch (Petravicz, 1938), one centrarchid (Keenleyside, 1972), and one cyprinodontid (Barlow, 1961), one wrasse (Warner *et al.*, 1975), and has been observed in one cichlid (Loiselle, unpublished data). It is difficult to evaluate the significance of such a breakdown in the lek system on the basis of these examples (but see Warner *et al.*, 1975). One would wish to know, in particular, whether the relative paucity of reports is an accurate reflection of rarity of such a breakdown, or simply an indication of failure to record its occurrence in other species.

An instance of a system in which selection seems to have operated against such cheating is cited by Ruwet for *Sarotherodon macrochir*. Resident males whose territories adjoin will display frenetically to an approaching female. Once the female has entered the territory of one of the competitors, however, all display by the unsuccessful rivals ceases. They turn away for the female and indulge either in nest-maintaining behavior or interact with other resident males.

In some lekking fishes, such as wrasses (Fiedler, 1964; Reinboth, 1973; Warner *et al.*, 1975) and parrotfishes (Barlow, 1976b), a form of cheating may be a regular feature of spawning (see p. 15). In some parrotfishes, and in some wrasses, the situation is complicated by a combination of intra- and intersexual competition. Many individuals are sequentially hermaphroditic (Reinboth, 1968, 1973). Some start life as males (primary males), but most are first females, who then change into males (secondary males). Large males are gaudy, and they lek. The young but sexually mature secondary and primary males resemble the drab females and are the cheaters. They are divergent in the context of this paper, and considering the implications of their biology here would carry us away from the main theme (see Barlow, 1976b; Warner *et al.*, 1975).

The existence of position effects among some lek birds and their probable occurrence in fishes raises the issue of female choice. Reproductive success, the number of offsping surviving to reproductive age, is the measure of evolutionary fitness common to all organisms. In lekking and most other promiscuous birds, the only measure of male reproductive success available to the observer is the number of successful copulations per breeding season, since the male plays no role in the rearing of the young. Many of the behavioral and morphological features that characterize males of lek birds, such as extreme sexual dimorphism and elaborate displays, are thus adaptations serving to maximize reproductive success.

The measure of female success, on the other hand, is the number of young she brings to independence. This will be determined by her own experience, crypticity, and ability as a mother, and by the genetic endowment of the hatchlings themselves. The latter is the only respect in which the male may make a significant contribution. It therefore behooves the female to select a male whose genetic material will maximize the chances of her young attaining independence and thus, presumably, sexual maturity. In the grouse the question of choice is yet more crucial, because the sperm storage means a female probably has but one chance a year to make an optimal choice or a mistake.

The exigencies of female choice and the nature of the mechanism that determines male succession to central sites within the lek may explain the existence of a position effect in some lek birds. When male succession is largely a function of age, a central male must possess a genome well adapted to its immediate environment. Otherwise he would not have survived long enough to attain such a rank. As Wiley (1974) has shown in one instance, the displays of older birds appear more attractive to females, thus providing a proximal behavioral mechanism for their selection of central males as mates.

Females may choose between different groups of communally displaying males. Females of the ruff preferentially visit arenas with a large number of satellite males. As the number of satellites present on an arena declines, so do the number of female visits and the number of copulations enjoyed by resident males (van Rhijn, 1973). Additional evidence comes from a colonially nesting species, the village weaverbird. Colonies with fewer than 10 displaying males attract disproportionately fewer females than do the typically larger colonies (Collias and Collias, 1969). Leks may be more attractive to females, and therefore to other males, in direct proportion to the number of displaying males, a point to which we will return.

Position effects, as indicated, are not as well documented in teleosts.

One would predict their existence in the following situations:

1. *Species Practicing Protocustodial or Paternal-Custodial Lekking.* When defense of the spawn is practiced in conjunction with lekking, the optimal strategy for a female is to mate with a male who can provide the most protection at the best location. In a lek situation, central males incidentally benefit from the screening provided through the interaction of peripheral resident males with intruders. Because they have fewer potential predators to contend with, central residents can render more effective defense of their spawn from the few intruders that penetrate the territories of peripheral or of satellite males. At the same time, they can devote a proportionately larger amount of time and energy to actual courtship, thus providing a proximal mechanism of female choice.

2. *Lekking in Relation to Predictability of the Environment.* In this section, and in later ones dealing with tradition and evolution, a key concept is predictability of environment. The present digression is necessary to explain how the term is employed. We use the concept relatively loosely and at times as being synonymous with stability of environment. For a more precise treatment of the concept as applied to periodic phenomena, the reader is referred to Colwell (1974).

Predictability with regard to lekking sites means merely that each year during the breeding season the same set of conditions is apt to prevail on the same lekking grounds. Thus in many species of grouse, the cocks are able to use precisely the same arena year after year (Lack, 1968).

Contrast this with the situation among gouramies of the genus *Trichogaster* in Thailand (Wright, 1976). These fishes commence breeding with the onset of the rainy season. The males build their bubble nests among floating and emergent vegetation in canals, pools, and flooded fields. As the rain continues, the rising water level submerges the vegetation at the original lek. The fish then decamp to find new, better suited sites. Thus the best place to lek is unpredictable. The seasonal pattern of rainfall, and consequent general pattern of movement of the fishes, however, are fairly predictable. Thus while the environment may be too unpredictable for traditionality of lek sites to develop, it may be highly predictable in the sense of a given male having the best genetic endowment for coping with it.

This brings us to the issue of predictability as a factor influencing female choice. Consider the female's problem: If the environment is relatively predictable, she should mate with the male best adapted to that situation. The predictability of the environment implies that the genome that is now the most fit will continue to be so in the next generation. If, however, the females' offspring are likely to find themselves in an environment or environments that differ from the present one, the female should not invest all her gametes in the male best adapted to the present situation. Her optimum course of action is to mate with a number of different males. By thus increasing the genetic variability of her offspring, she increases the probability that some of them will be optimally endowed for whatever environment they find themselves in.

Predictability of environment is relative to the species, as is the concept of the niche. Take the case of planktonic larvae of a marine fish that are widely dispersed to coral reefs scattered about the tropical sea. A small sedentary species, such as any of several damselfishes or gobies, faces a highly unpredictable community of other species of sedentary fishes when it settles out of the plankton onto a small coral head (Sale and Dybdahl, 1975). In contrast, a larger species such as a surgeonfish of the genus *Naso* can move about and average out local differences in community structure. Its environment is more predictable.

Similar arguments can be made for temporal predictability. If the climate is characterized by long cycles of suitable weather and water conditions, the female should pick the currently best adapted male, all else being equal. But if the onset and length of the breeding season and other features of the environment affecting the survival to maturity of the young are unpredictable, the female should be relatively polyandrous.

Annual cyprinodont fishes illustrate this point well. These fishes are able to survive in ephemeral pools by virtue of their drought-resistant eggs. The eggs are buried in the substratum of the pool; they survive the dry season and hatch with the onset of the next rainy season. Not all the eggs spawned in a given year hatch with the coming of the first rains of the next. In a proportion of each spawn, the diapause, or resting stage, of the embryo is prolonged, from several weeks up to, in some instances, several years. This is an adaptation to environments where the onset of the rainy season is characterized by one or more false starts. Even if many eggs do hatch after a light or unseasonal rainfall, and are subsequently lost, some resting eggs will survive the disappearance of the pool and will hatch with the true onset of the rainy season.

In a relatively predictable environment, selection will favor females who produce a large number of nonresting eggs. Such eggs will hatch immediately, giving the fry first access to the food resources of their environment. Such early fry can be expected to reach sexual maturity more rapidly than fry hatched later in the season and to enjoy a longer period of reproductive activity, thus producing more eggs. In an envi-

ronment where the onset of the rainy season is unpredictable, the reverse should be true. Females who produce a large number of resting
eggs will enjoy disproprotionate genetic representation in subsequent
generation.

While we have no evidence that the earliest hatched males or the
largest males in a population produce more nonresting eggs than do
smaller, later-hatched males, it is reasonable to assume some correlation
between these characteristics. There may well be aspects of the male's
behavior that make them variously adapted to competing, depending on
whether they enter the population early, mid, or late in the rainy season.
In any event, assuming that males differ in this regard, we would still
predict that the optimal strategy for a female attempting to hedge her
bets would entail spawning with a large number of males rather than
with one or a few individual males.

In predictable environments, mechanisms determining male position
on the lek may arise that reflect in a direct manner the adaptive value of
a particular genome. As an example, if male position is determined by
aggressive interactions, older, larger males, and/or those with a superior
energy balance, would be expected to dominate in such encounters.
Such males could then secure the nest sites that are best for the development of the eggs, and thus attract the most females. Evidence
suggesting this situation in the darter perch *Etheostoma nigrum* was presented by Winn (1958). Other males should crowd around this most
attractive male to maximize their own chances of attracting females, as in
the green sunfish (Hunter, 1963), the bluehead wrasse (Warner *et al.*,
1975), or gouramies of the genus *Trichogaster* (Wright, 1976). The male
attributes contributing to such victories are also correlated with adaptation to that particular environment: adaptations leading to increased
trophic efficiency result in larger size and/or superior energy balance. In
a relatively predictable environment, the genomes of such successful
males should converge upon an optimal configuration. Females would
then maximize their reproductive success by spawning with such males.

It should follow that sexual dimorphism is reduced in those lekking
species that are polyandrous. However, because of the brevity of mating, selection will still favor a high degree of dimorphism to enable rapid
unambiguous recognition of the opposite sex. This can be based purely
on coloration and shape (or possibly on sounds or chemicals), with size
dimorphism being more important when polyandry does not occur.

Thus we predict that when position effects are marked, the males will
be dimorphic for size and for color and shape. On the contrary, when
females are less discriminating, the males should be dimorphic for color
and shape but not necessarily for size. Size dimorphism should still be

expressed to some degree, however, because size can still be important in obtaining a position of the lek. In fact, when the breeding sites are in especially short supply, as may occur where some annual killifishes breed, size dimorphism should be pronounced.

We have written as if environments were either clearly predictable or not, which is not the case. There is a continuum of situations between highly predictable and unpredictable environments. Most will be relatively predictable or unpredictable to varying degrees and with regard to different properties of the environment. Consequently, most species of lekking fishes should reflect a mixed strategy. The more predictable the environment, the more prevalent should be dimorphism, polygyny, and position effect, and vice versa.

2.5 Persistence of the Lek and of the Occupation of Territories by Individual Males

Avian leks are typically occupied for part of each day during the breeding season. The resident males spend the remainder of the day foraging. Individual males of the ruff and several lekking grouse are faithful to a particular site within the lek, as are long-tailed and white-bearded manakins (Mercedes Foster, in prep.; Lill, 1974). There are no data available on site attachment in other lekking species. In some lekking grouse, males will revisit the lek site during the fall, well outside of the breeding season (Wiley, 1973).

Species inhabiting open habitats are active on the lek during the early hours of the day. One such species, the great snipe, even displays at night during the full moon (Gadamer, 1858). This is apparently an adaptation to minimize aerial predation faced by birds displaying in the open (Lack, 1968; Wiley, 1973).

The situation is less clear in forest dwelling species. The impression conveyed in the literature is that males of these species are active on the lek during the latter part of the day (Gilliard, 1962; Snow, 1970). In males of the long-tailed and white-bearded manakin, peaks of activity occur at different times in different parts of their long breeding season (Mercedes Foster, in prep.).

Such intermittent lekking, in which the lek is occupied for only part of each day, is also practiced by some teleosts. It is characteristic of lekking cyprinodonts, melanotaenids, and atherinids, and it may possibly occur in the Sacramento perch (Barlow, 1961; Echelle, 1973; Murphy, 1948; Loiselle, unpublished data). The period of sexual activity, as would be predicted in poikilothermous organisms, is correlated with water temperature and usually occurs in late morning and early afternoon. Occasionally, however, high temperatures interfere with lekking during the afternoon (Barlow, 1958, 1961). In most marine situations, or in large lakes, the temperatures are more stable and consequently less important as phasic triggers, though thermal effects have been reported (e.g., Fiedler, 1964).

Intermittent lekking is feasible in noncustodial species that produce demersal eggs, such as some cyprinodontids, and that habitually breed in environments into which few or no spawn predators penetrate. This allows males to practice intermittent lekking while accumulating eggs in their territories. It is also feasible for species that shed pelagic eggs into the plankton, such as parrotfishes (Barlow, 1976b), and wrasses (Reinboth, 1973). In neither case is the male's presence required to protect the spawn, nor is there an energetic investment in nest construction to be defended. Intermittent lekking may, nevertheless, be synchronous if for some reason the females have preferred times for spawning.

In contrast to some lekking birds (Wiley, 1973), there is no recorded instance of sexually inactive male fish visiting the lek site outside of periods of reproductive activity. This doubtless happens, however incidentally, in cyprinodontids confined to small pools and in other fishes.

Continuous lekking, in which the males occupy the lek without interruption for foraging, relying upon stored energy reserves to sustain their activity, is known only in teleosts. (The mating systems of penguins and albatrosses, and of pinnipeds, though not examples of lek systems, provide parallel cases among birds and mammals; see Ashmole, 1971; Bartholomew, 1970; LeBoeuf, 1972; LeBoeuf and Peterson, 1969.) Continuous lekking is predictable, for obvious reasons, in fish species practicing some type of defense of the spawn, be it constructing an elaborate nest or overtly repulsing predators. Sustained lekking in males of maternal mouth-brooding cichlids, however, cannot be thus explained. It may instead be correlated with the more overt competition for territories within their leks. Coe (1966), for example, reported that male *Sarotherodon grahami* that left their territories to forage lost them immediately to other males and had to contest their possession, often unsuccessfully, with the new proprietors.

There are few data on how long an individual male retains a site on the lek. Reighard (1913) stated that sexually active male logperch, *Percina caproides*, spend 10 to 14 days on the lek, then retire to deeper water. Neil (1964) found that sexually active male *Sarotherodon mossambicus* hold a nest site in the aquarium from three to ten days, with a mode around five to six days. Similarly, successful males of the green sunfish have a period of occupancy of around eight to nine days (Hunter, 1963). In

Thailand, each group of lekking male *Trichogaster trichopterus* lasts about one week (Wright, 1976). Otherwise, it is known only that the males remain on the lek for a substantial period of the reproductive cycle, a period of time that can vary from several hours, as in the Tanganyikan maternal mouth-brooders *Xenotilapia melanogenys* and *X. ochrogenys*, whose spawning is characterized by a remarkable degree of synchrony (Brichard, 1975), to several days at least.

As with intermittent lekking, activity appears correlated with water temperature and usually peaks in the late morning and early afternoon.

2.6 Environmental Factors as Determinants of Lek Sites

Traditionality of lek areas is one of the most remarkable features of avian lekking. In fact, Wilson (1975) gives traditionality as a criterion to distinguish lekking from the more general set called communal displaying (Table 2.2).

Armstrong (1947) documented traditionality in five galliform species (Argus pheasant, blackcock, prairie chicken, sharp-tailed grouse, and the extinct heath hen—a race of the prairie chicken), one charadriiform species (the ruff), and two forest-dwelling passeriform species (greater bird of paradise, Gould's manakin). Wiley (1973) presented persuasive evidence for traditionality in an additional galliform, the sage grouse, and Gilliard (1962) for another passeriform, the cock-of-the-rock. Traditionality is also well developed in long-tailed manakins (M. Foster, in prep.) and in white-bearded manakins (Lill, 1974). In contrast, nontraditionality appears to be an important feature of lekking as practiced by one charadriiform species, the buff-breasted sandpiper (Pitelka, personal communication).

This dichotomy of traditionality versus nontraditionality may be

TABLE 2.2 Circumstances associated with traditionality

A. Physical environment
  1. Relatively predictable
  2. More "best" arenas exist than are generally used
  3. Arenas often modified by the males' behavior
B. Animals
  1. Dispersed breeding population
  2. Relatively long-lived (at least more than one breeding period)
  3. Delayed sexual maturity in males
  4. Central nervous system complex enough to allow of learning and memory

explained by assuming that the location of avian lek sites is, or has been, determined by environmental factors. In the case of traditionalists, the factors are presumably a predictable environment coupled with the limited number of areas from which effective displays can be presented. These factors are particularly evident in the case of forest-dwelling species. Authors who have reported on the incidence of lekking in manakins (Chapman, 1935; Lill, 1974; Snow, 1963), bellbirds (Snow, 1970), cock-of-the-rock (Gilliard, 1962) and birds of paradise (Armstrong, 1947; Goodfellow, 1910) emphasize the following: (1) the performance of the displays requires open space; (2) special conditions of lighting are needed to emphasize the distinctive features of plumage; (3) the lek arenas are located in areas where environmental factors have disturbed the continuity of the predominantly closed forest canopy.

The situation in marsh- and prairie-dwelling birds may not be as obvious and is open to debate. Wiley (1973) and Hogan-Warburg (1966), however, implied that the traditional lek areas of the sage grouse and the ruff, respectively, were originally positioned in relatively open patches of habitat where edaphic or other environmental factors had thinned out the prevailing assemblage of forbs and grasses. Students of avian lekking regularly report the occurrence of behavior by resident males that intentionally or fortuitously preserves and perhaps enhances the suitability of the arena for lekking (e.g., Armstrong, 1947; Gilliard, 1962; Hogan-Warburg, 1966; L. H. Kermott, personal communication; Wiley, 1973).

Limited lek sites alone, however, could not account for the highly developed traditionality seen in some species. It requires in addition a relatively predictable environment coupled with a reasonably long life span and the ability of the males to remember the location of the lekking grounds. Otherwise, it would be difficult to account for the fact that some sites are used year after year by long-tailed manakins, while other sites that seem to have all the necessary features are not utilized (M. Foster, in prep.). It would also be difficult to account for the persistence of lek sites when the environment is unfavorably altered. A well-known example was provided by male ruffs who persisted in displaying on old sites that came to lie in a road (Armstrong, 1947).

In the case of the buff-breasted sandpiper, environmental factors impose nontraditionality. The sandpipers' leks are ephemeral and transitory, males gathering and displaying for periods of a week or two in a given spot, then apparently moving elsewhere to repeat the performance. Pitalka (personal communication) suggested to us that the placement of a lek in these sandpipers is influenced by the available supply of food for the nesting female and her brood and by year-to-year variations in the physical environment, such as unpredictable patterns of runoff from the melting ice and snow.

According to Pitelka's model, transitory lekking permits exploiting a patchy environment by moving over a wide area and settling in to display only where the terrain is suitable and food abundant. This maximizes the probability that females impregnated by them will be able to raise their broods successfully in the short Arctic nesting season. The occurrence of suitable areas depends on a multitude of local climatic factors and is therefore relatively unpredictable. Traditionality would be maladaptive under such conditions.

Lekking may also be correlated with population density. R. R. Warner and S. G. Hoffman (personal communication) are testing the following model, which was inspired by observations on wrasses and parrotfishes off the coast of Panama. A similar model is being developed for other vertebrates by S. T. Emlen and L. W. Oring (personal communication). We present the model in abbreviated form, with due apologies.

When the population density is low, the prevailing mating system is a territorial harem society. At intermediate densities lekking develops. At high population densities dominance relationships break down and territories are forsaken; a number of females may spawn synchronously, each with more than one male in attendance—the *conubium confusum* of Breder and Rosen (1966).

The intermediate population density at which lekking occurs must be considered relative to the species. It is our impression that lekking species of birds and fishes are relatively common. In general terms, lekking is probably favored by population densities that are relatively high, but not so high that social organization breaks down.

The dependence of many teleosts on a hygienic spawning location for their relatively vulnerable eggs means that environmental factors directly determine the location of lek sites in species practicing noncustodial, protocustodial, and paternal-custodial lekking. Traditionality in the avian sense is not well documented in such species. However, traditionality should be expected among mobile species occurring in relatively stable environments, such as the rocky littoral of the African Great Lakes or the protected coral reef. There the physical factors that dictate optimal spawning sites differ little from one year to the next. (However, the physical features of some coral reefs may at times be drastically altered in regions where violent storms occur (Barlow, personal observation; R. R. Warner, personal communication). In variable environments, in contrast, lek sites can change in location from year to year.

The bluehead wrasse provides an example of a coral reef fish with traditional lek sites. One population of this labrid used the same area as a spawning site over a period of five years (Reinboth, 1973). While this represents traditionality in the broadest sense, the reproductive modality of this species introduces complicating factors not encountered on avian leks. The bluehead wrasse sheds pelagic eggs into the plankton. It thus adjusts the precise location of its spawning site within a general area from day to day, and even within a day, apparently to remain in a down-current zone that favors the fertilized eggs being swept out to sea (R. R. Warner, personal communication).

Another instance of what may be lek traditionality in the avian sense is provided by the maternal mouthbrooding Tanganyikan chichlid *Cyathopharynx furcifer*. Brichard (1975) reported that males of this species construct sand nests on top of flat-crowned rock blocks. Sexually active males may be found using such areas continuously. Though the number of such sites is limited, intraspecific aggression is not pronounced, and resident males visit one another's territories in a manner reminiscent of such lek birds as the ruff and some grouse. Additional instances of apparent lek site traditionality have been reported for males of several other maternal mouth-brooding cichlids (Fryer, 1956; Iles, 1960; Kirchshofer, 1953; Lowe-McConnell, 1958).

Substratum-independent or "free-water" spawning behavior has been described for the maternal mouth-brooding Tanganyikan cichlids *Tropheus moorii, Limnochromis microlepidotus,* and *L. leptosoma* (Scheuermann, 1976; Wickler, 1969). In most instances, however, sexually active males prepare a nest from which courtship is directed and within which spawning occurs. Since their eggs do not remain in the male's nest during their development, these cichlids are not substratum-dependent in the same sense as are teleosts that produce demersal eggs. Even so their emancipation is not complete.

Regardless of their pattern of brood care, cichlds, gouramies, and other teleosts are limited in their selection of spawning sites by predation on both the breeding adults and their spawn. Ease of constructing nests will also vary among sites, as will the degree of shelter from wave action. These factors can adversely influence a male's reproductive success by obliging him to expend energy in nest preparation and maintenance that would otherwise be devoted to courting or to prolonging his time on the lek. The substratum preferences reported for the cichlid fish *Sarotherodon macrochir* by Ruwet (1962b) were probably in response to the suitability of the substrate. And the destruction of *Haplochromis* leks by wave action, reported by Kirchshofer (1953) and by Fryer and Iles (1972), suggests that shelter is indeed significant in selecting a lekking ground. The place where lekking is done can be important for still other reasons, as when mobile reef inhabitants seeks a favorable lauch window through which to shed their pelagic eggs.

In some instances, the siting of leks is constrained by adverse physiographic factors. An extreme case is provided by two cichlids(Coe, 1966, 1969). *Sarotherodon grahami* inhabits hot springs in Lake Magadi, *S. alcalicus* the hypersaline Lake Natron, both in the Rift Valley of Kenya and Tanzania. Thermal factors severely limit the areas available to sexually active males *S. grahami,* while salinity gradients restrict male *S. alcalicus* in their choice of nesting sites.

3   EVOLUTION OF LEKKING

Early attempts to determine the functional significance of avian lekking are exemplified by the following passage from Armstrong (1947: 225):

The conclusion is ineluctable that the advantage of arena or lek displays must be very great. It is highly probable that not only is sociality in itself stimulating, but that the psychological effects of pugnacious posturing have a beneficial effect on the race.

These remarks reflect the group-selectionist framework within which many previous workers approached the study of this animal reproductive adaptation and others.

In this account, we follow the lead of Hamilton (1964), Maynard Smith (1966), Williams (1966) in affirming that the functional basis of any reproductive adaptation is the increased reproductive success of the individual practicing it. Accepting this principle, we should be able to explain both the functional significance of lekking and how it evolved. This requires an examination of ecological factors together with an understanding of the limitations imposed by an organisms' reproductive biology (Table 2.3).

3.1   Avian Lekking in Relation to Feeding Adaptation

While the ability of the female to raise a brood unaided is a precondition for the evolution of lekking, lek birds are not the only species in which the male is divorced from a parental role. Alternative adaptations based on uniparental care of the brood are possible, ranging from harem polygyny to simple "promiscuity," practiced concurrently with or inde-

TABLE 2.3 Circumstances promoting lekking in birds

A. Properties of the physical environment
  1. Natural phasic stimuli for synchronization of mating, e.g., seasonal changes in photoperiod
  2. Best places for courtship and mating existing apart from feeding grounds, are characterized by:
     (a) Spatial properties that enhance signal propagation
     (b) Lack of ambush sites and/or unobstructed view of approaching predators
B. Trophic considerations
  1. Food resources either continuously or patchily dispersed.
     (a) Promote mobility, lack of site tenacity, and tendency to aggregate
     (b) Create need for effective long-range communication
  2. Peaks of superabundance
     (a) Remove necessity of biparental provisioning
     (b) Promote synchronous breeding
C. Predation
  1. Promotes clustering of displaying males, which confers some protection upon them
  2. Promotes either dispersal of camouflaged nests or clustering of nests in a secure place, well away from displaying males
D. Social factors
  1. Traditionality
  2. Male need satisfied by small space, since territory serves for mating only
  3. Relatively high population densities

---

pendent of colonial nesting. Such modes of reproduction probably arise when the trophic advantage of biparental care is outweighed by other factors, for example, by the increased risk of predation resulting from the more conspicuous activities of two parents around the next (Lack, 1968; Selander, 1972). This applies to lekking species as well. Furthermore, harem polygyny and/or simple "promiscuity" occur in such groups as grouse, pheasants, and hummingbirds—groups that contain lek species. There must be finer or overlooked differences in environmental factors that correlate with lekking. A brief digression to consider bird territoriality in its best-known form will help us bring out a salient difference.

Classical avian territoriality is feasible only if a resource, such as food, is sufficiently concentrated to make its defense economically profitable (Brown, 1964). In most territorial birds, the male's defense of his territory simultaneously assures the resources adequate to lodge and fledge a clutch, fixes his position in space, and advertises his presence to females. Conversely, the distribution of discrete advertised territories in a spatial mosaic increases the likelihood of a female encountering an unmated, territory-holding male. The system thus maximizes the fitness of both individuals in a pair.

The situation has to be different in lekking birds. Without exception, they forage widely for dispersed food, ranging from fruit or nectar to seeds and insects (Lack, 1968). In some instances, not only are the foods dispersed, but they also tend to be unevenly distributed in time and/or in space. And the higher the latitude, the more compressed in time is the period when food is maximally available.

Such a feeding adaptation has at least four consequences for the behavior of its practitioners:

1. The birds must be prepared to move on to a better location when the local supply of food dwindles. They are thus less likely to evolve the behavioral mechanisms necessary for sustaining large territories, notably high levels of aggressive responsiveness, a large individual distance, and site tenacity.

2. The nature of the food is such that when it is sufficiently abundant for breeding it is superabundant. Defense of the resource is thus economically unrewarding. Further, only one parent is then required, either as the provisioner, as in song birds, or as the caretaker of self-feeding offspring, as in gallinaceous birds.

3. Regardless of whether the food supply is uniformly dispersed or patchily distributed, there is still the risk of males and females foraging in different areas, or of individuals being widely separated. They need a communication system to bring them together.

4. We assume that there is a best place, or places, for the males to communicate to the females their presence, identity, and readiness to breed. We also assume that males, not females, congregate, because males mate repeatedly, and because the parental sex cannot afford to be conspicuous to the degree demanded by sexual competition. Males will therefore tend to congregate at, and compete among themselves for, the best sites. Selection will favor the larger, stronger males in such a situation, leading to the evolution of size dimorphism between the sexes. Further, the broadcast range and channel saturation of the communication system will be heightened through the summed activities of displaying males, increasing the individual fitness of each of them.

The initial stages of a trend toward lekking in birds are evident in nonlekking grouse and hummingbirds. There, male possession of discrete all-purpose territories contrasts with exclusively female brood care.

The common denominator of such territorial behavior is active defense of a suitable display site by the male. Such sites are prerequisite to reproductive success.

Birds whose foraging patterns preclude the defense of linked feeding and display territories have a serious problem. They must ensure access to essential display sites while maintaining a normal intake of food. The difficulty is apt to be acute when the physical setting or predation severely limit the number of sites available. Birds other than oceanic species like penguins are evidently unable to store sufficient energy to allow males to occupy their display sites continuously. They have to vacate the sites daily in order to feed.

Only two alternative solutions are therefore possible. The first is for the male birds to engage in physical competition for display sites after each foraging trip. Such activity would be bioenergetically wasteful. It would also increase the risk of injury to the combatants and make them more vulnerable to predators—in short, give them a pyrrhic victory. All these factors would reduce individual reproductive success.

The second alternative is to lessen overt competition by increasing the threshold of responses to stimuli eliciting aggression. That would permit males to occupy closely adjoining display sites without continual aggression. This solution also minimizes the expenditure of energy while diminishing the risk of injury and predation.

Lekking as practices by such forest species as the bearded bell bird and the cock-of-the-rock appears to illustrate this early grade of lek evolution. Their simple groupings of displaying males appear to lack such concomitants of classical avian leks as classes of males, rigid spatial distribution of display territories within an arena, marked position effects, and clear protocols of site succession.

Classical avian lekking, as typified by the ruff, blackcock, and sage grouse, is interpreted by us as aggregations of displaying males whose territories are arranged according to dominance relationships (see also Lill, 1974). Contrary to much widely accepted thought, the dichotomy between territoriality and dominance is not sharp (Brown, 1963). This type of lekking is characteristic of species inhabiting open country. The relatively undifferentiated topography there results in large aggregations of males, providing enhanced "artificial" land marks for females. In such large aggregations, competition for the best display sites would be increased. Selection should favor individual males who can compete for those vital positions while minimizing the risks inherent in combat. Such behavior is apt to produce distinct dominance relationships.

Following these hypotheses, all the classic features of such avian leks may be interpreted as manifestations of a hierarchial social structure.

Their existence therefore would be faciliated by long-term association of males outside of the breeding season. Those males would maintain or adjust their dominance relationships, obviating the need for high levels of aggression at the advent of the next breeding season. The delayed onset of male reproductive activity, another characteristic of birds with uniparental brood care, would also help in this respect: juvenile males are neither well equipped nor strongly motivated to contest for sites in the lek.

Lekking among birds implies the physical separation of display and nesting areas. With no further information, one can not predict whether such birds would lek or, alternatively, form polygynous colonies, as do village weaver birds, in which display and nesting occur in the same area (Crook, 1964). The missing element we believe to be the nature of nesting sites in relation to predation. As Crook pointed out, weaver birds concentrate their nests in the few trees that afford both a large measure of protection from predators and proximity to a rich supply of food. Thus when the predator-prey relationship favors clustered nests, given the foregoing ecological situation, a polygynous colony is predicted. But when the best antipredator adaptation is dispersed nests, as in grasslands, a lekking society will evolve.

The cock-of-the-rock provides an exception, but one that illustrates the importance of an adequate display arena. The females nest in colonies in rather dark caves with restricted entrances (Gilliard, 1962). Visual display within them must be ineffective. The males do not engage females there. Rather, they lek in forest galleries where shafts of sunlight strike their brilliant plumage.

We hypothesize, therefore, that the evolution of avian lekking requires first that food be maximally available for a relatively brief period. This leads to synchronization of reproductive activity. Second, the food must be superabundant, making its defense as a limiting factor economically unprofitable. This also permits males to confine their activities to courtship and insemination by facilitating the evolution of exclusively female brood care. Third, the distribution of the resource in space favors the evolution of a system of communication that will bring both sexes together.

Perhaps the most critical step in this process occurs when communal displays develop at the best available sites for their performance, determined largely by characteristic physical features of such locations. This defninition of "best" may include the presence of other males. Vocalizations and conspicuous movements of contrast-rich structures may thus undergo a multiplier effect that further enhances the detectability of each participating male by aiding females in finding the assemblage of displaying birds. The behavioral attributes of classical avian lekking will evolve, once this step has been taken, as selection pressures favor those modifications in behavior that facilitate the close proximity of sexually active males. Lastly, predation pressure must favor dispersed nesting. This will result in the movement of inseminated females away from the display ground. The end result is the complete spatial separation of display and nesting ground that is characteristic of lekking birds.

We also need to emphasize that the foregoing is a general scheme, and that the factors leading to lekking may have played relatively different roles in different species. In particular, we have slighted the possible importance of predation on the lekking birds (see Koivisto, 1965; Lack, 1968; Wiley, 1973). Lekking may have been, and may still be, crucial for birds that live in open country where little cover is available, but where the males must broadcast to attract females (Berger, Hammerstrom, and Hammerstrom, 1963). Then the males might congregate to reduce predation on themselves, as suggested for schools of fish (Williams, 1964) or any aggregating species (Hamilton, 1970; Wilson, 1975). In one mammal that leks in open country, the wildbeest, the males have been shown to be subject to heavy predation (Estes, 1969).

3.2 Lekking in Teleosts in Relation to Spawning-Site Dependence and Nest Predation

The evolution of lekking in teleosts (Table 2.4) is linked, we believe, to dependence upon suitable spawning sites, by the localized substrata for the deposition of demersal eggs or points assuring a favorable launch window for pelagic eggs. While synchrony of reproductive activity is imposed by environmental factors, as in birds, proximity is determined by the availability of suitable spawning sites. Where these spawning are limited in either occurrence or extensiveness, their sequestration, either totally or in part, by an individual may be a positive adaptation. Males would be in a better position to implement such an adaptation because of the greater energetic demand that the maturation of eggs places on females.

As in birds, however, total sequestration of a resource is reasonable only if its defense is economically profitable. Hence, while a male fish might, theoretically, enhance his fitness at the expense of conspecific competitors by monopolizing a spawning site *in toto*, such a strategy would be practical only if the energetic cost to its practitioner were exceeded in some manner by a positive return on the investment. Here the positive return would be enhanced reproductive success.

TABLE 2.4 Circumstances promoting lekking in teleosts

A. Properties of the physical environment
1. Natural phasic stimuli for synchronization of mating, e.g., seasonal changes in temperature, rainfall, or lunar/tidal cycles
2. Best places for courtship and spawning exist apart from feeding grounds. They are characterized by:
   (a) Hygienic properties that promote the development of the zygotes after spawning
   (b) Spatial and physical properties that enhance signal propagation
   (c) Relative freedom from predation due to
      (1) Inability of predators to penetrate the arena
      (2) Lack of ambush sites and/or unobstructed view of approaching predators
B. Trophic considerations
1. Lack of trophic component in brood care facilitates uniparental care of spawn
2. Ability to store metabolic reserves allows males to hold territories for extended periods of time
C. Predation
1. Promotes synchrony of breeding, as numbers of eggs and fry procured can "swamp" their predators
2. Promotes clustering of displaying males
   (a) Summated brood defense
   (b) Protection against predators of adult fish by "swamping" or by "selfish herd" phenomenon
D. Social Factors
1. Traditionality
2. Founder-male effect
3. Male needs satisfied by small space since
   (a) Territory used only for spawning or mating
   (b) Brood care strictly custodial
4. Relatively high population densities

We can find no record in the literature of any teleost whose reproductive pattern includes such behavior. Rather, the pattern that emerges is sequestration of a site only large enough to facilitate successful spawning. Because the lek site itself is unimportant in the nutrition of the offpsring in virtually all lekking teleosts, the defense of extensive territories is unnecessary.

Lekking therefore arises automatically in teleost fishes when the size of a discrete spawning territory sequestered by a male is small relative to extent of the available site. As the number of males entering the area and setting up territories increases, the size of each territory will contract to the smallest area required by each male in order to reproduce successfully. Under most circumstances, and for most animals, the resulting geometry will converge upon, but seldom achieve, an hexagonal array of territories (Barlow, 1974b; Grant, 1968).

We suspect that intermittent lekking is the most primitive manifestation of this reproductive strategy in teleosts. As males expend energy in obtaining and defending a site, selection will favor the evolution of site tenacity. From the standpoint of minimizing the chance of injuries sustained in intraspecific combat alone, this is a more efficient strategy than repeated contests for a suitable spawning site. The result of such selection would be the appearance of persistent lekking in the absence of any sort of parental care, such as is seen in some darter perches.

The defense of a spawning territory, even if only from conspecifics, confers serendipitously a degree of protection from predation to the eggs deposited therein. It requires little additional behavioral adjustment to broaden such defense to include heterospecific predators on the spawn. Natural selection would favor those fish who did practice such defense, or whose spawning behavior in some other manner favored the survival of their fry. Hence the widespread occurrence of some type of protective behavior among teleosts with demersal eggs.

Among teleosts that practice parental care, the primitive condition is for the male to establish a territory and for the female to visit him there (Barlow, 1963, 1964). The female then has four options: (1) She can remain with the male, an advanced condition shown by few kinds of fishes, and join in the care of the spawn. (2) She can assume full care of the eggs herself, while the male obtains further females elsewhere, as in some of the dwarf cichlids (Burchard, 1965). (3) She can pick up the eggs in her mouth and leave his territory. As previously noted, option (3) is confined to one family of fishes; it has clearly been derived from the first option—that is, joint parental care. (4) She can leave the eggs to the care of the male—the most general case. This solution permits the male to receive a number of females, accumulating eggs from them in his territory. However, if selection favors active paternal care, such as fanning the eggs, or assisting them to hatch, or dispersing the larvae, then the male will come to accept eggs for only a brief period in order to coordinate his care with the needs of the brood. Consequently, the reproductive system will become increasingly dissimilar to avian lekking.

We believe lekking to be prevalent among fresh-water teleosts because it is compatible with the third and fourth spawning options presented in the preceding paragraph. Indeed, it may actually facilitate their implementation in certain situations. Among maternal mouthbrooding cichlids, the advantages of lekking behavior must be similar to those that accrue to lek birds. Among custodial lekking fishes, participants in the lek may well benefit from a summed territorial defense, with centrally located males enjoying a reduced burden of defending the spawn because of the activities of peripherally located males. This factor appears to have influenced the evolution of lekking in gouramies of the genus *Trichogaster* (Wright, 1976). Regardless of whether they practice parental care or not, lekking teleosts have the potential advantage of swamping spawn predators with the sheer number of eggs and fry produced within a limited area, depending on the number of eggs and fry, and on predators and their capacity to devour eggs and fry.

Thus, just as predation upon nesting individuals has combined with feeding adaptations to produce lekking in birds, so has feeding biology and spawn predation, interacting with dependence upon hygienic spawning sites, led to the widespread occurrence of this type of mating system among teleosts.

4 AN OVERVIEW OF LEKKING IN FISHES

We would like in closing to be able to make a straightforward comparison of lekking in birds and in fishes (Table 2.5). That is not easily done, and for two reasons. First, there are more variations on the lekking theme within teleost fishes than exist among birds. Second, no one species of fish offers a pattern of lekking that is completely comparable to that seen in any bird. Yet all the cases previously cited fulfill our minimum prerequisites for lekking. These are synchrony of the breeding population, lekking grounds where males await females, sufficient mo-

TABLE 2.5 Characteristics of highly evolved lek systems in both birds and teleosts

---

A. General characteristics
   1. No feeding on the lek
   2. The more males present, the more females attracted
   3. Reduced aggression and increased intermale display
   4. Clear dominance relationships
   5. Well-developed sexual dimorphism
   6. "Cheating" by young or subordinate males rare
   7. Succession to central positions determined by a strict protocol
B. Characteristics of central males
   1. Largest and oldest are the most dominant
   2. Experience less interference with mating or spawning
   3. Devote relatively more time to courtship, less to status fights, territorial defense, or, in teleosts, antipredator behavior
   4. Females select central males
   5. Central males mate or spawn more than do other males

---

bility to move between separate areas for breeding and feeding, and performance of parental care, if it exists, by only one parent.

We do not include as a minimum prerequisite the absence of habitat constraints. Pitelka (personal communication) believes that it is necessary to show that there are available but unused alternate sites for lekking. Even when this can be demonstrated, it does not rule out the importance of suitable sites. For example, the long-tailed manakin apparently has a number of requirements for its arena, including a rare vine that is always present. Yet traditionality is highly developed, and some seemingly suitable sites are not used (M. Foster, in prep.). The issue is whether some attractive but limited features of the environment occur in only a few places, and thus help to concentrate the animals, or whether the animals themselves act as the focal point, given that adequate situations occur in a number of different places. We see these as interactive factors rather than opposing ones, and factors whose operation is effective to varying degrees, depending on the species.

A close parallel is exemplified by parrotfishes. The males take up positions on the lekking grounds for only a few hours during the day, as in grouse. And the situation is complicated by small males who resemble females and compete with the lekking males to fertilize the females' gametes.

Another reasonably close parallel is found in the desert pupfish whose reproductive pattern is probably typical of that of most cyprinodontid fishes. The males apparently leave the lek to feed and to sleep, as do classically lekking birds. There are even peripheral males that could be called satellites. The critical difference from birds, however, is that the demersal eggs are left in the male's territory, although the male provides no overt spawn care.

Most freshwater lekking fishes seem to be of the sunfish type. They differ among themselves in the extent to which they provide parental care, from protocustodial to paternal-custodial, and therefore remain continuously on the nest site. This mode of teleost lekking diverges most strongly from the avian paradigm in terms of the persistent occupancy of courts by sexually active males and the existence of a paternal custodial role.

The last type of lekking in fishes is that of maternal mouth-brooding cichlids. Cichlids parallel birds in that the females have their gametes fertilized at the lek, and then take them to separate brooding grounds to rear and, in many cases, shepherd the offspring. Unlike birds, the males stay on the lek for periods of a week or so. And unlike other fishes, the nature of the substrate is obviously not critical for the development of the eggs. The particular site, however, can be important for nest-building and courtship, and for the avoidance of predation.

Four factors in the biology of teleost fishes stand out as being responsible for the differences from birds. One is that they regularly store metabolic reserves, a practice that allows the males to remain on station without feeding for long periods of time. The second is external fertilization. The third is the sensitivity of their eggs to the medium that surrounds them. The fourth factor is the huge clutch size of teleosts, with a correspondingly lower investment per gamete.

Given this diversity within lekking by different species of teleosts, it is difficult and perhaps premature to attempt to explore how trophic adaptations might be of overriding importance in the evolution of lekking in fishes, as we attempted to do for birds (but see Barlow, 1976, for parallels in parrotfishes). However, some obvious generalizations can be made about ecological factors, even if they only serve as hypotheses to be disproved.

The trophic adaptations of lekking fishes must require a degree of mobility compatible with moving to breeding areas. The breeding areas must have some features that make them more suitable than those in which other activities take place, particularly feeding; these would include favorable physical conditions for the development of eggs and lessened vulnerability to predation on the fish and/or their eggs. Breeding must also be sharply phasic to bring a number of reproductively responsive animals together; phasing may be through trophic and climatic factors such as rainfall, or through tidal cycles linked to lunar periods.

The foregoing general features of lekking probably apply to any kind of animal that utilizes a lekking mode of reproduction.

5 CONCLUSION

We need to return, in closing, to our liberal usage of the term "lekking," for it is sure to antagonize those who take a purist point of view. We do not think it is important whether that which we call lekking in fishes corresponds exactly to that which has been described as lekking in birds. We have tried to extract the general features of the reproductive strategy of lekking and to relate it to possible ecological determinants. Further, we have purposely arrayed the types of lekking in fishes in a way that brings out the transitions to other reproductive adaptations—for example, by small steps from lekking to colonial breeding of the weaver bird or ballan wrasse type (Sjolander et al., 1972; Burchard, 1965). Lekking is then better understood in the broader framework of a fuzzy set of polygamous mating systems.

Finally, we are not enraptured by the term "lekking." Should ornithologists or others bridle at our adulteration of the concept, they may feel more comfortable retaining lekking as a special avian subset of a more inclusive and neutral term, such as arena breeding or communal displaying. If so, they will need to assure themselves of the homogeneity of the phenomenon among lekking birds.

In conclusion, we hope that this comparison of one behavior in two environments has produced a more general understanding of the reasons for one rather spectacular mode of reproduction, lekking.

6 ACKNOWLEDGMENTS

A simple "thank you" hardly does justice to Frank A. Pitelka for his contribution. He inspired this article through his stimulating and original lectures on avian lekking. If we have expressed what appear to be new views on that subject, they doubtless derive directly or indirectly from him. We are also grateful to Frank A. Pitelka, Jeffrey R. Baylis, Eric A. Fisher, M. H. A. Keenleyside, Pete Meyers, Stephen C. Stearns and Robert R. Warner for reading this paper and offering a number of suggestions for its improvement. The writing was supported by National Science Foundation grant GB 32192 to G. W. Barlow.

REFERENCES

Abel, E. F. 1961. Freiwasserstudien über das Fortplfanzungsverhalten des Mönchsfishes, *Chromis chromis* L., einem Vertreter der Pomacentriden im Mittelmeer. Z. Tierpsychol. **18:** 441–449.

Adams, C. C. and T. L. Hankinson. 1928. The ecology and economics of Oneida Lake fish. Roosevelt Wild Life Ann. **1:** 241–548.

Albrecht, H. 1969. Behaviour of four species of Atlantic damselfish from Columbia, South America (*Abudefduf saxatilis, A. taurus, Chromis multilineata, C. cyanea;* Pisces Pomacentridae). Z. Tierpsychol. **26:** 662–676.

Alexander, R. D. and T. E. Moore. 1962. The evolutionary relationships of 17-year and 13-year cicadas, and three new species (Homoptera, Cicadidae, *Magicicada*). Misc. Publ. Mus. Zool. Univ. Mich. **21:** 1–57.

Apfelbach, R. and D. Leong. 1970. Zum Kampfverhalten in der Gattung *Tilapia* (Pisces, Cichlidae). Z. Tierpsychol. **27:** 98–107.

Armstrong, E. A. 1947. *Bird Display and Behaviour.* Lindsay Drummond, London, 431 p.

Ashmole, N. P. 1971. Sea bird ecology and the marine environment. *In:* D. S. Farner and J. R. King, Eds. *Avian Biology.* Academic Press, New York. P. 223–286.

Baker, W. J. 1933. The blue-eye (*Pseudomugil signifer* Kner). Aquariana (San Francisco) **2:** 5–8.

Barlow, G. W. 1958. Daily movements of desert pupfish, *Cyprindon macularius*, in shore pools of the Salton Sea, California. Ecology **39:** 580–587.

Barlow, G. W. 1961. Social behavior of the desert pupfish, *Cyprinodon macularius* in the field and in the aquarium. Am. Midl. Nat., **65:** 339–359.

Barlow, G. W. 1963. Evolution of behavior. Science **139:** 851–852.

Barlow, G. W. 1964. Ethology of the Asian teleost *Badis badis*. V. Dynamics of fanning and other parental activities, with comments on the behavior of the larvae and postlarvae. Z. Tierpsychol. **21:** 99–123.

Barlow, G. W. 1974a. Contrasts in social behavior between Central American cichlid fishes and coral-reef surgeon fishes. Am. Zool. **14:** 9–34.

Barlow, G. W. 1974b. Hexagonal territories. Anim. Behav. **22:** 876–878.

Barlow, G. W. 1976a. The Midas cichlid in Nicaragua. *In:* T. B. Thorson, Ed. *Investigations of the Ichthyofauna of Nicaraguan Lakes*. School of Life Sciences, University of Nebraska, Lincoln, Nebraska. P. 333–358.

Barlow, G. W. 1976b. On the sociobiology of four Puerto Rican parrotfishes (Scaridae). Mar. Biol. **33:** 281–293.

Barlow, G. W. 1976c. Introduction. *Scientific American Reader in Ichthyology*. Freeman, San Francisco. P. 1–8.

Barney, R. L. and B. J. Anson. 1923. Life history and ecology of the orange-spotted sunfish, *Lepomis humilis*. U.S. Comm. Fish. (1922) (938) Appendix 15: 16 p.

Bartholomew, G. A. 1970. A model for the evolution of pinniped polygyny. Evolution **24:** 546–559.

Beeman, H. W. 1924. Habits and propagation of small-mouthed black bass. Trans. Am. Fish. Soc. **54:** 92–107.

Bendell, J. F. and P. W. Elliot. 1967. Behavior and the regulation of numbers in blue grouse. Can. Wildl. Serv. Rept., Ser. No. 4, Indian Affairs and Northern Development, Ottawa, p. 1–76.

Berger, D. D., F. Hammerstrom, and F. N. Hammerstrom. 1963. The effect of raptors on prairie chickens on booming grounds. J. Wildl. Manag. **27:** 778–791.

Beuchner, H. K. and H. D. Roth. 1974. The lek system in Uganda kob antelope. Am. Zool. **14:** 145–162.

Blache, J. 1964. Les poissons du bassin du Tchad et du bassin adjacent du Mayo Kebbi. Mem. Off. Rech. Sci. Tech. Outre Mer, Paris. 483 p.

Bradbury, J. W. 1972. The silent symphony: tuning in on the bat. *In:* T. B. Allen, Ed. *The Marvels of Animal Behavior*. National Geographic Society. P. 112–125.

Brattstrom, B. H. 1974. The evolution of reptilian social behavior. Am. Zool. **14:** 35–49.

Brawn, V. M. 1961. Aggressive behavior in the cod (*Gadus callarias* L.). Behaviour **18:** 107–147.

Breder, C. M. 1934. Ecology of an oceanic fresh-water lake, Andros Island, Bahamas, with special reference to its fishes. Zoologica (New York) **18:** 57–88.

Breder, C. M. 1936. The reproductive habits of the North American sunfishes (Family Centrarchidae). Zoologica (New York) **21:** 1–47.

Breder, C. M. and D. E. Rosen. 1966. *Modes of Reproduction in Fishes*. Natural History Press, Garden City (Am. Mus. Nat. Hist.) Pub. 941 p.

Brichard, P. 1975. Reflexions sur le choix de la nidification ou de l'incubation buccale comme mode de reproduction chez certaines populations de poissons cichlides du Lac Tanganyika. Rev. Zool. Afr. **89:** 871–888.

Brown, J. L. 1963. Aggressiveness, dominance, and social organization in the Steller's jay. Condor **65:** 460–484.

Brown, J. L. 1964. The evolution of diversity in avian territorial systems. Wilson Bull. **76:** 160–169.

Bruggen, A. C. van. 1965. Records and observations in the Port Elizabeth Oceanarium in 1960. Zool. Garten (Leipzig) **31:** 184–202.

Buck, J. B. 1938. Synchronous rhythmic flashing of fireflies. Qt. Rev. Biol. **13:** 301–314.

Burchard, J. E. 1965. Family structure in the dwarf cichlid *Apistogramma trifasciatum* Eigenmann and Kennedy. Z. Tierpsychol. **22:** 150–162.

Burchard, J. E. 1967. The family Cichlidae. *In:* W. Reed, Ed. *Fish and Fisheries of Northern Nigeria.* Ministry of Agriculture, Zaria. P. 123–143.

Campanella, P. J. and L. L. Wolf. 1974. Temporal leks as a mating system in a temperate zone dragonfly (Odonata: Anisoptera): I: *Plathemis lydia* (Drury). Behaviour **51:** 49–87.

Chapman, F. M. 1935. The courtship of Gould's manakin (*Manacus v. vitellinus*) on Barro Colorado Island, Canal Zone. Bull. Amer. Mus. Nat. Hist. **68:** 471–525.

Coe, M. J. 1966. The biology of *Tilapia grahami* Boulenger in Lake Magadi, Kenya. Acta Tropica **23:** 146–177.

Coe, M. J. 1969. Observations on *Tilapia alcalica* Hilgendorf, an endemic cichlid fish from Lake Natron, Tanzania. Rev. Zool. Bot. Afr. **80:** 1–14.

Collias, N. E. and E. Ç. Collias 1969. Size of breeding colony related to attraction of mates in a tropical passerine bird. Ecology **50:** 481–488.

Colwell, R. K. 1974. Predictability, constancy, and contingency of periodic phenomena. Ecology **55:** 1148–1153.

Constantz, G. O. 1975. Behavioral ecology of mating in the male Gila topminnow *Poeciliopsis occidentalis* (Cyprinodontiformes, Poeciliidae). Ecology **56:** 966–973.

Crook, J. H. 1964. The evolution of social organization and visual communication in the weaver birds (Ploceinae). Behaviour Suppl. **10:** 1–178.

Daget, J. 1954. Les poissons du Niger superieur. Mem. Inst. Fran. Afr. Noir., Dakar (65). 391 p.

Dawkins, R., and T. R. Carlisle. 1976. Parental investment, mate desertion, and a fallacy. Nature (London) **262:** 131–133.

Echelle, A. A. 1973. Behavior of the pupfish, *Cyprinodon rubrofluviatilis.* Copeia **1973:** 68–76.

Emlen, S. T. 1968. Territoriality in the bullfrog, *Rana catesbiana.* Copeia **1968:** 240–244.

Estes, R. D. 1969. Territorial behavior of the wildebeest (*Connochaetus taurinus* Burchell, 1823). Z. Tierpsychol. **26:** 284–370.

Fiedler, K. 1964. Verhaltensstudien an Lippfischen der Gattung *Crenilabrus* (Labridae, Perciformes). Z. Tierpsychol. **21:** 521–591.

Fishelson, L. 1970. Behaviour and ecology of a population of *Abudefduf saxatilis* (Pomacentridae, Teleostei) at Eilat (Red Sea). Anim. Behav. **18:** 225–237.

Fryer, G. 1956. Biological notes on some cichlid fishes of Lake Nyasa. Rev. Zool. Bot. Afr. **54:** 1–7.

Fryer, G. and T. D. Iles 1972. *The Cichlid Fishes of the Great Lakes of Africa.* Oliver and Boyd, Edinburgh. 611 p.

Gadamer, H. 1858. Das Balzen des *Scolopax major.* J. Ornithol. **6:** 235–237.

Geist, V. and F. Walther, Eds. 1974. *The Behaviour of Ungulates and Its Relation to Management.* International Union for Conservation of Nature and Natural Resources, Morges, Switzerland. Vol. 1 & 2. 940 p.

Gilliard, E. T. 1962. On the breeding behavior of the cock-of-the-rock. Bull. Am. Mus. Nat. Hist. **124:** 31–68.

Goodfellow, W. 1910. Notes on birds of paradise. Avic. Mag. **1:** 277–286.

Grant, P. R. 1968. Polyhedral territories of animals. Am. Nat. **102:** 75–80.

Greeley, J. R. 1927. Fishes of the Genesee region with an annotated list. *In: A Biological Survey of the Genesse River System.* Suppl. 16th Annual Rpt. (1926) N. Y. State Conserv. Dept. (Albany). Ser. 1, 4. P. 47–66.

Greeley, J. R. 1929. Fishes of the Erie-Niagra watershed. *In: A Biological Survey of the Erie-Niagara System.* Suppl. 18th Ann. Rept. (1928) N. Y. State Conserv. Dept. (Albany). Ser. 3, 6. P. 150–179.

Hamilton, W. D. 1964. The genetical evolution of social behaviour. J. Theor. Biol. **7:** 1–52.

Hamilton, W. D. 1970. Geometry for the selfish herd. J. Theor. Biol. **31:** 295–311.

Hankinson, T. L. 1920. Notes on life histories of Illinois fish. Trans. Illinois State Acad. Sci. **12:** 132–150.

Hildemann, W. H. 1959. A cichlid fish, *Symphysodon discus,* with unique nurture habits. Am. Nat. **93:** 27–34.

Hjorth, I. 1970. Reproductive behaviour in Tetraonidae. Viltrevy **7:** 184–596.

Hogan-Warburg, A. J. 1966. Social behaviour of the ruff, *Philomachus pugnax.* Ardea **54:** 109–229.

Hubbs, C. L. and G. P. Cooper. 1935. Age and growth of the long-eared and green sunfishes in Michigan. Papers Michigan Acad. Sci. Arts lett. **20:** 669–696.

Hubbs, C. L. and G. P. Cooper. 1936. Minnows of Michigan. Bull. Cranbrook Inst. Sci. **(8):** 1–95.

Hunter, J. R. 1963. The reproductive behavior of the green sunfish, *Lepomis cyanellus.* Zoologica (New York) **48:** 13–24.

Iersel, J. J. A. van. 1953. An analysis of the parental behaviour of the male three-spined stickleback (*Gasterosteus aculeatus* L.). Behaviour Suppl. **3:** 1–159.

Iersel, J. J. A. van. 1958. Some aspects of territorial behaviour of the male three-spined stickleback. Arch. Neerl. Zool. **13,** Suppl. 1: 384–400.

Iles, T. D. 1960. Prebreeding migration of common Lake Nyasa fishes. Con. Sci. Afr. 3rd Symp. Hydrobiol. Major Lakes. P. 131–132.

Jarman, P. J. 1974. The social organization of antelope in relation to their ecology. Behaviour **58:** 215–267.

Keenleyside, M. H. A. 1972. Intraspecific intrusions into nests of spawning longear sunfish (Pisces: Centrarchidae). Copeia **1972:** 272–278.

Kessel, E. L. 1955. The mating activities of balloon flies. Syst. Zool. **4:** 97–104.

Kirchshofer, R. 1953. Aktionssystem des maulbrüters *Haplochromis desfontainesi.* Z. Tierpsychol. **10:** 297–318.

Koivisto, I. 1965. Behavior of the black grouse, *Lyrurus tetrix* (L.), during the spring display. Finn. Game Res. **26:** 1–60.

Lack, D. 1968. *Ecological Adaptations for Breeding in Birds.* Methuen, London. 409 p.

Langlois, T. H. 1929. Breeding habits of the northern dace. Ecology 10: 161–163.

Larimore, R. W. 1954. Ecological life history of the warmouth (Centrarchidae). Bull. Illinois Nat. Hist. Surv. 27: 1–83.

LeBoeuf, B. J. 1972. Sexual behavior in the northern elephant seal *Mirounga angustirostris*. Behaviour 41: 1–26.

LeBoeuf, B. J. and R. S. Peterson. 1969. Social status and mating activity in elephant seals. Science 163: 91–93.

Leiner, M. 1930. Fortsetzung der ökologischen Studien an *Gasterosteus aculeatus*. Z. Morph. Okol. Tiere 16: 499–540.

Lill, A. 1974. Social organization and space utilization in the lek-forming white-bearded manakin, *M. manacus trinitatus* Hartert. Z. Tierpsychol. 36: 513–530.

Lloyd, J. E. 1973. Fireflies of Melanesia: bioluminescence, mating behavior, and synchronous flashing. (Coleoptera: Lampyridae). Ann. Entomol. Soc. Am. 2: 991–1008.

Loiselle, P. V. 1969. Monographie systematique et notes biologiques sur les possions de la lagune de Lome. Bull. Spec. l'Enseign. Sup. Benin (Lome). p. 1–37.

Loiselle, P. V. 1970. The biology of *Epiplatys sexfasciatus* Gill, 1862 (Teleostomi: Cyprinodontidae: Rivulianae) in southwestern Dahomey and the Togo hills. J. Am. Killifish Assoc. 7: 29–53.

Lorenz, K. 1962. The function of colour in coral reef fishes. Proc. Roy. Inst. Great Britain 39: 282–296.

Lowe, R. H. 1952. Report on the *Tilapia* and other fish and fisheries of Lake Nyasa, 1945–47. Colonial Off. Fish. Publ. 1: 1–26.

Lowe-McConnell, R. H. 1956. The breeding behavior of *Tilapia* species (Pisces: Cichlidae) in natural waters: observations on *T. karomo* Poll and *T. variabilis* Boulenger. Behaviour 9: 140–163.

Lowe-McConnell, R. H. 1957. Observations on the diagnosis and biology of *Tilapia leucosticta* Trewavas in East Africa. Rev. Zool. Bot. Afr. 55: 353–373.

Lowe-McConnell, R. H. 1958. Observations on the biology of *Tilapia nilotica* Linne in East African waters. Rev. Zool. Bot. Afr. 57: 129–170.

Lydell, D. 1926. Small-mouth black bass propagation. Trans. Am. Fish. Soc. 56: 43–46.

Marshall, A. J. 1960. Reproduction in male bony fish. Symp. Zool. Soc. London (1): 137–151.

Mathews, S. B. 1965. Reproductive behavior of the Sacramento perch, *Archoplites interruptus*. Copeia 1965: 224–228.

Maynard Smith, J. 1966. *The Theory of Evolution.* 2nd ed. Penguin, Baltimore. 336 p.

McKaye, K. R. and L. Hallacher. 1973. The Midas cichlid of Nicaragua. Pacific Discovery 5: 1–8.

Meral, G. H. 1973. The adaptive significance of territoriality in New World cichlids. Unpublished doctoral dissertation, University of California, Berkeley. 304 p.

Mertz, J. C. and G. W. Barlow. 1966. On the reproductive behavior of *Jordanella floridae* (Pisces: Cyprinodontidae) with special reference to a quantitative analysis of parental fanning. Z. Tierpsychol. 23: 537–554.

Munroe, J. L., V. C. Gaut, R. Thompson, and R. H. Reeson. 1973. The spawning season of Caribbean reef fishes. J. Fish. Biol. 5: 69–84.

Murphy, G. I. 1948. A contribution to the life history of the Sacramento Perch (*Archoplites interruptus*) in Clear Lake, Lake County, Cal. Cal. Fish Game 34: 93–100.

Myrberg, A. A., B. D. Brahy, and A. R. Emery. 1967. Field observations on reproduction of the damselfish *Chromis multilineata* (Pomacentridae), with additional notes on general behavior. Copeia **1967:** 819–827.

Neil, E. H. 1964. An analysis of color changes and social behavior of *Tilapia mossambica*. Univ. Calif. Publ. Zool. **75:** 1–58.

Newman, H. H. 1907. Spawning behavior and sexual dimorphism in *Fundulus heteroclitus* and allied fish. Biol. Bull. Woods Hole **12:** 314–348.

Noakes, D. L. G. and G. W. Barlow. 1973. Ontogeny of parent-contacting in young *Cichlasoma citrinellum*. Behaviour **46:** 221–255.

Penrith, M. J. 1972. The behaviour of reef-dwelling sparid fishes. Zool. Afr. **7:** 43–48.

Petravicz, J. J. 1936. The breeding habits of the least darter, *Microperca punctulata* Putnam. Copeia **1936:** 77–82.

Petravicz, J. J. 1938. The breeding habits of the black-sided darter, *Hadropterus maculatus* Girard. Copeia **1938:** 40–44.

Pitelka, F. A., R. T. Holmes, and S. A. McLean, Jr. 1974. Ecology and evolution of social organization in Arctic sandpipers. Am. Zool. 114: 185–204.

Randall, J. E. 1961. A contribution to the biology of the convict surgeonfish of the Hawaiian Islands, *Acanthurus triostegus sandvicensis*. Pacific Sci. **15:** 215–272.

Randall, J. E. and H. A. Randall. 1963. The spawning and early development of the Atlantic parrotfish, *Sparisoma rubripinne*, with notes on other scarid and labrid fishes. Zoologica (New York) **48:** 49–60.

Raney, E. C. 1939. Observations on the nesting sites of *Parexolglossum laurae* Hubbs and Trautman. Copeia **1939:** 112–113.

Raney, E. C. 1940. Comparison of the breeding habits of two subspecies of blacknosed dace, *Rhinichthys atratulatus* (Hermann). Am. Midl. Nat. **23:** 399–403.

Raney, E. C. 1947. Subspecies and breeding behavior of the cyprinid fish *Notropis procne* (Cope). Copeia **1947:** 103–109.

Raney, E. C. and E. A. Lachner. 1939. Observations on the life-history of the spotted darter, *Poecilichthys maculatus* (Kirtland). Copeia **1939:** 157–165.

Raney, E. C., R. H. Backus, R. W. Crawford, and C. R. Robins. 1953. Reproductive behavior in *Cyprinodon variegatus* Lacepede in Florida. Zoologica (New York) **38:** 97–104.

Rechnitzer, A. B. and C. Limbaugh. 1952. Breeding habits of *Hyperprosopon argenteum*, a viviparous fish of California. Copeia **1952:** 41–42.

Reeves, C. D. 1907. The breeding habits of the rainbow darter (*Etheostoma caeruleum* Storer). Biol. Bull. Woods Hole **14:** 35–59.

Reighard, J. 1910. Methods of studying the habits of fishes, with an account of the breeding habits of the horned dace (*Semotilus atromaculatus*). Bull. Wash. Bur. Fish. **28:** 1111–1136.

Reighard, J. 1913. The breeding habits of the log perch. (*Percina caproides*). (Preliminary account). Rep. Mich. Acad. Sci. **15:** 104–105.

Reinboth, R. 1968. Protogynie bei Papageifischen (Scaridae). Z. Naturforsch. **23:** 852–855.

Reinboth, R. 1973. Dualistic reproductive behavior in the protogynous wrasse *Thalassoma bifasciatum* and some observations on its day-night changeover. Helgoländer Wiss. Meersunters. **24:** 174–191.

Rhijn, J. G. van. 1973. Behavioural dimorphism in male ruffs. Behaviour **47:** 153–229.

Ricklefs, R. E. 1969. An analysis of nesting mortality in birds. Smithsonian Contr. Zool. No. 9, Washington, D. C. pp. 1–48.

Rippin, A. B. and D. A. Boag. 1974. Spatial organization among male sharp-tailed Grouse on arenas. Can. J. Zool. **52:** 591–597.

Robel, R. J. and W. B. Ballard. 1974. Lek social organization and reproductive success in the greater prarie chicken. Am. Zool. **14:** 121–128.

Robertson, E. F. and J. H. Choat. 1974. Protogynous hermaphroditism and social systems in labrid fish. Proc. 2nd Intern. Symp. Coral Reefs, Great Barrier Reef Comm., Brisbane. p. 217–225.

Ruwet, J. C. 1962a. Remarques sur le comportement de *Tilapia macrochir* Blgr. et *T. melanopleura* Dum. (Pisces: Cichlidae.) Ann. Soc. Roy. Zool. Belg. **92:** 171–177.

Ruwet, J. C. 1962b. La reproduction des *Tilapia macrochir* Blgr. et *T. melanopleura* Dum. au lac de la retenue de la Lufira (Katanga). Rev. Zool. Bot. Afr. **66:** 244–271.

Ruwet, J. C. 1963. Observations sur le comportement sexuel de *Tilapia macrochir* Blgr. (Pisces: Cichlidae) au lac de retenue de la Lufira (Katanga). Behaviour **20:** 242–250.

Sale, P. F., and R. Dybdahl. 1975. Determinants of community structure for coral reef fishes in an experimental habitat. Ecology **56:** 1343–1355.

Scheuermann, H. 1976. Some notes on *Limnochromis*—the Cypri-Cichlids. Buntbarsche Bull. **55:** 21–23.

Selander, R. K. 1972. Sexual selection and dimorphism in birds. *In:* B. Campbell, Ed. *Sexual Selection and the Descent of Man.* Aldine, Chicago. P. 87–104.

Selous, E. 1906–7. Observations tending to throw light on the question of sexual selection in birds, including a day-to-day diary on the breeding habits of the ruff (*Machetes pugnax*). Zoologist **(10):** 201–219, 285–294, 419–428; **11:** 60–65, 161–182, 367–380.

Selous, E. 1909–10. An observational diary on the nuptial habits of the blackcock (*Tetrao tetrix*) in Scandanavia and England. Zoologist **13:** 400–413; **14:** 23–29, 51–56.

Sibley, C. 1957. Evolutionary and taxonomic significance of sexual dimorphism and hybridization in birds. Condor **59:** 166–191.

Sjolander, S., H. O. Larson, and J. Engstrom. 1972. On the reproductive behaviour of two labrid fishes, the ballan wrasse (*Labrus berggylta*), and Jago's goldsinny (*Ctenolabrus rupestris*). Rev. Comp. Anim. **6:** 43–51.

Smith, I. D. 1956. Celebes sailfins or glass neons. Water Life Aquar. World, London **11:** 67–68.

Snow, B. K. 1970. A field study of the bearded bellbird in Trinidad. Ibis **11:** 229–316.

Snow, D. W. 1963. The evolution of manakin display. Proc. 13th Int. Ornithol. Congr. P. 553–561.

Soljan, T. 1930a. Nestbau eines adriatischen Lippfishes (*Crenilabrus ocellatus* Forsk.). Z. Morph. Okol. Tiere **17:** 145–153.

Soljan, T. 1930b. Die Fortpflanzung und das Wachstum von *Crenilabrus ocellatus* Forsk., einem Lippfish des Mittelmeeres. Z. Wiss. Zool. **137:** 150–174.

Spieth, H. T. 1968. Evolutionary implications of sexual behavior in *Drosophila*. Evol. Biol. **2:** 157–193.

Stout, J. F. and H. E. Winn. 1958. The reproductive behavior and sound production of the satinfin shiner. Bull. Ecol. Soc. Am. **39:** 136–137.

Stout, J. F. 1959. The reproductive behavior and sound production of the satinfin shiner. Anat. Rec. Philadelphia **134:** 643–644.

Sundara Raj, B. 1962. The extraordinary breeding habits of the catfish *Mystus aor* (Hamilton) and *Mystus seenghala* (Sykes). Proc. Nat. Inst. Sci. India **28:** 193–200.

Swerdloff, S. N. 1970. Behavioral observations on Eniwetak damselfishes (Pomacentridae: *Chromis*) with special reference to the spawning of *Chromis caeruleus*. Copeia **1970:** 371–374.

Tinbergen, N. 1951. *The Study of Instinct*. Oxford University Press, London, 228 p.

Ward, J. A. and G. W. Barlow. 1967. The maturation and regulation of glancing off the parents by young orange chromides (*Etroplus maculatus:* Pisces—Cichlidae). Behaviour **29:** 1–56.

Warner, R. R., D. R. Robertson, and E. G. Leigh, Jr. 1975. Sex change and sexual selection. Science **190:** 633–638.

Weiwandt, T. A. 1969. Vocalization, aggressive behavior, and territoriality in the bullfrog, *Rana catesbiana*. Copeia **1969:** 276–285.

Welcomme, R. L. 1970. Studies on the effects of abnormally high water levels on the ecology of fish in certain shallow regions of Lake Victoria. J. Zool. Lond. **160:** 405–436.

Wickler, W. 1962. Ei-Attrappen und Maulbrüten bei afrikanischen Cichliden. Z. Tierpsychol. **19:** 129–164.

Wickler, W. 1969. Zur Soziologie des Brabant buntbarsches, *Tropheus moorei* (Pisces, Cichlidae). Z. Tierpsychol. **26:** 967–987.

Wiebe, J. P. 1968. The reproductive cycle of the viviparous seaperch *Cymatogaster aggregata* Gibbons. Can. J. Zool. **46:** 1221–1233.

Wiley, R. H. 1973. Territoriality and nonrandom mating in sage grouse, *Centrocercus urophasianus*. Anim. Behav. Monogr. **6:** 85–169.

Wiley, R. H. 1974. Evolution of social organization and life history patterns among grouse. Q. Rev. Biol. **49:** 201–227.

Williams, G. C. 1964. Measurements of consociation among fishes and comments on the evolution of schooling. Mus. Mich. St. Univ. Biol. Ser. **2:** 351–383.

Williams, G. C. 1966. *Adaptation and Natural Selection*. Princeton University Press, Princeton. 291 p.

Wilson, E. O. 1975. *Sociobiology. The New Synthesis*. Belknap Press, Harvard Univ. Press, Cambridge, Mass. 697 p.

Winn, H. E. 1958. Comparative reproductive behavior and ecology of 14 species of darters (Pisces: Percidae). Ecol. Monogr. **28:** 155–191.

Wright, J. K. 1976. Inter- and intraspecific relationships of the anabantoid fish *Trichogaster trichopterus* (Pallas). Unpublished doctoral dissertation, University of California, Berkeley. 200 p.

3

THE EVOLUTION OF HERMAPHRODITISM AND UNISEXUALITY IN AQUATIC AND TERRESTRIAL VERTEBRATES

ROBERT R. WARNER

Marine Science Institute
and Department of Biological Sciences
University of California, Santa Barbara

1 INTRODUCTION

The purpose of this chapter is to explore the occurrence of hermaphroditism and unisexuality among the vertebrates. If we can show that a
particular sexual pattern should be advantageous under certain fairly
common ecological conditions, why don't more animals show such a
pattern? For example, why aren't any vertebrates other than fishes functionally hermaphroditic? Why does unisexuality find its greatest expression in reptiles? True, selection favoring a particular trait does not
guarantee that trait's appearance (cf. Bateson, 1963; Emlen, 1973: 88); but
the advantages of hermaphroditism, for example, can be enormous
under certain conditions. First, I demonstrate that these conditions exist
in many "higher" vertebrates. I then discuss the existence of several
other factors that have put constraints on intersexuality, most of them
involving the transition to life on land. Finally, I review unisexuality,
which shows a different and less explicable pattern of distribution than
hermaphroditism.

I define hermaphroditism as functional when it occurs among most or
all of the individuals in a species and presumably plays an adaptive role
in the life of those individuals. It can be either synchronous, in which
case an individual produces both eggs and sperm at the same time, or
sequential, where for part of the mature life-span the animal operates as
one sex and then successfully assumes the opposite sexual role. These
sexual patterns have evolved at least 10 separate times in the fishes
(Smith, 1975). Many invertebrate phyla contain hermaphroditic species
as well (for reviews see Ghiselin, 1969, 1974). This widespread occurrence has led to the genesis of a number of theories on the adaptiveness
of hermaphroditism (Smith, 1967, 1975; Ghiselin, 1969, 1974; Robertson
and Choat, 1974; Fishelson, 1975; Warner, 1975; Choat and Robertson,
1975; Warner et al., 1975).

Most of these overlapping ideas attempt to explain the advantages of
hermaphroditism in terms of a specific selective regime. Theoretically,
whenever this regime operates, selection should favor some type of
hermaphroditism, and the cooccurrence of the regime and hermaphroditism should provide support for the theory (for full discussion of
this approach, see Ghiselin, 1969). Where presumably strong selection
exists and the character is lacking, one can either assume (1) that there is
some stronger opposing selection pressure, (2) that the necessary
preadaptations have been lost or are unlikely to evolve in concert, or (3)
that the theory is incorrect. In no case do I attempt a complete review; I
mention only enough examples to lend an impression of the general
trend within a group.

2 HERMAPHRODITISM AND SEX DETERMINATION IN VERTEBRATES

2.1 Fishes

As mentioned above, hermaphroditism has apparently evolved numerous times in the fishes (reviews in Smith, 1975; Reinboth, 1970; Atz, 1964). The information is summarized in Table 3.1. Protogyny (females changing into males) is probably the most common pattern. It occurs in the freshwater symbranchid eels, in the wrasses (Labridae), parrotfishes (Scaridae), most of the larger sea basses (Serranidae), and in some porgies (Sparidae), all ubiquitous tropical marine families. There may be fewer protandric forms, and little is known of their ecology. Most of the protandric species studied have come from commercial fisheries, indicating that they occur in large aggregations. Most synchronous hermaphrodites are bathypelagic, but this is not universally so: many species of the subfamily Serraninae (Serranidae) are widely distributed in shallow water in tropical marine habitats.

The most complete information we have on sequential hermaphroditism deals with protogynous fishes, especially those in the families Labridae and Scaridae. In these species, sex change appears to be correlated with a social system in which large, dominant males have a high degree of reproductive success (Reinboth, 1973; Robertson and Choat, 1974; Warner et al., 1975). Sex change, at least in some species, appears to be socially controlled, with the females changing sex when the dominant males are removed (Robertson, 1972; Warner et al., 1975). In dense populations, this mating system can lead to sex ratios that are highly skewed toward females. In some common species, where population densities are high, nonhermaphroditic males exist that exploit this abundance of females by circumventing the standard mating hierarchy while they are young (Warner et al., 1975). These males will sneak into dominant males' territories and steal spawnings, or pursue, in large groups, a ripe female until she is induced to spawn. When they become large, they assume the behavior and coloration of the dominant males. These nonhermaphrodites are absent in rare species, and also in small populations of common species (Warner et al., 1975).

Correlated with this wide diversity of sexual expression, sex determination in fishes appears to be relatively labile (reviewed by Yamamoto, 1969; and Schreck, 1974). Small doses of mammalian sex hormones administered to developing larvae of species that normally do not change sex have resulted in permanent functional sex reversal and fertile adults (Young, 1965; Yamamoto, 1969; Schreck, 1974). However, Atz (1964) has

TABLE 3.1 Normally hermaphroditic fishes. Data from Reinboth (1970) and Smith (1975)

Type of Hermaphroditism	Order	Family	Degree of Occurrence Within Family	Habit of Hermaphrodites
I. Synchronous	Aulopiformes	All except Harpadontidae and Synodontidae	All species thus far studied	Bathypelagic
	Atheriniformes	Cyprinodontidae	One species (*Rivulus marmoratus*)	Still freshwater
	Perciformes	Serranidae	Subfamily Serraninae	Shallow marine
		Pseudogrammidae	One species (*Pseudogramma bermudensis*)	Shallow marine
II. Sequential				
A. Protogynous	Synbranchiformes	Synbranchidae	All species thus far studied	Still freshwater
	Perciformes	Serranidae	Most species in subfamilies Anthiinae, Epinephelinae	Shallow marine
		Grammistidae	All species thus far studied	Shallow marine
		Sparidae	Three species	Shallow marine
		Emmelichthyidae	Three species	Shallow marine
		Labridae	All species thus far studied	Shallow marine
		Scaridae	All species thus far studied	Shallow marine
		Cepolidae	One species (*Cepola rubescens*)	Shallow marine
B. Protandrous	Ostariophysi	Cobitidae	One species (*Cobitus taenia*)	Freshwater streams
	Stomiatiformes	Gonostomatidae	One species (*Gonostoma gracile*)	Mesopelagic
	Scorpaeniformes	Platycephalidae	At least three species	Shallow marine
	Perciformes	Sparidae	Seven species	Shallow marine
		Polynemidae	Several species	Shallow marine

correctly urged caution in making any generalization about the "primi-
tiveness" of sex determination in teleosts. The male is the heterogametic
sex in most fishes that have been investigated (Ebeling and Chen, 1970).
One poeciliid species, *Xiphophorus maculatus*, is polymorphic for
heterogamety; females may be the genotype *WY*, *WX*, or *XX*, and males
XY or *YY* (Gordon, 1957; Kallman, 1970).

2.2 Amphibians

There are no strictly hermaphroditic species of amphibians (Beatty,
1964), although they are very variable in the mechanisms of sex determination and sensitive to hormonally induced sex changes (Foote, 1964).

Rudimentary hermaphroditism (nonfunctional, *sensu* Atz, 1964) is typical of many amphibians, and is exemplified in *Bufo vulgaris* (reviewed in
Witschi, 1934, and Beatty, 1964). In this species, the Bidder's organ in
males is actually a rudimentary ovary. When the testes are removed, this
organ develops and produces mature, fertilizable eggs. Over the course
of time, the oviducts can develop into a functional state, and the male
secondary sexual characteristics are lost. A few naturally occurring synchronous hermaphrodites are found in this species as well.

Juvenile intersexuality has been described for six species of anurans
and two urodeles (Foote, 1964). In this case, either sexual development
from an undifferentiated hermaphroditic gonad or sex reversal to a testis
from a phenotypically female gonad occurs before maturity. In the best
studied species, *Rana temporaria*, some populations are 100% female
phenotypes at metamorphosis, but 50% change gradually into males
over the summer (Witschi, 1934; Beatty, 1964; Geisselman *et al.*, 1971).
Different races show varying degrees of differentiation. Berger (1971) has
recently shown that *Rana esculenta*, previously included as a species with
juvenile intersexuality, is an unstable, low-viability hybrid of *Rana les-
sonae* and *R. ridibunda*. The latter species produce equal number of males
and females with no intermediate types. Only in hybrid crosses and
backcrossses are skewed sex ratios and undifferentiated juveniles produced; *R. esculenta* may indeed be a hybrid form dependent upon the
other species for egg activation (Uzzell, 1975; see below). The possibility
of abnormal hybrid development should be closely investigated in other
species of amphibians that show juvenile hermaphroditism.

In *Rana temporaria*, old females occasionally transform into males
(Witschi, 1934; Mittwoch, 1973), a pattern reminiscent of the senile masculinization of secondary sex characteristics (arrhenoidy) of old females
in some species of poeciliid fishes (Atz, 1964). In amphibians, however,

the transformation is gonadal as well, and midway through the change, both fertile eggs and sperm are produced (Witschi, 1934; Mittwoch, 1973). Thus in *Rana temporaria*, at least, there is no inhibitory effect of the presence of one type of gamete on the other.

Hormone-induced sex changes have been successfully carried out on the larvae of a number of amphibian species (Chang and Witschi, 1956; Burns, 1961; Witschi, 1962; Foote, 1964; Young, 1965), and there appears to be no strongly canalized sex determination mechanism in amphibians.

2.3   Reptiles

Neither synchronous nor sequential hermaphroditism is found in reptiles (Cole, 1975). The only intersexuality found so far has been in two species of snakes. In *Bothrops insularis*, most of the females (and all the pregnant ones thus far encountered) have hemipenes (Hoge *et al.*, 1959). All females of *Pseudofimicia frontalis* have hemipenes, and the young males retain the oviducts after parturition (Hardy, 1970). There is no evidence of adult ovotestes or sex changes occurring in either species.

The reproductive system differentiates slowly in many reptiles, and there are many species in which embryonic and juvenile intersexual structures are characteristic, but these do not persist into adulthood (reviewed by Forbes, 1964).

No lasting or functional sex reversal has been achieved in reptile embryos under hormone treatment, although there may be some temporary modification of genetic males towards the female direction with estrogen administration (Forbes, 1964).

2.4   Birds

Birds are much better known than reptiles as experimental animals, and perhaps for this reason there exist more reports of ovotestes and sex reversal in this group. In no case is intersexuality a normal phenomenon in any avian species.

Only the left ovary is functional in most birds, and only the left gonad is covered by germinal epithelium in embryonic development. When the left ovary is damaged or removed, the medullary tissue in the left and right gonad can proliferate into sperm-producing tissue (Crew, 1923; Witschi, 1961; Van Tienhoven, 1961; Beatty, 1964; Taber, 1964; review in Mittwoch, 1973). This is the basis of the ancient legend of the deadly cockatrice, believed to be the offspring of the devil and hatched from a cock's egg. These egg-laying cocks were probably partially masculinized females, and a number of chickens were burnt at the stake in the Middle Ages for such incomplete sex reversal (see Marshall, 1964). The left gonad of genetic males can also generate ovarian tissue under hormone treatment (Mittwoch, 1973).

The degree of masculinization resulting from ovarian destruction is highly variable; there is one documented account of a previously functional female hen changing into male plumage and successfully fertilizing the eggs of a virgin hen (Crew, 1923). Autopsy of the individual revealed an infection of the left gonad that had arrested ovarian activity.

Ovotestes have been found in many chickens (Crew, 1923), and Riddle *et al.* (1945) bred a race of hermaphroditic pigeons in which 80% of the genetic males showed hermaphroditic features, including a left ovotestis and complete left oviduct. No mature eggs were formed, and I know of no reports of the simultaneous production of fertile eggs and sperm by any bird.

Hormone treatment of avian embryos results in partial (only some secondary sex characters are altered) masculinization of genetic females, or in partial to complete (internal and external anatomy completely altered) feminization of genetic males. The sex-reversed females tend to revert back to the male condition after hatching, and only a nonfunctional intersexual condition persists. No fully fertile sex-reversed individuals have been created thus far (reviewed in Taber, 1964; Burns, 1961).

2.5 Mammals

Sexual differentiation occurs very early in mammalian embryology, and there are no naturally occurring hermaphroditic species known (Bruner-Lorand, 1964). Only in the marsupial opossum, *Didelphis virginiana*, has ovarian development been induced by hormone treatment of newly born, very undeveloped male individuals (Burns, 1950; 1961). Phenotypically intersexual individuals can be produced by heterologuous hormone treatment of embryos *in utero* (reviewed in Young, 1965), or by testosterone deprivation (Goldman, 1975), but these have involved only secondary sexual characteristics, and no gonadal sex changes have been recorded.

Baker (1925) gives a delightful account of a race of pigs that produces a high frequency of phenotypically intersexual individuals much prized by the local inhabitants. These intersexes are genetic males, but their external genitalia are modified in the female direction to varying degrees.

3   WHERE IS HERMAPHRODITISM ADAPTIVE?

We now need to explore the conditions under which hermaphroditism would be favorable and see whether higher vertebrates fit into the theoretical framework. An answer to our question of why intersexuality is not found in mammals, birds, reptiles, and amphibians may be simply that in these animals selection for such a pattern does not exist.

This may indeed be the answer for synchronous hermaphroditism. The ability to reproduce with any other conspecific encountered has been viewed as an adaptation to extremely low density or low motility, where such encounters occur extremely rarely (Tomlinson, 1966; Scudo, 1969; Ghiselin, 1969, 1974). Synchronous hermaphrodites enjoy such an advantage. Among the invertebrates, functional ovotestes are found in many sessile or parasitic forms (Ghiselin, 1974). The bathypelagic aulopiform fishes (see Table 3.1) also appear to fit the model well, for their population density is presumably quite low. Their shallow water relatives in the families Harpodontidae and Synodontidae are not hermaphroditic (Smith, 1975). The freshwater cyprinodont fish *Rivulus marmoratus*, a self-fertilizing hermaphodite, may undergo periods of extreme low density due to alternate desiccation and tidal-pluvial floodings (Harrington, 1961). There is, however, a major anomaly to the low-density theory: the serranine sea-basses, a large group of synchronously hermaphroditic fishes, occur in shallow tropical waters in relatively high densities, and there is no reason to believe that they, in any way, encounter difficulties in finding a mate.

Like most fishes, the higher vertebrates are characterised by relatively high motility; I know of no species that suffer chronic low densities comparable to those envisioned for bathypelagic fishes except possibly some low-mobility forms like terrestrial turtles. In many of these species, however, the female stores sperm, which is an alternate method of alleviating the problem of a lack of mates. Even in cases where the nonbreeding population is spread sparsely over the habitat, as in some seals (Bartholomew, 1970) or pelagic sea-birds (Jameson, 1961; Ashmole, 1963), the species gather in large numbers for reproduction at specific sites.

Sequential hermaphroditism presents a more complicated picture, both in the diversity of opinions as to why it is adaptive in the first place, and also because it apparently would be advantageous in many species where it is not found. There are three principal hypotheses on the advantage of sex change. The first stresses the maximization (Smith, 1967) or optimization (Smith, 1975) of the zygote production of the population. Under conditions of high mortality in later ages, if all individuals were born as females and the survivors later changed into males, females would be concentrated in the more numerous younger age classes and zygote production thereby increased (Smith 1967, 1975; Nikolski, 1963). By a similar argument, with less harsh mortality, and where female fecundity increases greatly with age, protandry would increase zygote production.

Another explanation of sex change envisions periodic or chronic low density as the selective force; when local populations are small, sampling error might result in the absence of one sex, and sex change would obviate this difficulty and ensure reproduction (Liem, 1968; Smith, 1975). This model has obviously limited applicability (but for a contrary view, see Smith, 1975).

I believe that both explanations are based on group selection and that they overemphasize the role of females. They consider the production of eggs and the assurance of their fertilization as the main factors in the evolution of sex change. The role of males, and the fact that their genes constitute half of every zygote, are ignored: the only criterion is that there be an "adequate supply" (Smith, 1975:305) of males for fertilizing females. Who among a group will change sex? The contribution of a particular male to the next generation, although variable, can be much greater than that of a single female (Fisher, 1930; Bateman, 1948; Selander, 1965; Trivers, 1972). Any theory dealing with sex change must take into account the conditions under which an individual would most benefit from being a male or female relative to the rest of the breeding population.

For this reason, I shall deal exclusively from this point on with the remaining explanation, known as the size advantage model. First put forth by Ghiselin (1969), and since expanded and formalized (Robertson and Choat, 1974; Ghiselin, 1974; Warner, 1975; Warner et al., 1975), it simply states that sequential hermaphroditism would be adaptive in situations where it was more advantageous for the individual to be of one sex at a particular age or size and the other sex when larger or older. More formally, sex change is adaptive when male and female fertility are differentially distributed with age. The greater these differences are, the stronger the selection for sex change. When mating is random and large females have a higher fertility than smaller ones, protandry would be of advantage because small males can inseminate large females (Warner, 1975). Protogyny should be found in situations where male fertility is higher than the female's in later ages, as in many cases of polygyny and sexual selection (Warner, 1975; Warner et al., 1975). Such situations are most easily visualized (and most easily documented) where a few large males fertilize the eggs of most of the females in the population. Strong selection for sex change from female to male at later ages should exist in such a situation. Relative fertilities of males and females for protandric species are much more difficult to quantify because they usually involve random mating that is often not site-specific. Adequate data do exist for many species on the relative mating success of older, larger males, and therefore I shall concentrate on species that appear to fulfill the selective criteria for protogyny.

4 POLYGYNY IN FISHES AND HIGHER VERTEBRATES

Many protogynous fishes have mating behavior, such as harem establishment or leks, that should lead to high fertilities of old, large, and aggressively dominant, males (Randall and Randall, 1963; Fiedler, 1964; Robertson, 1972; Roede, 1972; Robertson and Choat, 1974; Choat and Robertson, 1975; Warner *et al.*, 1975). Differential reproductive success in large males has been quantified at least twice. For the cleaner wrasse, *Labroides dimidiatus*, a harem-forming species, mean harem size is six, and the male and females mate daily (Robertson, 1972). Thus the dominant male's fertility is six times that of females. For the lekking species *Thalassoma bifasciatum*, spawning also occurs daily, and large males spawn with over 40 females a day in large populations (Warner *et al.*, 1975).

While many protogynous fishes appear to be characterized by high fertility in older males, the converse is not true. There are many species of fishes that form leks but do not change sex (cf. Loiselle and Barlow, 1978). Many of these are freshwater species that show some form of male parental care, factors that may reduce the selective value of sex change (see below).

Differential reproductive success of older males is common in several higher vertebrate species (for references, see Trivers, 1972). Emlen (1968) has described how large male bullfrogs with established mating territories have a higher probability of mating. There is now good evidence for increased reproductive success with size of the male in anoles (Noble and Greenberg, 1941; Rand, 1967; Trivers, 1972) and other lizards (Evans, 1951; Blair, 1960; Harris, 1964).

Birds provide a rich source of information on polygyny. Verner and Willson (1969) estimate the 5% of North American passerines are polygynous. Polygyny appears to be strongly correlated with an ample food supply and lack of a large amount of male parental care (Orians, 1969; Selander, 1965; Amadon, 1959). In many of these species, the young males do not often reproduce, although they are capable of doing so, while females of similar age are successfully breeding (Verner, 1964; Selander and Hauser, 1965; Holm, 1973). Fertilities can be quite large in older males: 87% of the matings are performed by 3% of the males in the lek-forming sage grouse (Scott, 1942). In flocks of domestic chickens, the dominant cock is by far the most successful in siring chicks (Guhl, 1941, 1962).

Quantitative studies of age-specific mating frequencies of males and females are also available for a number of mammals. In elephant seals, the large harem masters inseminate a very high proportion of the available females (LeBouef and Peterson, 1969; Carrick et al., 1962). Young males are correspondingly restricted from breeding. In the southern species (*Mirounga leonina*), males mature at around age 7 but do not breed until at least age 12. If these males become dominant beach masters, they can hold as many as 150 females in a harem. Females, in contrast, mature at ages 3 to 6, and do not live past age 12 (Carrick et al., 1962). Similar, but less pronounced, harem structures have been described for other seals (for example, Bartholomew, 1970; Orr and Poulter, 1967). In the yellow-bellied marmot, males usually have at least two, and as many as eight, females in their harem (Downhower and Armitage, 1971).

Ungulates show a characteristic predominance of older, larger males in breeding (Geist, 1971; deVos, Brokx, and Geist, 1967; Schaffer and Reed, 1972), and the same effect has been noted for primates (Maslow, 1940; Carpenter, 1942; DeVore, 1965). For example, in baboons, males mature at age 5, but do not enter the hierarchy until age 8, and only at age 10 or 11 do they show the full range of mating behavior (DeVore, 1965).

5 BARRIERS TO THE EVOLUTION OF HERMAPHRODITISM

If, as indicated above, there exist many higher vertebrate species for which sequential hermaphroditism seemingly would be adaptive, why don't any of them change sex? In this section, I explore several factors that I think act to make the transformation from one sex to the other more complex in higher vertebrates than in fishes. The assumption is that the larger the suite of characters that must change for a particular adaptation to begin to operate, the less likely that adaptation is to evolve (cf. Bateson, 1963). The existence of hypothetical selection pressure for a trait in no way guarantees its appearance.

5.1   Terrestrial Life, Female Energy Expenditure, and Internal Fertilization

The transition to terrestrial life tended to magnify the difference between males and females. This was due to the increased need to protect and nurture the young to ensure their survival in a markedly less supportive environment. The production of great numbers of unprotected gametes, which unite and develop into planktotrophic larvae, is the primitive condition in marine fishes (Blaxter, 1969; Hoar, 1969); but it is no longer a viable option after the transition to fresh water or terrestrial existence, where conditions are much more harsh. There is a corresponding increase in the incidence of parental care from marine fishes to freshwater fishes, and from aquatic forms (including amphibians with aquatic larvae) to terrestrial ones (DeBeer, 1951; Berrill, 1955; Carter, 1967; Alexander, 1975). Animals that reproduce on land must additionally protect the developing eggs from water loss, and must provide an aquatic medium for the embryo until it develops the structures necessary for utilizing air (Carter, 1967).

The necessity of protecting the embryo and providing it with a large amount of the nutrition required for development has resulted in two different strategies: a large egg is enclosed in a tough case that is laid down after fertilization (as in birds and many reptiles); or the egg is retained inside the body, and the embryo develops to a relatively advanced state before birth (Alexander, 1975). Both of these strategies require internal fertilization.

The larger the egg or embryo produced by the female, the greater the differences in male and female anatomy. The delivery systems for eggs and sperms in many marine fishes are very similar, and if sex change occurs, it is accompanied by only slight modifications of external genitalia. As the fundamental dimorphism between males and females increases, so does the anatomical complexity of changing sex. The reduced incidence of sequential hermaphroditism in freshwater fishes relative to marine forms (Table 3.1) may be a reflection of this fact. In higher vertebrates, anatomical differences between the sexes become more pronounced, to the point of skeletal modifications, such as the widened pubic bones in some female birds and mammals (Romer, 1950; Welty, 1962).

Internal fertilization also leads to greater sex differences. Precise delivery of sperm becomes important, and the development of male external genitalia has often paralleled the development of systems in females for the production of advanced young. Even where the external anatomy is not greatly modified, the requirement for internal fertilization usually results in many sex-specific internal modifications and increases the need for close contact and precise mutual timing (e.g., Nelson, 1975). No sex-changing fish species have internal fertilization. The possible importance of experience in gaining precision in mating is discussed in more detail in a later section.

The increased specialization of males for sperm delivery and of females for the production of advanced young not only implies that any shift from one sex to the other is much more complex; it also implies that intersexuality is maladaptive. Essentially, male and female forms in higher vertebrates have become increasingly dichotomized adaptive peaks, with penalties attached to possessing some but not all of the attributes of the opposite sex.

5.2 Correlated Changes in the Sex Chromosomes

The selective value for specialization into either male or female forms is reflected in the increasing resistance to changes induced by heterologous sex hormones (mentioned above), which probably relates to the stringency of sex determination. Also, as one proceeds from fishes and amphibians to birds and mammals, the sex chromosomes become more and more dimorphic and isolated during meiosis (Ohno, 1967; Mittwoch, 1973; 1975).

The sex chromosomes are not heteromorphic in fishes and amphibians, and in fishes, at least, they have many homologous loci (Ohno, 1967; Mittwoch, 1973, 1975; see also Mehl and Reinboth, 1975). Both male and female heterogamety occur, but much of the control of sex determination may rest in the autosomes (Yamamoto, 1969; Beatty, 1964; Foote, 1964; but see Gordon, 1957). The case of both male and female heterogamety occurring in a single teleost species, *Xiphophorus maculatus*, has already been mentioned above.

Strictly terrestrial vertebrates show a more pronounced sexual difference in their chromosomes. Heteromorphic sex chromosomes are present in many but not all reptiles (Vorontosov, 1973; Cole, 1975; Mittwoch, 1975). Ohno (1967) has pointed out that in the primitive snake family Boidae there are no morphological differences in the sex chromosomes, while in the intermediate family Colubridae, the Z and W chromosomes of the heterogametic female differ by a pericentric inversion, and in the most advanced families (Crotalidae, Elapidae, and Viperidae), the W chromosome is minute relative to the Z. In contrast, the male is the heterogametic sex in some lizard species (cf. Cole, 1975).

In all species of birds and mammals that have been investigated, the sex chromosomes are dimorphic, there are few homologous loci, and the sex determining power of the Y or W chromosome is very great: in man, even an XXXY individual will be a phenotypic male (Mittwoch, 1975).

The overall impression of higher vertebrates is one of increasingly stringent separation of the sexes in development, strong canalization into a single sexual phenotype, and a consequent loss of bipotentiality. Under these circumstances, it is not surprising that sequential hermaphroditism has not evolved, even in species where the fertility of older males is much greater than that of females.

5.3   Behavior: The Role of Experience

The strength of selection for sex change depends upon the magnitude of the age-specific fertility differences between males and females. As pointed out above, more parental energy per offspring is required in terrestrial situations. Thus in many land animals, survival of the young may require that the female choose a male on the basis of his ability to share this burden in some way (cf. Trivers, 1972). The resulting investment by the male reduces his maximum potential number of mates, and thereby reduces selection for sex change. There is no reason to change sex in a strictly monogamous system, unless small males could induce large females to pair with them (protandry would result). This is unlikely in mating systems where females are choosing males on the basis of their ability to help raise the young.

While the above argument may help to explain why sex change should be less common in terrestrial animals, it sheds no light on why none of the polygynous species change sex. However, it is just in these species that prior experience may be important. For example:

In sex-changing fishes, the female can produce eggs and spawn as a female for several years. Then, given the proper cue (such as the removal of the dominant male), she can transform her ovary into a testis, destroy the remaining eggs, and begin producing sperm and courting as a male. A rapid transformation is advantageous, so that little reproductive time is lost while the change is being accomplished. For fishes that spawn year round, a sex-changing female can begin to demonstrate male behavior within a few hours of the removal of the previously dominant male, and can induce other females to spawn with them even though their testicular tissue is still undeveloped (Robertson, 1972; S. Hoffman, personal communication).

Fishes and amphibians that have undergone artificially induced sex reversal can show complete functional shifts in behavior (Humphrey,

1945; Beach, 1961; Witschi, 1962). Behavioral shifts are the most common and most easily induced sex change in the higher vertebrates, especially shifts from female to male behavior (detailed review by Beach, 1961). But there is also an increasingly large learned component in reproductive behavior in higher vertebrates, one that militates against mating success by inexperienced individuals.

Again, the role of learning is a consequence of the necessity for internal fertilization and for increased energy investment per gamete by the female. In such cases, female choice should be severe, because the loss of a batch of eggs represents a large waste of energy (Trivers, 1972). Under these conditions, male competition for mates is likely to be intense, and competence both in copulation and in between-male competition become determinants of fitness. The more intense the competition, the more experience may be needed before success is attained. Recently sex-changed individuals, although of a proper age or size for successful mating, may lack needed practice in their new sex role.

There are many examples of the necessity of prior experience for successful mating in birds (Selander, 1965) and in mammals, especially primates (Beach, 1947; Hediger, 1965; Harlow, 1965; DeVore, 1965). Additionally, sex play, long interpreted as mating practice, is characteristic of many young male mammals (Beach, 1947). However, some birds (domestic fowl: Beach, 1961) and mammals (rats, guinea pigs: Rosenblatt, 1965) do not appear to need practice before reproducing successfully. The key advantage of experience in many higher vertebrates may not lie in the mating act itself, but in increasing the ability of a male to fight successfully for females under conditions of intense male competition. This may be the case for many ungulates and seals.

In summary, whenever successful mating depends on experience gained in a particular sex role while young, sex changes may be disadvantageous because of the fact that a sex-changed individual may never be able to compete successfully for mates. The more complex the entire process of reproduction becomes, the more likely are practice and prior experience to be important.

5.4 Alternative Strategies

There are means other than sex change for avoiding and lessening the burden of being reproductively deprived while young. Energy not expended in reproduction as a young male may be redirected into growth or maintenance, leading to greater longevity or more rapid attainment of larger size relative to an individual functioning first as a female. Although females may virtually guarantee themselves reproduction while young, they must expend much energy in the production of offspring, and they thus reduce their chances of becoming a large competitive male. For example, in southern elephant seals (mentioned above), there is seemingly an excellent adaptive situation for sex change. But males must be very large to compete successfully for mates. Females do not grow as fast as males and generally die before equal-sized males even begin to mate. They bear only one pup a year, so clearly a mixed strategy (reducing litter size in order to grow larger) is impossible in this species.

These arguments are not new. The tactics of energy allocation into current reproduction (reproductive effort) or into future possibilities of reproduction (residual reproductive value) have been discussed in the past (Williams, 1966; Pianka and Parker, 1975; and references therein). Here the argument is recast to apply within a species, specifically to differential strategies between the sexes. I will deal in detail with this topic elsewhere, for, although it may help to explain why sex change is not generally more common, it offers little help in our search for the differences in sexual expression between fish and higher vertebrates. These strategies should apply equally well to all vertebrates, unless there is some block to efficient energy allocation peculiar to a particular group. I know of none; in fact, there is strong evidence for accelerated growth in young nonsex-changing males relative to hermaphroditic females in the striped parrotfish, *Scarus croicensis* (Warner and Downs, 1977).

6 UNISEXUALITY

The distribution of unisexuality (parthenogenesis) among the vertebrates is entirely different from that of hermaphroditism. There are about 35 "species" of naturally occurring parthenogenetic vertebrates (Uzzell and Darevsky, 1975). A few species of freshwater fishes in three families, and possibly three amphibians, have populations in which females give birth to all-female broods (MacGregor and Uzzell, 1964; Schultz and Kallman, 1968; Schultz, 1969; Yamamoto, 1969; Uzzell, 1970, 1975; Tunner, 1970). All these species require the presence of sperm from a male of a related form for activation of the eggs. In some poeciliid fishes and possibly *Rana esculenta*, the genome of the male parent is incorporated and expressed in the offspring, but is excluded *in toto* when those individuals in turn produce eggs (hybridogenesis: Schultz, 1969; Uzzell, 1975). The highest occurrence of parthenogenesis is in the reptiles, where 26 species of lizards in six different families, and one species of snake, are normally unisexual and do not require sperm for egg development (Cole, 1975). In all of the families, the majority of the species are gonochoristic, and multiple independent evolutions are indicated. There are no naturally occurring populations of unisexual birds, although certain carefully bred strains of some species (especially turkeys) have a high frequency of eggs that begin to develop without fertilization; some of these eggs, all male in phenotype, develop into adults (summarized in Beatty, 1967; Olsen, 1965; Olsen *et al.*, 1968). No mammals are unisexual; activated, unfertilized eggs generally do not even implant in the uterus (Beatty, 1967).

Why are there so many unisexual species of reptiles and so few unisexual species in other groups? Are there any special features of reptilian ecology that would make the evolution of parthenogenesis more likely? The most accepted explanation for the advantage to unisexuality lies in the preservation of adaptive genotypes, especially genotypes resulting from hybridization. Most parthenogenetic vertebrates appear to be hybrids (Cuellar, 1974; Uzzel and Darevsky, 1965); supposedly, a heterotic organism would be better adapted to a zone of overlap than either parent, and could maintain that advantage through unisexual reproduction undisturbed by recombination (White, 1970; Schultz, 1971; Uzzell, 1970; Maslin, 1971; Uzzell and Darevsky, 1975). Others have pointed out that a unisexual, hybrid or not, has an intrinsic advantage in any relatively stable environment, because recombination is wasteful and the rate of increase of a type that produces only female offspring can be twice that of a gonochorist (Maynard Smith, 1971a, b; Ghiselin, 1974; Williams, 1975). An additional suggested benefit to unisexuality is in an increased ability to colonize new habitats successfully (Suomalainen, 1950; Wright and Lowe, 1968; Bezy, 1972).

Concentrating on the most likely and most generally applicable model, that of preserving fit genotypes with high rates of reproduction, the prediction is that selection for unisexuality occurs whenever the environment of the offspring is somewhat predictable (cf. Williams, 1975). It does not appear that reptiles necessarily dwell in any more stable habitat than the other vertebrates. Nor do they appear more dependent on the invasion of new habitats for their existence.

Another possible explanation may rest in the long-term disadvantage of asexuality: the inability to develop new genotypes rapidly and constantly through recombination results in a higher probability of extinction (White, 1970; Maynard Smith, 1971a; Williams, 1975; Uzzell and Darevsky, 1975; Stanley, 1975). This explanation assumes that all vertebrate groups underwent the evolution of asexual species at similar rates, but that the rate of extinction of the unisexual reptiles was less than that of other groups. There is no reason to suppose that this would be so: do major changes in environmental conditions occur less often for reptiles?

Perhaps unisexuality is equally adaptive for all low-fecundity verte-brates in stable environments, but reptiles by chance possessed the preadaptations to overcome the obstacles to their evolution. The obsta-cle is mainly the development of meiosis-suppression or of other cytomechanical adaptations for preserving or reconstituting a highly heterozygous genotype (Schultz, 1969; Uzzell, 1970; Williams, 1975). I know of no way to test for such preadaptations.

Thus the basis of the pattern of unisexuality remains obscure and uncorrelated with any obvious changes, such as the shift to terrestrial life. It remains a challenge to evolutionary biologists.

7   SUMMARY AND CONCLUSIONS

Among the vertebrates, hermaphroditism, both synchronous (an indi-vidual producing both eggs and sperm at the same time) and sequential (assuming one functional sex, then the other) is restricted to the fishes. Synchronous hermaphroditism would be adaptive in situations where extremely low effective population density led to difficulty in finding a mate. These conditions do not appear to exist for higher vertebrate groups as they do for deep-sea fishes. Sequential hermaphroditism, however, which requires only differential distributions of fecundity be-tween males and females to be adaptive, would seemingly be advan-tageous to many polygynous species of reptiles, birds, and mammals. The reason it does not occur may lie in the fact that terrestrial life has led to greater differences between males and females. I assume that the greater the changes that must be made in order for functional sex change to operate, the less likely it is to evolve in the first place.

Females must invest much more energy per offspring when the pro-duction of small planktonically feeding larvae is impossible, and this energy expenditure results in greater internal anatomical differences be-tween the sexes in higher vertebrates than in fishes. The necessity for internal fertilization has often led to further anatomical separation of the sexes in the structure of the external genitalia. As the gap between successful male and female configurations has widened, sex determina-tion appears to have become more stringent, reflected in the evolution of dimorphic sex chromosomes. In addition, the more precise timing and positioning necessary for successful internal fertilization appears to have increased the learned component in mating, and the lack of experience of a newly transformed individual in the role of the opposite sex may place an additional barrier to sex change.

Unisexuality, which finds its fullest expression among the reptiles, does not offer as facile an explanation. Parthenogenesis should be adaptive if the environment of the offspring is similar to that of the parent, or if the probability of extinction is very low. Lizards and snakes do not appear to occupy any more stable habitats (in the short- or long-term sense) than other vertebrates, and the reason for the high incidence of unisexuality among the reptiles remains obscure.

8 ACKNOWLEDGMENTS

I am indebted to Egbert G. Leigh, Jr. for a continuing series of spirited discussions on the evolution of sexual patterns. Although our views often differ, he has proved a good listener and constructive critic. A suggestion of Gordon Orians' to Dr. Leigh was the genesis of the ideas on the role of experience. Isabel F. Downs aided me greatly in gathering data, and B. B. DeWolfe, S. G. Hoffman, E. G. Leigh, Jr., and S. I. Rothstein all provided helpful comments on an earlier draft. Any errors that remain are my own. This work was supported by a General Research Grant from the University of California, Santa Barbara.

REFERENCES

Alexander, R. McNeill. 1975. *The Chordates*. Cambridge University Press, London. 480 p.

Amadon, D. 1959. The significance of sexual differences in size among birds. Proc. Am. Phil. Soc. **103**: 531–536.

Ashmole, N. P. 1963. The regulation of numbers of tropical oceanic birds. Ibis **103B**: 458–473.

Atz, J. W. 1964. Intersexuality in fishes. *In*: C. N. Armstrong and A. J. Marshall, Eds. *Intersexuality in Vertebrates, Including Man*. Academic Press, New York. P. 145–232.

Baker, J. R. 1925. On sex-intergrade pigs: their anatomy, genetics, and developmental physiology. Brit. J. Exp. Biol. **2**: 247–263.

Bartholomew, G. A. 1970. A model for the evolution of pinniped polygyny. Evolution **24**: 546–559.

Bateman, A. J. 1948. Intrasexual selection in *Drosophila*. Heredity **2**: 349–368.

Bateson, G. 1963. The role of somatic change in evolution. Evolution **17**: 529–539.

Beach, F. A. 1947. A review of physiological and psychological studies of sexual behavior in mammals. Physiol. Rev. **27**: 240–307.

Beach, F. A. 1961. *Hormones and Behavior*. Cooper Square, New York. 368 p.

Beatty, R. 1964. Chromosome deviations and sex in vertebrates. *In*: C. N. Armstrong and A. J. Marshall, Eds. *Intersexuality in Vertebrates, Including Man*. Academic Press, New York. P. 106–115.

Beatty, R. A. 1967. Parthenogenesis in vertebrates. *In*: C. B. Metz and A. Monroy, Eds. *Fertilization: Comparative Morphology, Biochemistry, and Immunology*. Academic Press, New York. P. 413–440.

Berger, L. 1971. Sex ratio in the F_1 progeny within forms of *Rana esculenta* complex. Genetica Polonica **12**: 87–101.

Berrill, N. J. 1955. *The Origin of Vertebrates*. Clarendon Press, Oxford. 257 p.

Bezy, R. L. 1972. Karyotypic variation and evolution of the lizards in the family Xantusiidae. Contr. Sci., Nat. Hist. Mus., Los Angeles County No. 227: P.1 –29.

Blair, W. F. 1960. *The Rusty Lizard. A Population Study*. University of Texas Press, Austin. 185 p.

Blaxter, J. H. S. 1969. Development: Eggs and larvae. *In*: W. S. Hoar and D. J. Randall, Eds. *Fish Physiology*. Academic Press, New York. P. 177–252.

Bruner-Lorand, J. 1964. Intersexuality in mammals. *In*: C. N. Armstrong and A. J. Marshall, Eds. *Intersexuality in Vertebrates, Including Man*. Academic Press, New York. P. 310–347.

Burns, R. K. 1950. Sex transformation in the opossum: some new results and a retrospect. Arch. Anat. Microscop. et. Morphol. Expr. **39**: 467–481.

Burns, R. K. 1961. Role of hormones in the differentiation of sex. *In*: W. C. Young, Ed. *Sex and the Internal Secretions*. 3d Ed. Bailliére, Tindall and Cox, London. P. 76–158.

Carpenter, C. R. 1942. Sexual behavior of free-ranging rhesus monkeys (*Macaca mulata*). I. Specimens, procedures, and behavioral character of estrus. II. Periodicity of estrus, homosexual, autoerotic and nonconformist behavior. J. Comp. Psychol. **33**: 113–162.

Carrick, R., S. E. Csordas, and S. E. Ingham. 1962. Studies on the southern elephant seal, *Mirounga leonina* (L.). IV. Breeding and development. C.S.I.R.O. Wildl. Res. **7**: 161–197.

Carter, G. S. 1967. *Structure and Habit in Vertebrate Evolution*. University of Washington Press, Seattle. 520 p.

Chang, C. Y. and E. Witschi. 1956. Genetic control and hormonal reversal of sex differentiation in *Xenopus*. Proc. Soc. Exp. Biol. Med. **93**: 140–144.

Choat, H. and D. R. Robertson. 1975. Protogynous hermaphroditism in fishes of the family Scaridae. *In*: R. Reinboth, Ed. *Intersexuality in the Animal Kingdom*. Springer-Verlag, Heidelberg. P. 263–283.

Cole, C. J. 1975. Evolution of parthenogenetic species of reptiles. *In*: R. Reinboth, Ed. *Intersexuality in the Animal Kingdom*. Springer-Verlag, Heidelberg. P. 340–355.

Crew, F. A. E. 1923. Studies in intersexuality. II. Sex reversal in the fowl. Proc. Roy. Soc. B. **95**: 256–278.

Cuellar, O. 1974. On the origin of parthenogenesis in vertebrates: The cytogenetic factors. Am. Nat. **108**: 625–648.

De Beer, G. R. 1951. *Vertebrate Zoology, An Introduction to the Comparative Anatomy, Embryology, and Evolution of Chordate Animals*. Sidgwick and Jackson, Ltd., London. 435 p.

DeVore, I. 1965. Male dominance and mating behavior in baboons. *In*: F. Beach, Ed. *Sex and Behavior*. John Wiley and Sons, New York. P. 266–289.

de Vos, A., P. Brokx, and V. Geist. 1967. A review of social behavior of the North American cervids during the reproductive period. Am. Midl. Nat. **77:** 390–417.

Downhower, J. F. and K. B. Armitage. 1971. The yellow-bellied marmot and the evolution of polygamy. Am. Nat. **105:** 355–370.

Ebeling, A. W. and T. R. Chen. 1970. Heterogamety in teleostean fishes. Trans. Am. Fish. Soc. **99:** 131–138.

Emlen, J. M. 1973. *Ecology: An Evolutionary Approach.* Addison-Wesley, Reading, Mass. 493 p.

Emlen, S. T. 1968. Territoriality in the bullfrog, *Rana catesbiana.* Copeia **1968:** 240–243.

Evans, L. T. 1951. Field study of the social behavior of the black lizard, *Ctenosaura pectinata.* Am. Mus. Novitates **1493:** 1–26.

Fiedler, K. 1964. Verhaltensstudien an Lippfischen der Gattung *Crenilabrus* (Labridae, Perciformes). Z. Tierpsychol. **21:** 521–591.

Fishelson, L. 1975. Ecology and physiology of sex reversal in *Anthias squamipinnis* (Peters), (Teleostei: Anthiidae). *In:* R. Reinboth, Ed. *Intersexuality in the Animal Kingdom.* Springer-Verlag, Heidelberg. P. 284–294.

Fisher, R. A. 1930. *The Genetical Theory of Natural Selection.* Clarendon Press, Oxford. 272 p.

Foote, C. L. 1964. Intersexuality in amphibians. *In:* C. N. Armstrong and A. J. Marshall, Eds. *Intersexuality in Vertebrates, Including Man.* Academic Press, New York. P. 233–272.

Forbes, T. R. 1964. Intersexuality in reptiles. *In:* C. N. Armstrong and A. J. Marshall, Eds. *Intersexuality in Vertebrates, Including Man.* Academic Press, New York. P. 273–283.

Geisselman, B., R. Flindt, and H. Hemmer. 1971. Studien zur Biologie, Ökologie, und Merkmalsvariabilität der beiden Braunfrosharten *Rana temporaria* L. und *Rana dalmatia* Bonaparte. Zool. Jahrb. Syst. Bd. **98:** 521–568.

Geist, V. 1971. *Mountain Sheep: A Study in Behavior and Evolution.* University of Chicago Press, Chicago. 383 p.

Ghiselin, M. T. 1969. The evolution of hermaphroditism among animals. Qt. Rev. Biol. **44:** 189–208.

Ghiselin, M. T. 1974. *The Economy of Nature and the Evolution of Sex.* University of California Press, Berkeley. 346 p.

Goldman, A. S. 1975. Recent studies on the intersexual programming of the genetic rat male pseudohermaphrodite. *In:* R. Reinboth, Ed. *Intersexuality in the Animal Kingdom.* Springer-Verlag, Heidelberg. P. 422–437.

Gordon, M. 1957. Physiological genetics of fishes. *In:* M. E. Brown, Ed. *The Physiology of Fishes.* Vol. 2. Academic Press, New York. P. 431–450.

Guhl, A. M. 1941. The frequency of mating in relation to social position in small flocks of white leghorns. Anat. Rec., Suppl. **81:** 113.

Guhl, A. M. 1962. The behavior of chickens. *In:* I. S. E. Hafez, Ed. *The Behavior of Domestic Animals.* Bailliére, Tindall and Cox, London. P. 491–530.

Hardy, L. M. 1970. Intersexuality in a Mexican colubrid snake (*Pseudofimicia*). Herpetologia **26:** 336–343.

Harlow, H. F. 1965. Sexual behavior in the rhesus monkey. *In:* F. A. Beach, Ed. *Sex and Behavior.* John Wiley and Sons, New York. P. 234–265.

Harrington, R. W., Jr. 1961. Oviparous hermaphroditic fish with internal self-fertilization. Science **134:** 1749–1750.

Harris, V. A. 1964. *The Life of the Rainbow Lizard*. Hutchinson Tropical Monographs, London. 174 p.

Hediger, H. 1965. Environmental factors influencing the reproduction of zoo animals. *In*: F. Beach, Ed. *Sex and Behavior*. John Wiley and Sons, New York. P. 319–354.

Hoar, W. S. 1969. Reproduction. *In*: W. S. Hoar and D. J. Randall, Eds. *Fish Physiology*. Academic Press, New York. P. 1–59.

Hoge, A. R., H. E. Belluomini, G. Schreiber, and A. M. Penha. 1959. Sexual abnormalities in *Bothrops insularis* (Amaral) 1921. Mem. Inst. Butantan **29**: 17–88.

Holm, C. H. 1973. Breeding sex ratios, territoriality, and reproductive success in the red-winged blackbird (*Agelaius phoeniceus*). Ecology **54**: 356–365.

Humphrey, R. R. 1945. Sex determination in ambystomid salamanders: a study of the progeny of females experimentally converted into males. Am. J. Anat. **76**: 33–66.

Jameson, W. 1961. *The Wandering Albatross*. Rev. ed. Nat. Hist. Libr., Doubleday and Co., New York. 131 p.

Kallman, K. D. 1970. Sex determination and the restriction of sex-linked pigment patterns to the X and Y chromosomes in populations of a poeciliid fish, *Xiphophorus maculatus*, from the Belize and Sibun Rivers of British Honduras. Zoologica, New York **55**: 1–16.

Le Boeuf, B. J. and R. S. Peterson. 1969. Social status and mating activity in elephant seals. Science **163**: 91–93.

Liem, K. F. 1968. Geographical and taxonomic variation in the pattern of natural sex reversal in the teleost fish order Synbranchiformes. J. Zool. Lond. **156**: 225–238.

Loiselle, P. V. and G. W. Barlow. 1978. Do fishes lek like birds? *In*: E. S. Reese and F. J. Lighter, Eds. *Contrasts in Behavior*, Wiley-Interscience, New York. P. 31–75.

MacGregor, H. C. and T. M. Uzzell, Jr. 1964. Gynogenesis in salamanders related to *Ambystoma jeffersoneanum*. Science **143**: 1043–1045.

Marshall, A. J. 1964. Introduction. *In*: C. N. Armstrong and A. J. Marshall, Eds. *Intersexuality in Vertebrates, Including Man*. Academic Press, New York. P. 1–16.

Maslin, T. P. 1971. Parthenogenesis in reptiles. Am. Zool. **11**: 361–380.

Maslow, A. M. 1940. Dominance quality and social behavior in infrahuman primates. J. Soc. Psychol. **11**: 313–324.

Maynard Smith, J. 1971a. What use is sex? J. Theor. Biol. **30**: 319–335.

Maynard Smith, J. 1971b. The origin and maintenance of sex. *In*: G. C. Williams, Ed. *Group Selection*. P. 163–175.

Mehl, J. A. P. and R. Reinboth. 1975. The possible significance of sex-chromatin for the determination of genetic sex in ambisexual teleost fishes. *In*: R. Reinboth, Ed. *Intersexuality in the the Animal Kingdom*. Springer-Verlag, Heidelberg. P. 243–248.

Mittowch, U. 1973. *Genetics of Sex Differentiation*. Academic Press, New York. 253 p.

Mittwoch, U. 1975. Chromosomes and sex differentiation. *In*: R. Reinboth, Ed. *Intersexuality in the Animal Kingdom*. Springer-Verlag, Heidelberg. P. 438–446.

Nelson, G. G. 1975. Anatomy of the male urogenital organs of *Goodea atripinnis* and *Characodon lateralis* (Atheriniformes: Cyprinodontoidei) and *G. atripinnis* courtship. Copeia **1975**: 475–482.

Nikolski, G. V. 1963. *The Ecology of Fishes*. Academic Press, New York. 352 p.

Noble, G. K. and B. Greenberg. 1941. Induction of female behavior in male *Anolis carolinensis* with testosterone propionate. Proc. Soc. Exp. Biol. Med. **42**: 32–37.

Ohno, S. 1967. *Sex Chromosomes and Sex-Linked Genes*. Springer-Verlag, Heidelberg. 192 p.

Olsen, M. W. 1965. Twelve year summary of selection for parthenogenesis in Beltsville small white turkeys. Br. Poul. Sci. **6**: 1–6.

Olsen, M. W., S. P. Wilson, and H. L. Marks. 1968. Genetic control of parthenogenesis in chickens. J. Hered. **59**: 41–42.

Orians, G. H. 1969. On the evolution of mating systems in birds and mammals. Am. Nat. **103**: 589–603.

Orr, R. T. and T. C. Poulter. 1967. Some observations on reproduction, growth, and social behavior in the Stellar sea lion. Proc. Cal. Acad. Sci. **35**: 193–226.

Pianka, E. R. and W. S. Parker. 1975. Age-specific reproductive tactics. Am. Nat. **109**: 453–464.

Rand, A. S. 1967. The adaptive significance of territoriality in iguanid lizards. *In*: W. W. Milstead, Ed. *Lizard Ecology*. Univ. of Missouri Press, Columbia, Missouri. P. 106–115.

Randall, J. E. and H. A. Randall. 1963. The spawning and early development of the Atlantic parrotfish, *Sparisoma rubripinne*, with notes on other scarid and labrid fishes. Zoologica, New York **48**: 49–60.

Reinboth, R. 1970. Intersexuality in fishes. Mem. Soc. Endocrinol. No. **18**: 515–543.

Reinboth, R. 1973. Dualistic reproductive behavior in the protogynous wrasse *Thalassoma bifasciatum* and some observations on its day-night changeover. Helgoländer Wiss. Meeresunters. **24**: 171–191.

Riddle, O., W. F. Hollander, and J. P. Schooley. 1945. A race of hermaphrodite-producing pigeons. Anat. Record **92**: 401–423.

Robertson, D. R. 1972. Social control of sex reversal in a coral-reef fish. Science **177**: 1007–1009.

Robertson, D. R. and H. Choat. 1974. Protogynous hermaphroditism and social systems in labrid fishes. Proceedings of the Second Internat. Symposium on Coral Reefs. G. B. R. C. Brisbane **1**: 217–225.

Roede, M. J. 1972. Color as related to size, sex, and behavior in seven Caribbean labrid fish species (genera *Thalassoma*, *Halichoeres*, and *Hemipterinotus*). Studies on the fauna of Curacao and other Caribbean Islands **138**: 1–264.

Romer, A. S. 1950. *The Vertebrate Body*. W. B. Saunders Co., Philadelphia. 643 p.

Rosenblatt, Jay S. 1965. Effects of experience on sexual behavior in male cats. *In*: F. A. Beach, Ed. *Sex and Behavior*. John Wiley and Sons, New York. P. 416–439.

Schaffer, W. M. and C. A. Reed. 1972. The coevolution of social behavior and cranial morphology in sheep and goats (Bovidae, Caprini). Fieldeana Zool. **61**: 1–88.

Schreck, C. B. 1974. Hormonal treatment and sex manipulation in fishes. *In*: C. B. Schreck, Ed. *Control of Sex in Fishes*. Sea Grant Extension Division, Virginia Polytechnic Institute and State Univ., Blacksburg, Virginia. P. 84–106.

Schultz, R. J. 1969. Hybridization, unisexuality, and polyploidy in the teleost *Poeciliopsis* (Poeciliidae) and other vertebrates. Am. Nat. **103**: 605–619.

Schultz, R. J. 1971. Special adaptive problems associated with unisexual fishes. Am. Zool. **11**: 351–360.

Schultz, R. J. and K. D. Kallman. 1968. Triploid hybrids between the all-female teleost *Poecilia formosa* and *Poecilia sphenops*. Nature **219**: 280–282.

Scott, J. W. 1942. Mating behavior of the sage grouse. Auk **59**: 477–498.

Scudo, F. M. 1969. On the adaptive value of sexual dimorphism: II. Unisexuality. Evolution 23: 36–49.

Selander, R. K. 1965. On mating systems and sexual selection. Am. Nat. 99: 129–141.

Selander, R. K. and R. J. Hauser. 1965. Gonadal and behavioral cycles in the great-tailed grackle. Condor 67: 157–182.

Smith, C. L. 1967. Contribution to the theory of hermaphroditism. J. Theor. Biol. 17: 76–90.

Smith, C. L. 1975. The evolution of hermaphroditism in fishes. In: R. Reinboth, Ed. Intersexuality in the Animal Kingdom. Springer-Verlag, Heidelberg. P. 295–310.

Stanley, S. M. 1975. Clades versus clones in evolution: why we have sex. Science 190: 382–383.

Suomalainen, E. 1950. Parthenogenesis in animals. Adv. Genet. 3: 193–253.

Taber, E. 1964. Intersexuality in birds. In: C. N. Armstrong and A. J. Marshall, Eds. Intersexuality in Vertebrates, Including Man. Academic Press, New York. P. 285–310.

Tomlinson, J. 1966. The advantages of hermaphroditism and parthenogenesis. J. Theort. Biol. 11: 54–58.

Trivers, R. L. 1972. Parental investment and sexual selection. In: Bernard Campbell, Ed. Sexual Selection and the Descent of Man, 1871–1971. Aldine Publishing Co., Chicago. P. 136–179.

Tunner, H. 1970. Das serumeiweissbild einheimscher Wasserfrösche und der Hybridcharakter von Rana esculenta. Verh. Dtsch. Zool. Ges. 64: 352–358.

Uzzell, T. 1970. Meiotic mechanisms of naturally occurring unisexual vertebrates. Am. Nat. 104: 433–445.

Uzzell, T. 1975. Rana esculenta Conference. Copeia 1975: 194.

Uzzell, T. and I. S. Darevsky. 1975. Biochemical evidence for the hybrid origin of the parthenogenetic species of the Lacerta saxicola complex (Sauria: Lacertidae), with a discussion of some ecological and evolutionary implications. Copeia 1975: 204–222.

Van Tienhoven, A. 1961. Endocrinology of reproduction in birds. In: W. C. Young, Ed. Sex and Internal Secretions. 3d ed. Balliere, Tindall, and Cox, London. P. 1088–1169.

Verner, J. 1964. Evolution of polygamy in the longbilled marsh wren. Evolution 18: 252–261.

Verner, J. and M. F. Willson. 1969. Mating systems, sexual dimorphism, and the role of male North American passerine birds in the nesting cycle. Ornithol. Monogr. 9: 1–72.

Vorontosov, N. N. 1973. The evolution of the sex chromosomes. In: A. B. Chiarelli and E. Capanna, Eds. Cytotaxonomy and Vertebrate Evolution. Academic Press, New York. P. 619–657.

Warner, R. R. 1975. The adaptive significance of sequential hermaphroditism in animals. Am. Nat. 109: 61–82.

Warner, R. R. and I. F. Downs. 1977. Comparative life histories: growth vs. reproduction in normal males and sex-changing hermaphrodites of the striped parrotfish, Scarus croicensis. Proc. 3rd. Int. Coral Reef Symp. 1. Biology:275–281.

Warner, R. R., D. R. Robertson, and E. G. Leigh, Jr. 1975. Sex change and sexual selection. Science 190: 633–638.

Welty, J. C. 1962. The Life of Birds. W. R. Saunders Co., Philadelphia. 546 p.

White, M. J. D. 1970. Heterozygosity and genetic polymorphism in parthenogenetic animals. In: M. K. Hecht and W. C. Steeve, Eds. Essays in Evolution and Genetics in Honor of Theodosius Dobzhansky. Appleton-Century-Crofts, New York. P. 237–262.

Williams, G. C. 1966. *Adaptation and Natural Selection: a Critique of Some Current Evolutionary Thought*. Princeton University Press, Princeton, N. J. 307 p.

Williams, G. C. 1975. *Sex and Evolution*. Princeton University Press, Princeton, N. J. 200 p.

Witschi, E. 1934. Sex deviations, inversions, and parabiosis. *In*: E. Allen, Ed. *Sex and Internal Secretions*. Williams and Wilkins Co., Baltimore. P. 160–245.

Witschi, E. 1961. Sex and secondary sex characters. *In*: A. J. Marshall, Ed. *Biology and Comparative Physiology of Birds*, Academic Press, New York. P. 115–168.

Witschi, E. 1962. Sex reversal in animals and in man. Science in Progress, Yale University Press, New Haven. Ser. **12**: 171–193.

Wright, J. W. and C. H. Lowe. 1968. Weeds, polyploids, parthenogenesis, and the geographical and ecological distribution of all female species of *Cnemidophorus*. Copeia **1968**: 128–158.

Yamamoto, Toki-O. 1969. Sex differentiation. *In*: W. S. Hoar and D. J. Randall, Eds. *Fish Physiology*. Vol. 3, Academic Press, New York. P. 117–175.

Young, W. C. 1965. The organization of sexual behavior by hormonal action during the prenatal and larval periods of vertebrates. *In*: F. A. Beach, Ed. *Sex and Behavior*. John Wiley and Sons, New York. P. 89–107.

Part II

COMMUNICATIVE AND REGULATORY BEHAVIOR

4

LATERAL DISPLAYS
IN THE LOWER VERTEBRATES:
FORMS, FUNCTIONS, AND ORIGINS

DAVID CHISZAR

Department of Psychology
University of Colorado, Boulder

1   INTRODUCTION

The initial purpose of this paper was to organize the wealth of data on the topography, function, and causation of lateral displays in fish, amphibians, and reptiles. During the process of assembling these comparative data, several ideas emerged about the probable pathways involved in the evolution of this group of behaviors. Hence, I have also included descriptions and comparisons of these ethomorphological theories.

Whichever theory the reader eventually decides to accept, it is essential that some manner of evolutionary interpretation be attempted. Lateral displays occur frequently in the aggressive repertories of numerous vertebrate species, and it is unreasonable to suppose that all these animals could have acquired the same kind of response during individual experience. It is also necessary that lateral displays be subjected to psychological interpretation(s) that answer the question: What function do these behaviors serve? Since these responses commonly occur during aggressive episodes, it is typically assumed that they have an aggressive-threatening function. This belief is illustrated in the following quotation, which also reveals that the psychological interpretation of a behavior strongly disposes the theorist toward a particular direction of evolutionary speculation.

Ethologists use the term *threat* to refer to those gestures used to communicate higher social status as well as direct intentions of attack. There are two broad classes of initial threat postures among vertebrates. Either they present themselves to their opponent at right angles, called a *lateral* [italics in original] or broadside display, or they stand head-on, called a *frontal* display. The two display postures are very common and almost always are ritualized. The organs of intimidation are built around these different displays. The function of these auxiliary organs is to support the threat—to increase the opponent's likelihood of acknowledging with submission without fighting.

The two different threat displays have basically different intimidation organs. Those species which use a lateral display have structures that contribute to, or call attention to, their massive appearance when viewed from the side. Dewlaps (cattles, *Bos*; and moose, *Alces*), crests, or hair down the back (American Mountain Goat, *Oreamnos*), and erect manes (all wild horses and many African antelopes) are but a few examples from the mammals. Those species which depend more on a frontal display seldom have intimidation display organs on the posterior part of the body, but rather have them concentrated on the head and neck. [Guthrie, 1970, p. 259.]

It is fairly clear that Guthrie assumes that both lateral and frontal displays arose at least in part as ritualized combat postures or as ritualized combat-intention actions. A particular species shows one or the other response, depending upon whether lateral or frontal orientations regularly occurred during the fighting or during any stage of interaction leading to fighting (e.g., approach or ambivalent postures) in the ancestral stock. Species that exhibit both displays are probably derived from ancestors who employed both postures (sequentially or alternatively) during aggressive interaction. The displays are thus considered to be symbolic of aggressive intent or motivation, and the psychological and evolutionary implications of this view are fairly clear (see Sec. 3, "Lateral Displays as Aggressive-Intention Movements," for a more complete discussion).

I do not doubt that frontal displays have been derived mainly from combat-intention movements. Nor do I doubt that numerous mammalian morphological details (e.g., antlers, horns, hair caps, head crests, beards, sideburns, humps, etc.) can be understood in terms of the way they contribute to the effectiveness of these displays. However, I do question whether lateral displays should be lumped, motivationally, functionally, and evolutionarily, with frontal displays. Indeed, I think most ethologists would be reluctant to accept this view without introducing serious qualifications (Barlow, personal communication). For some species (e.g., large mammalian herbivores) I think the evidence suggests that this may be done (Geist, 1971). In other species, especially lower vertebrates, this sort of lumping may be an error, and the last section of this paper will be devoted to the presentation of an alternative view.

2 LATERAL DISPLAYS IN COMPARATIVE PERSPECTIVE

2.1 Fishes

Although I am not certain about the earliest paper to employ the term "lateral display," the behavior illustrated in Fig. 4.1 has probably been discussed often enough to deserve nominate status (see Tavolga, 1967, and Dijkgraaf, 1967, for discussions of the role of lateral-line organs in this and other aspects of fish behavior; see Barlow, 1963, for additional illustrations). The water jetting seen in this drawing can be strong enough that one fish could drive the other several centimeters away (Wickler, 1962, described such actions in the cichlid fish, *Apistogramma wickleri*). However, this intense degree of water fighting does not characterize the lateral display in all species of fish; in fact, many species that exhibit reciprocal lateral postures, often of long duration (i.e., 30 sec), show little or no water fighting (rainbow and brown trout, *Salmo gairdneri* and *S. trutta*; Jenkins, 1969; Chiszar, Drake and Windell, 1975; see Chapman, 1962, and Hartman, 1965, for illustrations). Barlow (1962, 1963) described a curious form of lateral display in the dwarf chameleon fish, *Badis badis*. Two males would assume reciprocal lateral display postures (head-to-tail = antiparallel orientation), and each individual would pass through a variety of color phases that represent varying intensities of threat. This "color fight" ends when one individual (the

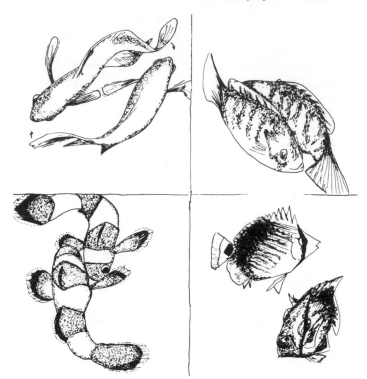

FIGURE 4.1   Various lateral displays. (a) Upper left: a typical lateral display involving water-jetting, wherein individuals may sweep each other away with "blows," and/or wherein individuals can derive an estimate of the opponent's strength by the force of the "blow" as well as from the massiveness of the profile. (Redrawn from Tinbergen, 1951.) (b) Upper right: the lateral display in bluegill sunfish, *Lepomis macrochirus*, may involve stationary antiparallel postures with erection of dorsal spines, or may develop into a vigorous carousel fight, with each animal attempting to nip the other's caudal fin. (c) Lower left: lateral display in the clown fish, *Amphiprion percula*, may involve the striking of real blows to the face with the pectoral fins. (Redrawn from Eibl-Eibesfeldt, 1960.) (d) Lower right: striped butterfly fish, *Chaetodon melanotus*, shown with erected spines (upper drawing) and in the act of tilting toward a source of threatening stimulation (lower drawing).

winner) remains in a dark phase while the loser pales and swims away. The entire episode can transpire without either fish "striking a blow." Although other species exhibit obvious color changes during social encounters, it is typical for the interaction to lead eventually to carousel fights and/or to mutual tail-nipping attempts (e.g., bluegill sunfish, *Lepomis macrochirus*; Stacey and Chiszar, 1975; Fig. 4.1b); or, in some species, the individuals may strike at each other with their pectoral fins (anemone or clown fish, *Amphiprion percula*; Eibl-Eibesfeldt, 1960; Fig.

4.1c). Individuals of species with long, sharp dorsal spines often assume a lateral-display posture until the other fish comes too close; then the former animal tilts the spines toward the latter in a defensive action called rolling or leaning (Fig. 4.1d). In such cases it has been hypothesized (e.g., Barlow, 1962; Lorenz, cited in Barlow, 1962) that the defensive response against conspecifics represents an evolutionary capitalization upon the presence of spines and associated behaviors that undoubtedly had an initial antipredation function (Hoogland, Morris, and Tinbergen, 1956/1957; see also Miller, 1948, and Vorhies, 1948, for an illustration of antipredatory spines in the horned lizard, *Phrynosoma solare*).

It is clear that lateral displays may incorporate a variety of offensive as well as defensive actions, and that great diversity exists among fish species in the composition of lateral displays. Indeed, the only general aspect of the display is the lateral positioning of the respective individuals. This leads to the hypothesis that lateral positioning is phylogenetically primary and that the supplementary components are more recent, each representing a unique adaptation to the particular anatomical substrate and/or ecological circumstances of the taxon under consideration. This is an important point because it specifies the direction of evolution: lateral displays (especially the lateral-positioning component) did not evolve from water fighting or pectoral-fin fighting or carousel fighting or color fighting; rather the latter behaviors all arose from, or were added to, the more basic, prior-existing tendency of fish to engage in reciprocal lateral posturing. Hence, although we now have some ideas about the origins of the fighting components, we have not begun to explain the origin of the lateral postures except to say that they may be phylogenetically older than the fighting components. This problem will be dealt with in detail later; for the moment it is intructive to examine the topography and socioecological roles of lateral displays in other vertebrates.

2.2 Amphibians

Although the term "lateral display" is not often employed in amphibian literature, there appear to be occasions where the label could be appropriate. For example, consider the following description of premating agonistic behavior among male pipid frogs (*Hymenochirus boettgeri*):

Most commonly a hot (i.e., reproductively motivated) male approaches another equally stimulated male and calls with his head oriented toward the second male's side. The second answers with a buzz. With movements amounting to a thrust and parry the first male usually passes by the second. However, there are variations in this action. The first male may follow his call with the dance before the second male buzzes, or charge the second animal head-on after he has buzzed. In charging the first male appears to butt his head against the head or throat of the second male. Occasionally the charging male passes above the second male's head and he may then attempt to clasp the second male head-on just behind the axilla. These encounters may be very violent, with the first male pumping his arms about the chest of the second and the second male buzzing after each pump. The first male unclasps in a short time and they quickly separate to distant parts of the tank. If the second male moves as the first calls, the second is grasped from the side and the resulting clasp is inguinal instead of head-on. [Rabb and Rabb, 1963, p. 221.]

This is a complex behavioral episode involving many components. Yet it seems that lateral posturing and lateral clasping justify the inclusion of this behavior in the present context; and it can be hypothesized that subsequent research might reveal threatening or other display significance of the lateral posturing of these frogs. Numerous additional papers (summarized by Rabb, 1973) describe combat in a variety of territorial male anurans and, although attention is usually given to chest-to-chest interaction, lateral postures are frequently seen prior to and after these struggles. Hence, the previous hypothesis is not confined to pipids, but extends at least to ranids, hylids, dendrobatids, pelobatids, and leptodactylids. In this context it should also be mentioned that many frogs and toads are known to assume "defense-fight" postures upon disturbance by humans and/or predators (Banta and Carl, 1967; Nobel, 1931; see Brodie, Johnson, and Dodd, 1974, for a similar phenomenon in salamanders). The lungs are inflated, the body is correspondingly swollen, often the forelimbs are stretched (the animal lifting the body off the ground and sometimes throwing it forward), and some species add an open-mouth display and/or an alarm cry to this pattern (Fig. 4.2). A swollen frog or toad is harder to grasp than a deflated one; and the lateral aspect of the animal is obviously enlarged by these actions.

There is no doubt that both the defensive and offensive components of this series of events are effective in warding off the attacks of both snakes and birds. The inflation of the body and the straightening of the limbs are part of the defensive mechanism of lizards, and hence at least this part of the response may be considered an ancient inheritance from early tetrapods. [Noble, 1931, p. 382–383.]

We may properly wonder if the lateral components of this display are derived from an even more ancient inher. ince: namely, from the piscine ancestors of the tetrapods, who had probably already employed

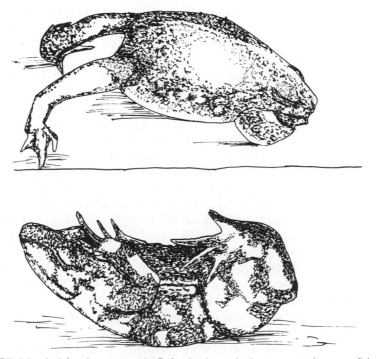

FIGURE 4.2 A defensive posture in *Bufo clamita* and other anurans (top panel) involves body swelling and, in some cases, movements of limbs and/or mouth. The lateral surfaces appear particularly large. (Redrawn from Noble, 1931.) The "unken relfex" (lower panel) of *Bombina bombina* also exposes lateral (as well as ventral) surfaces and may thereby expose defensive coloration. (Redrawn from Noble, 1931.)

lateral displays (as we may deduce from the ubiquity of lateral displays among contemporary fishes). Moreover, some anurans expose brightly colored and poisonous lateral surfaces in a remarkable action known as the "unken reflex" (Fig. 4.2), indicating another similarity with piscine lateral displays that expose special colorational and/or structural signals (e.g., Barlow, 1963; Neil, 1964; Waring, 1963).

Studies of aggression or other (nonreproductive) social behaviors have not been frequently reported for caudates or caecilians. However, it should not be assumed too quickly that these animals do not exhibit these types of behavior. Four factors suggest that such a view would be premature. First, almost nothing is known of the behavior of these animals during the nonreproductive parts of the year, during which most individuals are living a terrestrial or subterrestrial existence. Second, some responses that occur during courtship appear by their "violent" character to have aggressive significance. For example, the whipping motion in the courtship of newts of the genus *Triturus* (Halliday, 1974) would certainly be interpreted as a lateral display with aggressive meaning if males directed it at other males rather than at females. Perhaps it is employed as an alerting action during the early phase of courtship and as a warning or threat at other occasions; information on the latter point would be especially welcome at this time. Third, although most studies of courtship in newts and salamanders involve a single male and a single female, occasional observations of situations containing two or more males indicate that "competitive responses" may occur, that one male may attempt to disrupt the amplectic actions of another, and that an amplectic male may actively avoid and perhaps threaten an intruder (Storey, 1969). Clearly, descriptive research on aggression and other forms of social interaction in caudates may be rewarded by the discovery of hitherto unimagined kinds of behavioral displays. Fourth, the work of Brodie and his colleagues on defensive (i.e., antipredator) secretions in salamanders clearly indicates that these animals execute responses that have the effect of moving the noxious secretions toward or rubbing them on potential predators (Brodie, 1968; Brodie, Hensel, and Johnson, 1974; see Brodie and Gibson, 1969, for illustrations of defensive responses). Head-rubbing and tail-lashing are among these actions, and the latter, particularly, has a topography comparable to the lateral displays of other animals. Although the term "lateral display" is usually restricted to intraspecific behavior, we may not be overextending its meaning to employ it in this interspecific context. Indeed, if lateral displays involving ritualized tail-lashing and/or head-rubbing components were found to be characteristic of intraspecific social behavior in salamanders, it would be possible to argue that the display was derived from the antipredator repertory. At the moment, no such argument is warranted because we have no ethographic data on the topography or even the existence of nonreproductive social behavior in these organisms. Accordingly, it is of the utmost importance that such information be provided.

That such research is likely to reveal the presence of social responses is suggested by studies revealing the existence of aggregational tendencies in response to desiccatory stress (Alvarado, 1967) or in response to stimulus dimensions of breeding ponds (Rodda, 1975). In some cases aggregations may be a by-product of the fact that several individuals independently respond in the same manner to the same stimulus conditions, and no social "intentions" should be inferred in such situations. In other cases, aggregations appear to result from allelomimetic processes. For example, pairs of salamanders (*Ambystoma tigrinum*) placed into a uniformly illuminated observation arena spend more time in close spatial proximity than can be explained on the basis of chance directional movements of two independently responding animals (Thomas-Milton, in prep.). Also, the two animals spend more time with each other than does a single animal with a model, indicating that movement per se and/or reciprocal interaction may be at the basis of this "social attractiveness" phenomenon (see also papers by Latané and his coworkers for an analysis of a similar phenomenon in rats: Latané, 1969; Latané, Capell, and Joy, 1970; Latané, Edwards, Steele, and Walton, 1973; and Sloan and Latané, 1974). Accordingly, if individuals were indeed attracted to each other, they might also have responses that subserved communication and other functions resulting in the coordination of their activities. It is not unlikely that such responses would involve the presentation of lateral surfaces, particularly in larval and neotenic forms where the high caudal fins are so prominent when viewed from a broadside perspective, and where caudal movements are already known to be involved in interspecific communication (Brodie and Gibson, 1969).

However, at the moment we are forced to recognize that, although lateral displays are known in caudates, these responses appear to be restricted to courtship and antipredator situations. We must await the publication of new research findings before the additional suggestions made above can be evaluated.

2.3 Reptiles

The reptile situation is similar to that just encountered in amphibians: some reptiles (lizards) exhibit textbook examples of lateral displays, while others (turtles and snakes) perform behaviors that may be interpreted as lateral displays, but that have overall topographies containing many other components (Evans, 1955). Hence, the lateral aspects of these patterns may be submerged, sometimes to the point of near invisibility, in a context to which the term "lateral display" appears inappropriate.

Research on socioaggressive activities of lizards by Carpenter (1967), Evans (1953), Noble (1934), Noble and Bradley (1933), Ruibal (1957), and many others provides numerous examples of lateral displays that appear to be functionally and, to some extent, topographically similar to lateral displays in fish. For example, tail-lashing from a lateral or broadside position is well known in spiny-tailed and other agamid and iguanid lizards, and much of the morphology of the tail can be understood in relation to this behavior. In some iguanids, tail-lashing has become modified into a tail-curling lateral display that may or may not involve side-to-side movements (*Cophosaurus, Callisaurus* and *Holbrookia*; Clark,

1965; see also Fig. 4.3). The tail-curling display is employed by both sexes in eluding potential predators, by males in advertising territory to both males and females, and by gravid females in rejecting courtship advances of some males. Although there are taxon differences in the use

FIGURE 4.3 Tail displays in (a) *Holbrookia propinqua*, (b) *H. maculata*, (c) *H. lacerata*, (d) *Cophosaurus texanus*, and (e) *Callisaurus draconides*. These displays may accompany lateral posturings during assertion or challenge actions. Tail displays probably also have an antipredation function in that they draw a predator's attention toward the tail, which is detachable, and which will remain after the lizard has disappeared into cover. (Redrawn from Clarke, 1965.)

of the tail-curling display (Evans, 1953), it is nonetheless true that this display is widespread among iguanids and that it occurs in a variety of motivational contexts. Lorenz (1965) called such responses "behavioral tools," and one implication of this term is that the motivational context in which a response is first or most obviously seen may not be the one in which it evolved (see discussions by Eibl-Eibesfeldt, 1975, and Tinbergen, 1952, of the manner in which a behavior may undergo a change in motivation during phylogeny). Hence, tail-curling may not have evolved originally as an assertive or a defensive action, even though this hypothesis seems compelling. This point will be discussed again in the next two sections.

Figure 4.4 presents a variety of lateral displays that reveal differential involvement of the limbs, tail, mouth, and accessory structures (fringes, crests, dewlaps, etc.). One gets the impression that the major consistent theme is the broadside positioning and that there is great diversity in the manner in which this nuclear posture is supplemented. Further, it may be suggested that the broadside posture is phylogenetically primary and that the supplementation of this posture with limb, mouth, or other components is a more recent (and hence more variable) development. It is also useful to notice that lateral displays occur in lizards with laterally compressed bodies (i.e., arboreal lizards) as well as those with dorsoventrally flattened bodies (i.e., terrestrial lizards). Accordingly, this display probably appeared prior to the radiation of lizard body forms. Finally, it is noteworthy that frilled and bearded lizards (*Chlamydosaurus* and *Amphibolurus*) exhibit reciprocal lateral posturing, even though their remarkable appendages might initially lead to the prediction that their display would be primarily frontal (Carpenter, Badham, and Kimble, 1970; Schmidt and Inger, 1957). Perhaps this indicates that lateral posturing is a prepotent response because of phylogenetic seniority and/or greater motivational determination.

Aggressive behavior among the monitors is particualrly interesting because some species (e.g., the Komodo dragon, *Varanus komodoensis*) exhibit mostly unritualized combat (Auffenberg, cited in Murphy and Mitchell, 1974) while others (e.g., *V. salvator* and *gilleni*) exhibit highly developed rituals (Honneger and Heusser, 1969; Murphy and Mitchell, 1974). Hence, by comparison of these congeneric species, we may gain some insight into the derivation of response patterns, particularly those involving presentation of lateral surfaces. Although Komodo dragons may threaten each other (sometimes involving lateral compression of the trunk, open-mouth display, tail-lashing, and hissing), the contest usually ends up in an intense brawl, with the consequent production of bloody lacerations by reciprocal biting and clawing (Auffenberg, cited in

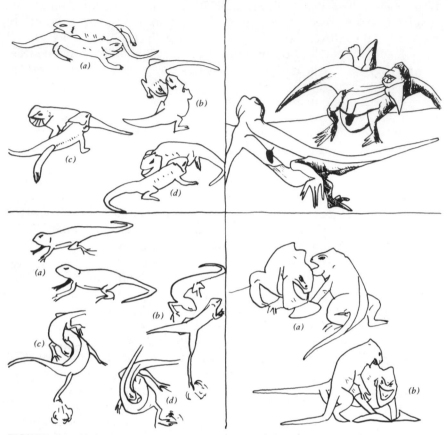

FIGURE 4.4 Various lateral displays (= "face-off postures") in lizards. (a) Upper left: note that an antiparallel lateral display occurs in the bearded dragon, *Amphibolurus barbatus*, even though the "beard" would suggest that frontal displays would be the most frequent form of display. (Redrawn from Carpenter *et al.*, 1970.) (b) Upper right: displaying fringe-toed lizards (genus *Uma*) reveal lateral compression of the bodies, exposure of special color-patches, and involvement of the limbs. (Redrawn from Carpenter, 1963.) (c) Lower left: aggressive interaction in the desert iguana, *Dipsosaurus dorsalis*, incorporates vigorous tail-slapping, suggesting that preliminary tail postures may have derived signal value as tail-slapping intention movements. (Redrawn from Carpenter, 1961.) (d) Lower right: postures of Galapagos land iguanas, genus *Conolophus*, incorporate erection of crests and mouth gaping into the antiparallel lateral display. (Redrawn from Carpenter, 1969.)

Murphy and Mitchell, 1974; Burden, 1928). In other varanids, initial intraspecific confrontations may involve lateral displays (with or without tail-lashing), open-mouth threats, or reciprocal bipedal postures that may, in turn, lead to a wrestling match. The latter posture seems to be similar to the "push-up" response, which is well known in both agamids and iguanids. However, it is doubtful that this relation represents anything more than an analogy, because the push-up response is normally executed in the context of a lateral display, whereas the rearing-up of varanids apparently occurs as part of a frontal threat. Indeed, the best phylogenetic hypothesis at present is that the rearing-up-onto-the-hindlimbs is a ritualized locomotory response that probably functioned initially as the first stage in a wrestling match and that has come to communicate aggressive intent (i.e., intention wrestling). The origin(s) of push-up behavior of agamids and iguanids is unclear (see Smith, 1946, and Jenssen, 1975), but in all probability this behavior has evolved independently of varanid bipedal rearing.

In *V. salvator* and *V. gilleni* we see the most highly ritualized combat found in the family *Varanidae*. Two males (flattened dorso-ventrally) approach each other and, unless one flees at this point, both rear up in the stance discussed above. Next, the males embrace each other with the front limbs (*V. gilleni* also uses the hindlimbs) in a venter-to-venter position, which they maintain while relying on their tails for balance. The males may lean and push against each other, or they may change the embrace so that they are side-against-side, in which case they may both lean backwards until their heads come to rest on the substrate. The venter-to-venter and side-against-side positions alternate with each other rapidly. Eventually one of the males will either flee or will become clearly subordinate. In the contest described by Murphy and Mitchell (1974), the victor and subordinate finally assumed postures comparable to the reciprocal (antiparallel) lateral display of other lizards, and the victor both bit and attempted to mate with the subordinate. The association of this lateral posturing with the termination of the contest and with mating behavior is potentially of great significance and will be dealt with in the last section of this chapter.

Snakes emit tail-lashing as a last resort when they have been grasped by a predator or a human handler. Often the tail movements are accompanied by the release of fecal materials or contents of musk glands. Hence, in addition to their potentially disorienting effects, tail lashes serve to spread these noxious fluids. However, it is unclear that these movements should be labeled as lateral displays. They involve lateral body surfaces, but they seem restricted to interspecific encounters. When we turn to intraspecific interaction, two related behavioral systems may be considered, both of which involve reciprocal contact between lateral body surfaces, and neither of which incorporates tail-lashing. First, courtship and copulation typically involve a prolonged period of mutual body-rubbing, which may be accomplished by the male and female crawling along each other's bodies, and which can also involve special structures, such as the spurs of the boas (males have been observed to sweep and scratch these structures against the body of the female while courting) and actions such as chin-rubbing and tail-stroking (in many snake species, the tail of the female is held by a loop of the male's tail during courtship and/or copulation; and, in at least one species, the western massasauga, *Sistrurus catenatus tergeminus*, this loop is actually employed to stroke the cloacal and postcloacal areas of the female's body; Chiszar, Scudder, Smith, and Radcliffe, 1976). Although the movements of head and tail sometimes obscure the lateral orientation of the bodies of the male and female, it is almost always the case that a more-or-less parallel orientation is maintained during the entire reproductive episode (Klauber, 1956; Oliver, 1956).

The second behavioral system involving lateral posturing is the so-called "combat dance" (Shaw, 1948; Thomas, 1961; see Klauber, 1956, Eibl-Eibesfeldt, 1975, and Schmidt and Inger, 1957, for illustrations). In the most frequently illustrated example, two male red rattlesnakes (*Crotalus ruber*) are seen with the front thirds of their bodies raised perpendicular to the substrate. The animals are touching each other at various points along their bodies, and their heads are facing each other. Pushing may occur, and either male may turn his head away from the other to shove his opponent by backing into him. In some respects this affair reminds the observer of wrestling in varanids. It is sometimes said that venomous snakes do not bite each other during this combat dance; however, photographs of water moccasins taken in the author's laboratory reveal that vicious bites can occur in these animals (*Agkistrodon piscivorous*). In this case, six moccasins were attempting to feed simultaneously, and competition for food was the factor that apparently precipitated the combat. Two snakes began twining about each other, and each attempted to push the other's raised head and neck. The ritual continued for approximately 15 mins, and at one point the participants locked mouths, with each snake stabbing its fangs into the other. It is not possible to say with certainty that venom was injected by either snake; however, blood was clearly visible, indicating that fang wounds were made. Hence, biting may occur during the combat dance, at least when the dance is initiated in a feeding situation. Yet it is noteworthy that the combat ritual appears to *inhibit* biting. It is not unusual for bites to occur in this group of moccasins during feeding or cage-cleaning sessions; indeed, one individual was observed to bite himself while he was excited as a consequence of transportation to an experimental apparatus. However, biting appears to occur infrequently if the combat ritual has first been activated. Hence, it seems reasonable to hypothesize that the ritual reduces the probability of biting and, therefore, of envenomation.

Although the combat dance contains many features of interest, for present purposes the lateral posturing is most important. The term "lateral display" may not be the best possible description for this phenomenon, but, just as in the case of courtship, the reciprocal lateral posturing and lateral pressing are nonetheless apparent. In fact, these activities seem to be the focus of the interaction. Accordingly, the behavior is included here as another potential kind of lateral display.

3   LATERAL DISPLAYS AS AGGRESSIVE-INTENTION MOVEMENTS

The manner in which intention or preparatory elements of a response sequence can become symbolic of the entire sequence and/or the motivational substrate underlying it has been well documented. Natural selection of such movements (as well as various other types of movements) for their signal value (i.e., releaser function) is called ritualization; and this process is considered to be one of the main ingredients in the evolution of animal communication (Baerends, 1950; Blest, 1961; Huxley, 1934, 1958; Lorenz, 1957; Morris, 1957; Selous, 1933; Tinbergen, 1952, 1959). Against the background of these major treatises, we may wonder about the extent to which the evolution of lateral displays can be explained on the basis of ritualization of aggressive-intention movements.

3.1   Reptiles

Lateral displays involving incipient tail-lashing (or related postures) in some lizards seem easily explicable in these terms. Some varanids are well known for the accuracy of their defensive tail-lashing; they may strike at and hit the eyes of their opponent (or handler) with great reliability (Cowles, 1930; Honneger and Heusser, 1969). A variety of other lizards are known to use their tails in comparable defensive actions. For example, spiny-tailed agamids (genus *Uromastix*) will first dash to a burrow or rock pile upon being molested by a predaceous snake or small mammal. However, a distal section of the tail is left outside the hiding place and, if touched, it is lashed to and fro with sufficient strength to strike a damaging blow. Tails with spines also occur among iguanids (e.g., *Hoplocerus spinosus*) and are employed in a similar manner; in addition, many long-tailed iguanids use the tail in a whiplash action reminiscent of the varanids. Although detailed ethological studies are not available for most lizard families, there is reason to believe that club-like and whip-like effects can be produced with the tail in the Cordylidae, Gerrhosauridae and possibly also in the Teiidae and Lacertidae (Schmidt and Inger, 1957). In view of the widespread occurrence of tail-lashing, it is easy to hypothesize that lateral displays may have evolved from an initial role as tail-lashing intention movements. That is, if movements preparatory to tail-lashing had communicative significance to other animals (especially conspecifics), then it is not unlikely that such movements and/or related postures could have been selected (i.e., ritualized) to serve threatening functions. Another alternative involves the use of Tinbergen's (1940) concept of "awakening movement." The lateral display might again be considered as an aggressive-intention movement, but in this case the display would be understood as a preliminary or incomplete manifestation of the overall aggressive pattern. Such a situation might arise when the intensity of the aggressive drive was relatively low, being sufficient to activate fractional components of the total pattern, but not the entire pattern. These ideas can explain two important facts concerning lateral displays in lizards: (1) that they resemble the initial components of movements employed in fighting; and (2) that they often occur during early phases of aggressive encounters before overt biting, clawing or tail-lashing movements are seen. Moreover, if lateral displays are derived from aggressive patterns, it is not surprising that they also appear to communicate status (as in assertion displays) and/or threat, sometimes being entirely sufficient to dissuade further encroachment from potential enemies.

Another aspect of lateral displays is not immediately explained by the above phylogenetic hypotheses, but it can be handled with an additional one. Often, lateral displays occur at a point during an aggressive episode when the tendencies to attack and to flee seem to be balanced (Barlow, 1962; Morris, 1955, 1958; Tinbergen, 1958). This latter idea is deduced when the respective individuals remain at least temporarily in a constant spatial relationship to each other, neither advancing and neither withdrawing (see the "face-off" postures of the bearded dragon, *Amphiboluros barbatus,* illustrated by Carpenter, Badham, and Kimble, 1970; and a similar posture in the fringe-toed lizards, genus *Uma,* illustrated by Carpenter, 1963). It is clear that these postures can have threatening significance; in fact, the terms "assertion display" and "challenge display" are employed as labels, depending upon the intensity of certain component responses (Carpenter, 1961, 1969). However, it is necessary to explain the fact that they sometimes also reflect conflict between the drive to attack and the drive to flee. On the behavioral level, it may be possible to understand the antiparallel-broadside posturing as a result of the simultaneous activation of an approach-attack response and a turn-away or flight response. As Huxley (1923, 1934) and Tinbergen (1952, 1958) have repeatedly stressed, many complex activities or postures with signal value can be explained only when we recognize that real-life situations frequently give rise to multiple drives and, hence, to multiple behaviors, or to a single behavior that incorporates components from two or more of the simultaneously aroused patterns. In the case of numerous species of lizards, the drive to attack gives rise to approach behavior, mouth-gaping, head-raising, head-tilting or lunging; but when the individual nears his opponent (or gets close to or past the boundaries of his territory), the drive to escape may activate such behaviors as stopping, turning the head and/or body away from the opponent, defensive tail-lashing, and running back to the center of the territory. If these two drives are of approximately equal strength for a brief period, then the animal is likely to exhibit some combination of response components drawn from both repertoires. For example, two animals, each experiencing a momentary balance between the drives to attack and to withdraw during a confrontation, may exhibit mouth-gaping while turning away from each other at the point of a face-to-face encounter. These antiparallel orientations would certainly be called reciprocal lateral displays, particularly if the posture should be shown through modeling experiments to have threatening or assertive significance. Hence we can now think of lateral displays as ambivalent intention movements, resulting from the simultaneous activation of two antagonistic drives.

This theory accounts for the topography of lateral displays in lizards. It seems to provide insight also into the combat dance of snakes. When a snake makes a sudden retreat, the head and forepart of the body are often lifted several inches off the ground during the initial change of direction. Hence, if the sight and/or odor of another snake elicits both attack and withdrawal, then the "dance" may be the result of the head-up and serpentine-locomotory components derived from the impulse to flee, together with face-to-face orientation, various head-jerking movements, and tail-lashing responses derived from the impulse to attack. This combination could result in the intertwining of bodies that is characterisitic of combat in many species. This view could be tested through studies that made careful comparisons of the movements comprising the combat dance with movements seen in situations that elicit pure escape and pure attack patterns. Also, it might be possible to produce the combat dance in experimental environments that created approach-avoidance conflicts (see papers by Kaufman and Miller, 1949, and Miller, 1959, for examples of the application of this methodology with rats as subjects).

3.2   Amphibians

Too little is known about threat behavior in amphibians to permit extensive speculation here. However, a few remarks can be made in the form
of hypotheses for future research. Can tail movements of some
salamanders be understood as intention movements of patterns that
have as their primary function the spreading of defensive secretions? If
threatening signals were of intraspecific value in species that exhibit
such interspecific defensive behavior, this pattern could have served as a
source for the ritualization of derived activities. Can threatening and/or
assertive vocalizations of anurans be explained through the simultaneous activation of respiratory movements involved in attack and escape?
Detailed analysis of sonograms of numerous vocalizations would be of
value in answering this question. Similarly, can the complex responses
involved in anuran threat postures and in overt wrestling matches
(Duellman, 1966; Emlen, 1968; Schroeder, 1968) be explained through
hypotheses emphasizing the balance of conflicting drives (in this case at
least three systems might be involved: attack, escape and mating)?

3.3   Fishes

When we return to the aggressive behavior of fish, the hypothesis that
lateral displays are ambivalent intention movements seems particularly
well supported. Both the topography and the function of piscine lateral
displays seem understandable through this view. For example, an antiparallel orientation might be derived from reciprocal approaching or
charging that at the last moment was thwarted by the impulse to withdraw. It would be expected that the impulse to attack would be high
when the individuals were separated by some minimal distance, and
that the impulse to withdraw would be aroused when the individuals
were close together. If these two drives balanced each other, we would
expect the fish to reach a distance from which they neither advanced nor
withdrew. Since the animals would have been approaching each other
before reaching this "conflict point," we would also expect them to be in
an antiparallel orientation when they reached this point. Although the
display is not automatically threatening as we have so far envisioned it,
evolution would surely capitalize on the reliability of this phenomenon
by adding movements and/or colorational attributes that could resolve
the aggressive encounter with minimal tissue damage. Accordingly, it is
possible to envision the lateral posture serving as a behavioral nucleus to
which natural selection would add components (within limits set by the

need for crypticity) that enhanced noticeability and, therefore, the ability to succeed in bluff, threat, assertion, and challenge. In some species, these added components have involved extraordinary colors and/or the ability to change color rapidly; perhaps the dwarf chameleon fish discussed earlier (Barlow, 1962, 1963) is the best example, and many others are available. In other species, additional movements have been added to the lateral posture, such as the vigorous wigwag movements in trout (Jenkins, 1969), water-fighting movements in various cichlids (Wickler, 1962) and actual striking movements with pectoral fins or caudal fins in *Amphiprion percula* (Eibl-Eibesfeldt, 1960).

3.4 Summary

It now seems possible to account for the ubiquity of lateral displays among the lower vertebrates in terms of more fundamental concepts (viz., "intention movements or postures" and "the balance of antagonistic drives"). Highly ritualized forms of lateral displays can be similarly explained on the basis of natural selection of additional signals that facilitate the informational role of the nuclear display (see Eibl-Eibesfeldt's 1975, concept of "semantization"). These hypotheses seem to go so far in explaining the natural history of lateral displays that the following statement by J. Huxley seems as appropriate here as it did in its original context:

This demonstrates how broad Darwinian principles can be applied to yield important conclusions even in the absence of genetic analysis. Granted certain capacities of visual perception, natural selection will produce certain kinds of results: and the results could not be produced by any other agency than selection. On this level of explanation, we now have a satisfactory interpretation of most of this sector of the evolutionary process. Genetic and experimental analysis would add new levels of explanation, but would not significantly alter the present picture. [Huxley, 1958, p. 16]

This statement may slightly overstate the confidence that ethologists have in the conclusion that lateral displays are derived from attack-intention movements, but it seems nonetheless true that so much faith has been placed in this general view that other avenues of thought have not been explored. Although it is hard to imagine that another set of hypotheses could constitute so strong a case, alternative arguments should be examined if for no other reason than to be shown unsatisfactory, because such results would strengthen the position of the primary theory. The following section is an attempt to explore an alternative hypothesis.

4   LATERAL DISPLAYS AS MATING-INTENTION MOVEMENTS

In numerous species of fish, amphibians, and reptiles (as well as birds and mammals), mating is preceded by a series of behaviors that are collectively referred to as "courtship" and that usually involve a good deal of body-rubbing (see Evans, 1955, for examples and photos). Sometimes the body-rubbing is reciprocal, and sometimes it is executed mainly by the male. In either case, the behavior can be interpreted as serving to synchronize the spatial and temporal aspects of courtship, so that both animals (in external fertilizers) deposit their gametes at the same time or that the female (in the case of internal fertilizers) is ready to accept the male or his spermatophore when he is ready. Since illustrations of courtship rubbing and other forms of body contact (e.g., see Koehn, 1965, for a discussion of nuptial tubercles) abound in the literature, only a few examples need be cited here. Bluegill sunfish, like most other centrarchids, begin the reproductive process when the male constructs a circular nest by sweeping silt and other debris from a small area in shallow water. Sweeping is accomplished by strong beats of the caudal fin, often when the male is perpendicular to the substrate, with the tail actually in contact with the debris. The same response often occurs after the nest is fully cleared, and it may play a role in attracting females, since the action also involves advertisement of the male's brightly colored ventral surface (Avila, 1973; Miller, 1963). When a female is attracted to the nest (i.e., territory) of a male, she may be greeted initially by an attack when she comes too near. However, if she endures the attack, remaining motionless with fins closed against the body, the male's aggressiveness wanes and is replaced by courtship responses (color changes by the female may also be involved; Stacey and Chiszar, 1975). Not infrequently, this transition is marked by postures in both the male and the female that are indistinguishable from lateral displays. The next phase in the interaction is called "swimming together" and is characterized by the two animals swimming side by side around the rim of the male's territory. Often the male and female touch each other along their opposed lateral surfaces while they are swimming together; and when the female is ready to spawn, the frequency and intensity of this touching increases to such a degree that the term "body-rubbing" becomes a better descriptor. The female now tilts her dorsum away from the male and rubs against his lateral and ventral surfaces with her belly. Eventually, this rubbing becomes concentrated around only the pericloacal tissues, and it is shortly afterwards that gametes are shed by both animals.

During this period of courtship, other nearby territorial males become excited by the female's presence and/or courtship activities. These males often swim around the rim of their nests (this rim-circling may be a form of nest advertisement), and some will intrude into the nest of the courting male, who immediately gives chase. However, while the territory owner is away, even for only a few seconds, still another male may enter the nest and execute fertilizing movements (Keenleyside, 1972). The high frequency of these intraspecific nest intrusions indicates that courting and spawning have great signal value for nearby conspecifics (females, territorial males, and nonterritorial males). Hence, although body-rubbing and body-rubbing intention responses are important for suppressing aggression and for the spatiotemporal coordination of the courting pair, the *sight* of these responses may also be significant in attracting and coordinating sexual excitation in other individuals. For our purposes, it is important to recognize that some aspects of body-rubbing and corresponding intention movements resemble the lateral displays seen in other social contexts. Other similarities between body-rubbing and lateral displays may indicate that the resemblance is more than superficial. For example, although lateral displays may eventually result in total intimidation of an adversary, *during* the period of ritualized combat the display can be said to provide a mechanism by which spatial proximity between the interactants can be maintained without bloodshed. "Fish (*Herichthys* and *Cichlasoma*) have an absolute inhibition against ramming each other's unprotected flank with their formidable teeth, as long as the other keeps on displaying and conforming to the 'Queensbury rules' of their ritualizations" (Lorenz, 1955, p. 291). It seems to go without saying that body-rubbing serves a comparable purpose in courtship.

It seems that the performance of rubbing (in the blue gourami, *Trichogaster trichopterus*) is mutually stimulating and is of value in keeping the pair in close proximity in a position favorable for subsequent curving and clasping. . . . It was also found that average duration of rubbing was higher in pairs in which one partner, usually the male, was highly aggressive. [Miller, 1964, p. 489]

According to the above descriptions, it appears that lateral displays and body-rubbing responses are both functional in the reduction of tissue-damaging aggression. Yet this correlation may not be indicative of a common derivation, since lateral displays derived as aggressive-intention movements would also be expected to be associated with reduced levels of tissue-damaging attacks:

Tail-beating (a response associated with lateral displays in many fish) is usually categorized as aggressive behavior in fishes, although on a lower level than such actions as charging and biting (Baerends and Baerends-van Roon, 1950; Barlow, 1962). Its effect as an appeasement behavior most likely stems from its role as a low-level threat; this would cause some fear in the aggressor, blocking overt attack (Dunham, Kortmulder, and van Iersal, 1968), but not enough to result in fleeing. [Barlow, 1968, p. 158]

But lateral displays have additional repertorial relationships that do not seem to follow directly from the hypothesis viewing them as aggressive-intention movements. For example, in the bluegill sunfish, the probability that a lateral display is followed immediately (intraactor analysis) by a nip or a butt is less than 0.05, whereas the probabilities that the other kinds of displays (frontal display, containment display, nip threat) are followed immediately by a nip or butt range from 0.10 to 0.36 (all p's comparing lateral displays to other displays < 0.05 by chi square tests; see Chiszar, Ashe, Seixas, and Henderson, 1976). This indicates different stochastic functions for lateral displays and frontal displays (and, perhaps, motivationally different functions as well). If lateral and frontal displays were both derived as aggressive-intention movements, we would expect them to have similar stochastic and motivational properties (unless lateral and frontal displays represented different levels of aggressive intent). Also, analyses of behavioral sequences in *Tilapia melanotheron* (Barlow and Green, 1970) have revealed that lateral displays (tail beats) tend to be correlated negatively with rates of charging and positively with reproductive responses. If lateral displays are representative of aggressive intention, we would probably expect a positive correlation between lateral displaying and charging. This "expectation" is actually more complicated, and depends upon whether intraactor or interactor analyses are performed. If intraactor correlations are calculated, the hypotheses that lateral displays are aggressive-intention postures would predict that a positive correlation should exist between frequency of lateral displays and frequency of nipping or other damaging acts. This prediction is made under the assumption that all or most sequences that eventuate in nipping begin with less violent rituals involving lateral displays. Hence, when aggressive motivation is low there should be relatively few displays and nips, but when aggressive motivation is high there should be relatively more of both responses. If interactor correlations are calculated, the above hypotheses would probably predict a negative correlation between lateral display frequency and nip frequency, because lateral displays would occur with high frequencies in animal A (subordinate) only when charging, nipping, and related behaviors were occurring with low frequency in animal B (dominant). When frequency of charging and nipping was high in animal B, animal

A would be expected to flee and hide, but not to attempt to threaten or bluff.

The hypothesis that lateral displays are derived from courtship responses makes predictions that are opposite to those above. In intraactor analyses, the frequency of lateral displays should be negatively correlated with the frequency of violent aggressive responses because the former are executed to inhibit fighting rather than to threaten. (Hence, the behaviors should be mutually exclusive). In interactor analyses, the correlations should be positive, because animal A would execute lateral displays with increased frequency when it was subjected to many attacks. Animal A would be attempting to inhibit B's aggressiveness. These conflicting predictions can be summarized as follows:

Direction of correlation between lateral display frequency and frequency of charging, nipping and other violent acts

	+	−
Intraactor analyses	Predicted by hypothesis of aggressive origin for lateral displays	Predicted by hypothesis of reproductive origin for lateral displays
Interactor analyses	Predicted by hypothesis of reproductive origin for lateral displays	Predicted by hypothesis of aggressive origin for lateral displays

Clearly, these predictions are complex and require sophisticated statistical treatment. (In fact, I'm not entirely convinced that this conceptual analysis is completely adequate.) Nonetheless, it is interesting to note that (with a few exceptions) the analyses of Barlow and Green (1970) seem to agree with the predictions of the hypothesis of reproductive origins. However, still other hypotheses (e.g., the "appeasement hypothesis," Tinbergen, 1959; Barlow, 1968) can explain these results, indicating a need for additional conceptual and empirical work aimed at specifying the similarities and differences between various theoretical positions and the consequences that derive from them.

Another view of the stochastic role of lateral displays can be had through the application of information theory (Dingle, 1972; Bekoff,

1975). Specifically, the *conditional information* present, given that a frontal display was performed by a male pumpkinseed sunfish (*Lepomis gibbosus*) during a territorial-aggressive episode, was 0.1509 bits, whereas the value was 0.4907 if the preponse was a lateral display. (Preponse = preceding response.) Models of sunfish were placed into the nests of territorial male pumpkinseeds at Sawhill Ponds, Boulder, Colorado (Summer, 1973 and 1974; see Stacey, 1975, for raw data). All analyses were performed on intraindividual (i.e., territorial male) response sequences. These values estimate the number of binary questions that must be asked in order to specify responses that follow the preponse. This is sometimes called "ambiguity." Hence, although a statistical evaluation of the difference between 0.1509 and 0.4907 bits is not possible at this time, it seems reasonable to conclude that the (human) observer of a lateral display is in a position almost three times more ambiguous (with respect to predicting the succeeding response) than the one he would be in if a frontal display had been observed. This means that more kinds of responses can follow a lateral display than a frontal display. This conclusion also holds if ambiguity is calculated for other sorts of displays in the sunfish repertory, or for responses such as charge or chase; in most cases ambiguity was less than 0.1000 bit. Hence, we conclude that the lateral display is one of the most ambiguous responses in the sunfish repertory. The only response with greater ambiguity is *orientation*, which can be followed by almost any other response. This finding needs to be replicated and extended to other species and to other situations.

Tentative explanations of the ambiguity property of lateral displays can proceed along at least three lines. It may be argued that: (1) resting and other postures are regularly mistaken for lateral displays such that when the bogus responses are lumped with real lateral displays, the result is that the aggregate possesses greater ambiguity than would pure lateral displays; (2) lateral displays actually represent a tenuous balance between approach and withdrawal and that at any moment either of these tendencies may predominate by a small margin with the result that numerous types of responses may follow a lateral display depending upon which of the conflicting drives is momentarily in ascendence (and by how much it is in ascendence); and (3) lateral displays may actually be serving to avoid tissue-damaging attacks by directly inhibiting them and/or by diffusing the behavior of the interactants into other channels. These ideas are not mutually exclusive, but they clearly emphasize different processes, namely: methodology, threat, and inhibition, respectively. The second hypothesis agrees perfectly with the notion that lateral displays evolved as ambiguous threat-intention movements, while the third hypothesis seems to agree more with the suggestion that lateral displays evolved as emancipated body rubbing-intention movements which actively function to inhibit aggressive responses. The present data are certainly not sufficient to support firm conclusions about any of these possibilities. However, it is hoped that some caution has been generated against the assumption that lateral displays are (functionally and phylogenetically) threat responses. Moreover, it is suggested that careful studies be designed to determine the extent to which lateral displays exert inhibitory and/or redirectional effects on aggression, *independently* of their intimidatory effects. This last point is crucial because the demonstration that aggressive responses occur less frequently in animal A after B has executed a lateral display (Dunham, Kortmulder and van Iersal, 1968) can always be explained on the basis of intimidation effects of the display. Procedures must be developed to allow independent assessment of potential sex-related inhibitory effects of lateral displays and threat-related inhibitory effects of lateral displays. Such data will, in turn, tell us if there is any need to speculate about the existence of a mating-intention motivation in the natural history of lateral displays. A similar suggestion was made by Wiepkema in his classic study of the bitterling (*Rhodeus amarus* Bloch):

It is interesting that the male during tail bending demonstrates the blue lateral line to the following female. The triple motivation of tail bending (sexual, aggressive and flight factors) suggests that it might have both a leading and a threatening function. However, this has to be examined in more detail. [Wiepkema, 1961, p. 166]

To my knowledge, no further analysis of this question has appeared in the literature; hence, it is not possible to decide which of the motivations is primary and which were added after the display began the process of ritualization.

A very similar story can be presented in the context of aggression in snakes. The similarity between courtship (and copulation) and the "combat dance" has already been discussed (similarities between courtship, copulation and aggressive rituals in lizards have been stressed repeatedly by Schmidt and Inger, 1957; see also Carpenter, 1961, 1963). Indeed, black rat snakes (*Elaphe obsoleta*), and water moccasins (*Agkistrodon piscivorous*) which have been excited by the presence of prey often engage in combat rituals containing responses comparable (if not identical) to some of those which might be seen in a reproductive episode, including eversion of a hemipenis (Chiszar and Radcliffe, unpublished data). Moreover, casual observation leads to the hypothesis that body-rubbing movements (involving either the head or other body surfaces) inhibit biting or thrashing rather than convey threat; and, such a function would probably be understandable if the "combat dance" was derived from courtship and/or copulation. In some lizards, rubbing of the female's lateral surfaces by the male's hind legs has been hypothesized to exert a calming influence on her, thereby facilitating intromission (Noble and Bradley, 1933; but see Cole, 1966, Burghardt, 1970, and Hathaway, 1964). If such movements or fractional components thereof have comparable effects on males, then we might expect such actions (or ritualized derivatives) to acquire some inhibitory function in the aggressive repertory; and, we might also expect these responses to manifest themselves as lateral displays. The extent to which this has actually occurred during the evolution of lizard aggressive behavior is an open question. These ideas, of course, do not rule out threatening functions for courtship-derived aggressive responses. But, they do suggest that threat and related ambivalent effects of these action patterns may represent secondary modifications of rituals which evolved initially for independent reasons. Again a great deal of research is required before these hypotheses can be evaluated properly; and, they are certainly not offered here as finished products. The main goal of this entire discussion has been to stimulate further interest in the phylogenesis and function of lateral displays by providing an alternative to the traditional lines of thought regarding this matter.

5   ACKNOWLEDGMENTS

I wish to thank the M. M. Schmidt Foundation for financial support during the preparation of this manuscript. I am indebted also to the City and County of Boulder for permission to work at the Sawhills Wildlife Refuge. Finally, I wish to thank George W. Barlow for his many helpful suggestions following a reading of an earlier draft of this paper.

REFERENCES

Alvarado, R.H. 1967. The significance of grouping on water conservation in *Ambystoma*. Copeia **1967:** 371–375.

Avila, V.L. 1973. A review and field study of nesting behavior of male bluegill sunfish (*Lepomis macrochirus* Rafinesque). Unpublished doctoral dissertation, University of Colorado. 108 p.

Baerends, G.P. 1950. Specializations in organs and movements with a releasing function. Soc. Exp. Biol. Symp. **4:** 337–360.

Banta, B.H., and G. Carl. 1967. Death-feigning behavior in the eastern grey treefrog *Hyla versicolor versicolor* Herpetologica **23:** 317–318.

Barlow, G.W. 1962. Ethology of the Asian teleost, *Badis badis:* III. Aggressive behavior. Z. Tierpsychol. **19:** 29–55.

Barlow, G.W. 1963. Ethology of the Asian teleost, *Badis badis:* I. Motivation and signal value of the colour patterns. Anim. Behav. **11:** 97–105.

Barlow, G.W. 1968. Effect of size of mate on courtship in a cichlid fish, *Etroplus maculatus.* Comm. Behav. Biol. **2,** Part A: 149–160.

Barlow, G.W., and R.F. Green. 1970. The problem of appeasement and of sexual roles in the courtship behavior of the blackchin mouthbreeder *Tilapia melanotheron* (Pisces: Cichlidae). Behaviour **36:** 84–115.

Bekoff, M. (1975). Animal play and behavioral diversity. Am. Nat.**109:** 60.

Blest, A.D. 1961. The concept of ritualization. *In:* W. H. Thorpe and O.L. Zangwill, Eds. *Current Problems in Animal Behavior.* Cambridge University Press, Cambridge. P. 102–124.

Brodie, E.D., Jr. 1968. Investigations on the skin toxin of the adult rough-skinned newt, *Taricha granulosa.* Copeia **1968:** 307–315.

Brodie, E.D., Jr., and L.S. Gibson. 1969. Defensive behavior and skin glands of the northwestern salamander, *Ambystoma gracile.* Herpetologica **25:** 187–194.

Brodie, E.D., Jr., J.L. Hansel, and J.A. Johnson. 1974. Toxicity of the urodele amphibians *Taricha, Notophthalmus, Cynops* and *Paramesotriton* (Salamandridae). Copeia **1974:** 506–512.

Brodie, E.D., Jr., J.A. Johnson, and C.K. Dodd, Jr. 1974. Immobility as a defensive behavior in salamanders. Herpetologica **30:** 79–85.

Burden, W.D. 1928. Observations on the habits and distribution of *Varanus komodoensis* Ouwens. Am. Mus. Novitates, No. 319: 1–10.

Burghardt, G.M. 1970. Chemical perception in reptiles. *In:* J.W. Johnson, Jr., D.G. Moulton, and A. Turk, Eds. *Communication by Chemical Signals.* Appleton-Century-Crofts, New York. P. 241–308.

Carpenter, C.C. 1961. Patterns of social behavior in the desert iguana *Dipsosaurus dorsalis.* Copeia **1961:** 396–405.

Carpenter, C.C. 1963. Patterns of behavior in three forms of the fringe-toed lizards (*Uma*–Iguanidae). Copeia **1963:** 406–412.

Carpenter, C.C. 1967. Aggression and social structure in iguanid lizards. *In:* W.W. Milstead, Ed. *Lizard Ecology: Symposium.* University of Missouri Press, Kansas City. P. 87–105.

Carpenter, C.C. 1969. Behavioral and ecological notes on the Galapagos land lizards of the genus *Uma.* Herpetologica **25:** 155–164.

Carpenter, C.C., J.A. Badham, and B. Kimble. 1970. Behavior patterns of three species of Amphibolurus (Agamidae). Copeia **1970:** 497–505.

Chapman, D.W. 1962. Aggressive behavior in juvenile Coho salmon as a cause of emigration. J. Fish. Res. Board Can. **19:** 1047–1080.

Chiszar, D., V. Ashe, S. Seixas, and D. Henderson. (1976). Social-aggressive behavior after various intervals of social isolation in bluegill sunfish (*Lepomis macrochirus* Rafinesque) in different states of reproductive readiness. Behav. Biol. **16:** 475–487

Chiszar, D., R.W. Drake, and J.T. Windell. 1975. Aggressive behaviour in rainbow trout (*Salmo gairdneri* Richardson) of two ages. Behav. Biol. **13:** 425–431.

Chiszar, D. and C.W. Radcliffe. Unpublished data. Topographical similarities between aggressive responses and courtship responses of crotalid snakes.

Chiszar, D., K. Scudder, H.M. Smith, and C.W. Radcliffe. 1976. Observations of courtship behavior in the western massasauga (*Sistrurus catenatus tergeminus*). Herpetologica, **32:** 337–338.

Clarke, R.F. 1965. An ethological study of the iguanid lizard genera *Callisaurus, Cophosaurus,* and *Holbrookia.* Emporia State Res. Stud. **13:** 1–66.

Cole, C.J. 1966. Femoral glands in lizards: A review. Herpetologica **22:** 199–206.

Cowles, R.B. 1930. The life history of *Varanus niloticus* (Linnaeus) as observed in Natal, South Africa. J. Entomol. Zool. **22:** 3–31.

Dijkgraaf, S. 1967. Biological significance of the lateral line organs. *In:* P. Cahn, Ed. *Lateral Line Detectors.* Indiana University Press, Bloomington. P. 83–95.

Dingle, H. 1972. Aggressive behavior in stomatopods and the use of information in the analysis of animal communication. *In:* H.E. Winn and B.L. Olla, Eds. *Behavior of Marine Animals.* Plenum Press, New York. P. 126–156.

Duellman, W.E. 1966. Aggressive behavior in dendrobatid frogs. Herpetologica **22:** 217–221.

Dunham, D.W., K. Kortmulder, and J.J.A. van Iersal. 1968. Threat and appeasement in *Barbus stoliczkanus* (Cyprinidae). Behaviour **30:** 15–27.

Eibl-Eibesfeldt, I. 1960. Beobachtungen und Versuche an Anemonen-fischen der Malediven und der Nicobaren. Z. Tierpsychol. **17:** 1–10.

Eibl-Eibesfeldt, I. 1975. *Ethology—the Biology of Behavior.* Holt, Rinehart and Winston, New York. 625 p.

Emlen, S.T. 1968. Territoriality in the bullfrog, *Rana catesbeiana.* Copeia **1968:** 240–243.

Evans, L.T. 1953. Tail display in an iguanid lizard, *Leiocephalus carinatus coryi.* Copeia **1953:** 50–54.

Evans, L.T. 1955. Group processes in the lower vertebrates. *In:* B. Schaffner, Ed. *Group Processes.* Madison Printing Company, Madison, N.J. P. 268–289.

Geist, V. 1971. *Mountain Sheep: A Study in Behavior and Evolution.* Chicago University Press, Chicago, 383 p.

Guthrie, R.D. 1970. Evolution of human threat display organs. *In:* T. Dobzhansky, M.K. Hecht, and W.C. Steere, Eds. *Evolutionary Biology.* Vol. 4. Appleton-Century-Crofts, New York. P. 257–302.

Halliday, T.R. 1974. Sexual behavior of the smooth newt, *Triturus vulgaris* (Urodela, Salamandridae). J. Herpetol. **8:** 277–293.

Hartman, G.F. 1965. The role of behavior in the ecology and interaction of underyearling Coho salmon (*Oncorhynchus kisutch*) and the steelhead trout (*Salmo gairdneri*). J. Fish. Res. Board Can. **22:** 1035–1081.

Hathaway, L.M. 1964. Suggested function of the femoral glands in *Crotophytus collaris collaris* (Say). Bull. Ecol. Soc. Am. **45:** 117 (Abstract.)

Honneger, R.E., and H. Heusser. 1969. Beiträge zum Verhaltensin-venter des Blindenwarans (*Varanus salvator*). Zool. Garten (NF) **36:** 251–260.

Hoogland, R., D. Morris, and N. Tinbergen. 1956/1957. The spines of sticklebacks (*Gasteros-*

teus and *Pygosteus*) as means of defense against predators (*Perca* and *Esox*). Behaviour **10:** 205–236.

Huxley, J.S. 1923. Courtship activities of the red-throated diver (*Columbus stellatus* Pontopp.); together with a discussion of the evolution of courtship in birds. J. Linn. Soc. **35:** 253–292.

Huxley, J.S. 1934. Threat and warning coloration in birds. *In:* Proceedings of the 8th International Ornithological Congress, Oxford University Press, Oxford. P. 430–455.

Huxley, J.S. 1958. The evolutionary process. *In:* J. Huxley, A.C. Hardy, and E.B. Ford, Eds. *Evolution As a Process.* Allen and Unwin, London. P. 1–23.

Jenkins, T.M. Jr. 1969. Social structure, position choice, and microdistribution of two trout species (*Salmo trutta* and *Salmo gairdneri*) resident in mountain streams. Anim. Behav. Mon. 2, Part 2:57–123.

Jenssen, T.A. 1975. Display repertoire of a male *Phenacosaurus heterodermus* (Sauria: Iguanidae). Herpetologica **31:** 48–55.

Kaufman, E.L., and N.E. Miller. 1949. Effect of number of reinforcements on strength of approach-avoidance conflict. J. Comp. Physiol. Psychol. **42:** 65–74.

Keenleyside, M.H.A. 1972. Intraspecific intrusions into nests of spawning longear sunfish (Pisces: Centrarchidae). Copeia **1972:** 272–278.

Klauber, L.M. 1956. *Rattlesnakes: Their Habits, Life Histories, and Influence on Mankind, Vol. I.* University of California Press, Berkeley. 708 p.

Koehn, R.K. 1965. Development and ecological significance of nuptial tubercules of the red shiner, *Notropis lutrensis.* Copeia **1965:** 462–476.

Latané, B. 1969. Gregariousness and fear in laboratory rats. J. Exp. Soc. Psychol. **5:** 61–69.

Latané, B., H. Cappell, and V. Joy. 1970. Social deprivation, housing density, and gregariousness in rats. J. of Comp. Physiol. Psychol. **70:** 221–227.

Latané, B., J. Edwards, C. Steele, and D. Walton. 1973. Social attraction among and between albino and hooded rats. Bull. Psychonomic Soc. **2:** 20–22.

Lorenz, K. 1955. Description of research on behavior of fighting fish. *In:* B. Schaffner, Ed. *Group Processes.* Madison Printing Company, Madison, N.J. P. 290–299.

Lorenz, K. 1957. Comparative study of behavior. *In:* C.H. Schiller, Ed. *Instinctive behavior: the Development of a Modern Concept.* International Universities Press, New York. P. 239–263.

Lorenz, K. 1965. *Evolution and Modification of Behavior.* University of Chicago Press, Chicago. 121 p.

Miller, H.C. 1963. The behaviour of the pumpkinseed sunfish *Leopmis gibbosus* (Linnaeus) with notes on the behaviour of other species of *Lepomis* and the pygmy sunfish *Elassoma evergladei.* Behaviour **22:** 88–151.

Miller, L. 1948. An enemy of the horned lizard. Copeia **1948:** 67.

Miller, N.E. 1959. Liberalization of basic S-R concepts: Extensions to conflict behavior, motivation, and social learning. *In:* S. Koch, Ed. *Psychology, a Study of a Science.* Vol. 2. McGraw-Hill, New York. P. 196–292.

Morris, D. 1954. The reproductive behavior of the river bullhead (*Cottus gobi* L.) with special reference to fanning activity. Behaviour **7:** 1–32.

Morris, D. 1958. The reproductive behavior of the 10-spined stickleback (*Pygosteus pungitius* L.). Behav. Suppl. **61:** 1–154.

Morris, D. 1957. The reproductive behaviour of the bronze mannikin (*Lonchura cucullata*). Behaviour **11:** 156–201.

Murphy, J. B., and L.A. Mitchell. 1974. Ritualized combat behavior of the pygmy mulga monitor lizard, *Varanus gilleni* (Sauria: Varanidae). Herpetologica **30:** 90–97.

Neil, E.H. 1964. An analysis of color changes and social behavior of *Tilapia mossambica*. University of California Publications in Zoology **75:** 1–58.

Noble, G.K. 1931. *The Biology of the Amphibia*. McGraw-Hill, New York. 577 p.

Noble, G.K. 1934. Experimenting with the courtship of lizards. Nat. Hist. **34:** 1–15.

Noble, G.K and H.T. Bradley. 1933. The mating behavior of lizards; its bearing on the theory of sexual selection. Ann. N. Y. Acad. Sci. **35:** 25–100.

Oliver, J.A. 1956. Reproduction in the king cobra, *Ophiophagus hannah* Cantor. Zoologica **41:** 145–153.

Rabb, G.B. 1973. Evolutionary aspects of the reproductive behavior of frogs. *In:* J.L. Vial, Ed. *Evolutionary Biology of the Anurans*. University of Missouri Press, Columbia, Missouri. P. 213–227.

Rabb, G.B. and M.S. Rabb. 1963. On the behavior and breeding biology of the African pipid frog *Hymenochirus boettgeri*. Z. Tierpsychol. **20:** 215–241.

Rodda, G. 1975. Activity of *Ambystoma tigrinum* from a foothills pond near Boulder, Colorado. Unpublished honors thesis, University of Colorado. 41 p.

Ruibal, R. 1967. Evolution and behavior in West Indian anoles. *In:* W.W. Milstead, Ed. *Lizard Ecology: a Symposium*. University of Missouri Press, Kansas City. P. 116–140.

Schmidt, K., and R.F. Inger. 1957. *Living Reptiles of the World*. Doubleday, Garden City, N.Y. 287 p.

Schroeder, E.E. 1968. Aggressive behavior in *Rana clamitans*. J. Herpetol. **1:** 95–96.

Selous, E. 1933. *Evolution of habit in birds*. Constable, London. 296p.

Shaw, C.E. 1948. The male combat "dance" of some crotalid snakes. Herpetologica **4:** 137–145.

Sloan, L.R. and B. Latané. 1974. Social deprivation and stimulus satiation in the albino rat. J. Comp. Physiol. Psychol. **87:** 1148–1156.

Smith, H.M. 1946. *Handbook of Lizards*. Comstock Publishing Company, Ithaca, N.Y. 557 p.

Stacey, P.B. 1975. Body pattern and the aggressive behavior of pumpkinseed sunfish (*Lepomis gibbosus*). Unpublished M.S. thesis, University of Colorado. 68 p.

Stacey, P.B., and D. Chiszar. 1975. Changes in the darkness of four body features of bluegill sunfish (*Lepomis macrochirus* Rafinesque) during aggressive encounters. Behav. Biol. **14:** 41–49.

Storey, R.A. 1969. Observations on the courtship of *Ambystoma laterale*. J. Herpetol. **3:** 87–97.

Tavolga, W. 1967. Relation of the lateral line to communication in fishes and the general problem of animal communication. *In:* P. Cahn, Ed. *Lateral Line Detectors*. Indiana University Press, Bloomington. P. 481–483.

Thomas, E. 1961. Fortpflanzungskämfe bei Sandottern (*Vipera ammodytes*). Zool. Anz. Suppl. **24:** 502–505.

Thomas-Milton, A. In preparation. Social attractiveness in bluegill sunfish (*Lepomis macrochirus*) and neotenic tiger salamanders (*Ambystoma tigrinum*).

Tinbergen, N. 1940. *The Study of Instinct*. Oxford University Press, New York. 228 p.

Tingerben, N. 1952. "Derived" activities, their causation, biological significance, and emancipation during evolution. Q. Rev. Biol. **27:** 1–32.

Tinbergen, N. 1958. The origin and evolution of courtship and threat display. *In:* J. Huxley, A.C. Hardy, and E.B. Ford, Eds. *Evolution As a Process.* Allen and Unwin, London. P. 233–250.

Tinbergen, N. 1959. Comparative studies of the behavior of gulls (*Loridae*): A progress report. Behaviour **15:** 1–70.

Vorhies, C.T. 1948. Food items of rattlesnakes. Copeia **1948:** 302–303.

Waring, H.H. 1963. *Color Change Mechanisms of Cold Blooded Vertebrates.* Academic Press, New York. 266p.

Wickler, W. 1962. Ei-attrapen und Maulbrüten bei afrikanischen Cichliden. Z. Tierpsychol. **18:** 129–164.

Wiepkema, P.R. 1961. An ethological analysis of the reproductive behavior of the bitterling (*Rhodeus amarus* Bloch). Arch. Néerl. Zool. **14:** 103–199.

5

TEMPORAL PATTERNING IN ACOUSTICAL COMMUNICATION

ARTHUR A. MYRBERG, JR.

Rosenstiel School of Marine and
Atmospheric Science
University of Miami
Miami, Florida

EHUD SPANIER

Institute of Evolution
University of Haifa
Mount Carmel, Haifa, Israel

SAMUEL J. HA

Millersville State College
Millersville, Pennsylvania

1 INTRODUCTION

One of the central themes of ethology has been the interpretation of signs and/or communication among an ever-increasing number and variety of animals, including man himself. One can easily ascertain the importance ascribed not only by examining its incredibly voluminous and diverse literature, but also by noting the multitude of techniques used for bringing forth data necessary for reasonable interpretation. Recent attempts to clarify problems in terminology, technique, and interpretation have been highly instructive; some have advocated new approaches to our thinking, while others have stressed innovative techniques for reaching appropriate solutions (e.g., Burghardt, 1970; Elsner, 1974; Hazlett and Bossert, 1965; Marler, 1961, 1967; Schleidt, 1973; Sebeok, 1965; Winn, 1964). Increased sophistication of instrumentation and experimentation, both in the laboratory and field, has also allowed workers to delve into problems that were largely unsolvable in the recent past. Many of these particular problems surround the signal used in a presumed communication-link; and the questions advanced fit well those mentioned by Marler (1967) when he advocated his addressee approach to studies in communication. (1) Are there correlations between variation in properties of the signal and variation in the patterns of response elicited? And (2) is some particular part or property of a signal responsible for evoking a given response?

In the consideration of acoustical communication, reasonable answers to the first question have been forthcoming from a variety of sources throughout the groups possessing the appropriate modality, with research continuing on many fronts. Answers to the second, and more difficult, question have only recently begun to appear regularly in the literature, and, though conclusions are based on studies of various species, most of the animals concerned belong to only three major groups: the insects, the amphibians, and the birds. Nonetheless, striking similarities are consistently apparent in many of the answers being provided by these disparate subjects. Interestingly, these similarities extend also to the results recently obtained from a limited sample of species from still another group—the fishes. Therefore, it is perhaps not unreasonable to stress that these common findings provide a factual basis for emphasizing the distinct importance of temporal patterning within the acoustical communication systems of animals that produce percussive or pulse-type sounds. The recognition of the importance of temporal patterning may, in turn, prompt heightened interest in formulating proper empirical means for determining valid model(s) of temporal coding (e.g., pulse rate modulation, pulse code modulation) for those transfer functions that must be operating between time-related environmental events, and for those occurring within appropriate neural processes.

2 RATIONALE FOR A PROGRAM OF RESEARCH

Within any animal community, intraspecific interactions will, for the most part, require those species utilizing a common modality to use a different signal code to avoid confusion (Konishi, 1970; Marler, 1974). A distinctive signal code seems particularly important in a complex community, such as the coral reef, where, often within a small area, myriads of animals, including many species of fishes, carry on their social activities. The reef is characterized, however, not only by the high densities of individuals belonging to many species, but also by its finite resources (e.g., space, food), which must eventually force keen competition among certain of its members (Hobson, 1972, 1974; Smith and Tyler, 1972). In such a competitive environment, any waste of energy must be considered highly detrimental not only to the individual(s) concerned, but, if persistent and widespread, to the continuity of a species itself in the area.

One can easily imagine a number of ways in which such an energy loss could occur; an obvious one would be inappropriate responsiveness to rather frequently occurring, but biologically unimportant or inadequate, stimuli. This could stem from a variety of sources and affect any appropriate modality. For purposes of this presentation, let's confine our thoughts to but one of these—the acoustic modality, and, further, in order to "set the stage," introduce the subjects of our work.

One of the most ubiquitous groups of fishes that abound on the coral reefs of southern Florida, the Bahamas, and the Caribbean is the damsel-fish genus, *Eupomacentrus*. Its nine or more species are all considered active sound producers, and among those studied thus far, courtship behavior is known to be influenced greatly by the occurrence of certain sounds (Emery, 1968; Ha, 1973; Myrberg, 1971, 1972a and b; Myrberg and Spires, 1972; Spanier, 1975). A provoking puzzle emerges, however, when this point is considered more closely. Males of all the species produce strikingly similar sounds (known as chirps; see Fig. 5.1) at the same critical moment during their almost identical courtship sequ-

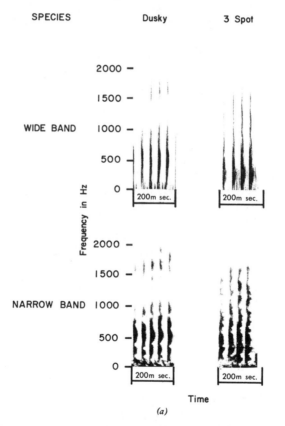

(a)

FIGURE 5.1a Sound spectrograms of representative chirps (a courtship sound) from males of two species of the damselfish genus, *Eupomacentrus: E. dorsopunicans* (dusky) and *E. planifrons* (threespot). Note the close structural similarity between the sounds and those shown in Fig. 5.1b.

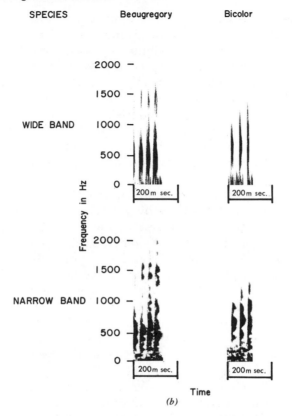

FIGURE 5.1b Sound spectrograms of representative chirps (a courtship sound) from males of two species of the damselfish genus, *Eupomacentrus: E. leucostictus* (beaugregory) and *E. partitus* (bicolor). Note the close structural similarity between the sounds and those shown in Fig. 5.1a.

ences. Such briefly pulsed sounds from a given male readily bring forth courtship behavior in nearby male conspecifics, especially if sounds and associated behavior continue for a short time. All species in a given area appear to have a common reproductive season, and congeners often maintain residences and territories (where courtship occurs) within a few meters of each other. Finally, it is not unreasonable to assume that the sounds produced by members of each species can be heard by members of all others, this being based on their extremely close anatomical (Emery, 1968) and physiological relationships (e.g., all have remarkably similar audiograms; Myrberg and Spires, in prep.). The puzzle thus becomes evident. Since chirps are known to influence courtship so strongly, a reasonable probability exists that such sounds are important for purposes of species-recognition. If such is the case, reproductively mature individuals must somehow distinguish their own species' chirps from those produced by their neighboring congeners. If such recognition is not accomplished, time and energy will be wasted in the performance of irrelevant behavior during inappropriate courtship rituals. This intriguing puzzle thus created the incentive to search not only for the behavioral correlates of the courtship sounds, but to determine whether some particular property(ies) might be responsible for providing the information necessary to reduce significantly, or to eliminate altogether, irrelevant behavior and its concomitant dissipation of energy.

The combined field and laboratory approach of the ensuing program furnished a most useful feedback by providing reasonable efficiency as well as valuable insight into the inherent limitations of each approach. At the same time, it pointed to the strengths gained when both are used in concert. The field approach became prominent, however, near the end of the program, since it was apparent that final proof of any biological hypothesis must inevitably rest with proper tests carried out on free-ranging members of one or more natural populations.

This report covers, by necessity, only the highlights of the intriguing story that unfolded during our search for answers to the various points mentioned above. Specific details not provided here can be obtained from reports of the original studies (Ha, 1973; Myrberg, 1972a; Myrberg and Spires, 1972; Spanier, 1975). Our research efforts were supported by National Science Foundation Grants GB11909, GB31000 and BNS7420067. Additional aid to E.S. was provided by a grant from Sigma XI. The manuscript was written at 6001 S.W. 65 Avenue, Miami, Florida. To update the literature that has appeared during the interim between the acceptance of this report for publication and its appearance, the reader is referred to Bentley, 1977; Capranica, 1976; Fine, *et al.* 1977; Gerhardt, 1976, Hoy *et al.*, 1977; and Sebeok, 1977.

3 MATERIALS

3.1 General

The program examined, bioacoustically, species-recognition in four closely related forms: the bicolor damselfish, *Eupomacentrus partitus*; the beaugregory, *E. leucostictus*; the dusky damselfish, *E. dorsopunicans*; and the threespot damselfish, *E. planifrons*. All species were found relatively near our Institute, providing, therefore, a ready supply of laboratory subjects and suitable field colonies. A few of the earliest experiments took place in the coastal waters of Bimini, Bahamas (Myrberg and Spires, 1972). Since the findings were consistent with those obtained during the remainder of the program, a zoogeographical interpretation might suggest, at least, similar mechanisms in widely separated populations of the same species. The avenues of investigation were broad, but for purposes of this report they can perhaps best be viewed in two perspectives: (1) sound characterization and (2) sound playback.

3.2 Laboratory

Numerous laboratory colonies were studied during the entire course of research, but the results of only two will be mentioned here. These were selected because of the many relevant findings they supplied. Both were comprised of bicolors; the first was used during the initial stages of the program (Myrberg and Spires, 1972), the second, during its critical midpoint (Ha, 1973). Each colony had been obtained from separate outcrops some weeks prior to testing. This provided time for all members to "settle down" in their new surroundings and to resume normal activities (e.g., feeding, agonism, territoriality, courtship, and reproduction). Both colonies (first—three males and five females; second—two males and a varying number of females) resided, at separate times, in the same 800-1 aquarium, the latter being equipped with appropriate substrate, filtration, and vibration-damping devices. Suitable food, temperature, and light regimes were provided, as was evidenced by frequent courtship and spawning behavior.

Sound recording systems included necessary hydrophones, preamplifiers, and tape recorders, all compatible with the acoustical features of the sounds encountered. Synthetic chirps, needed during specific experiments, were produced with an appropriate pulse generator and transient-free relays. Such sounds were instrumental in "dissecting" various parameters so that specific properties could be varied while others were held constant. All sounds were played back to colonies through an underwater loudspeaker via amplifier and tape-deck. Sounds were monitored (oscilloscope and millivolt meter) during playback sessions. All sound analyses were performed with a Kay Missilyzer and an oscilloscope.

3.3 Field

Recording gear included appropriate recorders, preamps, and hydrophones, while playback equipment included the same recorders with appropriate amplifiers and underwater speakers. The experimental design employed in the field during the final stages of the investigation required sound level calibrators and impact noise analyzers (Spanier, 1975). Sound analysis was performed with the same equipment as that mentioned above. Observations were often carried out through closed-circuit, underwater television (Myrberg, 1973), supplemented, when necessary, by SCUBA and snorkeling.

4 METHODS

Subsequent to sound analysis of a minimum of 30 chirps from each of the respective laboratory colonies and, invariably, of a larger number from the field, natural chirps were selected from recordings that were representative of each colony (laboratory) or area (field) sampled. Selection was based on clarity and structure, as well as on a low level of ambient noise accompanying the given sound. Selections were then placed separately onto tape-loops, such that a repetition rate was maintained between 22 and 25 chirps/min in the initial studies and 25 chirps/min thereafter. This rate was chosen because it reflected that produced by males (the sound producers) of all species whenever frequent courtship was evident in the laboratory or the field. The rate was subsequently verified by specific tests using bicolors, as well as by numerous records from the remaining species.

Experiments were conducted during the portion of the year when courtship was evident in the field, the specific time of testing occurring, generally, between 1000 and 1400 hours. This timing reduced possible complications due to diurnal changes in responsiveness. Although the entire investigation included results from various times of the year, specific experiments, dealing with one particular question or factor, were invariably completed within a short time. Thus, although responsiveness varied somewhat with the season, it did not affect the validity of the comparable levels of responsiveness within a given experimental series.

Free-ranging male damselfish often directed their courtship at nearby conspecific females, but the responses of the latter obviously depended not only upon male display, but upon some presently unmeasurable level of their own reproductive readiness. Thus, one noted that courtship by the males (including frequent chirping) often went unheeded by prospective mates (Myrberg, 1972a). On the other hand, if a given male continued such a pattern for only a few moments, nearby conspecific males invariably began performing the same patterns. Thus, frequent male responsiveness allowed sound playback to be used for assessing the value of specific elements in a given chirp or of the entire development of the chirp itself, for the presumed recognition process. Standard playback periods of 3 min invariably alternated with equally timed periods of silence (control). This procedure was used to show differences in responsiveness between periods of sound transmission and periods having none.

Although numerous patterns (motor, sonic, color) were followed during all experiments, one particular motor pattern was of special interest. This pattern, termed the "dip," is present in the repertoire of all species of *Eupomacentrus* studied thus far; and its conspicuousness makes for easy discernment. It consists, basically, of a rapid vertical, or near-vertical, dive of some centimeters near, or at, the prospective spawning area, accompanied by the unique species-specific courtship coloration and often by a distinctive chirp (Myrberg, 1972c). Most of the results provided in this report reflect the occurrence of this striking motor pattern; however, other motor patterns of courtship (i.e., nudge and lead) were, at times, included in the analysis (Ha, 1973).

Whenever an experimental series required that a number of different sounds be played back, the order of presentation was carried out in such a way that at the completion of the series, every sound had held each position in the given sequence an equal or near-equal number of times. Effects of possible habituation were minimized by the running of only a few tests each day.

Sound levels, adequate for playback, were determined early on in the program. It was found, for example, that levels could be halved or doubled (± 6 dB) with no apparent effect on responsiveness, at least in bicolor males (Ha, 1973). In any case, it was quite easy to match, aurally, playback levels, to within 3 dB or less, the levels of the chirps occurring "spontaneously" by the test males—considering, of course, distance from the source. This procedure was "tightened up a bit" during the final stages of the research: sounds were played back to field males at the sound level produced by their nearest conspecific neighbors (measured by an impact noise analyzer). In the laboratory, levels were adjusted to those measured in the field at similar distances under a calm sea. Finally, the underwater loudspeakers and their associated hardware were invariably set up well in advance of testing. Appropriate statistical treatments were applied to all data arising from the program, with the minimal criterion for significance being 0.05.

5 RESULTS

Prior research had demonstrated that males of the bicolor damselfish could selectively respond to different natural sounds of their own species under both laboratory and field conditions (Myrberg, 1972a). Yet the sounds used in those particular experiments, though similar in frequency spectrum, were strikingly different in temporal structure. The obvious question arose: would differential responsiveness still be shown if the sounds were similar in both frequency and time—resembling, for example, the similarity noted among chirps produced by congeners? The term "similar" was justified in that chirps from members of the genus possess broad and widely overlapping ranges in their frequency spectra (especially frequencies of greatest intensity), and temporal differences were at the order of msec (see Fig. 5.1). On the basis of past considerations of discriminative abilities by fishes in the time domain (e.g., see Wodinsky, 1964), such differences appeared slight indeed. Nevertheless, to insure even further similarity, chirps chosen for the earliest experiments contained three pulses—that is, the typical number for bicolors.

These playback series confirmed the fact that male bicolors could, indeed, discriminate between such sounds (Myrberg and Spires, 1972— laboratory results from one series are depicted in Fig. 5.2).

It was apparent, however, that chirps from congeners facilitated courtship to some extent in the test males. The notable difference was in the degree of such facilitation; significantly more responsiveness was shown by males to sounds of their own species than to sounds from congeners. An additional fact "brought to light" was that laboratory sounds were less effective in eliciting courtship than those recorded in the field. This effect was apparently the result of artifacts, such as slight reverberations and ringing within the pulse structure, brought about by such features as the walls of the aquarium. Subsequent studies, therefore, reduced significantly or eliminated entirely such sounds from experiments, relying on carefully recorded sounds from the field and their synthetic copies.

5.1   Chirp-Rate

Although a chirp-rate, common to all species, was used as the standard during the entire program, an effort was made to determine the importance of this factor for at least one of the species concerned, the bicolors (Ha, 1973). Findings showed that as chirp-rate increased from 10/min through 25/min, so did the intensity of courtship. This reflected the situation often noted during competitive courtship in this and the remaining species (Myrberg, 1972a): as courtship intensified, so did the number of chirps/min, until a point was reached where either dipping

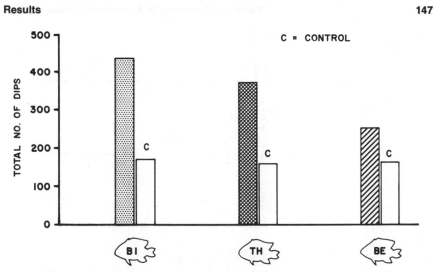

FIGURE 5.2 Differential responsiveness of male bicolors in the laboratory to three-pulse chirps from three species within its genus; BI = bicolor, TH = threespot, BE = beaugregory, C = control. Total sessions = 178. Significant differences ($\alpha = 0.05$) shown by differences in stippling.

occurred so rapidly that the corresponding chirp-rate could apparently no longer be maintained, or where other patterns replaced dipping in the courtship sequence. Chirping then ceased or was greatly reduced. It should also be mentioned that under free-ranging conditions, an increase in chirp-rate by a given male was invariably associated with a female approaching ever more closely a spawning site. Based on the competitive courtship of males, such an event clearly resulted in an increased probability that other nearby conspecifics would begin dipping, chirping, and approaching the vicinity of the female, in attempts to lead her to their respective residences. Thus there can be little doubt that chirp-rate reflected the state of relative arousal of the common causal factor(s) underlying courtship behavior in the bicolor and related damselfishes.

5.2 Pulse-Number

The number of pulses within chirps of a given species was not constant (Fig. 5.3). Each species did possess, however, a typical number of pulses within its chirps: dusky—6 or 7 (50%); threespot—4 (50%); beaugregory—4 (50%); bicolor—3 (75%). The question arising here was obvious: does the level of courtship vary with the number of pulses

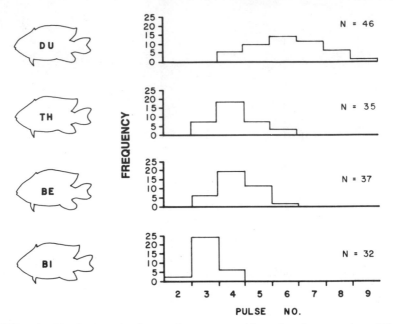

FIGURE 5.3 Distribution of pulse-numbers among chirps of various species within the genus, *Eupomacentrus;* DU = dusky, TH = threespot, BE = beaugregory, BI = bicolor.

present in a chirp? We attempted to answer this question for two of the four species involved, one under laboratory conditions and one in the field. Both provided basically the same answer. Let's consider the laboratory findings first (Ha, 1973).

Conspecific sounds, varying in pulse-number (maximum = 4), were presented to one of the bicolor colonies during two experimental series (both using the same playback and recording techniques.) Results of the first series (Fig. 5.4) showed that no significant difference existed between responsiveness to 3- and 4-pulse chirps, but the differences between these and the other sounds were, indeed, significant. Both 3- and 4-pulse sounds occurred in the reproductive context, while the 2-pulse sound was heard most often during the changeover from the nonreproductive phase to that of active reproduction. The 1-pulse sound (pop) is an agonistic sound, and it can even suppress reproductive behavior (Myrberg, 1972a). The second series (Fig. 5.4) showed that 3-pulse chirps are apparently "favored," however, over those having four pulses. A natural 4-pulse chirp was replicated thrice, and two of these replicates were altered by the removal of the first pulse and the first two pulses, respectively. Tests were then run on 4-, 3-, and 2-pulse sounds, all resulting from the same original chirp.

These findings thus provided further evidence for the conclusions reached in a previous study; that is, information relative to the major behavioral states and/or to their transitions appear to be transmitted by this property in the sounds of bicolors (Myrberg, 1972a). In addition, reasonable discreteness in the coding, perhaps, provides sufficient differentiation of state without excessive ambiguity. For example, the chirp, long chirp, grunt, and growl are all sounds of courtship in bicolors; the number of pulses included therein varies from 2 to 12, depending on the sound (Myrberg, 1971).

Let's turn now to the field (Spanier, 1975) and see if members of another species reflect the same ideas. The species was the dusky damselfish, *E. dorsopunicans*. Its chirp contains a greater number of pulses (4 to 8) than those shown by bicolors (2 to 4). Unfortunately, it has not been established whether the dusky possesses sounds equivalent to the grunt or growl of bicolors, but on the basis of findings from all other species (Myrberg, 1971), chances are excellent that it does. In any case, structural considerations indicate that the dusky appears capable of transmitting even more differentiations of state during the moment of dipping than

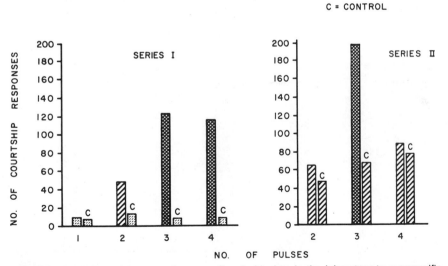

FIGURE 5.4 Differential responsiveness of male bicolors in the laboratory to conspecific chirps having different pulse-numbers. Total sessions: Series 1 = 64, Series 2 = 36, C = control. Significant differences (α = 0.05) shown by differences in stippling. For further clarification, see text.

those transmitted by bicolors. If so, one may expect a reasonable variation in responsiveness by conspecifics, based on the pulse-number of a
given chirp. This expectation was borne out in the results, as shown in
Fig. 5.5. Greatest responsiveness was shown to those chirps possessing
6 or 7 pulses, with subsequent reduction in responsiveness to chirps
having either higher or lower pulse numbers. Also, if one refers to Fig.
5.3, it is clear that these clines are paralleled perfectly by the distribution
of pulse-numbers within chirps. Thus, the story that was unfolded by
the bicolors appears to be told, once again, by the duskies.

5.3   Frequency Spectrum

All the courtship sounds of the genus have a reasonably broad frequency spectrum, ranging to 2400 Hz. Most energy is, however, concentrated between 250 and 1100 Hz. To place this information in its correct
perspective, a few comments are perhaps appropriate at this time. Audiograms from adults of all the species concerned here indicate that
frequencies higher than 800 Hz are most probably not "perceived" ex-

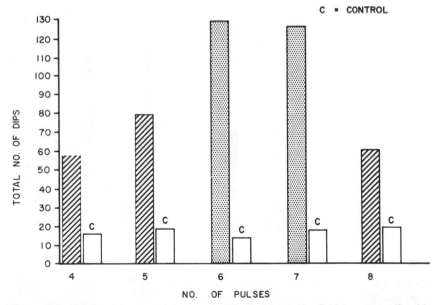

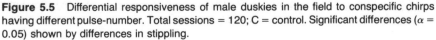

Figure 5.5 Differential responsiveness of male duskies in the field to conspecific chirps
having different pulse-number. Total sessions = 120; C = control. Significant differences (α =
0.05) shown by differences in stippling.

cept under most unusual conditions, such as being tested in a condition-ing paradigm with extremely loud tones. Attempts to obtain reliable responses from members of the genus above 1200 Hz have invariably failed (Myrberg and Spires, in prep.). Therefore only the spectrum below that point needed to be considered as possibly critical for pur-poses of species-specific communication. When that portion of the spec-trum was compared, however, among the sounds of the various species, all possessed, basically, the same frequencies of highest intensity (Fig. 5.6). This similarity indicated that frequency per se could not be playing a critical role in the presumed communication system. (Note: the possi-ble role of the spectrum in providing carrier frequencies is not being questioned here). Nevertheless, controlled tests were carried out in the laboratory, again with the use of our little "oceanic guinea pigs," the bicolors. Some tests pitted natural 3-pulse chirps against synthetic chirps containing a pure tone (550 Hz) or a noise band (200 to 1100 Hz), while others compared synthetic chirps of different bandwidths (all cen-tered at the same frequency). The former showed no significant differ-ence in responsiveness between the noiseband and the natural chirp, but the pure tone "chirp" had no value whatsoever (Ha, 1973). Results,

FREQUENCIES OF GREATEST INTENSITIES (HZ)

200 300 400 500 600 700 800 900 1000 1100 1200

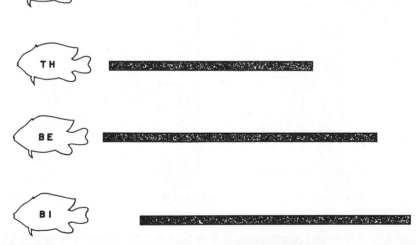

FIGURE 5.6 Comparison of frequencies of greatest intensity within chirps of the various species of damselfishes tested; DU = dusky, TH = threespot, BE = beaugregory, BI = bicolor.

using chirps of different bandwidths, are shown in Fig. 5.7. The bandwidth, mirroring the natural range (two octaves), did not differ significantly from a bandwidth one octave narrower in range; but responsiveness was significantly reduced for the 1/10 octave bandwidth. Thus, for chirps to have communicative value in courtship, they need not have much of their broad frequency spectrum, but if the latter is reduced excessively, responsiveness will cease. Relative lack of responsiveness to a severely restricted frequency spectrum indicated that if carrier frequencies are, indeed, being used for information purposes, they are in some form of a complex.

5.4   Pulse Duration

Sample-comparison diagrams of the many pulse durations measured from our original chirp samples are shown in Fig. 5.8. No significant difference appeared in this property between dusky and threespot, but both showed a significant difference from the samples of the other two species, the beaugregory has a longer pulse duration, the bicolor a shorter one (significance shown if 2 SE on either side of $\bar{x}$ provided no overlap among the samples compared). We can assume, therefore, that

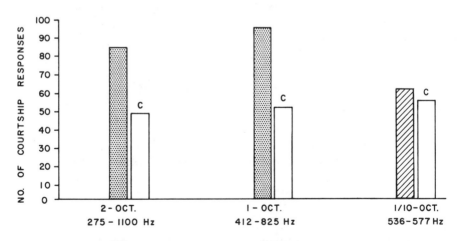

FIGURE 5.7   Differential responsiveness of male bicolors in the laboratory to three-pulse chirps having different frequency spectra. Sounds were synthesized, each pulse having a duration of 10 msec, with pulse interval being 40 msec. Total sessions = 24; C = control.

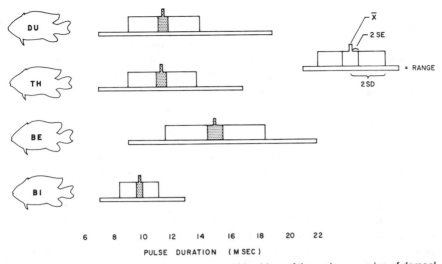

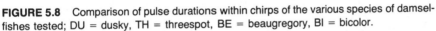

6   8   10   12   14   16   18   20   22

PULSE   DURATION   (M SEC)

FIGURE 5.8   Comparison of pulse durations within chirps of the various species of damsel-fishes tested; DU = dusky, TH = threespot, BE = beaugregory, BI = bicolor.

this property could not be used alone for purposes of species recognition between duskies and threespots. Yet, on the basis of the few msec differences that existed in this property among all the species (means separated by about 5 msec), is it possible that the pulses are too brief to permit discerning such minute differences? We turned, once again, to the laboratory bicolors in an attempt to answer this question (Fig. 5.9). Responsiveness was excellent for synthetic chirps that had pulse durations extending beyond their own range and even into the natural range of all the other species. Thus, it was unlikely that bicolors could use this property alone for purposes of species recognition. This test and the similar pulse durations of the dusky and threespot indicate that this property probably has little value, per se, in the communication system being considered here. A second series of tests then determined possible broad limits for the property regarding responsiveness. Results showed significantly reduced responsiveness when pulse durations were as brief as 2 msec or as long as 25 msec (Ha, 1973). It is possible that the former may well have been too brief to be perceived, and, if so, the playback series should have consisted, essentially, of transmitting no information whatsoever. This construct actually fits the data, since there was absolutely no difference in the occurrence of courtship patterns between the playback and control periods. There was neither "reversed-enhancement"—that is, increased courtship during control periods—nor even the slightest repression of courtship during the entire series.

(In an earlier study, repression and/or "reversed-enhancement" had been noted when unfamiliar or aggressive sounds were played back; see Myrberg, 1972a; see also below). Since the courtship-enhancing, 3-pulse chirp of the previous series (Fig. 5.9) had a 5 msec pulse duration and an "off-time" (i.e., silent period between two successive pulses = inter-pulse interval) of 35 msec, slight but important changes in one or both properties could have made the difference. If an excessive "off-time," rather than an imperceptible pulse, had been the critical factor causing lack of responsiveness,previous findings would lead one to expect that the sounds would have been treated as simply unfamiliar ones with appropriate "reversed-enhancement." This was not the case, and so a reasonable answer is that the 2 msec pulse had simply not been heard and, therefore, that the sounds had not been received by the subjects. If so, it is not unreasonable to assume that the threshold for pulse reception in adult male bicolors is probably less than 5 msec, but greater than 2 msec. It is noteworthy in this regard that Popper (1972) has shown that goldfish can also detect extremely brief pulses (as short as 5 msec duration), the threshold for such detection being no different from that associated with very long pulses.

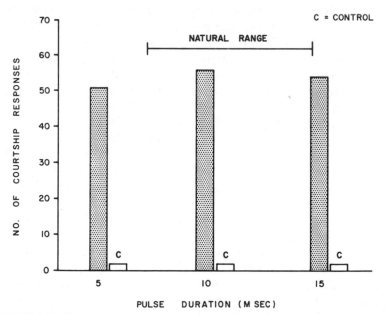

FIGURE 5.9   Responsiveness of male bicolors in the laboratory to three-pulse chirps having different pulse durations. Sounds were synthesized, using a pulse interval of 40 msec. Total sessions = 54; C = control.

significant difference in responsiveness between test and control periods for those chirps having pulse durations of 25 msec. First, almost twice the amount of courtship occurred during periods of silence, compared with that noted during playback periods. This typified "reversed-enhancement" of responsiveness, which apparently occurred when a particular sound possessed temporal properties well beyond the normal range of the species (e.g., pulse intervals; see below). These results, again, reflected those previously obtained during playback of unfamiliar sounds (Myrberg, 1972a). This suggested that not only were the pulses being perceived, but also that they were being "considered" as unfamiliar sounds. Although one may argue that the 15 msec "off-time" may have been too brief to be perceived, evidence militating against this conclusion is presented below.

5.5   Pulse Interval

The pulse interval was the next piece of the puzzle examined. This interval, by convention, includes the entire time between the onset of one pulse and the onset of the next, thus including within its time-frame both the duration and the "off-time." Sample-comparison diagrams of the many intervals measured in our original chirp samples are shown in Fig. 5.10. These samples, in contrast to those of pulse duration, show

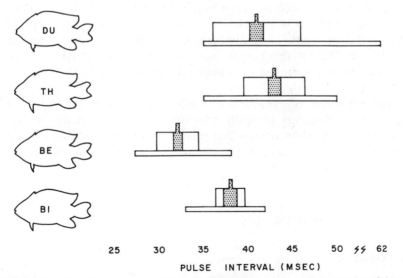

FIGURE 5.10   Comparison of pulse intervals within chirps of the various species of damselfishes tested; DU = dusky, TH = threespot, BE = beaugregory, BI = bicolor. See Fig. 5.8 for explanation of the sample-comparison diagrams.

that this property was significantly different among all the species concerned. The intervals of the dusky and threespot were very similar, their means being separated by only about 2 msec. These intervals were longer than those of the remaining species, the beaugregory having a distinctly shorter interval, the bicolor an intermediate one. Two series of experiments were directed at the laboratory colony of bicolors to determine the importance of this property to the presumed communication system (Ha, 1973). Results are shown in Fig. 5.11. Chirps having intervals of 40 msec (approximate center of sample distribution) were significantly superior to all others; and here a difference of only 5 to 10 msec produced a significant difference in levels of responsiveness. Smooth clines in responsiveness existed from 40 msec toward the limits tested; and at the extremes (20 and 60 msec), "reversed-enhancement" of courtship was again evident. Since all sounds possessed identical pulse durations, the only property varying throughout the series was the "off-time." This meant either that the latter property, alone, was supplying the information necessary for significant differential responsiveness, or that it was acting in concert with the pulse to provide the "correct" pulse interval. Experiments allowing the pulse interval, but not the "off-time," to vary were not conducted, and therefore, no decision can be made at this time about which possibility is the correct one. In any case, it is clear that the pulse interval itself, its "off-time," or a specific ratio of pulse duration to "off-time," was providing the essential information to members of the test colony, resulting in consistent, but different, levels of responsiveness. It is also clear from the findings that the responding fish were fully capable of distinguishing temporal differences between 5 and 10 msec. This amazing ability stands in marked contrast to the views that have been expressed on temporal discrimination in fishes (e.g., Wodinsky, 1964).

A second series of experiments varied specific aspects of the pulse interval, with findings basically the same as those already discussed. Other intriguing relationships that existed within the temporal structure of the pulse interval have been examined (Ha, 1973), but these will be covered elsewhere.

6   SPECIES RECOGNITION

6.1   General

The information provided above was used in examining species-recognition by the use of sound among our four species of damselfishes.

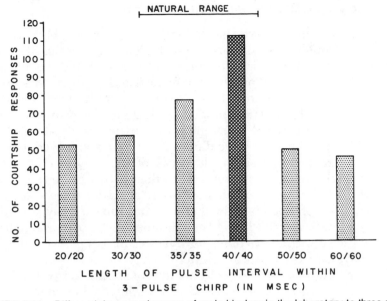

FIGURE 5.11 Differential responsiveness of male bicolors in the laboratory to three-pulse chirps having different pulse intervals (the two interval-durations within a given three-pulse chirp are given along the abscissa). A pulse duration of 10 msec was used in synthesizing sounds. Total sessions = 96. Significant differences (α = 0.05) shown by differences in stippling.

Basically, two types of sounds were used during this phase of the program. The first contained those chirps having the most prevalent number of pulses for each species (e.g., 3—bicolor; 4—threespot; 6—dusky). These were termed the "typical chirps." The second type contained 4-pulse chirps from all species, this number being chosen since it was present in the repertoire of all.

Each of these representative chirps was played back to field colonies of each species in "round-robin" fashion, in such a way that by the end of a given series, each chirp had been played back to each colony four times. This allowed each chirp to hold every position one time within all sequences.

A final set of experiments utilized both naturally and artificially modified chirps. Test subjects were males from a field colony of dusky damselfish. These males were confronted with normal 4-pulse chirps of a conspecific; normal 4-pulse chirps of the beaugregory (easiest courtship sound to discriminate by duskies; see below); and, finally, 4-pulse chirps of the beaugregory, which had been modified by a simple lengthening of the pulse intervals by a few msec (9), so that they equaled those produced by the duskies (Spanier, 1975).

6.2   The Dusky Damselfish, *E. dorsopunicans*

Results from playing back the "typical" and 4-pulse chirps of each
species to colonies of duskies are shown in Fig. 5.12. Duskies responded
significantly better to their own typical chirps than to those of the other
species. They responded next best to the typical chirp of the threespot, it
being "treated" significantly better than those of the two remaining
species. Although the latter produced little interest in duskies, their
courtship during playback was significantly better than that noted during the silent controls. Notable differences to the above were obvious,
subsequent to the analysis of playbacks of the 4-pulse chirps. First,
duskies did not respond differentially to their own 4-pulse chirp and to
those of the threespot. Next, their response appeared to be stronger for
4-pulse chirps of bicolors than that recorded during playback of the
corresponding "typical" chirps. The questions now posed are: could we
have predicted the pattern of responsiveness, and, if so, what property
would have best predicted that pattern?

It is apparent that duskies could not tell conspecific chirps from those
of a threespot when the pulse numbers of both were the same. No such
difficulties were evident, however, when both produced their own typi-

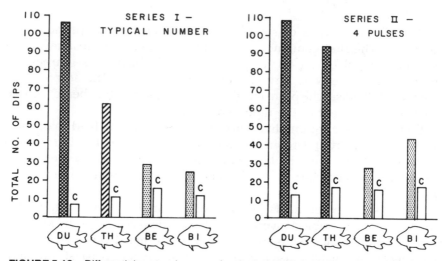

FIGURE 5.12   Differential responsiveness of male duskies in the field to chirps of the various
test species; DU = dusky, TH = threespot, BE = beaugregory, BI = bicolor, C = control. Total
sessions = 96. Significant differences ($\alpha = 0.05$) shown by differences in stippling. For further
clarification, see text.

cal numbers. Since 6-pulse chirps are relatively rare in the chirps of threespots (see Fig. 5.3), duskies can apparently use their most prevalent chirps as a means of species-recognition—with little risk of wasting energy at irrelevant times. They apparently have little trouble in distinguishing the chirps of the bicolor and beaugregory from their own sounds, and they can apparently distinguish most easily those of the beaugregory. The pattern of differential responsiveness to sounds of the various species would have been best predicted by information obtained from the pulse interval.

6.3   The Threespot Damselfish, *E. planifrons*

Playing back the "typical" and 4-pulse chirps of each species to colonies of threespots provided essentially the same "picture" as that recorded for the duskies. Threespots did not appear able to distinguish their own species' chirps from those of duskies if the pulse numbers were the same; but they could easily do so if the "typical" numbers were used. Thus, once again, the pulse number appeared as a means to convey "species-specificity." Threespots appeared to have no problem whatsoever in distinguishing their own chirps from those of the bicolor and the beaugregory. Their pattern of responsiveness to all sounds would have been best predicted from information on the pulse interval.

6.4   The Beaugregory, *E. leucostictus*

Results from playing back the "typical" and 4-pulse chirps of each species to colonies of beaugregories are shown in Fig. 5.13. This species apparently had little difficulty in distinguishing its own chirps from those of the other species. This finding held, also, for the chirps of the threespot (same "typical" pulse number). The relative ease shown by beaugregories in differentiating between their own chirps and those of the others rests, most probably, with the temporal structure of their own sounds. This structure was quite distinct, relatively speaking, from that present in the sounds of the other species (see Figs. 5.1, 5.8, and 5.10). Chirps of the bicolor received greater responsiveness when pulse numbers were equal, rather than unequal. This, again, indicated that pulse number was apparently being used, at least to some extent for species recognition, even by this species. The particular pattern of responsiveness that emerged from these series would have been equally predicted by the pulse interval and the "off-time."

6.5 The Bicolor Damselfish, *E. partitus*

Playing back the "typical" and 4-pulse chirps of each species to colonies of bicolors showed once again the basic patterns of differentiation evidenced by members of the other species. Their "typical" chirp was easily differentiated from those of the other species, but when pulse numbers were the same, they clearly differentiated only those chirps that possessed greatest dissimilarity from their own in pulse interval (or "off-time"); thus, pulse number was apparently again being used as a means of species-recognition. It is noteworthy, in this regard, that bicolors responded significantly better to the "typical" chirp of the dusky than they did to the sounds of the remaining two species. This response was indicative of the fact that the pulse number of the dusky was 6, just twice that of the bicolor. The particular pattern of responsiveness by bicolors to those sounds of the remaining species would have been best predicted, as in the case of the other species, by the pulse interval and/or the "off-time."

7 TESTING OF AN HYPOTHESIS

The above results, as well as others not considered here, appeared to demonstrate, unequivocally, that certain sounds were important elements within the total communication system underlying competitive courtship within the genus, *Eupomacentrus*. Additionally, their communicative value appeared to rest upon the unique temporal patterning of their individual pulses and intervals. Apparently, various types of information were being transmitted—not the least of which had to do with the problem of species-recognition. Since this particular problem had intrigued us from the very beginning, we felt that an effective coup de grace might be delivered to end the uncertainty of temporal involvement in this portion of the communication process.

This was accomplished in the following manner (Spanier, 1975). Four-pulse chirps were obtained from the beaugregory and dusky damselfish, and a number of replicates were made of each sound. The "off-time" of those chirps from the beaugregory was then artificially increased by 9 msec so as to produce a pulse interval equivalent to that of the dusky. Since this was the only modification made, everything else about the sound remained species-typical for the beaugregory (i.e., frequency spectrum, pulse number, pulse duration). Then, field tests were conducted on a colony of duskies to establish whether changes in the pulse interval, alone, could make beaugregory chirps, previously the easiest of all sounds to differentiate (see Fig. 5.12), now indistinguishable.

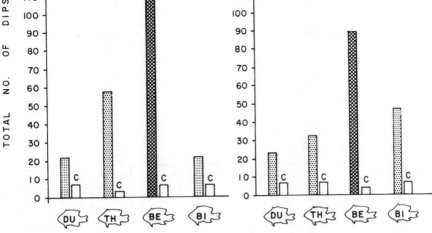

FIGURE 5.13 Differential responsiveness of male beaugregories in the field to chirps of the various test species; DU = dusky, TH = threespot, BE = beaugregory, BI = bicolor, C = control. Total sessions = 96. Significant differences ($\alpha = 0.05$) shown by differences in stippling. For further clarification, see text.

The ensuing results (Fig. 5.14) showed that equivalent responsiveness was indeed directed to their own chirps and to the altered chirps of the beaugregory, along with a significant reduction in responsiveness to the unaltered chirps of the latter species. This response meant that a mere 9 msec difference in the "off-time" effectively changed the entire "meaning" of a sound—and a very important sound, at that. This final series, using free-ranging members of a natural population, proved beyond any question that, indeed, the pulse interval (or possibly its "off-time") *was* the factor responsible for species recognition by at least this population of duskies. And thus its probable importance to all members of this, and other closely related species, was assured.

8   DISCUSSION

8.1   Fishes

On the basis of all results, including those highlighted above, it is reasonable to conclude that all species of damselfishes studied in this investigation possess complex and precise systems of acoustical communication. Also, since these species are so closely related and the sys-

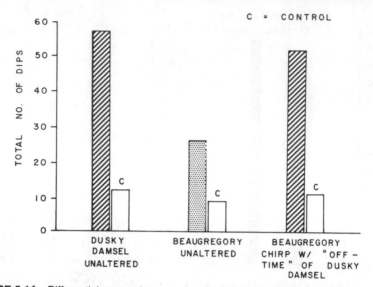

FIGURE 5.14 Differential responsiveness of male duskies in the field to altered and unaltered four-pulse chirps of the beaugregory; responsiveness to four-pulse, conspecific chirps, used as added control, also shown. Total sessions = 72; C = control. Significant differences (α = 0.05) shown by differences in stippling. For further clarification, see text.

tems they possess so similar, there is every reason to believe that the latter are, indeed, also homologous. Finally, since the systems all operate in the context of competitive courtship, one may assume that each probably provides a significant conservation of energy over that which might otherwise occur, owing to inconsequential courtship based on misidentification. It should be noted in this connection, however, that other modalities, such as vision (i.e., recognition of species-specific postures and coloration), probably augment any discrimination process in the natural situation, so long as appropriate stimuli are present. In the present experimental context, acoustical playback techniques precluded such possibilities.

The questions brought forth in the introductory section of this chapter have been answered in the affirmative: (1) the acoustical communication systems of damselfishes show clear correlations between variation in properties of the signals used and variation in the pattern of responses elicited; and (2) the signals do possess certain properties that appear to carry prime responsibility for evoking appropriate responses. Accordingly, these properties must be providing information relevant to the decision-making processes in the behavioral context(s) where the signals appear. One point should not be forgotten, however. The experimental designs used in our studies only allowed a role to be assigned to a variable when its removal or modification resulted in a significant reduction in responsiveness. If such a reduction was not evident, the only reasonable conclusion was that the variable in question could not, by itself, be essential to the communication process. This does not mean that it played no role—redundancy in information content and/or the combined effects of two or more parameters are fully adequate reasons for its role remaining unclarified. With this important point in mind, we can turn to the properties that appeared to contain the codes for the communication systems. In doing this, we believe that it is valuable to compare our findings with those obtained by others who have carried out similar studies with other groups of animals. We realize that such comparisons are fraught with methodological problems and terminological difficulties. Also, they are considered by many to be downright dangerous; important differences in levels of organization are apparently ignored, homology may be incorrectly implied, and coincidental appearances may well be misread (see Tavolga, 1970). Notwithstanding these arguments, it is nevertheless the responsibility of the behavioral scientist to attempt, wherever possible, to apply principles that may aid in reducing the number of variables needed to describe a system or process, irrespective of taxon or taxa. Any such attempt must be cautious, indeed, but it must be made.

The systems of communication that have been found in our damselfishes are all basically the same; so for purposes of simplicity we will consider all as a single system, except in those cases where such a convention may only confuse the issue.

It is abundantly clear that the acoustical communication system involving competitive courtship in damselfishes rests primarily, if not totally, upon the temporal organization or patterning of its included elements. Equally obvious is the fact that these elements differed in their apparent importance to the system. Some provided precise information relative to species-recognition (i.e., pulse interval, pulse number), while others appeared to function in expressing the major behavioral state of the animal involved (i.e., number of pulses/chirp) or the relative level of arousal (i.e., chirp-rate). Finally, certain elements did not seem, within broad limits, to be critical to the system—for example, frequency spectrum and amplitude (Ha, 1973).

Can we find similar types of acoustical communication systems operating in other animals, and if so, do the elements appear to carry the same type of information? To answer this question, a literature search was necessary. The search was very rewarding, although not exhaustive. Therefore, important contributions may have been overlooked.

Let's first look at the few studies that have "brought some light" to this question in fishes. The percussive or pulse-type sounds that comprise the repertoire of these animals make them excellent candidates for use in communication systems that apply the same principles of organization as those found in the damselfish system. Unfortunately, only one major research program has been conducted, and it did not deal specifically with the problem of species recognition. The subjects were toadfish, *Opsanus tau* (Fish, 1969, 1972; Winn, 1964, 1967, 1972). Males of the species announce their reproductive readiness by producing sounds called boatwhistles. A nearby male answered playbacks of such sounds with its own boatwhistles, so long as the former were loud enough (but not too loud) and their included units were comprised of a frequency spectrum within its hearing range (equal responsiveness shown to pure tones and to bands of noise). The duration of a boatwhistle is quite long—around 400 msec; if this was reduced to 75 to 150 msec, poor responsiveness resulted. The rate of calling also had to be above a threshold level (14 to 16/min) before response was given (maximum response maintained after rate reached some level, e.g., 18 to 20/min). Thus, amplitude and frequency appeared to have little control over the system, except at the extremes. This conclusion supported the contention by Winn (1964) that these two factors did not seem to have enough information for purposes of intraspecific communication. This conclusion is also consistent with our results. The remaining two properties of the boatwhistle appeared to play more decisive roles in the communication system, and both possess temporal organization—unit duration and repetition rate. Since pulse durations were not measured, the only reasonable comparison that can be made is between changes in the durations of the boatwhistle and appropriate changes in the duration of the chirp itself. This comparison, together with a comparison of the results from both repetition rates, makes it clear that the former provided information relative to species-specificity and the latter, to levels of arousal.

The remaining studies on fishes, though demonstrating acoustical communication systems, provided no information about essential properties (e.g., Delco, 1960; Gerald, 1971; Horch and Salmon, 1973; Stout, 1963). Delco (1960) did note, however, that two widely differing temporal elements existed in the sounds of the species he studied (*Notropis lutrensis* and *N. venustus*)—pulse duration and trills/sec. Gerald (1971) also noted in several species of North American sunfishes (*Lepomis* spp.) that the message-carrying parts of their courtship sounds, relative to species-recognition, were probably included in their temporal pattern. He further speculated that pulse rate, pulse number, and pulse duration were the important elements, based on consistent differences among the species. Caution should be exercised, however, in this regard, since in the case of our damselfishes, pulse duration was consistent within each species and significantly different among the species. Nevertheless, the property appeared nonessential per se to the system (see also Emlen, 1972, regarding consistency). Returning to the basic problem, Fay (1972) has expressed the notion that pitch perception, itself, in fishes may well be based on a temporal code.

Thus, though the sample is small, the same story has been repeated—that is, systems of communication based on the temporal organization of elements within the sounds of courtship. The data base includes precious few species at this time, however, and therefore it is possible that other aspects of sound (e.g., spectrum) may eventually be shown also to be important for communication purposes in other species.

8.2 Amphibians

We turn now to a group where far more work has been accomplished on acoustical communication systems: the Amphibia.

Numerous species of anurans are often found close together in small confined areas, each carrying on its own breeding and calling activities without heterospecific matings and rampant hybridization (Blair, 1958, 1964; Bogert, 1960). This absence of "biological confusion" has interested workers for many years, and attempts have been made to understand the intricate commmunication systems that must act as reproductive isolating mechanisms.

The crucial role of sound in these systems has now been established for all species studied thus far; and one sound, the mating call, has been investigated thoroughly (e.g., *Crinia* spp.—Littlejohn and Watson, 1974; *Dendrobates*—Bunnell, 1973; *Hyla* spp.—Gerhardt, 1974; Littlejohn, 1960a; Littlejohn and Loftus-Hills, 1968; Loftus-Hills and Littlejohn, 1971; Martof, 1961; Paillette, 1970, 1971; *Pseudacris* spp.—Capranica, Frishhopf, and Nevo, 1973; Littlejohn, 1960b, 1961; Littlejohn and Michaud, 1959; Martof, 1961; Michaud, 1962; *Rana*—Capranica, 1966, 1968; Capranica, Frishkopf, and Goldstein, 1967; Feng, Narins, and Capranica, 1975; Frishkopf, Capranica and Goldstein, 1968; *Scaphiopus* spp.—Capranica and Moffat, 1975; Forester, 1973).

Loftus-Hills and Littlejohn (1971) demonstrated that species-recognition was accomplished in *H. ewingi* and *H. verreaux* by means of the temporal patterning of pulses within their respective mating calls. They argued that pulse repetition rate was the important element.

It should, perhaps, be pointed out that the only difference between pulse repetition rate and pulse interval centers on the arbitrary time measure used in the former so that a rate can be provided. Pulse interval is most often used in cases where a given sound is extremely brief or interruptive in nature.

Gerhardt (1974) has recently shown that, in certain cases, hylids can be divided into two major groups: those that stress temporal organization in their communication systems (e.g., *H. avivoca, H. chrysoscelis,* and *H. femoralis*), and those that stress spectral composition (e.g., *H. cineria* and *H. gratiosa*). Regarding species-recognition, the system of the former group emphasized, again, pulse repetition rate as well as pulse train characteristics. Temporal patterning was also emphasized by Bunnell (1973) in intraspecific communication by *Dendrobates pumilis*. Capranica and Moffat (1975) have clear evidence that the auditory fibers of *Scaphiopus couchi* include elements for providing information on the spectral energy of sounds. Yet they have also demonstrated that the same system is capable of following the waveform periodicities of the trills found in mating and release calls. Thus, the neural system can faithfully encode the temporal pattern of amplitude modulations, as well as the spectral energy in each call. Finally, a model has been prepared for the acoustical communication system of *Rana catesbeiana*, based on the elegant results that have been obtained by Capranica and his coworkers over the last few years. In addition to three distinct types of auditory nerve fibers that provide information about the spectral energy of the incoming call (Capranica, personal communication), each of these units is tuned to a pulse train with the repetition rate of a conspecific's mating call (Frishkopf and Goldstein, 1963; Frishkopf, Capranica, and Goldstein, 1968).

Few studies have been carried out on the sounds of other amphibians (e.g., *Siren intermedia,* Gehlbach and Walker, 1970), but they do indicate that temporal patterning of sound may well be important in these forms, also.

Suffice it to state that anurans, and perhaps other soniferous amphibians, are receiving abundant information through the acoustical modality; and though the frequency spectrum is obviously important, so also is the temporal organization of structural elements within appropriate sounds. Finally, pulse repetition rate (or pulse interval) seems to be the important property within the temporal mode.

8.3 Reptiles

Little can be stated at this time about acoustical communication in reptiles. Frankenberg (1974) has noted sexual differences in the sounds of gekkos (*Ptyodactylus*), and Campbell (1973) concluded that, of the major species of crocodilians available to him at the time, only the *Caiman* responded exclusively to sounds of their own species. Hopefully, these and other workers will bring forth additional information in the near future about the functional significance of sound to this important group of animals.

8.4 Birds

The next group to be considered from the standpoint of acoustical communication has been intensively studied. We have, therefore, limited this discussion to only those studies that appeared to be most directly relevant.

The vocal repertoire of birds is not only rich and varied, but it also provides an inexhaustible source of information relative to the adaptive significance of that modality in meeting an enormity of environmental demands. It is obvious, however, that each modality must act in concert with others so that the gathering of relevant information is effective and efficient. Studies of such interaction have been carried out (Brockway, 1965, 1969; Cowan, 1974; Cowan and Evans, 1974; Evans, 1970, 1972; Evans and Mattson, 1972; Mattson and Evans, 1974). Another important phase of acoustical research in birds has involved individual recognition. Excellent reviews of this subject have recently appeared (Beer, 1970, 1972). They duly note the importance of temporal patterning to such recognition among various species—for example, pulse duration and interval in the luring calls of guillemots (Tschanz, 1958, 1965) and in the "caws" of the American crow (Thompson, 1969). Remarkable temporal organization also characterizes the antiphonal singing that has been described for various species (Thorpe, 1963, 1967; Thorpe and North, 1965; Grimes, 1965, 1966; Wickler, 1972, 1973; Wickler and Uhrig, 1969). Yet frequency spectrum certainly cannot be ignored (e.g., the laughing gull—Beer, 1972, Impekoven, 1973; the eastern whipbird—Watson, 1969). The general "rule of thumb" used to differentiate those properties important for individual recognition from those important for species recognition is that the former are generally highly variable among individuals, but consistent for any given individual, while the latter are constant and unvarying among all members of a given species. For example, individual differences in frequency characteristics have been found in the white-crowned sparrow (Borror and Gunn, 1965; Falls, 1969), the *Hylocichla* thrushes (Stein, 1956), and the brown towhee (Marler and Isaac, 1960). Hutchinson *et al.* (1968) concluded that three properties of the "fish calls" of sandwich terns were likely used for individual recognition, on the basis of this "rule." On the other hand, the problem of species recognition has been answered also by these and other birds (see below). Appropriate experiments, in fact, have left little doubt that temporal patterning is a most important factor in that respect among many, if not most, species.

"Classic" examples of acoustical communication systems in birds are found in Fall's detailed studies of the ovenbird (Falls, 1963; Weeden and Falls, 1959) and white-throated sparrow (Falls, 1963, 1969). Elements concerned with species-recognition in the former were phrases of a characteristic structure (i.e., frequency), repeated in a specific temporal pattern; those of the latter included primarily unvarying pure tones of the song and secondarily (although still important) its temporal pattern (i.e., note duration and interval). The fine study carried out by Emlen (1972) on the indigo bunting emphasized also the physical structure (frequency) and the rhythmic variation of the song itself (i.e., temporal pattern). Species-recognition by sound in the wood lark seemed to be mediated by the tonal quality and phrase structure (Tretzel, 1965); while the same purpose was being effected by syntax (i.e., alternation of high and low frequencies) in the European robin (Bremond, 1963, 1967). Interestingly, temporal features in the latter case appeared to play little role in the recognition process because of extreme variability. Again, both pitch and timing appeared important for species recognition in the European nightjar (Abs, 1963).

In summary, many birds obviously use both temporal and frequency information for purposes of species-recognition. Although the same principle operates also in the anurans, it appears to be either more widespread or at least easier to demonstrate in birds; and though the frequency spectrum appears to carry little weight in species recognition among the few fishes studied thus far, the "rules" that seemed to be operating in fishes, with regard to temporal patterning, appear to be operating in birds and amphibians also. Even the same elements are being used—pulse interval and unit duration. The decision as to which parameter (time or spectrum) to use for a given recognition process apparently rests, at least in birds, with the unique morphological and physiological nature of the species involved. Information on the latter subject has been carried out by Schwartzkopff (1963), Schwartzkopff and Winter (1960), Pumphrey (1961), and others.

8.5 Mammals

Man has, without doubt, the most flexible and (regarding the perception of periodic change in amplitude modulation, see Harbert *et al.*, 1968), complex system of acoustical communication in the animal kingdom. It is also relatively well understood in comparison with that of any other mammal. At first, this phenomenon appears surprising; but a moment's consideration probably recalls the numerous major difficulties encountered when dealing with animals at this level of organization. They include not only the extremely rich and varied repertoires of sounds, but also a complex nature of gradients between recognizable utterances (e.g., Rowell, 1972). Yet, it is obvious from even the few studies that have been carried out to date that temporal patterning often plays a critical role (e.g., various rodents: Hoffman and Searle, 1967; Farentinos, 1974; small insectivores, bats, and carnivores: Tembrock, 1963; Vaughan, 1972; pinnipeds: Caldwell and Caldwell, 1972; LeBoeuf and Petrinovich, 1974; small cetaceans: Caldwell and Caldwell, 1967, 1968, 1970; Caldwell et al., 1972a and b; monkeys: Marler, 1973). These studies, as well as others, point to sound as a means not only for species-recognition and individual recognition, but also for conveying information relative to major motivational states and differing levels of arousal (even under differing environments; see Marler, 1974). These are often expressed within the temporal organization. We do not wish to imply, however, that the frequency spectrum plays no role in these matters. Recent neurophysical evidence shows, for example, that the frequency spectrum is, indeed, supplying information to higher centers (the squirrel monkey, Newman and Wollberg, 1973).

Thus, the systems of acoustical communication used in mammals do not appear to be qualitatively different from those of either the birds or even the amphibians. Members of all three groups clearly make use of information from the frequency spectrum, and, to date, that pattern of the three groups appears to differ from that noted in fishes (except for effects based on extremes).

8.6 Arthropods

The final group to be touched on is the Arthropoda. Various studies have been included in this section, based on their relevance to the general problem at hand. Certain of them have empirically demonstrated that specific acoustic properties are responsible for species-recognition. Although frequency modulation may be a possibility for information coding relative to species-recognition (a thesis based on the apparent ability of certain insects to discriminate frequencies, e.g., *Schistocerca greyaria*—Michelsen, 1966, 1971a and b, 1974), most workers agree that temporal patterning of the pulsatile sounds is the prime factor responsible for the recognition process. Nowhere is this made more clear than in the studies carried out by Elsner (1974) on the gomphocerine grasshoppers, and by Bennet-Clark and Ewing (1967, 1970) on selected species of *Drosophila*. The findings were basically the same in both cases. Elsner concluded that the impulse rate of stridulations supplied the information necessary for species-specificity; modulations in this rate were based on variable velocities of stridulation. These points were then followed by effective arguments that the receptor cells could, indeed, follow these rates, individually or as envelopes. The studies of Bennet-Clark and Ewing (1967, 1970) have shown that the pulse interval of the respective mating calls constitutes a major effective isolating mechanism in the fruit flies. Since females could not be deceived when they were presented signals that were 0.5 or $2x$ the normal value, the underlying basis for discrimination must be a rather complex one.

Findings basically similar to those just mentioned have been obtained on a variety of insects, including crickets (Hoy, 1974; Walker, 1957; Shuvalov and Popov, 1973), katydids (Shaw, 1968) and grasshoppers (Bailey and Robinson, 1971; Busnel, 1963; Dumortier, 1963; Helversen, 1972). The frequency spectrum per se appears to play little, if any, direct role in the specificity shown, but some workers do differ in their opinion regarding the importance of the pulse itself, within the waveform.

Other temporally related phenomena that have to do with intraspecific interactions have been investigated in crickets. These studies have shown that increasing chirp-rate results not only in increasing responsiveness to chirp, but also in heightening aggressive actions. Moreover, if chirp-rate becomes high enough, attempts are made to sing antiphonally (Heiligenberg, 1966, 1969). It has also been shown that, within limits, increasing amplitude of chirping induces crickets to chirp more rapidly (Jones, 1966). Various neural correlates to these and related studies on temporal pattern recognition in crickets have been supplied by Huber (1962), Kutsch and Huber (1970), and Stout and Huber (1972).

The above findings are, in principle, remarkably similar to those reported in the acoustical studies conducted on fishes—pulse interval and pulse rate again being the prime elements used in species-recognition, and chirp-rate apparently reflecting levels of arousal. In fact, as far as temporal patterning goes, these findings are not basically dissimilar from those summarized in all the groups covered by this report. The only major apparent difference is that in amphibians, birds, and mammals, the frequency spectrum is obviously carrying information (in the FM mode) in addition to (and *not* rather than) that supplied by the temporal properties.

9 CLOSING STATEMENT

The preceding "journey" has allowed us to look only briefly at a miniscule portion of the total organization responsible for species recognition
and courtship behavior in various animals. Yet it has provided the opportunity to see how basically similar even these portions are to one
another. Is this simply coincidental and without meaning for us? On the
basis of what is presently known, we find ourselves agreeing with the
conclusion reached by Capranica (1972), ". . . it is hard to believe that
each species has evolved a completely different encoding scheme in its
auditory system." Instead, the principles of encoding the temporal information contained in a complex sound may be similar in different
mammals, perhaps basically the same, or, at least, similar in the birds,
and perhaps similar even in the insects. Many will probably disagree
with this, arguing that different levels of organization preclude such a
possibility. Since such disagreement often rests upon basically different
philosophical approaches, it is perhaps best to leave this contention for
future studies to prove or disprove. In any case, temporal patterning
pervades many forms of interactions other than those few covered in
this report. It forms, for example, the basis of the acoustical "war
games" between bats and noctuid moths (Griffin, 1958; Roeder, 1966),
and the electrolocating responses of the weakly electric fishes (Bullock,
1973; Heiligenberg, 1973, 1974; Hopkins, 1974). The phenomenal precision of the temporal mechanisms underlying these processes (see Bullock, 1973), and of those serving intraspecific communication, provides
an ever-expanding base from which empirical consideration can be directed at those appropriate models of temporal coding that allow the
most reasonable transfer functions between time-related, environmental
events and those events occurring within appropriate neural processes.
Such models have been discussed recently by Bullock, 1973; Mayo, 1968;
and Schleidt, 1973. The thought-provoking article by Schleidt centering
on tonic communication and pulse-rate modulation, has special relevance, since many of his examples deal specifically with sonic communication.

Temporal patterning of events, thus, appears to be essential not only
to acoustical communication systems of a wide variety of animals—
aquatic and terrestrial alike—but also to processes associated with
neurological function and signal detection. This common denominator
suggests the presence of properties that possess a relatively high level of
efficiency in terms of the conservation of energy at various levels of
integration. This efficiency is exemplified, perhaps, by those acoustical
systems that must operate in environments possessing a variety of im-

peding barriers, such as shallow-water surfaces, coral heads, rocks, leaves and trees, or those noisy with the sounds of many animals, the wind, or even the sea.

Any given communication or information-transfer system must be considered also as an evolutionary product that has been shaped by a variety of often quite divergent selection pressures. Specific pressures now operating on any such system may well differ greatly from those that influenced it in the past. Thus, it is obvious that we will probably never know how a particular system attained its present level of achievement. This does not preclude in any way, however, the fantastic opportunities that await future research in extending our knowledge about the principles upon which such systems operate.

REFERENCES

Abs, M. 1963. Field tests on the essential components of the European nightjar's song. Proc. 13th Int. Ornithol. Congr., Cornell, **1962:** 202–205.

Bailey, W. J. and D. Robinson. 1971. Song as a possible isolating mechanism in the genus *Homorocoryphus* (Tettigonioidea, Orthoptera). Anim. Behav. **19:** 390–397.

Beer, C. J. 1970. Individual recognition of voice in the social behavior of birds. *In* D. S. Lehrman, R. A. Hinde, and E. Shaw, Eds. *Advances in the Study of Behavior.* Vol. 3. Academic Press, New York. P. 27–74.

Beer, C. J. 1972. Individual recognition of voice and its development in birds. Proc. 15th Int. Ornithol. Congr., Leiden, **1972:** 341–356.

Bennet-Clark, H. C. and A. W. Ewing. 1967. Stimuli provided by courtship of male *Drosophila melanogaster.* Nature **215:** 669–671.

Bennet-Clark, H. C. and A. W. Ewing. 1970. The love song of the fruit fly. Sci. Am. **223:** 84–92.

Bentley, D. 1977. Control of cricket song patterns by descending interneurones. J. Comp. Physiol. A. **116:** 19–38.

Blair, W. F. 1958. Mating call in the speciation of anuran amphibians. Am. Nat. **92:** 27–51.

Blair, W. F. 1964. Isolating mechanisms and interspecies interactions of anuran amphibians. Quart. Rev. Biol. **39:** 334–344.

Bogert, C. 1960. The influence of sound on the behavior of amphibians and reptiles. *In:* W. E. Lanyon and W. N. Tavolga, Eds. *Animal Sounds and Communication.* Publ. 7. Am. Inst. Biol. Sci., Washington, D.C. P. 38–92.

Borror, D. J. and W. W. H. Gunn. 1965. Variation in white-throated sparrow songs. Auk **82:** 26–47.

Bremond, J. C. 1967. Reconnaissance de schémas reáctogènes liés à l'information contenue dans le chant territorial du rouge-gorge. Proc. 14th Int. Ornithol. Congr., Oxford, **1966:** 217–229.

Bremond, J. C. 1963. Acoustic behaviour of birds. *In:* R. G. Busnel, Ed. *Acoustic Behaviour of Animals.* Elsevier, Amsterdam. P. 709–750.

Brockway, B. F. 1965. Stimulation of ovarian development and egg laying by male courtship vocalization in budgerigars (*Melopsittacus undulatus*). Anim. Behav. **13:** 575–578.

Brockway, B. F. 1969. Roles of budgerigar vocalization in the integration of breeding behaviour. *In:* R. A. Hinde, Ed. *Bird Vocalizations: Their Relation to Current Problems in Biology and Psychology.* Cambridge University Press, Cambridge. P. 131–158.

Bullock, T. H. 1973. Seeing the world through a new sense: electroreception in fish. Am. Sci. **61:** 316–325.

Bunnell, P. 1973. Vocalizations in the territorial behavior of the frog (*Dendrobates pumilio*). Copeia **1973:** 277–284.

Burghardt, G. M. 1970. Defining "communication." *In:* J. W. Johnston, Jr., D. G. Moulton, and A. Turk, Eds. *Advances in Chemoreception.* Vol. 1: *Communication by Chemical Signals.* Appleton-Century-Crofts, New York. P. 5–18.

Busnel, R-G. 1963. On certain aspects of animal acoustic signals. *In:* R-G. Busnel, Ed. *Acoustic Behaviour of Animals.* Elsevier, Amsterdam. P. 69–111.

Caldwell, D. K. and M. C. Caldwell. 1972. Senses and communication. *In:* S. H. Ridgway, Ed. *Mammals of the Sea: Biology and Medicine.* Charles C. Thomas, Springfield. P. 419–465.

Caldwell, M. C. and D. K. Caldwell. 1967. Intraspecific transfer of information via the pulsed sound in captive odontocete cetaceans. *In:* R-G. Busnel, Ed. *Les Système Sonar Animaux Biologiques et Bioniques,* Laboratoire de Physiologie Acoustique, INRA-CNRZ—Jouy-en-Josas. P. 879–936.

Caldwell, M. C and D. K. Caldwell. 1968. Vocalization of naive captive dolphins in small groups. Science **159:** 1121–1123.

Caldwell, M. C. and D. K. Caldwell. 1970. Etiology of the chirp sounds emitted by the Atlantic bottlenosed dolphin: a controversial issue. Underwat. Nat. **6:** 6–8 and 43.

Caldwell, M. C., D. K. Caldwell, and N. R. Hall. 1972a. Ability of an Atlantic bottlenosed dolphin (*Tursiops truncatus*) to discriminate between and potentially identify to individual, the whistles of another species, the common dolphin (*Delphinius delphis*). ONR Tech. Rept. 9, Contract N 00014-70-C-0178. St. Augustine, Fla., Marineland Research Lab. 7 p.

Caldwell, M. C., N. R. Hall, and D. K. Caldwell. 1972b. Ability of an Atlantic bottlenosed dolphin to discriminate between and respond differentially to whistles of eight conspecifics. Tech. Rept. 10, Contract N 00014-70-C-0178. St. Augustine, Fla. Marineland Research Lab., 5 pp.

Campbell, H. W. 1973. Observations on the acoustic behavior of crocodilians. Zoologica **58:** 1–11.

Capranica, R. R. 1966. Vocal response to natural and synthetic mating calls. Acoust. Soc. Am. **40:** 1131–1139.

Capranica, R. R. 1968. The vocal repertoire of the bullfrog (*Rana catesbeiana*). Behaviour **31:** 302–325.

Capranica, R. R. 1972. Why auditory neurophysiologists should be more interested in animal sound communication. Physiologist **15:** 55–60.

Capranica, R. R. 1976. Morphology and physiology of the auditory system *In:* R. Llinas and W. Precht, Eds. *Frog Neurobiology.* Springer Verlag, Berlin. P. 551–575.

Capranica, R. R. and A. J. Moffat. 1975. Selectivity of the peripheral auditory system of spadefoot toads (*Scaphiopus couchi*) for sounds of biological significance. J. Comp. Physiol. **100:** 231–249.

Capranica, R. R., L. S. Frishkopf, and M. Goldstein, Jr. 1967. Voice and hearing in the bullfrog. *In:* W. Wathen-Dunn, Ed. *Models for the Perception of Speech and Visual Form.* MIT Press, Cambridge, Mass. P. 244–246.

Capranica, R. R., L. S. Frishkopf, and E. Nevo. 1973. Encoding of geographic dialects in the auditory system of the cricket frog. Science **182:** 1272–1275.

Cowan, P. J. 1974. Selective responses to the parental calls of different individual hens by young *Gallus gallus:* Auditory discrimination learning versus auditory imprinting. Behav. Biol. **10:** 541–545.

Cowan, P. J. and R. M. Evans. 1974. Calls of different individual hens and the parental control of feeding behavior in young *Gallus gallus*. J. Exp. Zool. **188:** 353–360.

Delco, E. A. 1960. Sound discrimination by males of two cyprinid fishes. Tex. J. Sci. **12:** 48–54.

Dumortier, B. 1963. The physical characteristics of sound emissions in arthropoda. *In:* R-G. Busnel, Ed. *Acoustic Behaviour of Animals.* Elsevier, Amsterdam. P. 583–654.

Elsner, N. 1974. Neuroethology of sound production in gomphocerine grasshoppers (Orthoptera: Acrididae). I. Song patterns and stridulatory movements. J. Comp. Physiol. **88:** 67–102.

Emery, A. R. 1968. Comparative ecology of damselfish (Pisces: Pomacentridae) at Alligator Reef, Florida Keys. Unpublished doctoral dissertation, University of Miami. 258 p.

Emlen, S. T. 1972. An experimental analysis of the parameters of bird song eliciting species recognition. Behaviour **42:** 130–171.

Evans, R. M. 1970. Parental recognition and the "mew call" in black-billed Gulls (*Larus bulleri*). Auk **87:** 503–513.

Evans, R. M. 1972. Development of an auditory discrimination in domestic chicks (*Gallus gallus*). Anim. Behav. **20:** 77–87.

Evans, R. M. and M. E. Mattson. 1972. Development of selective responses to individual maternal vocalizations in young *Gallus gallus*. Can. J. Zool. **50:** 777–780.

Falls, J. B. 1963. Properties of bird song eliciting responses from territorial males. Proc. 13th Int. Ornithol. Congr., Cornell, **1962:** 259–271.

Falls, J. B. 1969. Functions of territorial song in the white-throated sparrow. *In:* R. A. Hinde, Ed. *Bird Vocalizations: Their Relation to Current Problems in Biology and Psychology.* Cambridge University Press, Cambridge. P. 207–232.

Farentinos, R. C. 1974. Social communication of the tassel-eared squirrel (*Sciurus aberti*): A descriptive analysis. Z. Tierpsychol. **34:** 441–458.

Fay, R. R. 1972. Perception of amplitude-modulated auditory signals by the goldfish. J. Acoust. Soc. Amer. **52:** 660–666.

Feng, A. S., P. M. Narins, and R. R. Capranica. 1975. Three populations of primary auditory fibers in the bullfrog (*Rana catesbeiana*): Their peripheral origins and frequency sensitivities. J. Comp. Physiol. **100:** 221–229.

Fine, M. L., H. E. Winn, and B. Olla. 1977. Communication in fishes. *In* T. Sebeok, Ed. *How Animals Communicate.* Indiana University Press, Bloomington. P. 472–518.

Fish, J. F. 1969. The effect of sound playback on the toadfish (*Opsanus tau*). Dissertation Abstract, University of Michigan, Microfilm No. 70–14, 148. 3 p.

Fish, J. F. 1972. The effects of sound playback on the toadfish. *In:* H. E. Winn and B. L. Olla, Eds. *Behavior of Marine Animals: Current Perspectives in Research.* Vol. 2: *Vertebrates.* Plenum Press, New York. P. 386–432.

Forester, D. C. 1973. Mating call as a reproductive isolating mechanism between *Scaphiopus bombifrons* and *S. hammondii*. Copeia **1973:** 60–67.

Frankenberg, E. 1974. Vocalizations of males of three geographical forms of *Ptyodactylus* from Israel (Reptilia: Sauria: Gekkoninae) J. Herpetol. **8:** 59–70.

Frishkopf, L. S. and M. H. Goldstein. 1963. Responses to acoustic stimuli from single units in the eighth nerve of the bullfrog. J. Acoust, Soc. Am. **35:** 1219–1228.

Frishkopf, L. S., R. R. Capranica, and M. H. Goldstein, Jr. 1968. Neural coding in the bullfrog's auditory system—a teleological approach. Proc. IEEE **56:** 969–980.

Gehlbach, F. R. and B. Walker. 1970. Acoustic behavior of the aquatic salamander, *Siren intermedia*. Bio-Science **20:** 1107–1108.

Gerald, J. W. 1971. Sound production during courtship in six species of sunfish (Centrarchidae). Evolution **25:** 75–87.

Gerhardt, H. C. 1974. The vocalizations of some hybrid treefrogs: Acoustic and behavioral analyses. Behaviour **49:** 130–151.

Gerhardt, H. C. 1976. Significance of two frequency bands in long distance vocal communication in the green tree frog. Nature **261:** 692–694.

Griffin, D. R. 1958. *Listening in the Dark.* Yale University Press, New Haven. 413p.

Grimes, L. 1965. Antiphonal singing in *Laniarius barbarus* and the auditory reaction time. Ibis **107:** 101–104.

Grimes, L. 1966. Antiphonal singing and call notes of *Laniarius barbarus*. Ibis **108:** 122–126.

Ha, S. J. 1973. Aspects of sound communication in the damselfish *Eupomacentrus partitus*. Unpublished doctoral dissertation, University of Miami. 78 p.

Harbert, F., I. M. Young and C. H. Wenner. 1968. Auditory flutter fusion and envelope of signal. J. Acoust. Soc. Am. **44:** 803–806.

Hazlett, B. and W. H. Bossert. 1965. A statistical analysis of the aggressive communication systems of some hermit crabs. Anim. Behav. **13:** 357–373.

Heiligenberg, W. 1966. The stimulation of territorial singing in house crickets (*Acheta domesticus*). Z. Vergl. Physiol. **53:** 114–129.

Heiligenberg, W. 1969. The effect of stimulus chirps on a cricket's chirping (*Acheta domesticus*). Z. Vergl. Physiol. **65:** 70–97.

Heiligenberg, W. 1973. Electrolocation of objects in the electric fish *Eigenmannia* (Ramphichthyidae, Gymnotoidei). J. Comp. Physiol. **87:** 137–164.

Heiligenberg, W. 1974. Electrolocation and jamming avoidance in a *Hypopygus* (Ramphichthyidae, Gymnotoidei), an electric fish with pulse-type discharges. J. Comp. Physiol. **91:** 223–240.

Helversen, D. V. 1972. Gesang des Mannchens und Lautschema des Weibchens bei der Feldheuschrecke, *Chorthippus biguttulus* (Orthoptera, Acrididae). J. Comp. Physiol. **81:** 381–422.

Hobson, E. S. 1972. Activity of Hawaiian reef fishes during the evening and morning transitions between daylight and darkness. Fish. Bull. **70:** 715–740.

Hobson, E. S. 1974. Feeding relationships of teleostean fishes on coral reefs in Kona, Hawaii. Fish. Bull. **72:** 915–1031.

Hoffman, H. S. and J. L. Searle. 1967. Acoustic and temporal factors in the evocation of startle. J. Acoust. Soc. Am. **43:** 269–282.

Hopkins, C. D. 1974. Electric communication in fish. Am. Sci. **62:** 426–437.

Horch, K. and M. Salmon. 1973. Adaptations to the acoustic environment by the squirrelfishes (*Myripristis violaceus*) and *M. pralinus*. Mar. Behav. Physiol. **2:** 150–157.

Hoy, R. R. 1974. Genetic control of acoustic behavior in crickets. Am. Zool. **14:** 1067–1080.

Hoy, R. R., J. Hahn, and R. C. Paul. 1977. Hybrid cricket auditory behavior: evidence for genetic coupling in animal communication. Science **195:** 82–83.

Huber, F. 1962. Central nervous control of sound production in crickets and some speculations on its evolution. Evolution **16:** 429–441.

Hutchinson, R. E., J. G. Stevenson, and W. H. Thorpe. 1968. The basis for individual recognition by voice in the sandwich tern (*Sterna sandvicensis*). Behaviour **32:** 150–157.

Impekoven, M. 1973. The response of incubating laughing gulls (*Larus atricilla* L.) to calls of hatching chicks. Behaviour **46:** 94–113.

Jones, M. D. R. 1966. The acoustic behavior of the bush cricket (*Pholidoptera griseoaptera*). J. Exp. Biol. **45:** 15–44.

Konishi, M. 1970. Evolution of design features in the coding of species specificity. Am. Zool. **10:** 67–72.

Kutsch, W. and F. Huber. 1970. Zentrale versus periphere kontrolle des Gesangs von Grillen (*Gryllus campestris*). Z. vergl. Physiol. **67:** 140–159.

LeBoeuf, B. J. and L. F. Petrinovich. 1974. Elephant seals: Interspecific comparisons of vocal and reproductive behavior. Mammalia **38:** 16–32.

Littlejohn, M. J. 1960a. Call discrimination by female frogs of the *Hyla versicolor* complex. Copeia **1960:** 47–49.

Littlejohn, M. J. 1960b. Call discrimination and potential reproductive isolation in *Pseudacris triseriata* females from Oklahoma. Copeia **1960:** 370–371.

Littlejohn, M. J. 1961. Mating call discrimination by females of the spotted chorus frog (*Pseudacris clarki*). Tex. J. Sci. **13:** 49–50.

Littlejohn, M. J. and J. J. Loftus-Hills. 1968. An experimental evaluation of premating isolation in the *Hyla ewingi* complex (Anura: Hylidae). Evolution **22:** 659–663.

Littlejohn, M. J. and T. C. Michaud. 1959. Mating call discrimination by females of Streckers chorus frog (*Pseudacris streckeri*). Tex. J. Sci. **11:** 86–92.

Littlejohn, M. J. and G. F. Watson. 1974. Mating call discrimination and phonotaxis by females of the *Crinia laevis* complex (Anura: Leptodactylidae). Copeia **1974:** 171–175.

Loftus-Hills, J. J. and M. J. Littlejohn. 1971. Pulse repetition rate as the basis for mating call discrimination by two sympatric species of *Hyla*. Copeia **1971:** 154–156.

Marler, P. 1961. The logical analysis of animal consumption. J. Theor. Biol. **1:** 295–317.

Marler, P. 1967. Animal communication signals. Science **157:** 769–774.

Marler, P. 1973. A comparison of vocalizations of red-tailed monkeys and blue monkeys, (*Cercopithecus ascanius* and *C. mitis*) in Uganda. Z. Tierpsychol. **33:** 223–247.

Marler, P. 1974. Animal communication. *In:* L. Kramer, T. Alloway, and P. Pliner, Eds. *Nonverbal Communication.* Plenum Press, New York. P. 25–50.

Marler, P. and D. Isaac. 1960. Song variation in a population of brown towhees. Condor **62:** 272–283.

Martof, B. S. 1961. Vocalization as an isolating mechanism in frogs. Am. Midl. Nat. **61:** 118–126.

Mattson, M. E. and R. M. Evans. 1974. Visual imprinting and auditory-discrimination learning in young of the canvasback and semiparasitic redhead (Antidae). Can. J. Zool. **52:** 421–427.

Mayo, J. S. 1968. Pulse code modulation. Sci. Am. **218:** 102–108.

Michaud, T. C. 1962. Call discrimination by females of the chorus frogs *Pseudacris clarki* and *P. nigrita*. Copeia **1962:** 213–235.

Michelsen, A. 1966. Pitch discrimination in the locust ear: observations on single sense cells. J. Insectic. Physiol. **12:** 1119–1131.

Michelsen, A. 1971a. The physiology of the locust ear. I. Frequency sensitivity of single cells in the isolated ear. Z. Vergl. Physiol. **71:** 46–92.

Michelsen, A. 1971b. The physiology of the locust ear. II. Frequency discrimination based upon resonances in the tympanum. Z. Vergl. Physiol. **171:** 63–101.

Michelsen, A. 1974. Hearing in invertebrates. *In:* W. D. Keidel and W. D. Neff, Eds. *Auditory System-Anatomy, Physiology (Ear): Handbook of Sensory Physiology.* Vol. 5. Springer, New York. P 389–422.

Myrberg, A. A., Jr. 1971. Hearing and allied senses in fishes. Final Rept., NSF. 52 p.

Myrberg, A. A., Jr. 1972a. Ethology of the bicolor damselfish, *Eupomacentrus partitus* (Pisces: Pomacentridae): a comparative analysis of laboratory and field behaviour. Anim. Behav. Monogr. **5:** 197–283.

Myrberg, A. A. Jr. 1972b. Social dominance and territoriality in the bicolor damselfish. *Eupomacentrus partitus* (Poey) (Pisces: Pomacentridae). Behaviour **41:** 207–231.

Myrberg, A. A. Jr. 1972c Using sound to influence the behaviour of free-ranging marine animals. *In:* H. E. Winn and B. L. Olla, Eds. *Behavior of Marine Animals.* Vol. 2: *Vertebrates.* Plenum Press, New York. P. 435–468.

Myrberg, A. A., Jr. 1973. Underwater television—a tool for the marine biologist. Bull. Mar. Sci. **23:** 824–835.

Myrberg, A. A., Jr., and J. Y. Spires. 1972. Sound discrimination by the bicolor damselfish, *Eupomacentrus partitus.* J. Exp. Biol. **57:** 727–735.

Newman, J. D. and Z. Wollberg. 1973. Multiple coding of species-specific vocalizations in the auditory cortex of squirrel monkeys. Brain Res. **54:** 287–304.

Paillette, M. 1970. Conditions biophysiques du declenchement du signal sonore chez *Hyla meridionalis* (Amphibien, Anoure). Extrait de la Teu. et la Vie (2-1970): 251–300.

Paillette, M. 1971. Communication acoustique chez les Amphibiens Anoures. J. de Psychol. Norm. et Pathol. (3–4): 327–351.

Popper, A. N. 1972. Auditory threshold in the goldfish (Carassius auratus) as a function of signal duration. J. Acoust. Soc. Am. **52:** 596–602.

Pumphrey, R. J. 1961. Hearing in birds. *In:* A. J. Marshall, Ed. *Biology and Comparative Physiology of Birds.* Vol. 2. Academic Press, New York. P. 55–68.

Randall, J. E. 1967. Food habits of reef fishes of the West Indies. *In:* F. M. Bayer *et al.,* Eds. *Studies in Tropical Oceanography.* No. 5. University of Miami, Miami. P. 665–847.

Roeder, K. D. 1966. Auditory system of noctuid moths. Science **154:** 1515–1521.

Rowell, T. C. 1972. Agonistic sounds of the rhesus monkey (*Macaca mulatta*). Symp. Zool. Soc. London **8:** 91–96.

Schleidt, W. M. 1973. Tonic communication: continual effects of discrete signs in animal communication systems. J. Theor. Biol. **42:** 359–386.

Schwartzkopff, J. 1963. Morphological and physiological properties of the auditory system in birds. Proc. 13th Int. Ornithol. Congr., Cornell, **1962:** 1059–1068.

Schwartzkopff, J., and P. Winter. 1960. Zur Anatomie der Vogel—Cochlea unter natür-lichen Bedigungen. Biol. Zbl. **79:** 607–625.

Sebeok, T. A. 1965. Animal communication. Science **147:** 1006–1014.

Sebeok, T. Ed. 1977. *How Animals Communicate.* Indiana University Press, Bloomington. 1128 p.

Shaw, K. C. 1968. An analysis of the phonoresponse of males of the true katydid, *Pterophylla camelliofolia* (Fabricius). Behaviour **31:** 203–260.

Shuvalov, V. F. and A. V. Popov. 1973. [Significance of some of the parameters of the calling songs of male crickets, *Gryllus bimaculatus*, for phonotaxis of females]. Zh. Evol. Biokhim. Fiziol. **9:** 177–182.

Smith, C. L. and J. C. Tyler. 1972. Space resource sharing in a coral reef fish community. *In:* B. Collette and S. Earle, Eds. *Results of the Tektite Program: Ecology of Coral Reef Fishes.* Los Angeles County, Nat. Hist. Mus. Sci. Bull. (14). P. 125–170.

Spanier, E. 1975. Sound recognition by damselfishes of the genus, *Eupomacentrus*, from Florida waters. Unpublished doctoral dissertation, University of Miami. 145 p.

Stein, R. C. 1956. A comparative study of "advertising song" in the *Hylocichla* thrushes. Auk **73:** 503–512.

Stout, J. F. 1963. The significance of sound production during the reproductive behavior of *Notropis analostanus* (Family Cyprinidae). Anim. Behav. **11:** 83–92.

Stout, J. F. and F. Huber. 1972. Responses of central auditory neurones of female crickets (*Gryllus campestris* L.) to the calling song of the male. Z. vergl. Physiol. **76:** 302–313.

Tavolga, W. N. 1970. Levels of interaction in animal communication. *In:* L. R. Aronson, D. S. Lehrman, J. S. Rosenblatt, and E. Tobach, Eds. *Development and Evolution of Animal Behavior.* Freeman Press, San Francisco. P. 283–302.

Tembrock, G. 1963. Acoustic behavior of mammals. *In:* R-G. Busnel, Ed. *Acoustic Behavior of Animals.* Elsevier, Amsterdam. P. 751–786.

Thompson, N. S. 1969. Individual identification and temporal patterning in the cawing of common crows. Commun. Behav. Biol. Commun. No. 09690044.

Thorpe, W. H. 1963. Antiphonal singing in birds as evidence for avian auditory reaction time. Nature **197:** 774–776.

Thorpe, W. H. 1967. Vocal imitation and antiphonal song and its implications. Proc. 14th Int. Ornithol. Congr., Oxford, **1966:** 245–263.

Thorpe, W. H. and M. E. W. North. 1965. Origin of significance of the power of vocal imitation with special reference to the antiphonal singing of birds. Nature **1208:** 219–222.

Tretzel, E. 1965. Artkennzeichnende und reaktionsauslösende Komponeten im Gesang der Heidlerche (*Lullula arborea*). Verh. Dtsch. Zool. Ges. Jena: 367–380.

Tschanz, B. 1958. Trottellumen. Die Entstehung der persönlichen Beziehung zwischen Jungvögel und Eltern. Z. Tierpsychol. **4:** 1–103.

Tschanz, B. 1965. Beobachtungen und Experimente zur Entstehung der "Persönlichen" Beziehung zwischen Jungvögel und Eltern bei Trottellummen. Verh. Schweiz. Naturforsch. Ges., Zurich: 211–216.

Vaughan, T. A. 1972. *Mammology.* W. B. Saunders Co., Philadelphia. 463 p.

Walker, T. J. 1957. Specificity in the response of female tree crickets (Orthoptera, Gryllidae, Oecanthinae) to calling songs of the males. Ann. Entomol. Soc. Am. **50:** 626–636.

Watson, M. 1969. Significance of antiphonal song in the Eastern whipbird, *Psophodes olivaceus.* Behaviour **35:** 157–178.

Weeden, J. S. and J. B. Falls. 1959. Differential responses of male ovenbirds to recorded songs of neighboring and more distant individuals. Auk **76:** 343–351.

Wickler, W. 1972. Duettieren zwischen artverschiedenen Vögeln im Freiland. Z. Tierpsychol. **31:** 98–103.

Wickler, W. 1973. Artunterschiede im Duettgesang zwischen *Trachyphonus d'arnaudii usambiro* und den anderen Unterarten von *T. d'arnaudii*. J. Ornithol. **114:** 123–128.

Wickler, W., and D. Uhrig. 1969. Bettelrufe, Antwortszeit, und Rassenunterschiede im Bergrüssungsduett des Schmuckbartvogels *Trachyphonus d'arnaudii*. Z. Tierpsychol. **26:** 651–666.

Winn, H. E. 1964. The biological significance of fish sounds. *In:* W. N. Tavolga, Ed. *Marine Bio-Acoustics.* Vol. 2. Pergamon Press, New York. P. 213–231.

Winn, H. E. 1967. Vocal facilitation and the biological significance of toadfish sounds. *In:* W. N. Tavolga, Ed. *Marine Bio-Acoustics,* Vol. 2. Pergamon Press, New York. P. 283–303.

Winn, H. E. 1972. Acoustic discrimination by the toadfish with comments on signal systems. *In:* H. E. Winn and B. L. Olla, Eds. *Behavior of Marine Animals.* Vol. 2. Plenum Press, New York. P. 361–385.

Wodinsky, J. 1964. [Comments in General Discussion]. *In:* W. N. Tavolga, Ed. *Marine Bio-Acoustics.* Pergamon Press, New York. P. 249–250.

6

STABILITY OF TEMPERATURES PREFERRED BY CENTRARCHID FISHES AND TERRESTRIAL REPTILES

JOHN J. MAGNUSON
Laboratory of Limnology
Department of Zoology
University of Wisconsin, Madison

THOMAS L. BEITINGER
Department of Biological Sciences
North Texas State University
Denton, Texas

1 INTRODUCTION

Temperature regulation and other adaptations that allow animals to function in a varied thermal habitat are biologically important. They constitute chapter subjects in physiological texts (Bartholomew, 1968; Prosser, 1973; Hoar, 1975; Schmidt-Nielson, 1975) and numerous reviews (Dill, 1964; Rose, 1967; Kinne, 1970; Whittow, 1970; Hoar and Randall, 1971; Hamilton, 1973; Prechtel *et al.*, 1973; Wieser, 1973; Roberts, 1974), and they are active areas of research. Faced with varying thermal habitats, animals can thermoregulate physiologically, adjust biochemically to the changes, reduce the array of their vital functions, or thermoregulate behaviorally. In aquatic animals, behavioral thermoregulation is limited to the occupation of temperatures available in the habitat. Terrestrial animals can, in addition, posture themselves to alter rates of heat loss or gain.

Behavioral thermoregulation is the only means by which most fishes regulate body temperature. The distribution of fishes in space and time is strongly influenced by orientation or other behavioral responses to temperature gradients in nature. Temperature has been considered a primary environmental variable by zoogeographers (Hesse, Allee, and Schmidt, 1951; Ekman, 1967; Briggs, 1974); by fish physiologists and ecologists (Fry, 1947; Fry and Hochachka, 1970; Brett, 1970; Fry, 1971); by students of the effects of electrical power generation on aquatic organisms (Krenkel and Parker, 1969; Coutant, 1975); and by fishermen who earn a living by locating and capturing fishes at sea (Hela and Levastu, 1962). There is evidence that fishes have specialized in regard to thermal features of their habitat in the same manner as they have specialized relative to food type and size, active times in the diel cycle, predator avoidance, and so on. Specialization for a particular temperature regime, even in small lakes, can segregate fish species spatially in the habitat.

The purposes of this chapter are to: (1) examine the precision and stability of temperature preference in the sunfishes, family Centrarchidae, (2) consider those features of the environment that repress or alter temperature preference, and (3) compare these results with general features of temperature preference by terrestrial reptiles. Most data on fishes are taken from three Ph.D. theses at the University of Wisconsin-Madison (Neill, 1971; Beitinger, 1974a; Stuntz, 1975) and concern primarily the bluegill (*Lepomis macrochirus*), a common freshwater species in temperate lakes of North America. Data on terrestrial reptiles are from the general literature and are limited to diurnal species.

We thank Timothy C. Moermond, William H. Neill, Arthur A. Myrberg, Jr., William W. Reynolds, and Warren E. Stuntz for reading the manuscript and providing valuable comments.

2 TEMPERATURE PREFERENCES OF CENTRARCHIDS

2.1 Preferred Temperatures

2.1.1 Precision and Methods

Temperature preference has usually been measured by means of recording the position of fish in either horizontal or vertical temperature gradients in space (Fry and Hochachka, 1970). The final preferendum (Fry, 1947) is obtained when preferred temperature and acclimation temperature are equal, or when an active fish resides at a particular temperature in a spatial gradient of temperature after one or more days of experience.

Measurements of temperature preference (final preferendum) of fishes at the Laboratory of Limnology have been obtained by the alternate method of a temperature gradient in time (Neill, Magnuson, and Chipman, 1972). The temperature of the test aquarium is continually changing—either steadily upward or steadily downward (usually at 3°C/hour). An individual fish is given control of the direction of temperature change and, by alternating cooling and warming periods, can regulate the aquarium temperature. In this design, active behavioral thermoregulation is required—an inactive fish will either "cook" or "freeze." Cooling or heating is controlled when the fish swims past a pair of photocells located in a short tunnel connecting two halves of the tank (Fig. 6.1). Swimming in one direction activates heating; in the other direction, cooling. The two halves of the tank, separated by a partition, differ in temperature by 2°C. This difference provides a fish initial information about which side of the tank it should occupy to activate either warming or cooling. Both sides warm and cool at the same rate, and the 2°C difference is maintained.

In the above apparatus, centrarchid fishes maintain temperatures

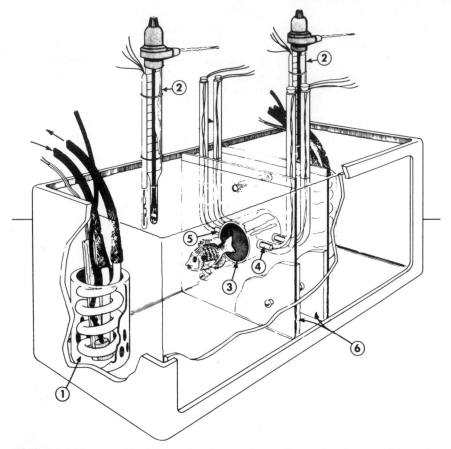

FIGURE 6.1 Diagram of tank to measure temperature preference in a temporal temperature gradient. (Adapted from Fig. 33 in Neill, 1971.) Components are indicated as follows: (1) cooling and heating elements; (2) thermistors and mercury contact thermometer; (3) tunnel; (4) photocells; (5) light source; (6) insulated partition.

within narrow limits. Maximum or minimum temperatures can be averaged to provide estimates of upper- and lower-avoidance temperatures. These two temperatures delimit a preferred range that has a width and a midpoint or preferred temperature. Data, collected several days after a fish is in the device, provide estimates of the final preferendum. Green sunfish (*Lepomis cyanellus*) provide an example of results (Fig. 6.2). While green sunfish allowed tank temperatures to fluctuate over a 10°C range, the preferred range was only 3.7°C wide. Fish maintained temperatures within the preferred range 71% of the time, and within 0.5°C of the preferred temperature 39% of the time. The grouped values are repeata-

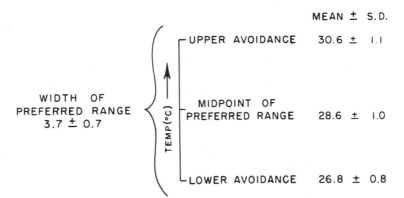

MEAN ± S.D.

UPPER AVOIDANCE 30.6 ± 1.1

WIDTH OF
PREFERRED RANGE
3.7 ± 0.7

MIDPOINT OF
PREFERRED RANGE 28.6 ± 1.0

LOWER AVOIDANCE 26.8 ± 0.8

FIGURE 6.2 Temperature preference statistics for 13 green sunfish measured over three diel periods. (Calculated from Beitinger *et al.*, 1975.)

ble and reasonably precise (S.D.= 0.7 and 1.1°C). Means and medians yield similar values (Beitinger *et al.*, 1975; Reynolds and Casterlin, 1976). Behavioral thermoregulation is similarly precise for other species (Neill and Magnuson, 1974). Measurements on the same species are repeatable at different laboratories (Reynolds and Casterlin, 1976; Beitinger, 1977).

Temperatures within the preferred range are strongly sought. Bluegill chose to thermoregulate actively in a temporal gradient rather than remain at constant temperatures only 1 to 2°C outside their preferred range (Beitinger, 1977). If preferred temperatures are not available in a temporal gradient, bluegill keep the tank temperatures as close as possible to their preferred range (Beitinger, 1977).

2.1.2 Comparisons among Species

Centrarchids prefer warm water (Table 6.1). In temporal gradients of temperature with single fish, their preferred temperature varied from 27.3 to 30.8°C among six species tested. The bluegill has the highest preference of 30.8°C and is closely followed by the black basses (*Micropterus* sp.). Other sunfish (*Lepomis* sp.), crappies (*Pomoxis* sp.), and rock bass (*Ambloplites rupestris*) prefer slightly cooler water, from 27.3 to 28.3°C. The similarity among species is perhaps more striking than the differences: all are within only 3.5°C of each other. All prefer temperatures warmer than surface temperatures and littoral-zone temperatures of most temperate-climate lakes in summer. This response would tend to attract centrarchids to the warmest temperatures available in most lakes; during summer these occur in the littoral zone or in powerplant outfalls.

TABLE 6.1 Temperature preference determined under laboratory conditions for centrarchids in temporal and spatial gradients. Based on summer conditions. Various measures of central tendency were used by different authors.

Species	Temporal Gradient		Spatial Gradient	
	°C	Source	°C	Source
Micropterus				
Smallmouth bass	30.1[a]	Reynolds & Casterlin (1976)	28.0	Fry (1950)
			30.0	Barans & Tubb (1973)
			30.1	Barans & Tubb (1973)
			31.0[c]	Peek (1965)
Largemouth bass	28.4[a]	Reynolds & Casterlin (1976)	30.0–32.0	Fry (1950)
	29.0[b]	Neill & Magnuson (1974)		
	30.1[a]	Reynolds, Casterlin, & Covert (1976)		
	30.2	Reynolds et al. (1976a)		
Mean	29.4			
Lepomis				
Redear sunfish			>32.0	Hill, Schnell, & Pigg (1975)
Bluegill	30.0[a]	Stuntz & Magnuson (1976)	26	Crawshaw, 1975
	30.4[b]	Neill & Magnuson (1974)		
	30.5[a]	Reynolds, Casterlin, & Covert (1976b)		
	31.0[a]	Reynolds & Casterlin (1976)	27.4	Reutter & Herdendorf (1974)
	31.2[a]	Beitinger & Magnuson (1975)	27.2	Hill, Schnell, & Pigg (1975)

Species				
	31.2 [a]	Beitinger (1974b)	31.7	Cherry et al. (1975)
	31.4 [a]	Beitinger (1975)	31.8	Fry & Pearson (1952)
Mean	30.8			
Green sunfish	28.2 [a]	Beitinger et al. (1975)	27.3	Jones & Irwin (1965)
			30.7	Cherry et al. (1975)
			>32.0	Hill, Schnell, & Pigg (1975)
Pumpkinseed			27.7	Reutter & Herdendorf (1974)
			28.5	Müller & Fry (1976)
			31.5	Anderson (1951)
Longear sunfish			23.5	Hill, Schnell, & Pigg (1975)
			29.2	Neill (1967)
Orangespotted sunfish			20.0	Hill, Schnell, & Pigg (1975)
Pomoxis				
Black crappie	27.9 [b]	Neill & Magnuson (1974)	21.7	Reutter & Herdendorf (1974)
White crappie			19.4	Reutter & Herdendorf (1974)
Ambloplites				
Rock bass	27.5 [b]	Neill & Magnuson (1974)	18.7	Reutter & Herdendorf (1974)

[a] Mean of day and night.
[b] Midpoint of day and night from Fig. 17 in original paper.
[c] Dominant fish.

Temperature preferences in spatial gradients are more variable than in temporal gradients (Table 6.1), including values as low as 18.7°C and as high as >32°C. We believe that these estimates are biased, either by the inactivity of fish at low temperatures, by interference in thermoregulatory behavior owing to social interactions, or by interference from water currents. Barans and Tubb (1973), testing individual smallmouth bass in a spatial gradient, obtained estimates identical to those derived from temporal gradients. Data on bluegill and a review of the literature (Beitinger and Magnuson, 1975) make it clear that agonistic behavior can bias results of temperature-preference experiments. Results of Hill, Schnell, and Pigg (1975) may be confounded by water currents.

Temperature perferences of centrarchids appear to be relatively independent of fish size, on the basis of measurements in temporal gradients. Beitinger and Magnuson (1975) observed no correlation ($r = -0.03$) between preferences and lengths of 35 bluegill from 7 to 14 cm. Their grand median, 31.2°C, was only 0.8°C warmer than the median preference of 13 smaller bluegill between 5 and 8 cm long (Neill and Magnuson, 1974). Similarly, 20 largemouth bass, 10 to 15cm long (Reynolds and Casterlin, 1976), had a preference only 0.6°C cooler than eight smaller largemouth 6.5 to 7.5 cm long (Neill and Magnuson, 1974). Measurements in spatial gradients provide more varied results for smallmouth bass and suggest that young-of-the-year fish prefer warmer water than adults, especially in fall and spring (Barans and Tubb, 1973). Temperatures occupied in the gradient were 1 to 7°C warmer for the young fish. This result may be confounded by a difference in the initial acclimation state betweeen small and large fish. Clarification of whether these conflicting results are due to interspecific differences or methods of measurement requires additional study.

In conclusion, temperature preference by centrarchids is a species-specific characteristic that varies little within the family. It can be precisely determined in laboratory experiments. For centrarchids, experiments with temporal gradients or solitary fish produce the most consistent results.

2.1.3   Relation to Distribution in Nature

Temperature preference is an important determinant of distribution in nature. Neill and Magnuson (1974) compared the distribution of centrarchids in the thermal outfall of a power plant at Lake Monona, Wisconsin, with temperatures preferred in the laboratory. Temperature in the littoral zone ranged from 27 to 35°C and spanned the preferred temperatures of the species. The highest temperatures were from the influence of the thermal effluent of a power generating plant. Temperatures occupied in the field were estimated from body temperatures of fishes captured by electroshocking. Body temperature was measured with a thermistor as soon as each fish was caught and provided a best estimate of recent thermal history of the fish. Correspondence between laboratory and field results are dramatic (Table 6.2), and it is clear that temperature preference plays an important role in segregation of various centrarchids in aquatic habitats, even though differences in preferences are slight. Body temperatures of largemouth bass monitored via an ultrasonic tag indicate that maximum temperatures occupied in the field average 27°C, even when temperatures as warm as 32°C are nearby (Coutant, 1975). These temperatures are only 2°C below the preferred temperatures of young fish.

Warm temperatures preferred by centrarchids would certainly be important in their segregation from mesothermal species, such as the yellow perch (*Perca flavescens*) and the walleye (*Stizostedion vitreum*), or the cold water stenotherms, such as the salmonids.

2.2 Sensitivity to Changes in Physical Conditions

The stability of temperature preference of centrarchids is considered below in regard to physical features of the habitat. Seasonal and diel changes in light regimes and temperature might be expected to influence greatly the thermal behavior of a fish in temperate climates. In addition, patterns of the physical structure of the habitat might be expected to repress the distributional responses to temperature.

TABLE 6.2 Relation between preferred temperature and temperature occupied during daylight in the thermal plume from a power plant at Lake Monona, Wisconsin (Neill and Magnuson, 1974)

Species	Laboratory Preference (°C)	Body Temperature in Lake (°C)	Difference (°C)
Bluegill	30.3	29.4	+0.9
Largemouth bass	29.1	29.7	−0.6
Black crappie	28.3	28.3	0.0
Rock bass	27.3	27.5	−0.2

2.2.1 Light

Temperature preferences of centrarchids in temporal gradients are similar during day and night, even though centrarchids are diurnal or somewhat crepuscular animals in regard to feeding and locomotor activity (Fig. 6.3). Day and night differences in both upper-avoidance temperatures and lower-avoidance temperatures were not significant for largemouth bass, black crappie, or rock bass (Neill and Magnuson, 1974), or for green sunfish (Beitinger et al., 1975). The mean temperature of the tanks being regulated by centrarchid species were compared for day and night by Beitinger (1975), and Reynolds and Casterlin (1976). Thermal behavior did not differ significantly betweeen day and night for bluegill, largemouth bass, or smallmouth bass. All differences, however, were in the direction of being cooler at night. Reynolds and Casterlin (1976) observed that temperature distribution was more skewed to the low temperatures at night and that modal temperatures were 1 to 3°C cooler at night. Thus, in the laboratory, centrarchids behave very similarly during day and night but demonstrate a slight tendency to regulate at cooler temperatures at night. Significant day and night differences in median body temperature of centrarchids in the field (as much as 3°C for large bluegill), documented by Neill and Magnuson (1974), apparently do not result from a diel change in temperature preference. Temperature preference is remarkably stable throughout the diel period.

Seasonal changes in temperature preference of bluegill are not induced by changes in photoperiod, nor is temperature preference altered

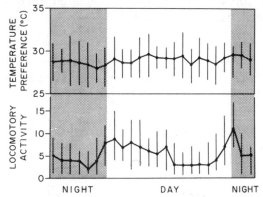

FIGURE 6.3 Diel changes in the temperature preference and locomotory activity of green sunfish. Preferred temperatures are indicated by upper- and lower-avoidance temperatures and the midpoint of this range. Locomotor activity is indicated by median and quartiles of the number of tunnel passes/fish/hr. (Adapted from Beitinger et al., 1975.)

by exposure to unnatural photoperiods (Table 6.3). Experiments with a variety of acclimation temperatures and feeding regimes are grouped by photoperiods characteristic of summer, spring and fall, winter, and unnatural. For each condition, means of lower-avoidance temperature ranged from 28.8 to 30°C; for upper-avoidance temperature, from 32.2 to 33.4°C; and for midpoints of preferred range, from 29.6 to 31.6°C. In a matched experiment of fish acclimated to 25°C, but at photoperiods of 15:9 and 9:15 (see footnote in Table 6.3), thermal preferences were almost the same, 31.0 and 29.9°C respectively. Thus, the temperature preferred by bluegill and the seasonal changes in the temperatures they occupy in temperate lakes are not altered by changed photoperiods.

During all seasons, centrarchids would be expected to occupy the warmest waters available, namely the littoral zone or surface waters in summer and the deep (4°C) waters in winter. Direct observations during daylight show that they concentrate in the littoral zone in summer (Stuntz, 1975) and in deeper water in winter (Magnuson and Karlin, 1970). Largemouth bass in nature occupied the warmest waters available until water temperatures exceeded 27°C (Coutant, 1975).

In spatial gradients, seasonal differences in temperature preference were observed for smallmouth bass (Barans and Tubb, 1973) and for pumpkinseed (*Lepomis gibbosus*), white crappie (*Pomoxis annularis*), and rock bass (Reutter and Herdendorf, 1974). For smallmouth bass, winter and summer preferences differed by as much as 18°C. We think the differences result because in the spatial gradient a fish is not forced by changing temperatures to thermoregulate actively, and, as a consequence, the experiments were too brief for fish to attain the final preferendum. In Fig. 2 of Barans and Tubb (1973), it is apparent that the fish in winter are rapidly changing acclimation state, yet the estimates of preferred temperature included the periods of change. In addition, the fish were not fed during the experiment, and the declining temperature preference common in Fig. 2 of Barans and Tubb (1973) may be a consequence of the feeding regime. Stuntz and Magnuson (1976) present evidence that bluegill with a negative energy budget choose lower temperatures than those with a positive energy budget.

Light intensity might also influence temperature preference. Warmer temperatures are found near the surface where light is bright. A preference for low light levels could interfere, override, or suppress the expression of a temperature preference. Bluegill do prefer lower light intensities when given the choice between two light levels in a shuttle box (Stuntz, 1975). In the laboratory, they chose the dim light even when it took them out of their preferred temperature. Thus, a gradient of light intensity alters the expression of temperature preference by the bluegill

TABLE 6.3 Relation between preferred temperature of bluegill and photoperiod measured in a temporal gradient tank

Photoperiod	Hours (light–dark)	Source	Temperatures		
			Lower Avoidance	Midpoint	Upper Avoidance
Summer	15–9	Beitinger (1974a), Table 15	—	31.0[a]	—
		Beitinger (1975)	29.8	31.4	33.0
		Beitinger (1974a)	30.2	31.8	33.4
		Beitinger (1974a)	29.9	31.8	33.6
		Beitinger (1974a)	30.3	32.0	33.7
Mean			30.0	31.6	33.4
	14–10	Neill & Magnuson (1974)	28.5	30.4	32.4
		Beitinger (1976)	29.5	31.2	33.1
		Beitinger (1974b)	29.4	31.2	33.1
Mean			29.1	30.9	32.9
Spring and fall	12–12	Beitinger (1975)	29.1	31.1	33.1
		Stuntz & Magnuson (1976), growing	—	31.2	—
		Stuntz & Magnuson (1976), not growing	—	29.8	—
Mean			29.1	30.7	33.1
Winter	9–15	Beitinger & Magnuson (1976)	—	29.2[b]	—
		Beitinger (1974a), Table 15	—	29.9[a]	—
Mean			—	29.6	—
Unnatural	24–0	Beitinger (1975)	29.9	31.4	33.0
	6–6	Beitinger (1975)	28.8	30.9	33.0
Mean			29.4	31.2	33.0

[a] Matched experiment with acclimation temperature of 25°C. Sample size: 10 and 9 fish.
[b] Acclimated to 5°C.

in the laboratory. Stuntz (1975) points out that cover from aquatic-rooted vegetation and fallen trees can reduce light intensity in the littoral zone, and a response to light intensity may influence distribution in shallow warm areas.

In summary, of the effects of light on temperature preference of centrarchids, preference in a temporal gradient is generally the same during day and night and is unchanged by seasonal changes in photoperiod. However, the expression of temperature preference can be repressed by a preference for low light levels in a light gradient.

2.2.2 Temperature

The final temperature preferendum by definition should not be influenced by acclimation temperature unless adequate time is not provided for the fish to change its acclimation state. Reynolds and Casterlin (1976) reported that fish acclimated to temperatures above 15 to 20°C should be able to attain their final preferendum within 24 hours owing to the rapid rate at which they can change acclimation state upward. Our work at the Laboratory of Limnology strongly supports this conclusion.

Beitinger (1974a) acclimated bluegill to 5, 21, 25, 27, 31, and 34°C, and then measured their temperature preference from 24 to 72 hours after they were placed in a temporal gradient tank. Estimates of preferred temperature differed by less than 0.5°C for fish acclimated to 21 to 31°C. Fish acclimated to 5°C for more than a month allowed the temperature of their tank to increase so rapidly that all died unless the temperature rise was stopped at 19°C for 24 hours. This apparently allowed their acclimation state to catch up with their preference (Beitinger and Magnuson, 1976). After this, a preference of 29.2°C was recorded, which is within 2.2°C of fish acclimated to temperatures between 21 and 31°C. Hence the long-term acclimation to 5°C had little effect on the bluegills' preferred temperature. Interestingly, bluegill acclimated to 34°C preferred temperatures of 28.2°C, or almost 3°C below those preferred by fish acclimated to 21 to 31°C. The explanation for this is unclear. The 34°C temperature is the upper-avoidance temperature for bluegill and is only 2 to 3°C below their incipient lethal temperature (Speakman and Krenkel, 1971). Perhaps there was some damage to the fishes' thermal regulatory machinery. Stuntz and Magnuson (1976) noted that bluegill in a negative-energy budget chose cooler temperatures. Perhaps holding fish for 1 month at 34°C prior to testing placed fish in a negative-energy balance and therefore induced selection of cooler water. Whatever the cause, the final preferred temperatures, ranging from 28.2 to 31.4°C, were relatively insensitive to acclimation temperatures from 5 to 34°C.

However, as expected, temperatures preferred after only one hour in a spatial gradient tank did differ among acclimation temperatures of 16, 21, and 26°C for five centrarchid species (Hill, Schnell and Pigg, 1975). Preferences differed by 0.5 to 6.5°C for a 5°C change in acclimation temperature.

Temperature preference of bluegill is little influenced by short-term exposure to extreme temperatures. Bluegill acclimated to 31°C and exposed for 30 min to either 36.1 or 21°C had preferred temperatures within 0.7°C of control fish (Beitinger, 1974b).

The temperatures preferred by bluegill do not depend on the rate of temperature change (Beitinger, 1976). In most of our experiments in temporal gradients, the temperature changed 3°C/hour. If the rate of heating was only one half the rate of cooling, or vice versa, bluegill had upper- and lower-avoidance temperatures within 0.3°C of controls with equal rates of heating and cooling (Beitinger, 1976).

The temperature preferred in a temporal gradient also did not depend on a temperature difference between the two sides of the test tank (Neill, Magnuson, and Chipman, 1972). An experiment on a bluegill with the temperature the same on both sides gave similar results to one with a 2°C difference. Apparently, bluegill are able to respond to temporal changes in temperature alone and do not depend on a comparison of temperature differences in space to thermoregulate accurately.

In summary, long- and short-term exposure to temperatures different from the final preferendum, as well as rates of warming and cooling, had little or no influence on the temperatures preferred by bluegill after 24 hours in a temporal gradient.

2.2.3 Physical Structure of the Habitat

Bluegill in a shuttle-box-preference tank were given a choice of sparse or dense cover, and of fine or coarse substrate (Stuntz, 1975). They usually chose the side of the tank with coarse substrate. Fish also selected the side with dense cover during day, but chose the side with sparse cover at night. Stuntz argued that preference for coarse substrate and, during day, for dense cover were adaptations to avoid predation. He considered that choice of sparse cover at night might also make escape from a predator easy.

Assuming that choice of suitable cover and substrate do reduce predation, it is interesting to see whether these preferences repress temperature preference. Stuntz (1975) gave the fish a choice of their preferred temperature in their unpreferred cover or substrate. In both cases, the fish chose the preferred temperature over their preferred cover or substrate. Thus, preferred substrate structure and macrophyte density, at least at the levels measured, do not appear to suppress temperature preference.

2.2.4 Summary of Responsiveness to Physical Conditions

Behavioral thermoregulation by centrarchids seems little influenced by changes in physical properties, such as day versus night, photoperiod, acclimation temperature, exposure to extreme temperatures, and cover and substrate structure. Only a preference for dim light seemed to override a highly stable, unresponsive character-temperature preference. The stability of temperature preference appeared greater when estimates were made in temporal gradients of temperature than in spatial gradients of temperature, apparently because the temporal system demands rapid, active, and precise behavioral thermoregulation, whereas a spatial gradient does not. Apparently, most seasonal, diel, and other changes in temperature occupied by centrarchids are not induced by changes in temperature preference. Their thermal behavior seems reasonably straightforward. They almost always prefer a temperature warmer than available in their natural habitat (exclusive of thermal effluents from power plants). This behavior would contribute to their presence in the warmer littoral zone in summer and (apparently) in warmer deep water in winter.

2.3 Sensitivity to Changes in Biotic Conditions

This section deals with temperature preference in relation to biotic factors at the individual organism level and considers whether thermoregulatory behavior of centrarchids is influenced as little by biotic factors as by the physical factors discussed in Section 2.2.

Within a preferred physical habitat, of which temperature is one feature, a successful animal must locate and efficiently process food, must avoid predation, and must relate to a number of possible competitors, parasites, and mutualists. Thermoregulatory behavior evolved in concert with these biotic factors; hence, biotic factors most likely contributed importantly to the selective presssures that led to a species' preferred temperature. Yet a rigid adherence to preferred temperatures is likely to be disadvantageous in the complexity of real environments. Thus, learning also is probably important in an animal's compromise between occupying preferred temperatures and avoiding predators and social dominants (negative stimuli) or obtaining food (a nonthermal reward).

Departure from preferred temperature is in itself a negative reinforcement, and the animal apparently is able to scale and balance these assorted reinforcements and behave accordingly.

2.3.1 Food Supply and Its Distribution

The abundance and distribution of food influences the thermoregulatory behavior of centrarchids. The quantity of food eaten by a centrarchid in a day is not only influenced by habitat temperature, but in turn influences the temperatures the fish select (Stuntz, 1975; Stuntz and Magnuson, 1976). The distribution of food, especially if more abundant outside a fish's preferred temperature range, can repress a fish's preferred temperature response (Neill and Magnuson, 1974).

Daily ration of centrarchids is influenced by habitat temperature (Stuntz, 1975). When provided earthworms in excess, bluegill increased their consumption from almost nothing at 4°C to an equivalent of about 12% of the body weight per day (wet weight) at 19°C. Over the range of 19 to 31.5°C, consumption leveled off at about 11 to 13% of body weight. Consumption increased to 15.5% at 34°C, but this increase was not statistically different from consumption levels at lower temperatures. To reiterate, food consumption varied directly with temperature in the cool range but was relatively constant from 19 to 34°C—a 15°C range that includes the 4°C preferred range of 29 to 33°C. Data on the efficiency of food utilization and growth at various temperatures are somewhat contradictory (Banner and Van Arman, 1973; Beitinger, 1974a; Stuntz, 1975) for centrarchids, but growth generally increases with temperature at cooler temperatures, is relatively constant from 22 to 31.5°C, and declines near 35°C.

If a bluegill can only obtain a ration so small that the fish loses weight, then occupation of a cooler temperature might reduce metabolic demands sufficiently to bring energy gains and losses into more favorable balance. Kitchell *et al.* (1974) observed that bluegill in nature stopped growing in midsummer, and concluded that high metabolic demands induced by high temperatures were the explanation. Stuntz and Magnuson (1976) recorded the thermal behavior of bluegill at four rations, some of which resulted in gains and others in losses in body weight. Bluegill that were losing weight preferred temperatures in a 6 day test of 29.8°C, or 1.4°C lower than those that were gaining weight. This difference, while small, was statistically significant. Fish receiving a ration of 2% body weight/day were most interesting. At their pretest acclimation temperature of 25°C, they had been gaining weight. When allowed to thermoregulate, these fish increased their tank temperature into the preferred range, but then began to lose weight at these warmer tempera-tures. After three days of regulating within the preferred range, prefer-red temperatures began to decline at a rate of about 2°C/day. Median preferred temperatures were near 24°C, or well out of the preferred temperature range of bluegill, at the end of the 6 day experiment. A disconcerting observation to the validity of these experiments was that fish not fed did not exhibit a declining temperature preference. Perhaps it can be argued that fish being fed nothing could not balance their energy budget by preferring cooler temperatures, but those at a 2% ration could. Interestingly, bluegill acclimated to 34°C presented the only other example of a progressive decline in preferred temperature (Beitinger, 1974a). Eight out of nine fish had a lower preferred tempera-ture on day 4 than day 1, with a mean decrease of 1.2°C during the 4 day experiment. Feeding experiments of Stuntz (1975) indicate that during pretest acclimation, 34°C fish probably were not receiving an adequate daily ration and, hence, were also in a negative-energy budget.

The influence of ambient temperature upon maintenance metabolism (and required daily food ration) and their relationship to temperature-preference behavior requires further study. For further discussion of the relation between energetic and thermal ecology of fish, readers are refer-red to Brett (1971).

In summary of the above, bluegill losing weight prefer slightly cooler temperatures than those gaining weight and may decrease their prefer-ence by at least 6°C when such a change has the effect of apparently producing a positive energy budget.

If food is unavailable within the preferred range, fish could forage into warmer or cooler temperatures to obtain food. An experiment (Neill and Magnuson, 1974) estimated what extremes of temperature bluegill, 6 to 9 cm long, will enter to obtain food. Aquaria in Fig. 6.1 were adapted so that the preferred temperature was on one side of the partition, and temperatures as much as 12°C different from preferred were on the other side. When food was presented on the side with nonpreferred tempera-tures, a bluegill could swim through the tunnel, thus activating a feeder that provided one food pellet for each 5 min spent at the nonpreferred temperatures. Control experiments where food was presented on the side with the preferred temperature were also conducted.

At the beginning of the experiments, when temperatures were the same on both sides of the tank, bluegill spent 73% of their time on the side where food was available (Fig. 6.4). Bluegill voluntarily exposed themselves to temperatures at least 5°C above and 11°C below the mid-point of the preferred range to obtain food. Fish occupied the extreme temperature of about 4.5°C above and 9°C below preferred temperatures for about 8% of the daylight period to obtain a ration of up to 2% body weight per day (Fig. 6.4). High temperatures imposed a more restrictive limit on feeding activity than did cool temperatures, probably because the preferred temperature of bluegill is so near their upper-lethal temperature. In the controls, when food was provided only on the side with the preferred temperature, bluegill spent 3% or less of their daylight hours at any temperature that exceeded either the upper- or lower-avoidance temperature—that is, outside of their preferred range. Thus, when food is present at preferred temperatures, bluegill are expected to stay within their preferred range, but when food is available only outside their preferred range, bluegill will violate the limitation of their avoidance temperatures to obtain food.

In summary, the abundance and the spatial distribution of food in relation to temperature can significantly alter and repress the thermal regulatory behavior of centrarchids.

2.3.2 Distribution of Conspecifics

The density of fish in an area or the presence of larger dominant fish may alter the thermal selection of centrarchids. Crowded fish may tend to disperse from preferred habitat, and subordinate animals may be displaced from preferred habitat. Although the influence of density has

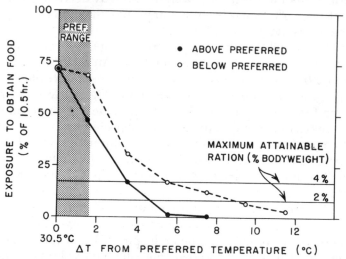

FIGURE 6.4 The percentage of daylight hours that young bluegill will expose themselves to nonpreferred temperatures to obtain food. 30.5°C is the midpoint of the preferred range, and the abscissa is °C either above or below that temperature. See text for explanation. (Adapted from Fig. 18a in Neill and Magnuson, 1974.)

not been examined, intraspecific social behavior has been shown to alter thermal behavior of subordinate centrarchids (Peek, 1965; Beitinger and Magnuson, 1975). A number of authors have commented that social behavior interferes with determinations of unbiased estimates of temperature preference (Pearson, 1952; Neill, 1967; Barans and Tubb, 1973; Beitinger and Magnuson, 1975).

Data from Peek (1965) indicate that the largest smallmouth bass in a spatial-temperature gradient occupied the preferred temperatures typical of the species, and progressively smaller individuals were forced to occupy sequentially lower temperatures. Position in the social hierarchy determined the temperature occupied, and the smallest fish in three separate experiments were found dead in the compartment with the lowest temperature (21 or 17°C). Bluegill 9 to 11 cm long spent less than 1% of their time at the preferred temperature when given a choice between their preferred temperature plus a larger bluegill, 13 to 16 cm long, and temperatures either 4°C below or 3°C above the midpoint of their preferred range (Beitinger and Magnuson, 1975). The highest temperature (34°C) they occupied was only 2 to 3°C below incipient upper-lethal temperature (Speakman and Krenkel, 1971). In these experiments, food was provided only on the side of the tank at preferred temperatures. Thus, social hierarchy exerted a great influence on the location of the smaller fish. Subordinate bluegill occupied an area without food and at nonpreferred temperatures to avoid a dominant conspecific.

In conclusion, under laboratory conditions, fish with low social rank are forced to occupy temperatures that are not preferred, even if that position also restricts them from obtaining food or locates them in a lethal temperature. The location of a dominant animal appears to exert a greater influence on a bluegill's response to temperature than did the distribution and abundance of food discussed in Section 2.3.1.

2.3.3 Distribution of Predators

The influence of predators on the expression of thermal selection by centrarchids has not been examined. One might expect that the presence of a predator would repress temperature preference, as an obvious generalization from the effect of dominant conspecifics described in Section 2.3.2. A number of predators of centrarchids have temperature preferences that are similar to those of centrarchids, and some centrarchids are piscivorous themselves—for example, largemouth and smallmouth bass. Since small centrarchids share their preferred thermal range with predators, they might be expected to escape by taking refuge in nonpreferred temperatures.

Several arguments can be raised to counter this idea. First, predators could pursue prey into nonpreferred temperatures and, because of their greater mass, their body temperatures would be less immediately affected by the temperature change than would the body temperature of the prey. Second, sudden temperature shock modifies the activity of bluegill (Beitinger, 1974b) and the swimming performance of juvenile largemouth bass (Hocutt, 1973). These changes could be expected to increase the susceptibility of the small centrarchids to predation, not only during their exposure to extreme temperature but also on return to the preferred temperature. Increased susceptibility to predation resulting from exposure to extreme temperatures is well documented in young salmonids (Sylvester, 1972; Coutant, 1973). Third, when approached by the predator largemouth bass, bluegill in the littoral zone seek cover in vegetation and fallen trees, rather than in deeper, cooler water offshore (Stuntz, 1975). In addition, their preference in the laboratory for low-light, dense, simulated macrophyte cover and coarse substrate appears to be related to predator avoidance within the warm waters of the littoral zone.

In summary, while no data are available on the direct effect of a predator on the temperature-selection behavior of centrarchids, we expect that, in field situations, occupation or penetration of nonpreferred temperature to avoid a predator is not likely to be a successful adaptation.

2.3.4 Response to Infection

Reynolds *et al.* (1976*b*) injected centrarchids with a bacterium, *Aeromonas hydrophila*, that causes haemorrhagic septicaemia and compared the thermal selection behavior with controls. After the injections of the bacterium, the mean temperature preferred in a temporal gradient tank increased 2.1°C for two largemouth bass and 2.7°C for eight bluegill. These resulting preferred temperatures are above the upper-avoidance temperatures recorded for these species as listed in Table 6.1. One unusual bluegill preferred 37.2°C, which is above the lethal temperature. Control fish did not alter their thermal-selection behavior. Reynolds *et al.* (1976b) concluded that this "behavioral fever" may be adaptive.

2.3.5 Summary of Responsiveness to Biotic Conditions

In contrast to the minimal influence of physical factors on thermal-selection behavior, biotic factors had a large influence on the expression of temperature preference (Table 6.4). Centrarchids were willing to violate both their upper- and lower-avoidance temperature, and occupied temperatures frequently differing 2 to 14°C from the midpoint of the preferred-temperature range. On the high-temperature side, they occupied temperatures of at least 34°C to obtain food and avoid social dominants, and 33.2°C when injected with a pathogenic bacterium. On the low-temperature side, they occupied temperatures at least as low as 21.5°C to obtain food, and 17°C to avoid a dominant conspecific. In addition, at low daily rations, preferences declined at least 6°C, while with no food, preferences were about 2°C below fish that were eating enough to grow. Violations of the lower-avoidance temperature were greater than for the upper-avoidance temperature, perhaps because the upper-avoidance temperature is so close to the upper-lethal temperature. Biotic factors repress temperature preference and greatly expand the range of temperatures that centrarchids can be expected to occupy in nature.

3 COMPARISON WITH TERRESTRIAL REPTILES

Comparisons of temperature-selection behavior of centrarchids will be limited almost exclusively to terrestrial reptiles that are diurnally active and that behaviorally regulate their body temperature during the day. These reptiles regulate their body temperatures mainly, but not exclusively, by contact with warm or cool substrates—that is, thigmothermic behavior, or by controlled exposure to the sun's radiation—that is, heliothermic behavior (see Templeton, 1970; Dawson, 1967, 1975). Regulation of their body temperature is similar in form to that of a fish in a temporal-gradient tank. For example, by moving from sun to shade— that is, by alternating periods of heating and cooling—a heliothermic reptile can regulate body temperature. Devices to determine thermoregulation of reptiles take advantage of this principle (Stebbins, 1963; Licht et al., 1966; DeWitt, 1967a; Vaughn et al., 1974).

3.1 Precision and Methods

The precision of temperature selection will be compared primarily between the green sunfish (Beitinger et al., 1975) and the desert iguana, *Dipsosaurus dorsalis* (DeWitt, 1967a; Vaughn, Bernheim, and Kluger, 1974), because similar data sets are available. Beitinger et al. (1975) used the temporal gradient described in Section 2.1; DeWitt (1967a) utilized a heliothermic apparatus in which the desert iguana could move back and

TABLE 6.4 Stability of temperature preference by bluegill related to physical and biotic features as determined in laboratory experiments

Condition	Maximum Influence on Preferred Temperature (ΔT in °C)	Maximum Influence on Temperature Occupied to Obtain or Avoid Nonthermal Factor (ΔT in °C)	Source
Physical			
Day vs. night	0.25	—	Beitinger (1975)
	0.1	—	Reynolds & Casterlin (1976)
Photoperiod (winter vs. summer)	0.1	—	Table 3 for fish acclimated to 25°C
Photoperiod (natural vs. unnatural)	0.5	—	Table 3
Light intensity (bright vs. dim)	—	At least 3.0	Stuntz (1975)
Acclimation temperature			
(21–31°C)	0.4	—	Beitinger (1974a)
(5–34°C)	3.2	—	Beitinger (1974a)
Temperature shock			
(31–21°C)	0.1	—	Beitinger (1974b)
(31–36.1°C)	0.7	—	Beitinger (1974b)

Cover (dense vs. sparse)	—	0	Stuntz (1975)
Substrate (coarse vs. fine)	—	0	Stuntz (1975)
Biotic			
Food deprivation (14 days)	1.4	—	Stuntz & Magnuson (1976)
Negative energy budget at a ration of 2% body weight per day	6.0	—	Stuntz & Magnuson (1976)
Food available only above[a] preferred temperature	—	4.5	Neill & Magnuson (1974)
Food available only below[a] preferred temperature	—	9.0	Neill & Magnuson (1974)
Presence of larger dominant bluegill at preferred temperatures	—	at least 4.0 at least 14.0	Beitinger & Magnuson (1975) Peek (1965)
Presence of predator at preferred temperatures	—	?	—
Bacterial infection	2.7	—	Reynolds, Casterlin, & Covert (1976)

[a] Volitional exposure for 8% of time to obtain ration of up to 2% body weight per day.

forth from low to high radiation; Vaughn, Bernheim, and Kluger (1974) had a thigmothermic bichambered cage in which the iguana could move back and forth from warm and cool substrate. For the fish, water temperatures were monitored as close estimates of fish body temperature (see Reynolds *et al.*, 1976). In the iguana experiments, body temperatures were monitored directly.

The desert iguana prefer temperatures about 10°C warmer than do green sunfish, but the similarity in the precision of their thermoregulatory behavior is remarkable (Fig. 6.5). The full range of temperatures obtained is 10°C in both species, and the percentage of time spent at various temperatures within the range is similar. Upper- and lower-avoidance temperatures bracket a preferred range of 3.7°C for green sunfish and 3.9°C for desert iguana. Standard deviations of upper and lower avoidance temperatures are about 1°C for both species. The major difference in precision is that the iguana data seem more skewed to the left than those for the green sunfish; however, data for other centrarchids are also skewed to the left (Reynolds and Casterlin, 1976).

The similarity in precision of behavioral thermoregulation may be more general. The widths of the preferred ranges for four centrarchids other than green sunfish are 3.6 to 3.8°C (Neill and Magnuson, 1974), and repeated measurements on the bluegill (Table 6.3) average 3.7°C. In

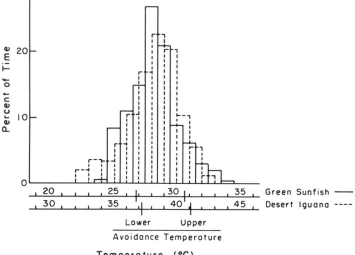

FIGURE 6.5 Comparison of the precision of thermoregulation of the green sunfish and the desert iguana. Data on green sunfish from Beitinger *et al.* (1975). Data on desert iguana from DeWitt (1967a) for histogram, and from Vaughn, Bernheim, and Kluger (1974) for avoidance temperatures.

the case of lizards, the preferred range averaged 3.9°C for six species of horned lizards, *Phrynosoma* sp. (Heath, 1962). These values were measured as the difference in body temperature between times of seeking shade and of reentering the sun under field conditions. Laboratory data of colon temperatures of the blue-tongued lizard, *Tiliqua scincoides*, are not quite as precise, and the preferred ranges averaged 6.8°C on three individuals (Hammel, Caldwell, and Abrams, 1967).

Many data on preferred range of temperatures in reptiles are based on averages of maximum and minimum body temperature observed in a given time interval, and are not mathematically equivalent to the preferred range as defined and used here. For our purposes the preferred range is defined as the interval between upper- and lower-avoidance temperatures. Measurements by Licht *et al.* (1966) are more equivalent to the full range of temperatures obtained by an animal in a gradient. These full ranges in a temporal gradient are 6 to 9°C wide during day for three centrarchids, and they average 7.6°C (Reynolds and Casterlin, 1976). Comparable ranges are: 3 to 10°C for 28 species of agamid, scincid, and gekkonid lizards, with a mean range of 6.1°C (Licht *et al.*, 1966); 6.3 to 7.6°C in three *Anolis* sp. (Corn, 1971); 6 to 10°C, mean 7.8°C, from repeated measurements by McGinnis (1966) on the western fence lizard; and 9°C for the gecko, *Coleonyx variegatus* (Vance, 1973). Other workers measured wider ranges of 17°C for the skinks, *Eumeces laticeps* (Pentecost, 1974); 16.2°C for the western fence lizard, and 16.5°C for the sagebrush lizard, *Sceloporus graciosus* (Mueller, 1970); and 10°C and 25°C for the smooth snake, *Coronella austriaca* (Spellerberg and Phelps, 1975).

Green sunfish and the desert iguana, and perhaps fishes and reptiles generally, have similar abilities to thermoregulate accurately. The similarities lie in precision of control and in the basis of the control process. Heath (1962) referred to one of the control processes used by reptiles as the simplest possible. It depends on an "on" and an "off" setting on an internal "thermostat," at the lower- and upper-avoidance temperatures. In response to these two limits, reptiles and fishes alternate periods of heating and cooling. Other control mechanisms also were discussed by Heath (1960).

Differences in the abilities of fishes and reptiles to thermoregulate accurately are to be found in the array of behavioral and physiological mechanisms available for thermoregulation. For example, posturing in relation to radiation, and panting for evaporative cooling, allow reptiles to maintain body temperatures as much as 30°C above (Pearson, 1954) and 5°C below (Whitfield and Livezey, 1973) ambient air temperature. In addition, some reptiles can elevate temperatures with endothermic heat production (Bartholomew and Tucker, 1964; Hutchison, Dowling, and

Vinegar, 1966; Vinegar, Hutchison, and Dowling, 1970). These and other mechanisms possible for reptiles are discussed in Porter and Gates (1969), Templeton (1970), Porter *et al.* (1973), and Dawson (1975). Fish, unless rapidly moving between two different temperatures or producing considerable endothermic heat, will have the same temperature as the habitat they occupy. Conduction of heat across the body and gill surfaces is essentially the only physical process of heat exchange between fish and their habitat. With large gill surfaces in direct contact with water, equilibration between the temperature of a fish and water is rapid, at least in small fish (Stevens and Fry, 1970, 1974). With the exceptions of tunas and lamnid sharks (Carey *et al.*, 1971; Stevens and Neill, 1976), the body temperatures of fishes at equilibrium are seldom more than 1°C higher than ambient.

3.2   Correspondence with Field Data

As with the centrarchids (Table 6.2), the relations between preferred temperature measured in the laboratory and temperature of reptiles in the field is close, provided the habitat has features that allow behavioral thermoregulation. Deviations between preferred temperatures of reptiles and those measured during day in the field without regard to sign averaged 1.2°C for all species (Licht *et al.*, 1966), 1.1°C for five species (Bradshaw and Main, 1968), and 0.3 to 1.8°C for five species (McGinnis and Dickson, 1967; McGinnis, 1966; Pianka and Parker, 1975; Huey, 1974a; Pentecost, 1974). Occasional differences as high as 3.5°C (Licht *et al.*, 1966), 4.6°C during winter (McGinnis, 1966), 3.1°C (DeWitt, 1967b), and 1.6 to 3.5°C (Vernon and Heatwole, 1970) are reported but are the exceptions. They are usually believed to result because the habitat does not allow better regulation, or because the energetic costs of shuttling between shade and basking sites are too high (Huey, 1974b).

In contrast to the close agreement between preferred temperatures and temperatures of active diurnal species, temperatures of active nocturnal species are 5 to 20°C below their preferred temperatures (Licht *et al.*, 1966).

3.3   Sensitivity to Physical Conditions

In contrast to centrarchids, preferred temperatures differ greatly between day and night for diurnal reptiles. Day-active, terrestrial reptiles often retreat to burrows or cover at night, become inactive, and allow their body temperatures to cool (Templeton, 1970). Apparently, some lizards even prefer a cooler temperature at night, and do not merely tolerate a cooler temperature (Regal, 1967; Hutchison and Kosh, 1974; Myhre and Hammel, 1969; Spellerberg, 1974). Temperatures preferred at night were below those voluntarily occupied during day, and median temperatures were 10 to 16°C below those preferred during day. Regal (1967) reasons that the active selection of cooler temperatures at night is adaptive for desert reptiles because it prevents confusion in their shelter-seeking behavior during the time when habitat temperatures are declining. Some reptiles, such as the water snake, *Natrix erythrogaster*, prefer similar temperatures throughout the diel period (Gehrmann, 1971). Centrarchids differ from most reptiles by preferring similar temperatures during day and night. Similarly, the water habitat of centrarchids is not characterized by large diel variations in temperature, such as those found in desert habitats.

Diurnal terrestrial reptiles have similar preferred temperatures throughout the year that are little influenced by photoperiod and acclimation temperature. The same is true of centrarchids. Differences among seasons for lizards collected from the field and tested in laboratory gradients averaged only 1.2°C for *Anolis carolinensis* (Licht, 1967), 0.9°C for the western fence lizard (McGinnis, 1966), and 3.4°C for the sagebrush lizard (Mueller, 1969). Stebbins (1963) found no significant shifts in the preferred temperatures of surface-active, striped plateau lizards, *Sceloporus virgatus*, examined in laboratory photothermal gradients during winter, spring, and summer. The *A. carolinensis*, acclimated at photoperiods of 6 and 14 hours of light, preferred temperatures within 1°C of each other, and those in constant darkness were within 1.0 to 1.3°C of those with 14 hours of light (Licht, 1968). In constant light, two *Lacerta* sp. preferred temperatures within 0.3°C of those with 12 hours of light (Spellerberg, 1974), and the water skink, *Sphenomorphus quoyi*, in continuous light preferred temperatures 1.2°C warmer than in continuous darkness (Vernon and Heatwole, 1970). Only one experiment seems to show an influence of photoperiod (Ballinger, Hawker, and Sexton, 1969). The lizard, *Sceloporus udatus*, in a thigmotactic gradient selected temperatures that averaged about 6°C cooler with 6 hours of light than with 12 hours of light. In this case, the substrate temperature rather than body temperature was recorded, and measurements were apparently averaged over light and dark periods. We think these data may be biased by the averaging of day and night preferences when selection of cooler temperatures in darkness is for longer periods, when days are short.

Temperature acclimation has little effect on preferred temperature.

Temperature acclimation to 20°C to 32°C, and to temperature fluctuation from 20 to 32°C altered temperature preference by less than 1.5°C in *A. carolinensis* (Licht, 1968). A skink, *Eumeces laticeps,* acclimated to 14, 22, or 28°C, preferred temperatures within 1.2°C (Pentecost, 1974). The western fence lizard, acclimated to 12 and 25°C, preferred temperatures within 0.5°C of each other (Wilhoft and Anderson, 1960), but those acclimated to 35°C chose temperatures 3.5°C below controls. The 35°C was 2 to 3°C above the temperature preferred by these lizards. In conclusion, the only significant effect of photoperiod and temperature acclimation is the selection of cooler temperature by those acclimated to temperatures above their preferred level. These features are consistent with the response of the bluegill to temperature acclimation.

In summary of sensitivity to physical conditions, centrarchids and diurnal terrestrial reptiles do not have the same diel pattern of temperature preference, but do have the same response to photoperiod and temperature acclimation.

3.4 Sensitivity to Biological Interactions

Ingestion of a meal seems to increase the temperature preferred by reptiles. This relationship may be analogous to the decrease in preference noted in centrarchids when deprived of food (see Sec. 2.3.1). Lizards (Regal, 1966), snakes (Regal, 1966; Kitchell, 1969), and turtles (Gatten, 1974) chose temperatures when fed that averaged 1.1 to 16°C warmer. Higher temperatures of reptiles after a meal have been reasoned to enhance digestion and to result from increased basking after eating. Cooler preferences by fish when fed low rations (Stuntz and Magnuson, 1976) have been inferred to adaptive reduction of energy expenditure when less food is available.

We found no references particularly relevant to invasion of nonpreferred temperatures by lizards in order to obtain food, but foraging behavior was observed to continue at temperatures outside the preferred range (Huey and Webster, 1975).

Desert iguana involved in territorial fighting allowed body temperature to rise to 45.9°C, or 7.4°C above their preferred temperature (DeWitt, 1967a). Hertz (1974) suggested that selection of a perch site by forest *Anolis* sp. was little constrained by the need to thermoregulate. He suggested that resource partitioning among species, social interactions, and predator avoidance were more important. Huey (1974b) noted that in open habitat, *Anolis cristatellus* maintained good control of body temperature, but in the forest it did not. He concluded that to remain in suitable basking sites in the forest required considerable movement from tree to tree and would be a significant energy expenditure for thermoregulation. Regardless of explanation, a number of forest species have broad ranges of body temperature in the field (Ruibal and Philibosian, 1970).

Temperatures of 46.4 to 46.8°C, or about 8°C above preferred temperatures, were observed in desert iguana that remained motionless in the direct sun near an observer (see DeWitt, 1967a). Apparently, the behavior was an antipredator response. Bustard (1967) suggested that nocturnal feeding in some lizards may have evolved in response to higher predation hazards during the day. These lizards are active at temperatures below those preferred in a gradient.

The desert iguana also has been demonstrated in the laboratory to exhibit a behavioral fever of about 2°C after injection of *Aeromonas* bacteria (Vaughn, Bernheim, and Kluger, 1974). The fever may be a useful adaptation because, when the fever is repressed by drugs, mortality is higher (Bernheim and Kluger, 1976).

Data on responses of reptiles to biotic factors are very limited, but are similar to those noted for centrarchids. Feeding history, agonistic behavior, and bacterial infection alter or override temperature preference.

3.5 Summary of Similarities and Differences

The similarities and differences between centrarchids and diurnal terrestrial reptiles are summarized in Table 6.5. In spite of the fact that these animals are in different classes (fishes and reptiles) and dwell in different habitats (aquatic and terrestrial), there are a surprising number of similarities in their thermoregulatory behavior. Comparable data on the influence of predators and the distribution of food supply are not available, but our guess is that the influence of these biotic factors on thermal behavior would be similar for centrarchids and terrestrial reptiles. The three major differences (Table 6.5) seem closely related to differences in the thermoregulatory potentials for an ectotherm in a terrestrial and an aquatic habitat. The centrarchids prefer the warmest temperature available to fishes from temperate climates, and cannot take thermoregulatory advantage of the sun's radiation or of evaporative cooling to maintain body temperatures different from the medium. In the absence of radiation or evaporation, reptiles are also dependent on the habitat temperature. Their body temperatures, for example, decline markedly at night along with the temperature of the habitat.

TABLE 6.5   Similarities and differences in the thermoregulatory behavior of centrarchid fishes and diurnal, terrestrial reptiles

Similarities

1. Precision of regulation
2. High correspondence between temperature preference in laboratory gradients and body temperatures in nature
3. No marked seasonal changes in preferred temperature
4. Photoperiod does not influence preferred temperature
5. Only acclimation to temperatures above preferred temperature alter preferred temperature
6. Food deprivation lowers preferred temperature
7. Agonistic behaviors cause animals to violate their preferred temperature range
8. *Aeromonas* bacterial infections induce a behavioral fever

Differences

1. Some reptiles prefer temperatures 10°C warmer than centrarchids
2. Reptiles can regulate temperatures above or below air temperature. Centrarchids are essentially the same temperature as the water they inhabit
3. Reptiles prefer cooler temperatures at night; centrarchids do not

4   POSTSCRIPT

The purpose of this chapter has been to relate the thermal behavior of centrarchids and to compare it, from general reviews, with a terrestrial group. This exercise has led us to several conclusions. First, review articles and literature on temperature preference dwell on differences rather than similarities and have, we think, occasionally masked the general view. Review articles in themselves were not adequate for comparisons between fish and reptiles because they were not sufficiently detailed. Comparisons made here required reference to primary literature. Second, centrarchids and terrestrial reptiles are much alike in regard to many features of thermoregulation. The similarity between groups so widely separated in phylogeny and habitat suggests that other fishes may have thermal-selection behavior much like that of centrarchids. Temperature preferences (final preferenda) in other fishes may be equally precise, generally insensitive to changes in physical conditions, and significally altered by biotic factors. Finally, a point well recognized in the reptile literature but often confused in the fish literature, is that preferred temperature is measured in the laboratory where interfering factors can be eliminated. Temperature preference is only one of many factors that relate to habitat selection and temperature occupation in nature. Biotic factors, such as distribution of food, social interaction, and the location of predators, have the effect of significantly widening the thermal habitat of centrarchids and, most likely, of other fishes as well.

REFERENCES

Anderson, R. C. 1951. Preferred temperature of a sample of *Lepomis gibbosus,* the pumpkinseed. Ontario Fisheries Research Laboratory Library, Toronto (from Ferguson, 1958).

Ballinger, R. E., J. Hawker, and O. J. Sexton. 1969. The effect of photoperiod acclimation on the thermoregulation of the lizard, *Sceloporus udatus.* J. Exp. Zool. **171:** 43–48.

Banner, A. and J. A. Van Arman. 1973. Thermal effects on eggs, larvae, and juveniles of bluegill sunfish. Ecol. Res. Ser. E. P. A. R3-73-041. 111 p.

Barans, C. A. and R. A. Tubb. 1973. Temperatures selected seasonally by four fishes from western Lake Erie. J. Fish. Res. Board Can. **30:** 1697–1703.

Bartholomew, G. A. 1968. Body temperature and energy metabolism. *In:* M. S. Gordon, G. A. Bartholomew, A. D. Grinell, C. B. Jorgensen, and F. N. White, Eds. *Animal Function: Principles and Adaptations.* Macmillan, New York. P. 290–354.

Bartholomew, G. A. and V. A. Tucker. 1964. Size, body temperature, thermal conductance, oxygen consumption, and heart rate in Australian varanid lizards. Physiol. Zool. **37:** 341–354.

Beitinger, T. L. 1974a. Influence of abiotic and biotic factors on the stability of behavioral thermoregulation in fishes, particularly the bluegill. Unpublished doctoral dissertation, University of Wisconsin–Madison. 240 p.

Beitinger, T. L. 1974b. Thermoregulatory behavior and diel activity patterns of bluegill, *Lepomis macrochirus,* following thermal shock. Fish. Bull. **72:** 1087–1093.

Beitinger, T. L. 1975. Diel activity rhythms and thermoregulatory behavior of bluegill in response to unnatural photoperiods. Biol. Bull. **149:** 96–108.

Beitinger, T. L. 1976. Behavioral thermoregulation by bluegill (*Lepomis macrochirus*) exposed to various rates of temperature change. *In:* G. W. Esch and R. W. McFarlane, Eds. *Thermal Ecology II. Proceedings of a Symposium Held at Augusta, Ga., April 2–5, 1975.* A. E. C. Symposium Series, CONF-750425. P. 176–179.

Beitinger, T. L. 1977. Thermal preference behavior of bluegill (*Lepomis macrochirus*) subjected to restrictions in available temperature range. Copeia, **1977:** 536–541.

Beitinger, T. L. and J. J. Magnuson. 1975. Influence of social rank and size on thermoselection behavior of bluegill (*Lepomis macrochirus*). J. Fish. Res. Board Can. **32:** 2133–2136.

Beitinger, T. L. and J. J. Magnuson. 1976. Low thermal responsiveness in the bluegill, *Lepomis macrochirus.* J. Fish. Res. Board Can. **33:** 293–295.

Beitinger, T. L., J. J. Magnuson, W. H. Neill, and W. R. Shaffer. 1975. Behavioral thermoregulation and activity patterns in the green sunfish, *Lepomis cyanellus.* Anim. Behav. **23:** 222–229.

Bernheim, H. A. and M. J. Kluger. 1976. Fever: effect of drug-induced antipyresis on survival. Science **193:** 237–239.

Bradshaw, S. D. and A. R. Main. 1968. Behavioral attitudes and regulation of temperature in *Amphibolurus* lizards. J. Zool. (London) **154:** 193–221.

Brett, J. R. 1970. Fishes, functional responses. *In:* O. Kinne, Ed. *Marine Ecology, a Comprehensive, Integrated Treatise on Life in Oceans and Coastal Waters.* Vol. I. *Environmental factors, Part I.* Wiley-Interscience, New York. P. 515–560.

Brett, J. R. 1971. Energetic responses of salmon to temperature. A study of some thermal relations in the physiology and freshwater ecology of sockeye salmon (*Oncorhynchus nerka*). Am. Zool. **11:** 99–113.

Briggs, J. C. 1974. *Marine Zoogeography.* McGraw-Hill, New York. 475 p.

Bustard, H. R. 1967. Activity cycle and thermoregulation in the Australian gecko *Gehyra variegata*. Copeia **1967:** 753–758.

Carey, F. G., J. M. Teal, J. W. Kanwisher, and K. D. Lawson. 1971. Warm-bodied fish. Am. Zool. **11:** 137–145.

Cherry, D. S., K. L. Dickson, and J. Cairns, Jr. 1975. Temperatures selected and avoided by fish at various acclimation temperatures. J. Fish. Res. Board Can. **32:** 485–491.

Corn, M. J. 1971. Upper thermal limits and thermal preferenda for three sympatric species of *Anolis*. J. Herpetol. **5:** 17–21.

Coutant, C. C. 1973. Effect of thermal shock on vulnerability of juvenile salmonids to predation. J. Fish. Res. Board Can. **30:** 965–973.

Coutant, C. C. 1975. Temperature selection by fish—a factor in power-plant impact assessments. *In: Environmental Effects of Cooling Systems at Nuclear Power Plants. I A E A Proc. IAEA-SM-187/11:* 575–597.

Crawshaw, L. I. 1975. Twenty-four hour records of body temperature and activity in bluegill sunfish (*Lepomis macrochirus*) and brown bullhead (*Ictalurus nebulosus*). Comp. Biochem. Physiol. **51A:** 11–14.

Dawson, W. R. 1967. Interspecific variation in physiological responses of lizards to temperature. *In:* W. W. Milstead, Ed. *Lizard Ecology, a Symposium.* University of Missouri Press, Columbia, Missouri. P. 230–257.

Dawson, W. R. 1975. On the physiological significance of the preferred body temperature of reptiles. *In:* D. M. Gates and R. B. Schmerl, Eds. *Perspectives of Biophysical Ecology.* Springer-Verlag, New York. P. 443–473.

DeWitt, C. B. 1967a. Precision of thermoregulation and its relation to environmental factors in the desert iguana, *Dipsosaurus dorsalis*. Physiol. Zool. **40:** 49–66.

DeWitt, C. B. 1967b. Behavioral thermoregulation in the desert iguana. Science **158:** 809.

Dill, D. B., Ed. 1964. *Handbook of Physiology.* Sec. 4: Adaptations to the environment. American Physiological Society, Washington, D.C. 1056 p.

Ekman, S. 1967. *Zoogeography of the Sea.* Sidgwick and Jackson, London. 417 p.

Ferguson, R. G. 1958. The preferred temperature of fish and their midsummer distribution in temperate lakes and streams. J. Fish. Res. Board Can. **15:** 607–624.

Fry, F. E. J. 1947. Effects of the environment on animal activity. Univ. Toronto Stud., Biol. Ser. 55; Publ. Ontario Fisheries Research Laboratory 68. 62 p.

Fry, F. E. J. 1950. Temperature preference and cruising speed of largemouth and smallmouth bass in relation to acclimation temperature. Ontario Fisheries Research Laboratory Library, Toronto. (from Ferguson, 1958).

Fry, F. E. J. 1971. The effect of environmental factors on the physiology of fish. *In:* W. S. Hoar and D. J. Randall, Eds. *Fish Physiology.* Vol. VI. *Environmental Relations and Behavior.* Academic Press, New York. P. 1–98.

Fry, F. E. J. and P. W. Hochachka. 1970. Fish. *In:* G. C. Whittow, Ed. *Comparative Physiology of Thermoregulation.* Vol. 1. Academic Press, New York. P. 79–134.

Fry, F. E. J. and B. E. Pearson. 1952. Some temperature relations of the pumpkinseed and bluegill sunfish. Publ. Ontario Fisheries Research Laboratory. 10 p.

Gatten, R. E., Jr. 1974. Effect of nutritional status on the preferred body temperature of the turtles *Pseudemys scripta* and *Terrapene ornata*. Copeia **1974:** 912–917.

Gehrmann, W. H. 1971. Influence of constant illumination on thermal preference in the immature water snake, *Natrix erythrogaster transversa*. Physiol. Zool. **44:** 84–89.

Hamilton, W. J. III. 1973. *Life's Color Code*. McGraw-Hill, New York. 238 p.

Hammel, H. T., F. T. Caldwell, Jr., and R. M. Abrams. 1967. Regulation of body temperature in the blue-tongued lizard. Science **156:** 1260–1262.

Heath, J. E. 1962. Temperature regulation and diurnal activity in horned lizards. Univ. Calif. Pub. Zool. **64:** 97–129.

Hela, I., and T. Laevastu. 1970. *Fisheries Oceanography*. Fishing News Books Ltd. 238 p.

Hertz, P. E. 1974. Thermal passivity of a tropical forest lizard, *Anolis polylepis*. J. Herpetol. **8:** 323–327.

Hesse, R., W. C. Allee, and K. P. Schmidt. 1951. *Ecological Animal Geography*. 2nd ed. John Wiley and Sons, New York. 715 p.

Hill, L. G.; G. D. Schnell, and J. Pigg. 1975. Thermal acclimation in sunfishes (*Lepomis*, Centrarchidae). Southwest. Nat. **20:** 177–184.

Hoar, W. S. 1975. *General and Comparative Physiology*. 2nd ed. Prentice-Hall, Englewood Cliffs, N. J. 848 p.

Hocutt, C. H. 1973. Swimming performance of three warm-water fishes exposed to a rapid temperature change. Chesapeake Sci. **14:** 11–16.

Huey, R. B. 1974a. Winter thermal ecology of the iguanid lizard *Tropidurus peruvianus*. Copeia **1974:** 149–155.

Huey, R. B. 1974b. Behavioral thermoregulation in lizards: importance of associated costs. Science **184:** 1001–1003.

Huey, R. B. and T. P. Webster. 1975. Thermal biology of a solitary lizard: *Anolis marmoratus* of Guadeloupe, Lesser Antilles. Ecology **56:** 445–452.

Hutchison, V. H. and R. J. Kosh. 1974. Thermal regulatory functions of the parietal eye in the lizard *Anolis carolinensis*. Oecologia (Berlin) **16:** 173–177.

Hutchison, V. H., H. G. Dowling, and A. Vineger. 1966. Thermoregulation in a brooding female Indian python, *Python molurus bivittatus*. Science **151:** 694–696.

Jones, T. C. and W. H. Irwin. 1965. Temperature preferences by two species of fish and the influence of temperature on fish distribution. Proc. 16th Annual Conf. Southeast Game and Fish Comm.: 323–333.

Kinne, O. 1970. *Marine Ecology, a Comprehensive, Integrated Treatise on Life in Oceans and Coastal Waters*. Vol. I: *Environmental factors*, Part I, Chapter 3—Temperature. Wiley-Interscience, New York. 681 p.

Kitchell, J. F. 1969. Thermophilic and thermophobic responses of snakes in a thermal gradient. Copeia **1969:** 189–191.

Kitchell, J. F., J. F. Koonce, R. V. O'Neill, H. H. Shugart, Jr., J. J. Magnuson, and R. S. Booth. 1974. Model of fish biomass dynamics. Trans. Am. Fish. Soc. **103:** 786–798.

Krenkel, P. A. and F. L. Parker. 1969. *Biological Aspects of Thermal Pollution*. Vanderbilt University Press, Nashville, Tenn. 407 p.

Licht, P. 1968. Response of the thermal preferendum and heat resistance to thermal acclimation under different photoperiods in the lizard *Anolis carolinensis*. Am. Midl. Nat. **79:** 149–153.

Licht, P., W. R. Dawson, V. H. Shoemaker, and A. R. Main. 1966. Observations on the thermal relations of Western Australian lizards. Copeia **1966:** 97–110.

Magnuson, J. J. and D. J. Karlin. 1970. Visual observations of fish beneath the ice in a winterkill lake. J. Fish. Res. Board Can. **27:** 1059–1068.

McGinnis, S. M. 1966. *Sceloporus occidentalis:* preferred body temperature of the western fence lizard. Science **152:** 1090–1091.

McGinnis, S. M. and L. L. Dickson. 1967. Thermoregulation in the desert iguana *Dipsosaurus dorsalis*. Science **156:** 1757–1759.

Mueller, C. F. 1969. Temperature and energy characteristics of the sagebrush lizard (*Sceloporus graciosus*) in Yellowstone National Park. Copeia **1969:** 153–160.

Mueller, C. F. 1970. Temperature acclimation of two species of *Sceloporus*. Herpetologica **26:** 83–85.

Müller, R. and F. E. J. Fry. 1976. The preferred temperature of fish: a new method. J. Fish. Res. Board Can. **33.** In press.

Myhre, K., and H. T. Hammel. 1969. Behavioral regulation of internal temperature in the lizard *Tiliqua scincoides*. Am. J. Physiol. **217:** 1490–1495.

Neill, W. H. 1967. Factors affecting heat resistance and temperature selection in the longear sunfish, *Lepomis megalotus*. Unpublished M.S. thesis, University of Arkansas. 63 p. (as cited in Neill, 1976).

Neill, W. H. 1971. Distributional ecology and behavioral thermoregulation of fishes in relation to heated effluent from a steam-electric power station (Lake Monona, Wisconsin). Unpublished doctoral dissertation, University of Wisconsin–Madison. 203 p.

Neill, W. H. 1976. Mechanisms of behavioral thermoregulation in fishes. Electric Power Research Institute Special Report 38. *In: Report of a Workshop on the Impact of Thermal Power Plant Cooling Systems on Aquatic Environments.* Vol. 2. P. 156–169.

Neill, W. H. and J. J. Magnuson. 1974. Distributional ecology and behavioral theremoregulation of fishes in relation to heated effluent from a power plant at Lake Monona, Wisconsin. Trans. Am. Fish. Soc. **103:** 663–710.

Neill, W. H., J. J. Magnuson, and G. D. Chipman. 1972. Behavioral thermoregulation by fishes: a new experimental approach. Science **176:** 1443–1445.

Pearson, B. E. 1952. The behavior of a sample of hybrid trout (*Salvelinus fontinalis X Cristivomer namaycush*) in a vertical temperature gradient. Ontario Fisheries Research Laboratory Library, Toronto. 24 p.

Pearson, O. P. 1954. Habits of the lizard, *Liolaemus multiformis multiformis,* at high altitudes in southern Peru. Copeia **1954:** 111–116.

Peek, F. W. 1965. Growth studies of laboratory and wild population samples of smallmouth bass, *Micropterus dolomieu* Lacépède, with application to mass marking of fishes. Unpublished M.S. thesis, University of Arkansas. 116 p.

Pentecost, E. D. 1974. Behavior of *Eumeces latipes* exposed to a thermal gradient. J. Herpetol. **8:** 169–173.

Pianka, E. R. and W. S. Parker. 1975. Ecology of horned lizards: A review with special reference to *Phrynosoma platyrhinos.* Copeia **1975:** 141–162.

Porter, W. P. and D. M. Gates. 1969. Thermodynamic equilibria of animals with environment. Ecol. Monogr. **39:** 245–270.

Porter, W. P., J. W. Mitchell, W. A. Beckman, and C. B. DeWitt. 1973. Behavioral implications of mechanistic ecology, thermal and behavioral modeling of desert ectotherms and their microenvironment. Oecologia (Berlin) **13:** 1–54.

Precht, J., J. Christophersen, H. Hensel, and W. Larcher. 1973. *Temperature and Life.* Springer-Verlag, New York. 779 p.

Prosser, C. L. 1973. *Comparative Animal Physiology,* 3rd ed. W. B. Saunders, Philadelphia. 966 p.

Regal, P. J. 1966. Thermophilic response following feeding in certain reptiles. Copeia **1966:** 588–590.

Regal, P. J. 1967. Voluntary hypothermia in reptiles. Science **155:** 1551–1553.

Reutter, J. M. and C. E. Herdendorf. 1974. Laboratory estimates of the seasonal final temperature preferenda of some Lake Erie fish. Proc. 17th Conf. Great Lakes Res. **1974:** 59–67.

Reynolds, W. W., and M. E. Casterlin. 1976. Thermal preferenda and behavioral thermoregulation in three centrarchid fishes. *In:* G. W. Esch and R. W. McFarlane, Eds. *Thermal Ecology II: Proceedings of a Symposium Held at Augusta, Ga., April 2–5, 1975.* A. E. C. Symposium Series CONF-750425. P. 185–190.

Reynolds, W. W., M. E. Casterlin, and J. B. Covert. 1976. Behavioural fever in teleost fishes. Nature **259:** 41–42.

Reynolds, W. W., R. W. McCauley, M. E. Casterlin, and L. I. Crawshaw. 1976. Body temperatures of behaviorally thermoregulating largemouth blackbass (*Micropterus salmoides*). Comp. Biochem. Physiol. **54A:** 461–463.

Roberts, J. L. 1974. Temperature acclimation and behavioral thermoregulation in cold-blooded animals. Fed. Proc. **33:** 2155–2161.

Rose, A. H., Ed. 1967. *Thermobiology.* Academic Press, New York. 653 p.

Ruibal, R. and R. Philibosian. 1970. Eurythermy and niche expansion in lizards. Copeia **1970:** 645–653.

Schmidt-Neilsen, K. 1975. *Animal Physiology, Adaptation and Environment.* Cambridge University Press, New York. 699 p.

Spellerberg, I. F. 1974. Influence of photoperiod and light intensity on lizard voluntary temperatures. Br. J. Herpetol. **5:** 412–420.

Spellerberg, I. F. and T. E. Phelps. 1975. Voluntary temperatures of the snake, *Coronella austriaca.* Copeia **1975:** 183–185.

Speakman, J. N. and P. A. Krenkel. 1971. Quantification of the effects of rate of temperature change on aquatic biota. Report No. 6. Department of Environmental and Water Resources Engineering, Vanderbilt University. 178 p.

Stebbins, R. C. 1963. Activity changes in the striped plateau lizard with evidence on influence on the parietal eye. Copeia **1963:** 681–691.

Stevens, E. D. and F. E. J. Fry. 1970. The rate of thermal exchange in a teleost, *Tilapia mossambica.* Can. J. Zool. **48:** 221–226.

Stevens, E. D. and F. E. J. Fry. 1974. Heat transfer and body temperatures in nonthermoregulatory teleosts. Can. J. Zool. **52:** 1137–1143.

Stevens, E. D. and W. H. Neill. In press. Body temperature in tuna. *In:* W. S. Hoar and D. J. Randall, Eds. *Fish Physiology.* Vol. 7: *Locomotion.* Academic Press, New York.

Stuntz, W. E. 1975. Habitat selection and growth of bluegills. Unpublished doctoral dissertation, University of Wisconsin—Madison. 125 p.

Stuntz, W. E. and J. J. Magnuson. 1976. Daily ration, temperature selection, and activity of bluegill, *Lepomis macrochirus. In:* G. W. Esch and R. W. McFarlane, Eds. *Thermal Ecology II. Proceedings of the Second Thermal Ecology Symposium, Augusta, Ga., May 1975.* A. E. C. Symposium Series, CONF 750425-42. P. 180–184.

Sylvester, J. R. 1972. Effect of thermal stress on predator avoidance in sockeye salmon. J. Fish. Res. Board Can. **29:** 601–603.

Templeton, J. R. 1970. Reptiles. *In:* G. C. Whittow, Ed. *Comparative Physiology of Thermoregulation.* Vol. I. Academic Press, New York. P. 167–221.

Vance, V. J. 1973. Temperature preference and tolerance in the gecko, *Coleonyx variegatus*. Copeia **1973:** 615–617.

Vaughn, L. K., H. A. Bernheim, and M. J. Kluger. 1974. Fever in the lizard *Dipsosaurus dorsalis*. Nature **252:** 473–474.

Vernon, J. and H. Heatwole. 1970. Temperature relations of the water skink, *Sphenomorphus quoyi*. J. Herpetol. **4:** 141–143.

Vinegar, A., V. H. Hutchison, and H. G. Dowling. 1970. Metabolism, energetics, and thermoregulation during brooding of snakes of the genus *Python* (Reptilia, Bordae). Zoologica **55:** 19–50.

Whitfield, C. L. and R. L. Livezey. 1973. Thermoregulatory patterns in lizards. Physiol. Zool. **46:** 285–296.

Whittow, G. C., Ed. 1970. *Comparative Physiology of Thermoregulation*. Vol. I. Academic Press, New York. 333 p.

Wieser, W., Ed. 1973. *Effects of Temperature on Ectothermic Organisms. Ecological Implications and Mechanisms of Compensation*. Springer-Verlag, New York. 298 p.

Wilhoft, D. C., and J. D. Anderson. 1960. Effect of acclimation on the preferred body temperature of the lizard, *Sceloporus occidentalis*. Science **131:** 610–611.

Part III
FEEDING BEHAVIOR

7

AGGREGATING AS A DEFENSE AGAINST PREDATORS IN AQUATIC AND TERRESTRIAL ENVIRONMENTS

EDMUND S. HOBSON

Tiburon Laboratory
Southwest Fisheries Center
National Marine Fisheries Service and
Scripps Institution of Oceanography
Tiburon, California

1 INTRODUCTION

Many animals characteristically aggregate. They include creatures from the simplest to the most complex, and their assemblages are as diverse in form as the animals themselves. Undoubtedly, aggregations offer selective advantages that vary according to species and circumstances, with differences occurring between aquatic and terrestrial habitats. Nevertheless, strong parallels exist between schools of fishes, flocks of birds, herds of mammals, and other animal assemblages. Among the selective advantages animals reportedly gain by aggregating are: available mates, more efficient swimming or flying, standardized behavior, thermoregulation, obtaining of food, and thwarting of predators. Probably each of these possibilities is in force at times; but this chapter, which centers on vertebrates, considers only the impact of aggregating on animals threatened by predators. I draw comparisons between aquatic and terrestrial habitats, but, since my experience has been largely with fishes, the views expressed favor features that are most pronounced underwater.

2 IMPACT OF AGGREGATING ON THE FREQUENCY OF ENCOUNTERING PREDATORS

Several theoretical studies have contended that prey reduce their encounters with predators by aggregating. The essence of these works, however, are mathematical models that, while provocative, rest on questionable assumptions.

Speculating on fishes and envisioning a sea where visually feeding predators and their prey move randomly, Brock and Riffenburg (1960) calculated that prey in schools are less likely to be sighted than prey swimming alone. They assumed that the predators always feed to capacity upon sighting prey but reasoned that this capacity is limited during any one feeding. Over the long run, they concluded, when prey swim in schools, fewer are eaten. Making the same assumptions, and elaborating on search theory, Olsen (1964) similarly concluded that fishes, by schooling, are sighted by fewer predators.

Vine (1971) modeled predator-prey interactions among terrestrial mammals and reached similar conclusions. He envisioned a flat habitat without natural cover or camouflage, where predators hunt prey by vision alone. Vine, too, assumed that predators feed at every opportunity, so that mechanisms reducing prey sightings would reduce predation. In designing his model, Vine assumed that a predator's relative success in sighting prey while scanning a new habitat is influenced by how much it must turn its head from the midline to sight a given target. He reasoned that the more the predator must turn its head, the less likely it is to sight the target, and thus the more likely it is to move elsewhere. Vine assumed that, on the average, predators must turn their heads more to sight prey herded together than scattered about, an assumption that led him to conclude that prey would be advantaged in aggregations.

But can one generally measure a selective advantage of aggregating by noting how often predators detect prey, especially when one also assumes that attack follows each detection? This situation may hold for predators like wolves, which reportedly are constantly alert for food while traveling over their range and attack every suitable prey they encounter (Mech, 1970). But many predators and their prey often remain within sight of one another for long periods without overtly interacting. On marine reefs, for instance, many large predatory fishes swim peacefully among schooling fishes during most of the day (Fig. 7.1), even though they will prey on these fishes under appropriate circumstances (Hobson, 1968). Similarly, wolves coexist with caribou herds during much of the year, and though the wolves prey on these mammals, the coexistence generally is peaceful (Banfield, 1954). Because predators and their prey so often coexist intimately, the question of detection, as used in the models, is frequently irrelevant. The models overstress spatial relationships. Obviously, relative positions are important, but so are other variables unconsidered in the models, including time of day, distance to cover or to conspecifics, attentiveness, and physical condition (Hobson, 1968, 1972).

Furthermore, it is often unrealistic to assume that predators or prey are distributed randomly, or that predators hunt by random search. Although wolves may often depend on chance encounters for a successful hunt (Murie, 1944; Mech, 1970), many predators benefit from predictable movements of their prey. During morning and evening twilight, for example, certain large predatory reef fishes visit specific places where small schooling fishes moving along established migration routes are briefly vulnerable to them (Hobson, 1965, 1968). Undoubtedly, similar situations exist on land, as for instance when lions sometimes lie in wait for prey moving to or from water holes (Schaller, 1972).

Models that consider only visual predation often distort reality, an opinion also expressed by Treisman (1975). Many predators use senses other than vision to detect distant prey. Certain sharks, for example, locate prey well beyond their visual ranges by using olfactory or auditory stimuli (Hobson, 1963; Nelson and Gruber, 1963), and among terrestrial predators wolves usually locate their prey by odor (Mech, 1970). Modeling requires simplification, but in simplifying there is danger of overlooking inconsistencies with the assumptions on which the models are based. Models that examine the adaptive value of aggregating in reducing predation should recognize the senses used by all major predators on aggregating species.

In both terrestrial and aquatic habitats, the cues that lead predators to prey are multiplied when the prey aggregate. Predators that locate prey

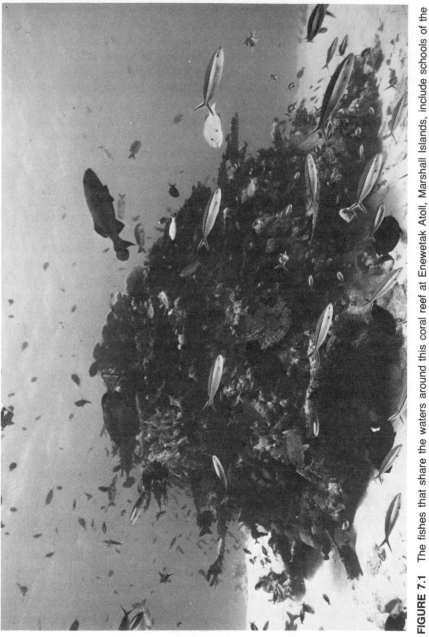

FIGURE 7.1 The fishes that share the waters around this coral reef at Enewetak Atoll, Marshall Islands, include schools of the planktivorous lutjanid *Pterocaesis tile* (foreground), and large groupers, *Epinephelus leopardus* (hovering above the reef in the background), a predator that feeds on these and other smaller fishes.

by their sense of smell will find a greater odor emanating from a group than from an individual, just as those that respond to sounds of prey will find that aggregations generate more of these stimuli. Similarly, aggregated prey should be visible at greater distances than prey standing alone. [This view was rejected by Vine (1971), who, in support of his model, contended that on flat terrain, aggregated prey are visible at no greater distance than solitary prey. Later, however, Vine (1973) admitted that this contention, based on a misinterpretation of studies in human vision, is incorrect, a fact that weakens his model.] Bird flocks in flight, having an added dimension (compared to animals assembled on the ground), would be even more visible at a distance. One might assume the same would hold for fish schools, which also have the added dimension, but the relationship between size and visibility is much weaker underwater. Owing to backscatter and absorption—optical peculiarities of even the clearest water—aquatic objects of all sizes are invisible beyond about 70 m (Brock and Riffenburgh, 1960). Even so, however, schools of fish are more readily perceived than solitary fish. For these reasons, I not only question the contention that aggregating reduces encounters with predators but in fact consider the opposite view more probable. Significantly, most ways suggested to explain how aggregating reduces predation deal not with avoiding encounters, but rather with thwarting predators already on the scene. The following sections discuss some of these suggested ways.

3   REDUCED PREDATION THROUGH COLLECTIVE MIMICRY

Some observers have suggested that prey are more secure in aggregations than alone because predators regard the group as some inedible, or even frightening, object. Hass (1945) introduced the term "collective mimicry" in reference to aggregations of African grasshoppers that he felt resembled large black caterpillars. Most examples of collective mimicry later suggested, however, have included speculations on dense aerial or aquatic concentrations of birds or fish. The ebb and flow of individuals within these three-dimensional assemblages produce many forms that stimulate imaginative interpretations. For the most part, however, these interpretations have been questionable. Crawford and Powers (1953) and Randall and Randall (1960) described members of fish schools oriented so that their assemblages resembled submarine plants. Springer (1957) observed what he described as a warty red-spotted blob, at first thought to be a ray, moving rapidly close beneath the surface of the sea, and he realized only later that it was a tightly packed school of small fish. Perhaps making too much of having been misled himself, Springer concluded that the small fish were protected by the "frightening appearance" of the group. Conceivably, prey could benefit in aggregating because collectively they resemble inedible objects, but the idea is inconsistent with at least one major aspect of widespread predator-prey interactions: many predators attack aggregations most effectively in the diminished light of twilight (Hobson, 1968), and one would expect collective mimicry, which depends on misinterpreting a visual impression, to be most effective when visibility is reduced.

4   IMPORTANCE OF AGGREGATING IN DETECTING PREDATORS

The greater number of sensory receptors in a group of animals provides increased capacity to sense threatening predators. This is the advantage most often attributed to prey in aggregations, and it is one likely to be important. Although the idea has been widely applied to both terrestrial and aquatic forms (e.g., birds, by Tinbergen, 1951; and fishes, by Bowen, 1931), it would seem that the prey who benefit most would be among those terrestrial animals concerned with the actions of predators some distance away. Mech (1970), for example, noted that it is critical for moose, deer, and other animals to sense the wolves that stalk them before these predators get too close.

The advantage is particularly valuable in allowing animals in aggregations to feed, and to follow other necessary pursuits, without becoming unduly vulnerable to surprise attacks (Lack, 1954). Certainly it would be a strong asset to species experiencing complex social interactions. A solitary animal cannot remain constantly on guard, and when its attention is diverted even momentarily, it can readily miss the warning signs that frequently precede an attack. In an aggregation, however, some individuals can be alert to danger even while most of the group is sleeping or otherwise resting. And the overt response of these watchful few quickly alerts the rest. Members of fish schools and bird flocks are especially sensitive to the actions of their fellows, so that alarm in one almost instantly spreads throughout the group. This is an important aspect of the "group cohesion" that Welty (1934) found characteristic of fish schools.

5   AGGREGATIONS AS PLACES TO HIDE

An animal on the edge of a group is more exposed to attackers than one within the group, and this fact undoubtedly has influenced the defenses of various animals. Thus, when the vulnerable young of some hoofed mammals are threatened, they often move to the center of the herd, leaving older, more able, members of the group to confront the predators (Schaller, 1972). Logically, behavior of this sort should be expected to have evolved among aggregating animals. The basic concept, however, has been greatly expanded by some investigators to account for the aggregating habit itself.

One view has it that animals aggregate because historically certain individuals found advantage in taking positions that put others of their kind between themselves and predators. In developing this position with studies of fishes, Williams (1964) reasoned that because individuals on the periphery of a group are the first to be sighted and pursued, individuals that take positions within the group are selected for in the presence of vision-dependent predation. Hamilton (1971) thought that Williams' position explains why aggregations of many different kinds of animals, including herds of mammals, flocks of birds, and schools of fish, close ranks when threatened. This response, he contended, is a simultaneous attempt by members of these assemblages to occupy the more secure interior positions. The advantage of being inside the group was similarly stressed by Pulliam (1973), who, also taking his lead from Williams, reasoned that the relatively secure interior positions within bird flocks would be monopolized by the more dominant individuals, while positions on the exposed periphery would be left to disadvantaged subordinates.

But I know of no good evidence that animals in aggregations generally do in fact compete for the interior positions when threatened. I have seen nothing among fishes that I could interpret this way. The relative positions of fish in a school continuously change, and I doubt that a given individual habitually swims in any particular segment of the group—be it on the periphery or in the interior. When the school is threatened, the members swim faster and also increase their rate of changing relative positions. The school tightens (a phenomenon discussed further in the next section), but I have failed to note concerted efforts among those on the periphery to bury themselves in the assemblage. Perhaps one can construe the activity in this way—the action is difficult to follow—but it has seemed to me that as many insiders are moving out as outsiders are moving in. The net result, in my view, is that the schoolers simply move closer together. Radakov (1973) expressed a similar opinion after analyzing motion picture sequences of fish schools under attack. If the relative positions of fishes in schools change as fluidly as it seems, then all members probably have an equal chance of being on the periphery (or deep within the school) when a predator strikes.

I believe all members of a school share the advantage offered in reducing predation. Thus, as I stated earlier (Hobson, 1968), I disagree with Williams' (1964) thesis that the selective advantage of schooling lies with those individuals that have others of their kind between themselves and predators—that is, those occupying the interior positions. If schooling protected only those within the assemblage, then those on the periphery would increase their availability to predators when they came together in dense numbers, and this would put the school's future in doubt. It is well documented that many schools are regularly attended by predators that will feed when they have a chance (e.g., Hobson, 1968), and if fish swimming on the periphery were vulnerable, they would be quickly taken. Furthermore, every member of the school would ultimately experience a turn on the periphery as the numbers declined, so that if they became vulnerable here, the entire assemblage would be progressively annihilated under continuous attacks. This does not happen, of course—a fact most logically explained if the peripheral individuals, along with their fellow schoolers, are relatively secure at least most of the time. A possible reason why this may be so is discussed next.

6   THE CONFUSION EFFECT

It has been suggested that predators confronted by the many targets in an aggregation may have trouble concentrating on individual prey (Allen 1920a, 1920b; Eibl-Eibesfeldt, 1962; Manteifel and Radakov, 1961; Hobson, 1965, 1968; Starck and Davis, 1966; Neill and Cullen, 1974). If this were so, aggregating would benefit prey threatened by predators that had to direct their attacks on individuals. Perhaps significantly, most advocates of this "confusion effect" have drawn their examples from fish schools or from bird flocks in flight. Predators on fishes and birds generally attack individuals, and it would seem more difficult to isolate individuals from the three-dimensional aggregations of these animals than from the two-dimensional assemblages that other animals form on the ground. Sharp (1951), however, believed that eagles attacking flying ducks are unable to concentrate on individuals, even when the ducks are in groups of as few as two. Apparently, the distracting influence of even a single alternative target can hamper an attack.

The confusion effect is probably widespread in varying degrees where predators seek prey from aggregations. The many animals that tighten their aggregations when threatened place more individuals within the visual field of attacking predators, thus further hindering those predators troubled by multiple targets. In refining this strategy more than most, fishes have emphasized features that make it difficult for pre-

FIGURE 7.2 The flatiron herring, *Harengula thrissina*, a major target of piscivorous predators in the Gulf of California, illustrates the silvery hues so common among small schooling fishes.

FIGURE 7.3 The Mexican goatfish, *Mulloidichthys dentatus*, hovering in a relatively inactive daytime school in the Gulf of California, illustrates the striped color pattern common among near-shore schooling fishes.

dators to concentrate on individuals. All members of a school are about the same size and look much alike (schooling fishes are noted for lacking external differences between the sexes). As noted above, when threatened they increase not only their swimming speed but also the rate at which they dart in and out among one another. Coloration can be important too. Many schoolers are silvery (Fig. 7.2), and sunlight reflecting from their bodies at rapidly changing angles during evasive maneuvers presents the attacker with a bewildering shower of brilliant flashes (Hobson, 1968). Many others are barred or striped (Fig. 7.3), and when they swim in schools, these patterns blend together as a shifting maze of lines that conceal the individuals (Starck, 1966). Some fishes are barred or striped only when they school: the goatfish *Mulloidichthys samoensis*, for example, carries a prominent yellow stripe on its sides when schooling, but when it forages independently, or in small groups, the stripe is replaced by a solitary black spot (Hobson, 1974). Dissimilar members of a school seem vulnerable. Walter A. Starck II (personal communication) placed prominent marks on certain individuals from a school and found these individuals quickly taken by predators when he returned them to their school, even though he judged that they were behaving normally. Just as uniform appearance is important among members of a school, so is uniform behavior. When a school is being watched by predators, any individual that behaves abnormally—as for example because of injury—is more likely to be taken (Hobson, 1968).

The confusion effect, being a close-range phenomenon, is particularly suited to the aquatic environment, where visual ranges are short and most large predators myopic (Walls, 1942). Furthermore, the aquatic medium permits fishes their living integument and thus the highly developed and changeable colorations that so often contribute to masking individuals. Because terrestrial animals have nonliving integuments—a corollary to living on land, they cannot match fishes in this respect.

7   A DELICATE BALANCE

Clearly, interactions between predator and prey are delicately balanced. Whereas predators in most of their feeding activities depend on recognizing momentary opportunities for successful attack, prey depend for their survival on adaptations that reduce such opportunities. These opposing selective pressures have established a thin line across which advantage shifts back and forth between predator and prey in response to even slight changes in circumstance. Breder (1959) doubted that a confusion effect exists when he failed to observe hesitancy or indecision in predatory fishes attacking schools of prey. But certainly the success or failure of these attacks are so finely separated that decisive elements in most instances are imperceptible to human observers.

Some general trends, however, can be recognized during the course of the diel cycle. Prey in aggregations seem advantaged during most of the day, judging by how seldom they are attacked by predators that are within clear striking range. This advantage is especially evident among fishes on marine reefs, where most of the relatively few individuals taken during midday are among those failing for some reason to maintain a normal station in the school (Hobson, 1968). During twilight, however, the advantage swings abruptly toward the predators (Fig. 7.4). Predators become more active at this time, both on land and underwater (Kavanau, 1971; Hobson, 1968). Nevertheless, the phenomenon is better documented underwater, especially regarding relative advantages of aggregating (Hobson, 1972; McFarland and Munz, 1976). Crepuscular predation is perhaps more pronounced underwater, since it seems to be accentuated by physical features of the aquatic habitat, as noted below, and involves primarily close-range interactions, which are particularly suited to the limited visual ranges of this realm.

Fishes in schools are significantly more vulnerable during twilight

FIGURE 7.4   The Pacific amberjack, *Seriola colburni*, which commonly exceeds a length of 1 m and weight of 50 kg, is much larger and faster than the many schooling fishes that are its major prey. This fish is swimming above a reef at Cocos Island, Costa Rica.

than during the day (Hobson, 1968), a fact that probably relates to major changes in the visual setting underwater at this time. The predator's twilight advantage probably occurs at that final phase of the attack, when it strikes its prey. Generally this strike is visually directed, even in predators led to the scene by olfaction or audition—for example, certain sharks (Hobson, 1963). The sky is still light for some time after sunset and before sunrise, and this light is reflected in the brightness of the water's surface when viewed from below. Little of this light penetrates underwater, however, and from a position in the water column, vision to the sides and, especially, below, is limited (Hobson, 1966, 1968; see also Munz and McFarland, 1973). Under these conditions, many of the features that generally protect schooling fishes lose their effectiveness. The fishes' colorations, for example, no longer are a factor. Predatory fishes typically attack from below during twilight, so that each member of the school is silhouetted against the still-bright water's surface overhead—a distinct target (Hobson, 1966). But being more readily perceived is only part of the problem that prey face under these conditions. It is also likely that they are slower in reacting to attacks launched from darkness. And because, in the final analysis, a prey's survival depends on how quickly it reacts to the predator's charge, even momentary delays will often prove fatal.

Although these considerations would seem most evident underwater, terrestrial predators that attack aggregated prey should enjoy a similar crepuscular edge. Although in general they probably cannot match the advantage enjoyed by fishes whose prey are silhouetted against bright surface waters, at least one aerial predator may use the twilight sky this way. When Texas night hawks attack flying insects during the crepuscular periods, they typically swoop up from below and toward the illuminated sector of the sky (George W. Barlow, University of California, personal communication.) And terrestrial prey, like their aquatic counterparts, probably are delayed in reacting to attacks launched in semidarkness. In both environments, the predator chooses the moment and place of attack; the prey can only respond. Because response suffers more than attack when visibility is reduced, the attacker should consistently benefit from crepuscular conditions, so long as light is sufficient for its own actions.

8 SOME CLOSING THOUGHTS

Among fishes and mammals, dominant forms in the aquatic and terrestrial realms, the benefits of aggregating in deterring predators seem to differ primarily in emphasis, with a strong influence exerted by prevailing physical and biological considerations. On land, where animals often interact over considerable distances, mammals in herds are about the same size, or even larger, than most of the predators that threaten them. Flight is a common response to these threats, for many can outrun their attackers, especially if the danger is recognized early (Mech, 1970). Under these circumstances, where there is a high premium on advance warning, the benefits of aggregating probably emphasize increasing awareness of impending danger. On the other hand, underwater, where animals usually interact over much shorter distances, fishes in schools are much smaller than most of the predators that threaten them (compare Figs. 7.2, 7.3, and 7.4). Flight is an uncommon response to these threats, except for those fish that can find cover in a reef or other structure close at hand (Hobson, 1968, 1974). This is predictable because few can outswim their attackers, especially as the danger usually is at close quarters before it is recognized. Under these circumstances, where the prey must tolerate a charging predator in their midst, the benefits of aggregating likely emphasize the confusion effect. Thus, it would seem that these two different kinds of animals, herding mammals and schooling fishes, which live under highly dissimilar conditions, each derive benefits from aggregating that reflect their particular circumstances. And yet the major benefit of one likely is a secondary benefit of the other. That is, herding mammals probably derive some benefit from the confusion effect, and schooling fishes probably gain some benefit from earlier detection of threatening predators.

Finally, some accounts suggest that certain predators in fact benefit when prey aggregate. This is probably true, at least under specific circumstances. Because effective defenses create pressures that lead to modified offenses, it should be expected that certain predators have acquired solutions to the defensive characteristics of aggregations. Thus, the long tail of the thresher shark may be an effective weapon when attacking fish schools (Nichols and Murphy, 1916), as may be the sword of the swordfish and the saw of the sawfish (Williams, 1964). But the impact of such predators remains insignificant when balanced against the many more predators whose attacks seem frustrated by various features of aggregations.

REFERENCES

Allen, W. E. 1920a. Behavior of loon and sardines. Ecology **1**: 309–310.

Allen, W. E. 1920b. Behavior of feeding mackerel. Ecology **1**: 310.

Banfield, A. W. F. 1954. Preliminary investigation of the barren ground caribou. Part II.

Life history, ecology, and utilization. Can. Wildl. Serv. Wildl. Manag. Bull. **1**(10B): 412 p.

Bowen, E. S. 1931. The role of the sense organs in aggregations of *Ameiurus melas*. Ecol. Monogr. **1:** 1–35.

Breder, C. M., Jr. 1959. Studies on social groupings in fishes. Bull. Am. Mus. Nat. Hist. **117:** 397–481.

Brock, V. E. and R. H. Riffenburgh. 1960. Fish schooling: a possible factor in reducing predation. J. Cons. Int. Explor. Mer **25:** 307–317.

Crawford, R. W. and C. F. Powers. 1953. Schooling of the orange filefish, *Alutera schoepfi*, in New York Bight. Copeia **1953:** 115–116.

Eibl-Eibesfeldt, I. 1962. Freiwasserbeobachtungen zur Detung des Schwarmverhaltens verschiedener Fische. Z. Tierpsych. **19:** 165–182.

Hamilton, W. D. 1971. Geometry for the selfish herd. J. Theor. Biol. **31:** 295–311.

Hass, F. 1945. Collective mimicry. Ecology **26:** 412–413.

Hobson, E. S. 1963. Feeding behavior in three species of sharks. Pac. Sci. **17:** 171–194.

Hobson, E. S. 1965. Diurnal-nocturnal activity of some inshore fishes in the Gulf of California. Copeia **1965:** 291–302.

Hobson, E. S. 1966. Visual orientation and feeding in seals and sea lions. Nature **210:** 326–327.

Hobson, E. S. 1968. Predatory behavior of some shore fishes in the Gulf of California. U. S. Fish Wildl. Serv. Res. Rept. 73. 92 p.

Hobson, E. S. 1972. Activity of Hawaiian reef fishes during the evening and morning transitions between daylight and darkness. Fish. Bull., U.S. **70:** 715–740.

Hobson, E. S. 1974. Feeding relationships of teleostean fishes on coral reefs in Kona, Hawaii. Fish. Bull., U.S. **72:** 915–1031.

Kavanau, J. L. 1971. Locomotion and activity phasing of some medium-sized mammals. J. Mamm. **52:** 386–403.

Lack, D. 1954. *The Natural Regulation of Animal Numbers*. Clarendon Press, Oxford. 343 p.

Manteifel, B. P. and D. V. Radakov. 1961. The adaptive significance of schooling behavior in fishes. Russ. Rev. Biol. **50:** 338–345.

McFarland, W. N. and F. W. Munz. 1976. The visible spectrum during twilight and its implications to vision. *In*:G. C. Evans, R. Bainbridge, and O. Rackam, Eds. *Light As an Ecological Factor*. Blackwell Scientific Publications, Oxford. P. 249–270.

Mech, L. D. 1970. *The Wolf: The Ecology of an Endangered Species*. Natural History Press, New York, 384 p.

Munz, F. W. and W. N. McFarland. 1973. The significance of spectral position in the rhodopsins of tropical marine fishes. Vis. Res. **13:** 1829–1874.

Murie, A. 1944. The wolves of Mount McKinley. Fauna of the Natl. Parks of the U. S., Fauna Ser. 5. Washington, D.C. 238 p.

Neill, S. R. St. J. and J. M. Cullen. 1974. Experiments of whether schooling by their prey affects the hunting behavior of cephalopods and fish predators. J. Zool. (Lond.) **172:** 549–569.

Nelson, D. R. and S. H. Gruber. 1963. Sharks: attraction by low-frequency sounds. Science **142:** 975–977.

Nichols, J. T. and R. C. Murphy. 1916. Long Island fauna IV, the Sharks. Brooklyn Mus. Sci. Bull. **3:** 1–34.

Olson, F. C. W. 1964. The survival value of fish schooling. J. Cons. Int. Explor. Mer **29:** 115–116.

Pulliam, H. R. 1973. On the advantages of flocking. J. Theor. Biol. **38:** 419–422.

Radakov, D. V. 1973. *Schooling in the Ecology of Fish.* Halsted Press, New York. 173 p.

Randall, J. E. and H. A. Randall. 1960. Examples of mimicry and protective resemblance in tropical marine fishes. Bull. Mar. Sci. Gulf Caribb. **10:** 444–480.

Schaller, G. B. 1972. *The Serengeti Lion. A Study of Predator-Prey Relations.* University of Chicago Press, Chicago, 480 p.

Sharp, W. M. 1951. Observations on predator-prey relations between wild ducks, trumpeter swans, and golden eagles. J. Wildl. Manag. **15:** 224–226.

Springer, S. 1957. Some observations on the behavior of schools of fishes in the Gulf of Mexico and adjacent waters. Ecology **38:** 166–171.

Starck, W. A., II. 1966. Marvels of a coral realm. Nat. Geogr. Mag. **130:** 710–738.

Starck, W. A., II and W. P. Davis. 1966. Night habits of fishes of Alligator Reef, Florida. Ichthyol. Aquar. J. **38:** 313–356.

Tinbergen, N. 1951. *The Study of Instinct.* Clarendon Press, Oxford. 228 p.

Treisman, M. 1975. Predation and the evolution of gregariousness. I. Models for concealment and evasion. Anim. Behav. **23:** 779–800.

Vine, I. 1971. Risk of visual detection and pursuit of a predator and the selective advantage of flocking behavior. J. Theor. Biol. **30:** 405–422.

Vine, I. 1973. Detection of prey flocks by predators. J. Theor. Biol. **40:** 207–210.

Walls, G. L. 1942. *The Vertebrate Eye and Its Adaptive Radiation.* Reprinted 1963. Hafner, New York. 785 p.

Welty, J. C. 1934. Experiments in group behavior of fishes. Physiol. Zool. **7:** 85–128.

Williams, G. C. 1964. Measurement of consociation among fishes. Mich. State Univ. Mus. Biol. Ser. **2:** 349–384.

8

COMPARATIVE FEEDING BEHAVIORS OF MARINE AND TERRESTRIAL VERTEBRATES (FISH AND MAMMALS) IN A TROPICAL ENVIRONMENT

MIREILLE L. HARMELIN-VIVIEN
Station Marine d'Endoume
Marseille, France

1 INTRODUCTION

The most primitive vertebrates, the fish, evolved in the ancestral oceanic environment, whereas the most advanced vertebrates, the mammals, attained dominance on dry land. For both, success depends on adjusting to the essential problems of survival: feeding, escape from predators, and reproduction.

The solutions to these problems are often similar in the various groups of animals when the problems posed by environmental conditions are similar. Examples of these convergences are numerous and well known. On the other hand, and precisely because of the fundamental differences between the aquatic environment and the terrestrial one, it seems of particular interest to make a comparative study of the ways fish and mammals solve their feeding problem. To illustrate this discussion, the comparison will be limited to the tropical zone, with an Indian Ocean coral reef representative of the aquatic environment and a shrubby African savannah representative of the terrestrial environment. A complete review of previous studies on the feeding behavior of reef fishes and tropical mammals is not the purpose of this paper. Rather, I present a summary of the various problems associated with feeding in the two environments. A detailed review of these problems still needs more studies, especially on the variations in diets and feeding rhythms. The examples selected to illustrate this discussion are essentially taken from the papers of Hiatt and Strasburg (1960), Hobson (1965, 1968, 1974) and Vivien (1973) for the reef fishes, and from Bourlière (1951), Brosset (1969), Matthews (1972), and Pierre (1968) for the tropical mammals.

Before actually dealing with the problems related to feeding behavior, the essential differences between these two environments should be reviewed. The marine tropical environment appears remarkably stable, be it on a daily scale or on a yearly scale. The temperature of the water around a coral reef varies little throughout the year, at the most a few degrees Celsius between summer and winter. Day to day variations, which affect only the most superficial water layer, do not have any effect upon the fishes' behavior. In contrast, the variations of temperature on land, even in a tropical zone, are large. The daily, and, moreover, seasonal temperature variations may reach several degrees in a sparsely wooded ground like the savannah, where the vegetation is too scattered to play the role of a thermal screen, as it does in rain forests.

Other climatic factors in the terrestrial environment, such as the availability of water and relative humidity (Matthews, 1972; Brosset, 1969), are even more important in a tropical environment than is temperature, and they play a significant role in the ecology of mammals. Water is an essential metabolite for terrestrial mammals. However, the requirements for water are not identical from one species to another and can be satisfied in various ways. Available water, from rivers, pools, seasonal water spots, or dew, determines in part the distribution of terrestrial mammals according to the importance of their specific needs, and it commands daily and seasonal migrations. Numerous large African herbivores, as well as a great number of carnivores, must drink every day and thus may at times cover long distances to reach a water hole. Other species, requiring less water, are satisfied with licking the dew that accumulates on plants during the night, and still others find in their food enough water to satisfy their requirements.

Relative humidity plays a part in the distribution of mammals, being greater in the forests, under the shelter of trees and in burrows, than in an open savannah. The joint action of temperature, moisture, and light has an effect upon the behavior and the feeding rhythm of mammals. During the hottest part of the day, a great number of species will tend to look for shade under the shelter of trees and bushes and will more or less cease their feeding activity. Whereas small variations of temperature in tropical waters do not apparently affect fishes, variations of light determine the biological rhythms for most species. This effect can also be observed in terrestrial mammals. Light is an important factor and must be considered in the study of the feeding behavior of animals. Its effects on the feeding periods of terrestrial mammals have been known for a long time (Bourlière, 1951), but its effect on the feeding of fishes, and particularly of reef fishes, was only recorded some 10 years ago (Hobson, 1965; Vivien, 1973). Daily light variations are, directly or indirectly, the basis of the nyctemeral feeding rhythm observable in many species. Species are classified as diurnal, nocturnal, or crepuscular, according to their feeding period. Yearly luminosity variations also affect the feeding behavior of animals by way of the seasonal fluctuations of vegetation.

Finally, one of the fundamental differences between fishes and terrestrial mammals lies in the space available for their evolution, which results from differences in the density of mediums, in gravity, and in morphological characteristics. Whereas most mammals, bats excepted, live in a two-dimensional space and are in permanent contact with the ground, the fish evolved in a three-dimensional space, a great number having in fact only occasional relations with the bottom. These differences provide various possibilities for the evolution of behaviors adapted to each environment.

2 FEEDING BEHAVIORS

Generally, the diet of a certain species is likely to vary in time and in space, independently of the alterations linked to the age of individuals. Strictly specialized diets, consisting of one certain kind of food, are rare, and they often constitute a heavy handicap for the survival of the species, these being threatened by the smallest change in environmental conditions (Bourlière, 1951).

Most species show a certain natural disposition to modify their feed-ing habits according to whatever is available at the moment. The study of the feeding habits of marine and terrestrial vertebrates will con-sequently be all the more difficult. In the settings chosen, it has been established that the environmental characteristics of terrestrial mammals were much more diversified than those of the fishes. The surroundings being more varied on land, the feeding habits are consequently multip-lied and the complexity of food webs increased (Romer, 1970; Pierre, 1968). The food webs of a coral reef, not yet well known, though already extremely complex in appearance, seem relatively simple when com-pared to the food webs existing in an African savannah.

The three main categories of feeding behavior, usually classified as herbivorous, omnivorous, and carnivorous, are to be found on land as well as in the sea. Feeding similarities, differences, and peculiarities of each of these categories, observable in comparative study of the two environments, are discussed below.

2.1 The Herbivores

Most terrestrial and marine herbivores use a highly productive vegeta-tion consisting of small-sized elements. In the marine environment, the plant-eating fishes use algae as their primary food. On the other hand, the marine spermatophytes are most often neglected, as are the large brown algae with rather rigid thalli, such as the sargassoes or *Turbinaria*, which appear in summer. Filamentous or unicellular algae and shoots of multicellular algae are the most often used. These algae form an epilithic or epiphytic padding that grows rapidly on any available area. Plant consumption on land follows a comparable pattern. A certain number of mammals, such as elephants or giraffes, browse on leaves from the trees, but the plants most often used are found, by far, in the highly productive grassy meadows. These wide herbaceous stretches form the grazing areas for the large herds of such mammals as antelopes, zebras, and buffaloes (Matthews, 1972; Pierre, 1968).

The similarity on land and in the sea between this type of plant con-sumption extends itself to the level of certain behaviors. The primarily plant-eating animals are large-sized ones with gregarious and generally diurnal habits. The schools of surgeon fishes (Acanthuridae) and par-rotfishes (Scaridae), often plurispecific, can be compared, allowances being made, with the herds of large ungulates such as zebras, antelopes, gnus, and buffaloes. Their grouping in herds or schools protect to a certain extent the individuals against predators. The similarity of behaviors between these fishes and these grass-eating mammals is, however, limited to the feeding activity period. The herd of antelopes, indeed, remains compact day and night, whereas the schools of Acanthuridae and Scaridae break apart every night. These fishes individually find a shelter for the night and then gather every morning, first in small groups, progressively reuniting until a large school or aggregation is again formed.

Herds and schools represent the most important units of both biomass and social organization among the herbivores. However, there exist also small-sized diurnal herbivores living in small groups or singly and having relatively secretive habits. In the marine environment, examples are the blennies (Blenniidae), damselfishes (Pomacentridae), and filefishes (Monacanthidae). Terrestrial examples are rodents such as terrestrial squirrels (*Xerus*), Daman rats (*Petromus*), and, among the Hyracoids, the Damans (Procaniidae).

The great diversity of plants on land results in the possibility of a great diversity in the diets of the herbivores in this environment. In the tropical coral reef marine environment, only algae constitute the general and constant food of herbivorous fishes. On land, in contrast, the plants used are varied and numerous: graminaceae, leaves from trees and bushes, fruits, seeds, mushrooms and lichen, and even the sap of plants and flowers. Fruits and seeds are the basis of the diet of numerous small terrestrial mammals, such as rodents (Sciuridae, Anomaluridae, Pedetidae, Cricetidae) and bats (fruit-eating Megachiroptera).

The food available to the herbivores, being much more varied in the terrestrial environment than in the marine one, affects not only the diets but also the feeding time and duration. On the reefs, the herbivorous fishes are nearly all diurnal in their feeding activity (Hobson, 1965). The same is not true for the savannah mammals. In addition to the diurnal herbivores, whose biomass is, moreover, very important, there are in the savannah a certain number of nocturnal herbivorous species. These species spend the daytime away from the heat in the rivers (hippopotamus), not far from water holes or under the shelter of trees (Potamochoerus, elephants, rhinoceros), or crouched in their resting places or their burrows (lagomorphs, rodents) (Matthews, 1972). At nightfall, these animals come out of their shelters to seek food. This behavior probably appeared in the terrestrial environment under the pressure of other, better-adapted herbivorous vertebrates becoming too competitive during the day, or because of the presence of dangerous diurnal predators. However, in spite of the various behaviors and diets observed among herbivorous terrestrial or marine vertebrates, a certain convergence in the digestive system must be noted: cutting and masticatory teeth and a very long digestive tract with symbiotic bacteria to digest the cellulose.

2.2 The Omnivores

The omnivores ingest both animal and plant material. There is, however, no strict omnivorous diet; rather, a multitude of diets adapted to the needs of each species have evolved. Omnivorous species show great adaptability in their food and feeding behavior. In the marine environment, most of the species having an omnivorous diet feed during the day (Hobson, 1965; Vivien, 1973). These species include damselfishes (Pomacentridae), certain species of butterflyfishes (Chaetodontidae), gobies (Gobiidae), pufferfishes (Canthigasteridae), and filefishes (Monacanthidae). In the terrestrial environment, the rhythm of omnivorous mammals appears to be more diversified. The largest ones, such as the Primates (baboons, cercopithecus) have generally a diurnal feeding activity. Numerous other species, members of the families Soricidae, Muridae, and Dendromuridae, come out during the night. These small mammals are in general very prolific and adapt themselves very well to various situations. Large-sized nocturnal omnivores include the African porcupines (Hystricidae), which remain concealed in their burrows during the day and emerge at night to search for tubers, roots and insects, which constitute their omnivorous diets.

2.3 The Carnivores

The terrestrial and marine carnivores present the most diversified diets and feeding behaviors, and yet many of them share common morphological and physiological adaptations: sharp-pointed teeth, a short digestive tract, and rapid assimilation of food.

The different groups of carnivores having a diurnal feeding activity are examined first. On tropical reefs, most of the carnivorous fishes that feed during the day present particular adaptations in their morphology and in their behavior, enabling them to catch prey accessible during the day. Certain fishes feed on prey that are permanently accessible and that possess passive protective devices: spicules, spines, shells, and so on. Some fishes, such as angelfishes (Pomacanthidae), are thus specialized in the predation of sponges (Randall, 1963), and others, as some Balistidae, feed more particularly on urchins or on gastropods, as do some large wrasses (Labridae). Other species, thanks to the shape of their body and their snout, are able to reach prey hidden in reef crevices during the day. Thus, the Labridae *Gomphosus*, with its long and tubular snout, can catch small crustaceans hidden between the coral branches (Vivien, 1973). Some species of goatfish (Mullidae) have peculiar foraging organs, the barbels, with which they can detect invertebrates living in the sediment. In addition to these invertebrate feeders, a certain number of piscivorous fishes feed during the day. These species, lizardfishes (Synodontidae) and flatheads (Platycephalidae), remain motionless on the bottom or on the corals, waiting for a fish to pass within their reach. They seize it with a rapid lunge (Hiatt and Strasburg, 1960). Such fishes are often referred to as ambush predators. Other piscivorous fishes, some groupers (Serranidae) for example, feed indifferently by day and at night.

In the African savannah, carnivores with a strictly diurnal feeding activity are not numerous. A few representatives are to be found among Macroscelididae (*Elephantulus*) and among Viveridae, certain species of mongooses. However, large carnivores that hunt essentially during the evening or the night (lions, cheetahs, lycaons) also catch prey during the day when the opportunity occurs.

Nocturnal carnivores, either terrestrial or marine, far outnumber diurnal ones. In the aquatic environment, nocturnal carnivores are often more primitive than diurnal ones, and they present few adaptations to nocturnal life: namely, increase in the size of the eyes or development of the sense of smell. Most nocturnal carnivorous fishes, squirrelfishes (Holocentridae), cardinalfishes (Apogonidae), scorpionfishes (Scorpaenidae), snappers (Lutjanidae), conger-eels (Congridae), and the like, feed on invertebrates emerging at night from the reef crevices or from the sediment. Other piscivorous fishes, groupers (Serranidae) and jackfishes (Carangidae), actively hunt their prey throughout the night, often increasing their activity at dusk. In the African savannah, nocturnal carnivores are also more numerous than the diurnal ones. The largest mammals are the principal predators of large ungulates, including the Felidae (lions, panthers, jaguars, and cheetahs) and the Canidae (lycaons). The smaller ones (Mustelidae, Viveridae) also are very numerous, feeding on other small mammals, on birds, reptiles, and insects.

A greater similarity is evident between terrestrial and marine carnivores, if one considers the kinds of prey caught and not the feeding period.

Thus, in each environment, the carnivores can be divided into two groups: the predators of vertebrates and the predators of invertebrates. The first group includes, for the terrestrial environment, all the carnivores catching other mammals, reptiles, and birds and, for the marine one, the piscivorous fishes. The second group includes the fishes feeding on invertebrates and all the small mammals feeding on insects and on other arthropods. It has already been noted that the invertebrate-eating fishes were numerous and diurnal or nocturnal according to the species. On land, most of the mammals feeding entirely or partly on insects have a nocturnal feeding behavior. Insects are preyed upon by numerous terrestrial vertebrates: batrachians, reptiles, birds, and even mammals. Insects are frequently included in the diet of omnivorous mammals, but they also constitute almost all the prey caught by some typical insectivores, such as Erinaceidae, Chrysochloridae, and Soricidae. To that list must be added an impressive number of insectivorous bats (Microchiroptera) and the *Proteles* among Hyaenidae. Certain terrestrial insectivores are extremely specialized, notably the orycterope (Tubulidentae), which feeds exclusively on ants and termites during the night. The orycteropes, as well as the Macroscelididae, also anteaters, have powerful claws enabling them to destroy anthills and termitaries.

In the marine environment, among the invertebrate-feeders, there exists a very important group of fishes with a particular diet; these are planktophagous fishes. The marine environment is characterized by the presence of plankton. Plankton represents an important food resource, not only for the pelagic fishes but also for the littoral and reef fishes swimming above the bottom, as indicated by the important number of planktophagous fishes encountered on a reef. Certain planktophagous fishes, such as certain Pomacentridae and Nasidae, feed during the day. Others have nocturnal behavior (Holocentridae, Apogonidae, Atherinidae) and catch the organisms that become planktonic at night, in addition to those which are always part of the plankton.

Only the insectivorous bats (Microchiroptera) can be considered, among the mammals, as the terrestrial equivalent of these planktophagous fishes. These flying mammals are the only ones to have conquered the aerial environment, and they are able to move about in a three-dimensional space comparable to that of the aquatic environment of fishes. The flying insects used as their food can be likened to various planktonic organisms.

One category of carnivores typical of the terrestrial environment includes the carrion-eaters, which feed on the abandoned carcasses of animals. This diet seems to be particularized only in the terrestrial surroundings. Hyaenidae (*Hyaena, Crocuta*) are the well-known representatives of that category. They feed on the scraps of meat left by large flesh-eating animals, this being in addition to other small mammals on which they feed. Their powerful crushing teeth enable them to use the bones of their prey as well.

This phenomenon is not as well established among the fishes. In the marine environment, leftovers from the prey do not seem constant and abundant enough to allow a group of fishes to specialize in the collecting of scraps. In the sea, the role of carrion-eaters is played most of the time by invertebrates such as crustaceans (especially pagurids), echinoderms, and mollusks (especially gastropods).

To conclude the comparative study on the marine and terrestrial carnivores, the principal methods of catching prey are considered. Two main ways of hunting exist among the fishes as well as among the terrestrial mammals; they either lie in wait for prey, or they actively hunt it.

Lying in wait for prey is common among certain reef fishes, either diurnal (Platycephalidae) or nocturnal (Scorpaenidae) (Hobson, 1968). These fishes generally are camouflaged by their shape and color and have a strong resemblance with the bottom where they hide. They escape notice and suddenly dash at their prey when the latter passes within their reach. The same behavior—camouflage, expectation, sudden attack—can be observed in numerous terrestrial carnivores (Matthews, 1972; Bourliere, 1951). One example is provided by the hunting technique of the panther, often lying in ambush in a tree or crouching in tall grasses near an antelope passage and pouncing on the prey when it comes within reach.

The same technique, more active, however, consists of approaching the prey unexpectedly and generally catching it after a short pursuit. On the reefs, this method is used by trumpetfishes (Aulostomidae) and cornetfishes (Fistulariidae). These species slowly approach another fish, and when they are at a suitable distance, they dart upon the prey, open mouthed, to snatch it. In the savannah, this method of hunting is often used by large felines, such as lions or cheetahs, which in this instance hunt alone. Great carnivores have a very strong odor that large herbivores with a well-developed sense of smell can detect from a distance. For these felines, the problem is not so much to be seen or heard, as, rather, not to be smelled.

Another way of catching prey, hunting in a cooperative group, seems to be a specialization of terrestrial mammals and does not have any equivalent among fish. Group hunting at an advanced social level involves the use of a certain strategy and the distribution of roles among the participants. Lions hunt in groups, and certain individuals move the prey toward other lions lying in ambush in a predetermined place. Hunting in groups is even better organized among the Canidae. Lycaons, for example, hunt in packs and force the prey to run, several individuals taking turns at the head of the group during the pursuit. In all these examples, only one prey is seized by several individuals and will be used as food for the whole group. On the reefs, such behaviors have not been observed. Some species of fishes prey to advantage in groups (Hobson, 1968), but pursuing one prey that is afterwards divided among the hunters does not seem to exist among fishes. A prey is in general eaten by only one individual fish, the size of the prey being generally in proportion to that of the predator.

3   FEEDING RHYTHMS

Having discussed the main types of diet encountered in the marine and terrestrial environments, I consider the daily and seasonal migrations and feeding rhythms.

3.1   Daily Migrations

The animals are in general unprotected during their feeding period and are thus the most accessible to predators. During their resting time, or relative inactivity, it is necessary for them to protect themselves against predators. In the marine and terrestrial environment, the animals essentially protect themselves in two different ways. One way consists of gathering all the individuals of the same species into a compact flock that discourages predators. Carnivores rarely attack a group; they rather attack isolated individuals or those separated from the group. This protective device is generally used by large herbivores of the savannah, both day and night, but the group becomes tighter during the inactive period. In the marine environment, this strictly defensive behavior can be observed in certain diurnal herbivores (Scaridae, Acanthuridae) or in certain nocturnal carnivores. During the day, snappers (Lutjanidae), some goatfishes (Mullidae), and silversides (Atherinidae) form compact schools breaking apart at nightfall.

The second protective device consists of staying out of the predator's reach, hiding either in a burrow built by the animal itself or in any preexisting shelter. This behavior is generally used in the marine and terrestrial environments among diurnal as well as nocturnal species. On land, a great number of mammals build their burrows, as the Orycterope, certain lagomorphs (rabbits), and numerous rodents do. These burrows generally serve the same individual for several months. Other species frequently use these shelters alternately with the main resident. For example, the burrows built by the Orycterope, a nocturnal carnivore, shelter diurnal species during the night. Other mammals use natural shelters, such as hollow trunks of trees, holes under stones, or crevices in rocks. Damans, for example, hide in preexisting shelter in their territory. Finally, other species, such as hares (Leporidae), spend the daytime in holes in the ground.

On the reefs, most species hide during their inactive period. During the night, diurnal species seek shelter between coral branches, in reef crevices, or even in the sediment, as numerous wrasses do. During the day, the same hiding places are generally used by nocturnal carnivores, sheltering in groups under the overhanging rocks or in reef crevices (Pempheridae, Holocentridae), or hiding individually in corals or crevices (Scorpaenidae, Plesiopidae, etc.). Reef fishes rarely build permanent burrows, although this phenomenon can be observed in certain families, such as the Gobiidae.

On land, another kind of daily migration has already been noted in connection with the necessity for certain animals to drink. These daily migrations to water holes generally occur twice a day, once in the morning, and again in the evening. Each species follows characteristic schedules.

3.2 Seasonal Migrations

Yearly variations of temperature and light have a great effect on terrestrial vegetation. In a tropical environment, the savannah comes under a seasonal cycle that follows the cycle of rainfall. During the dry season, the vegetation withers or becomes dormant. In contrast, during the rainy season, shrubs, grasses, and trees grow green again, develop actively, and produce seeds, berries, and flowers. These yearly variations of vegetation play a direct role in the feeding of herbivores and an indirect one on their predators. As food becomes scarce, these species are forced to migrate towards richer regions or to store food in order to survive the critical period without leaving the area.

Seasonal migrations toward more hospitable grazing areas can be observed in most of the large herbivores. Antelopes, zebras, gnus, buffaloes, and elephants migrate every year at the same time throughout Africa along traditional routes. The need for food is only one of the numerous factors determining these migrations. Although the same phenomenon is not observed in reef fishes, a marine equivalent can be found among pelagic fishes such as the Thunnidae and Carangidae, which travel in search of food according to seasonal cycles.

Among terrestrial mammals, storing food is a relatively frequent phenomenon, observed for varying periods of time. Certain carnivores keep a part of their prey for one or several days. A panther, for example, keep what remains of the carcass up in a tree, out of the carrion-eaters' reach, in order to feed on it the following day. It is, however, among the rodents that the habit of storing is the most conspicuous. Although more pronounced in a temperate zone, this behavior nevertheless exists among certain tropical species.

In contrast, however, the storing of food is not observed in the tropical marine environment, for food, although varying from one season to another, is always sufficiently abundant.

4   CONCLUSION: COMPARATIVE SURVEY OF FOOD WEBS

In this concluding section, the findings on food webs of a coral reef and of an African savannah are compared. Articles on the feeding of reef fishes (Hiatt and Strasburg, 1960; Randall, 1963; Vivien, 1973) provide a general idea of food webs existing on the coral reef. Herbivorous and omnivorous fishes as well as a small percentage of carnivorous fishes are diurnal. Most carnivorous fishes are nocturnal in their feeding activity. It should be noted, therefore, that the different trophic levels of a coral reef are not simultaneously consumed. The lowest trophic levels (the primary and secondary levels) are essentially used during the day while the highest trophic levels (the tertiary and quaternary levels) are consumed at night.

This alternation of two trophic cycles, one diurnal, the other nocturnal, is not observed in the case of the African savannah, which is certainly one of the terrestrial environments where the biological balance is the most complex and is still poorly understood. Food webs are extremely complex and imbricated. Whereas most carnivorous mammals have a nocturnal or crepuscular feeding activity like their marine counterparts, terrestrial herbivores and omnivores can be diurnal or nocturnal according to the species. All the trophic levels are thus used regardless of the time of day or night.

In the same way that the food web existing in these two environments are fundamentally different, the pyramids of biomass by feeding categories also are dissimilar among the fishes and the mammals. In an African savannah, the biomass of herbivores is assessed at about 20% of the plant biomass (Pierre, 1968) and that of carnivores at 1% of the biomass of herbivores. Effectively, most carnivorous mammals in the savannah feed on other mammals, herbivores, omnivores, and small carnivores. The other groups of animals (birds, reptiles, etc.) constitute only a small part of their diet. The number of carnivorous mammals thus is directly linked to the number of herbivorous ones, which explains why their biomass is small when compared to that of herbivores.

The situation is quite different on the reefs. The biomass of herbivorous fishes hardly reaches 25 to 30% of that of the total reef ichthyofauna (Randall, 1963; Bakus, 1967). The most important component of the biomass on reefs is represented by carnivorous fishes. This can be explained by the fact that these species are not dependent for survival on herbivorous fishes, which constitute only a small part of the diet of the carnivorous fishes. Most of the prey used by these carnivores are in fact invertebrates (crustaceans, polychaetes, and mollusks). The pyramid of biomass, then, is reversed on the reefs, if the fishes only are considered, with carnivores being more important than herbivores.

It is thus clear that fishes in the marine environment and mammals in the terrestrial setting have adapted their food and feeding behaviors to the different environmental conditions that they encounter. The terrestrial environment, with its seasonal fluctuations, offers a greater variety of diets and behaviors.

Although convergences of feeding habits can be observed among these two groups of vertebrates, the peculiarities proper to each group appear as the consequence of fundamental differences between the two environments.

5 ACKNOWLEDGMENTS

I thank Dr. E. S. Hobson, National Marine Fisheries Service and Scripps Institution of Oceanography, Tiburon, California, for his comments and criticisms.

REFERENCES

Bakus, G J. 1967. The feeding-habits of fishes and primary production at Eniwetok, Marshall Islands. Micronesica **3**: 135–149.

Bourlière, F. 1951. *Vie et Moeurs des Mammifères*. Payot, Paris. 250 p.

Brosset, A. 1969. La vie des Mammifères. Les Moeurs, rapports avec le milieu et classification. *In:* P. P. Grassé, Ed. *La Vie des Animaux*. Vol. 3. Larousse, Paris P. 227–380.

Hiatt, R. W. and D. W. Strasburg. 1960. Ecological relationships of the fish fauna on coral reefs of the Murshall Islands. Ecol. Monogr. **30:** 65–127.

Hobson, E.S. 1965. Diurnal-nocturnal activity of some inshore fishes in the Gulf of California. Copeia **1965:** 291–302.

Hobson, E. S. 1968. Predatory behavior of some shore fishes in the Gulf of California. Res. Rept. U.S. Fish. Wildl. Serv. **73:** 1–92.

Hobson, E. S. 1974. Feeding relationships of teleostean fishes on coral reefs in Kona, Hawaii. Fish. Bull. U.S. **72:** 915–1031.

Matthews, L. H. 1972. La vie des Mammifères. *In:* Bordas, Ed. *La Grand Encyclopedie de la Nature.* Paris, Vols. 1 and 2. P. 1–767.

Pierre, F. 1968. L'Afrique, terre des grands fauves et des antilopes. *In:* P. P. Grassé, Ed. *La vie des Animaux.* Vol. 1. Larousse, Paris P. 147–199.

Randall, J. E. 1963. An analysis of the fish populations of artificial and natural reefs in the Virgin Islands. Caribb. J. Sci. **3:** 31–48.

Randall, J. E. 1967. Food habits of reef fishes of the West Indies. Proc. Int. Conf. Trop. Oceanogr. **1965:** 665–840.

Romer, A. S. 1970. L'évolution animale. *In:* Editions Rencontre, *La Grande Encyclopedie de la Nature.* Vols. 2 and 3. Lausanne, Paris. P. 1–767.

Vivien, M. L. 1973. Contribution à la connaissance de l'éthologie alimentaire de l'ictyofauna du platier interne des recifs coralliens de Tuléar (Madagascar). Tethys Supp. **5:** 221–308.

Part IV

SOCIAL BEHAVIOR

9

SOCIAL BEHAVIOR IN SOME MARINE AND TERRESTRIAL CARNIVORES

BURNEY J. LE BOEUF

Crown College
University of California, Santa Cruz

1 INTRODUCTION

Once upon a time, around 37 million years ago, when primitive fissiped carnivores were evolving from their miascid predecessors, some of them forsook their way of life on land and went to sea to find food. This move must have worked out well, because many of the descendants of these pioneers—the seals, sea lions, and walruses—are still making a living in the sea today. Of course, descendants of the carnivores that remained on land fared well, too. Because land and sea are such different environments, we might expect the two animal groups to have diverged in many ways since their separation. Indeed, it should be interesting to compare representatives of the two groups because of what they have in common, an ancestor, and because of the obvious differences in the environments in which they live. In this chapter, I point out some differences and similarities between seals and their terrestrial conterparts with respect to gross morphology, feeding and predatory behavior, reproductive behavior, and various aspects of social life. As is necessary when comparing two large groups of animals, I document points with examples from a few selected species. My selection is biased toward those species that have been studied most systematically, those that are of greatest theoretical interest, and those studies with which I am familiar.

The similarities between seals and land carnivores were obvious to laymen and early scientists (Fig. 9.1). Fifteenth and 16th century sailors described the seals they saw as marine carnivores and called them "sea lions," "sea bears," or "lobos de mar" (sea wolves). Linnaeus and several later taxonomists classified seals, sea lions, and walruses in the order Carnivora. However, as early as 1811, there was an attempt to place these animals in a separate order (Illiger, 1811). At present, many investigators class these marine mammals in their own separate order, the Pinnipedia (e.g., King, 1964). However, classification of these animals is far from settled. Some maintain that the new order is inappropriate and that pinnipeds should be considered merely a suborder of the Carnivora (McKenna, 1969). Others argue that the pinnipeds can be classified into two living families (walruses are placed in the same family as sea lions) under the superfamily, Canoidea, in the order Carnivora (Mitchell and Tedford, 1973).

Before I make specific comparisons, it may be useful to present a sketch of pinniped evolutionary history. Their history, although poorly documented, may provide clues to differences we might expect between them and terrestrial carnivores.

The earliest pinnipeds probably entered the sea in one of the following areas: the Arctic Basin, the northwest coast of North America, or the Tethyan-Mediterranean area (Matthew, 1939; Davies, 1958a; McLaren, 1960; Repenning, 1970). It is not clear whether seals and sea lions (including the walrus) were already differentiated at this time. The oldest pinniped remains are from the Miocene era, a time when they were already well adapted for aquatic life and when seals and sea lions were already distinguishable (Downs, 1956; Mitchell and Tedford, 1973). One opinion holds that all pinnipeds derived from canoid or dog-bear stock (e.g., Matthew, 1939; Simpson, 1945; Davis, 1958a; Sarich, 1969). An opposing view is that sea lions and the walrus derived from ursine stock, and seals derived from lutrine stock (e.g., Mivart, 1885; McLaren, 1960; King, 1964; Repenning, 1970). This question is far from settled. Nevertheless, there is agreement that all pinnipeds are more closely related phylogenetically to members of the superfamily Canoidea of the order Carnivora—the

FIGURE 9.1 The head, face, and muzzle of California sea lions resemble those of dogs and bears.

dogs, raccoons, bears, weasels, and the like—than to the feloid carnivores.

After they entered the water, the distribution and diversity of pinnipeds were influenced by geomorphic and climatic barriers, distance between land falls, ocean currents, and water temperature (Davies, 1958a; King, 1964; Hendey, 1972). Davies (1958b) hypothesizes that pinnipeds are, and always have been, tied to a cold-water environment. He argues very persuasively that the distribution and differentiation of present-day northern pinnipeds reflects periods of expansion and contraction of sea and glacial ice that occurred during the Pleistocene era. Scheffer (1958, p. 37) points out that "as local shore lines and islands rose and fell and glacial barriers came and went, pinnipeds moved back and forth in order to maintain favorable breeding grounds along the edge of the sea." On land, many contemporary carnivores were being forced into extinction by periodic fires, floods, droughts, and dust storms.

Scheffer suggests that the early pinnipeds moved out along the shores of continents, from island to island and later to polar ice fields. The rate of evolution was faster at the frontiers of the advancing lines where immigration was unidirectional. He speculates further:

The primitive populations were small, composed of family groups, not very sociable. The members did not wander far, had no well-developed homing instinct, were not migratory, and did not need to rendezvous in special places in order to find mates. Polygyny had not developed in any of the pinniped stocks. The animals were perhaps smaller than most recent pinnipeds (Cope's rule), had less fat, lived in more temperate waters, and perhaps made crude dens in beach grasses and among boulders. The advancing pinnipeds met, from sea birds and cetaceans, little competition for food. They met no competition for breeding room, nor do they often today. Pinnipeds early lost the habit of feeding on beach organisms such as crabs, mussels, periwinkles, and blennies. [Scheffer, 1958, p. 36–37]

As each generic stock became isolated, it was transformed in response to the local physical and biotic environment and adapted to its peculiar niche. Among species frequenting isolated bays, gulfs, islands, inland seas, or lakes, there has been, and still is, rapid evolution.

In the last few centuries, the effect of commercial sealing upon island and continental pinniped populations has been catastrophic. Millions of seals have been slaughtered and entire breeding populations wiped out. It is doubtful that some species will ever recover genetically from undergoing such a severe population "bottleneck" (Le Boeuf, 1977). In one recently exploited species, absolutely no polymorphic variation was found in 21 blood proteins from 159 seals representing five rookeries (Bonnell and Selander, 1974)! In this regard, some land carnivore populations have suffered a similar fate at the hands of man—for example, the wolf. The increasing range of human populations is changing the distribution of both land carnivores and pinnipeds.

Although pinnipeds are marine, all species have retained an attachment to land. In this respect, they differ from the Cetacea, descendants of a primitive ungulate ancestor, who have become completely aquatic. All pinnipeds give birth on land or ice, and some species spend the majority of their time resting out of the water.

Pinnipeds have exploited the marine niche for food. A few carnivores, such as the sea otter, *Enhydra lutris*, and the polar bear, *Thalarctos maritimus*, also obtain food from the sea, but they have not undergone the same degree of morphological transformation to aquatic living as the pinnipeds. The anatomical and behavioral adaptations of the pinnipeds to life in the sea clearly distinguishes them from the land carnivores. Since these adaptations influence their behavior on land, it is worth reviewing some of the major ones.

2 MORPHOLOGICAL COMPARISONS

Many morphological differences between pinnipeds and land carnivores are simply a reflection of the different environments in which they live. The average body size of pinnipeds is greater than that of carnivores. The smallest pinniped, the ringed seal, *Pusa hispida*, weighs 90 kg. The largest pinniped, the southern elephant seal, *Mirounga leonina*, weighs about 3629 kg and is 650 cm long (Scheffer, 1958). Several seal species are larger than the largest land carnivore, the grizzly bear, *Ursus arctos*, which weighs 771 kg (Erdbrink, 1953). Many land carnivores, such as the foxes of Africa (Bekoff, 1975), weigh less than 4 kg. The Fennec fox, *Fennecus zerda*, weighs less than 1 kg! The greater body size of pinnipeds evolved mainly in response to the marine environment. Large body size is better for heat retention in the cold sea. Moreover, since the water medium gives more support than air, large size could more easily evolve in the sea than on land.

The pinniped body is adapted for swimming and diving. Body shape is streamlined to reduce drag. The external ears are reduced or absent, external genitalia and mammary teats are drawn into the body, limbs are enclosed within the body and extremities are flattened—the tail is short and the head is flattened, and the eyes are situated well forward. The neck, in particular, is thick and muscular and considerably more flexible than in most large carnivores. The skin is adapted to a water environment (Montagna and Harrison, 1957), and the hair is flattened. Pinnipeds never groom the pelage with the mouth or tongue (Scheffer, 1958). The terrestrial carnivore body is a picture of contrast. The canid body, especially the large one, is designed for long-distance running (see Romer, 1966; Mech, 1970; Fox, 1975).

Subcutaneous fat forms a substantial part of all pinniped bodies. Skin and blubber make up more than 25% of the weight of the Weddell seal, *Leptonychotes weddelli* (Bruce, 1951) and almost 50% of the body weight of the southern elephant seal (Laws, 1953). Blubber provides reserve energy during fasts and lactation, thermal insulation, buoyancy, and the padding necessary for a streamlined profile. The proportion of body fat to total weight in land carnivores is apparently much smaller, even in dormant or hibernating bears, skunks, and raccoons.

Although the pinniped brain has not been studied in great detail, it is evidently large, like that of terrestrial carnivores, but more spherical and more highly convoluted (King, 1964). The sea lion brain resembles that of bears, while the seal brain looks more like that of cats and dogs. Compared to a dog's brain, the cerebellum is large, probably because of the increased coordination demanded in swimming. The auditory nerve is large and the olfactory lobes are reduced. Pinniped eyes (the walrus excepted) are larger than those of land carnivores, and they function well at low levels of illumination. Seal vision is excellent both in water and on land (Schusterman, 1972).

Pinnipeds have fewer and more uniform teeth than most land carnivores (except for the walrus, a special case once again). All species have the pronounced upper and lower canines but lack the carnassial cusps characteristic of land carnivores. The postcanines in most species are rudimentary pegs functioning to hold prey that is swallowed whole. Variation in pinniped teeth reflects the type of flesh the animal feeds on, and, as in many mammals, it is a useful taxonomic indicator. Generally, the teeth, mouth, jaw, and associated structures of pinnipeds are designed for grasping, tearing, and swallowing prey whole or in chunks, rather than for chewing, shearing, or crushing large bones. In contrast with land carnivores, the deciduous teeth of pinnipeds disappear before or soon after birth.

Pinnipeds have made numerous physiological adjustments to aquatic life that set them apart from land carnivores. These adaptations in respiration, circulation, renal physiology, and the like are important and interesting, but it would be too much of a digression to cover these topics here. Ridgeway (1972) provides an excellent review of marine mammal adaptation to the aquatic environment.

3 PREY, FOOD HABITS, AND FEEDING BEHAVIOR

Pinnipeds deviated from land carnivores in form and function because of adaptations that took place as a result of seeking food in the sea. It is therefore most important to compare these two animal groups from the point of view of hunting and feeding habits, and in relation to their respective prey.

Both pinnipeds and land carnivores are meat eaters, but only the marine mammals eat flesh exclusively. Seals and sea lions feed mainly on crustacea, molluscs, fish, penguins, and other sea birds. Although diet varies with the species, the majority of pinnipeds feed on a variety of prey. The Alaska fur seal, *Callorhinus ursinus*, is the best studied pinniped from the point of view of food habits. Its catholic diet is representative of the wide range of fishes and squid eaten by the Otariids (the earred seals or sea lions and fur seals, as opposed to the Phocids, the earless, true seals). Alaska fur seals feed on more than 30 kinds of marine organisms: at least 27 species of fish, 1 species of octopus, and 5 species of squid (Fiscus, Niggol, and Wilke, 1961). The most common prey of fur seals are northern anchovy, *Engraulis mordax*, squid, and Pacific herring (*Clupea harengus*). Various rockfish, Pacific hake, *Merluccius Productus*, Pacific saury, *Cololabis saira*, salmon, *Oncorhynchus* spp., and American shad, *Alosa sapidissimia*, are eaten in lesser quantities. Hermit crabs, amphipods, and various diving sea birds (e.g., Rhinocerous Auklet, *Cerorhinca monocerata*, Red-throated Loon, *Gavia stellata*, and Beal Petrel, *Oceanodroma leucorhoa* beali) are eaten occasionally, but they seem to play only a minor role in the seals' diet (Niggol, Fiscus and Wilke, 1959).

Fur seals, like most other pinnipeds, are opportunistic feeders. What is eaten depends on the seasonal distribution and the abundance of prey. Since fur seals commonly feed on schooling fishes, stomach contents of several animals collected in the same area often contain only one type of fish. The Steller sea lion, *Eumetopias jubata* (Spaulding, 1964), and the California sea lion, *Zalophus californianus* (Fiscus and Baines, 1966), eat similar fishes and squid, especially where the feeding range of the three species overlaps. Steller males in the Bering Sea and off Alaskan islands supplement their diet with Alaska fur seal pups (Roger Gentry, personal communication).

Most true seals, such as the harbor seal, *Phoca vitulina*, and the grey seal, *Halichoerus grypus*, are mainly fish eaters, but they occasionally feed on an assortment of crustacea, octopus, eels, and molluscs (Spaulding, 1964; Kenyon, 1965; Anderson *et al.*, 1974). The northern elephant seal, *Mirouna angustirostris*, is a deep diving seal that feeds primarily on squid, skates, rays, small sharks, and ratfish, *Hydrolages collier* (Huey, 1930; Morejohn and Baltz, 1970). The small ringed seal, *Pusa Hispida*, which inhabits the circumpolar Arctic coasts, feeds on up to 72 different species of small pelagic amphipods, euphausians, and other crustacea, as well as on small fish (King, 1964).

Only two of the 32 different pinniped species in King's classification (King, 1964) are rather specialized feeders that exploit one type of prey species almost exclusively. The Crabeater, *Lobodon carcinophagus*, feeds on krill, small shrimp-like animals that it catches in quantity and strains from the water through its multicusped cheek teeth, much as a mysticete whale sieves krill through its baleen. The walrus, *Odobenus rosmarus*, feeds primarily on three genera of bivalve molluscs, *Mya*, *Saxicava*, and *Cardium*, for which it forages in shallow coastal waters less than 40 fathoms deep. Bivalves on the sea bottom are examined and sorted by the lips and whiskers; feet and fleshy parts are torn off and swallowed whole or sucked out. But when molluscs are scarce, the walrus may eat young ringed seals, bearded seals, *Erignathus barbatus*, and even young walruses. It is the only pinniped that apparently feeds on Cetacea. Occasionally a narwhal, *Monodon monoceros*, or a beluga, *Delphinapterus leucas* is eaten. However, it is not known whether walruses acturally kill them or feed on corpses (King, 1964).

The diversity of foods eaten by canids and ursids is even greater than that of pinnipeds. According to Mech (1970), "probably every kind of backboned animal that lives in the range of the wolf has been eaten by the wolf." Wolves, *Canis lupus*, eat mice, mink, muskrats, squirrels, rabbits, various birds, fish, lizards, snakes, grasshoppers, earthworms, and berries. But predation on small animals plays only a minor role in the wolf's diet. The main prey of the wolf, like those of the African wild dog, *Lycaon pictus*, are large animals. The wolf's primary prey in the United States and Canada are: white-tailed deer, mule deer, moose, caribou, elk, Dall sheep, bighorn sheep, and beaver. Wild dogs kill mostly Thomson's gazelles, juvenile wildebeests and Grant's gazelles (Estes and Goddard, 1967), and, occasionally, warthogs and zebras (van Lawick-Goodall and van Lawick-Goodall, 1971). African foxes feed mostly on rodents and small reptiles, birds's eggs, insects and vegetable matter; jackals eat similar foods in addition to small mammals and carrion (Bekoff, 1975). Additional information on other canids can be found in Fox (1975).

Of all the land carnivores, bears have the most diverse tastes. The grizzly, before man virtually annihilated it, was an omnivorous opportunist *par excellence*. The California grizzly (Storer and Tevis, 1955) ate almost anything and everything that was available. This long list included: meat, fresh or putrid from whales, water birds, fish, elk, deer, antelope, gophers, lizards, frogs, and domestic livestock; a wider variety of plant materials than herbivorous animals ate, some of which were various berries, clovers, nuts, wheat, corn, potatoes, tree bark, and various bulbs; and assorted foods like honey, ants and their larvae, yellow-jacket nests, and mushrooms. Polar bears, *Thalarctos maritimus*, have a much more restricted diet. Although they consume some vegetation and carrion during the summer (Russell, 1975), they feed primarily on the ringed seal during most of the year (Stirling and McEwan, 1975).

The remarkable thing about the feeding habits of the large canids is that the prey is often larger than the predator. In this respect, the large canids differ from all of the pinnipeds. Wild dogs, whose average weight does not exceed 18 kg, bring down impala and reedbucks that are double or triple their size (Estes and Goddard, 1967) and zebras that are even larger. Wolves weighing 36 to 45 kg kill moose and bison that may weigh over 500 kg. These canids overcome large prey by hunting in packs that range from a few animals up to a score or more of them. One dog usually selects a quarry from a retreating herd of gazelles, and the other dogs follow it. The quarry is coursed for 1 to 3 km until it becomes exhausted. The lead dog catches up to it and grabs it or bowls it over. Once overtaken, the prey is fallen on by all the following dogs, and it is dismembered and eaten with great dispatch. Wolves bring down deer or moose in a similar way (Mech, 1970). The first wolf to catch up to the fleeing prey attempts to grab hold of the rump, flanks, neck, or nose. Once the prey is down, others attack from every side. Although the technique may vary with prey species, the strategy of the individual quarry, and the composition of the hunting pack, it is clear that these pack hunters get help from each other in getting their food. Lone wolves or even small packs are at a disadvantage in bringing down large prey. In black-backed jackals, *Canis mesomelas*, Wyman (1967) observed that two hunters were more than four times as successful as one in bringing down gazelle fawns.

Like land carnivores, the size of prey eaten by pinnipeds varies greatly, but, except for the dubious possibility that walruses kill small whales, pinnipeds always kill and eat animals that are much smaller than themselves. Prey size determines how Alaska fur seals, Steller sea lions, and harbor seals eat their food. Small fishes less than 30 cm long, such as anchovy, herring, saury, or squid, are consumed whole under water (Niggol, Fiscus, and Wilke, 1959; Spaulding, 1964). Except for very small food items like lanternfish, the prey is swallowed head first. Larger prey measuring more than 30 cm long, such as hake, rockfish, or salmon, is brought to the surface, grasped by the head, shaken violently, and reduced to chunks that are swallowed piecemeal. As fur seals get older and larger, large fish up to 92 cm make up an increasingly high proportion of their diet (Spaulding, 1964).

Some pinnipeds feed in groups, but, unlike the case with canids, grouping does not enable them to exploit larger animals. Rather, grouping seems to make it easier for them to exploit large aggregations of small prey. Fiscus and Baines (1966) saw Steller sea lions leaving their hauling grounds in the vicinity of Unimak Pass, Alaska, in compact groups of several hundred to several thousand animals. They swam out to feeding areas, where they dispersed into smaller groups of less than 50 animals containing both sexes and mixed sizes of animals. Massings of this type fed on large schools of fish or squid. Casual observations suggest that groups of sea lions feed more efficiently on schools of fish because cooperation among the hunters enables them to herd and control the movements of the school. When large fish schools are absent, sea lions feed singly or in small groups of two to five animals. Similar behavior has been observed in the California sea lion (Fiscus and Baines, 1966; Michael Bonnell, personal observation).

Before Steller sea lion females leave the rookery and their pups to go to sea and feed, they may engage in activities that resemble, and that may have an analogous function to, the prehunt greeting ceremony of wild dogs (Estes and Goddard, 1967; van Lawick-Goodall and van Lawick-Goodall, 1971). Several females may gather at water's edge, where they mill about restlessly in close contact with each other. They may vocalize repeatedly and engage in what appears to be low-intensity aggressive behavior before swimming off as a group to feed. In both species, these activities may reinforce group cohesion and unity as well as synchronize the time of departure.

Similarly, canids and pinnipeds may travel several kilometers to get a meal. Van Lawick-Goodall and van Lawick-Goodall (1971) report that wild dogs did not start their first chase until they were 8 km from where they started. The chase itself covered a distance of 5½ km. Wolves may pursue moose or caribou for up to 5 to 8 km but usually give up sooner (Mech, 1970). They may range up to 32 km from their den (Kelsall, 1957). Steller sea lions and California sea lions travel much further from their rookeries or hauling grounds to feed. The former have been seen feeding as far as 112 to 136 km from land (Kenyon and Rice, 1961) and the latter as far as 62 km from land (Fiscus and Baines, 1966; Le Boeuf, unpublished data). Usually, only small groups of less than 30 individuals are seen this far from land. Large groups of sea lions (100 or more) are seldom seen feeding more than 16 to 24 km from a hauling ground or rookery. It would be interesting to compare land carnivores and pinnipeds on the success of their respective hunting and fishing expeditions, but the difficulties inherent in observing seals feeding in the water makes this impossible at present. However, some indirect evidence is pertinent. Virtually all fur seals collected early in the day by the U. S. Fish and Wildlife Service had food in their stomachs (Niggol, Fiscus, and Wilke, 1959).

Although both pinnipeds and the larger land carnivores are nomadic, the former travel greater distances in their annual feeding migrations. The record holder is the Alaska fur seal, which migrates from its breeding grounds in the Bering Sea to its winter feeding grounds along the shores of the eastern and western Pacific as far south as San Diego, California, and Hokkaido, Japan, a distance of some 5000 km. Wolves may follow caribou on their annual migrations (Kelsall, 1968).

Wild dogs and dholes, *Ceron alpinus,* prefer to hunt in early morning or early afternoon or evening, although hunts occur on moonlight nights as well (Estes and Goddard, 1967; van Lawick-Goodall and van Lawick-Goodall, 1971; Davidar, 1975). Wolves and bears may hunt by day or night. Most of the smaller foxes are nocturnal feeders (Bekoff, 1975). Fur seals and sea lions are primarily night and early morning feeders. Stomach contents of animals collected at various hours after sunrise show decreasing amounts of food. However, in some areas where large schools of fish are present, daytime feeding also occurs. Typically, the midday hours are spent resting, and feeding activities gradually resume in late afternoon (Niggol, Fiscus, and Wilke, 1959; Spaulding, 1964). The harbor seal is a daytime feeder (Spaulding, 1964).

Canids eat great amounts of food in a single feeding bout. A wolf may gorge 9 kg of meat in a single meal; this may represent 20% of its body weight. However, estimates of a little more than half that amount per day per wolf may be more representative (Mech, 1970). Estes and Goddard (1967) estimate that wild dogs average 2.72 kg of meat per day, or approximately 6.7% of their body weight. But these canids may have to go without eating for several days at a time. Five to 7 day fasts have been recorded in wolves, and one wolf went for 17 days without food (Mech, 1970). It is common knowledge that domestic dogs can go for several days without eating, particularly when sexual activity is probable. Grizzlies and black bears in the more northerly parts of North America may go dormant for varying periods of time during the winter when food is scarce. In general, all of the land carnivores will feed regularly if possible. Even bears will actively feed throughout the year when food is available.

Most pinnipeds feed daily except at certain times of the year, usually the breeding season, when they undergo long fasts. Thus, feasts and famine are even more extreme in their annual cycle. When they are feeding, fur seals and sea lions ingest less food relative to body weight than the canids mentioned above. Spaulding (1964) estimates that fur seal, sea lion, and harbor seal food requirements range from 2 to 11% of body weight per day, with 6% being the average. During the breeding season, fur seal and sea lion males fast for approximately 6 weeks; harbor seals do not appear to fast during this time. The record for long fasts in pinnipeds goes to male northern elephant seals. They may go without food for 3 months (Le Boeuf, and Peterson 1969). Throughout this time they are actively fighting and attempting to copulate, and they may lose over 450 kg. Females of this species fast for an average of 34 days during the period in which they give birth and nurse their pups daily for 28 days (Le Boeuf, Whiting, and Gantt, 1972). A female's total body weight may be reduced by almost 50% during this fast. During the nonbreeding season, males and females fast again for approximately 30 days while undergoing the annual molt.

Most canids and ursids scavenge for food at some time. Perhaps bears exploit carrion more than any other land carnivore. Carrion was a major part of the California grizzly's diet more than 100 years ago, before man killed the grizzly and its prey. It is said that these bears kept the California coast clean of pinniped and whale carcasses that repeatedly washed ashore. There are numerous reports of 12 to 15 bears feeding at the same time on a single whale carcass (Storer and Tevis, 1955). Many of the larger land carnivores typically desert the remains of a kill and cache it away and return to eat from it later. Polar bears are an exception to this rule. They do not cache ringed seal carcasses that they kill, despite the fact that they may only feed on the blubber and leave the meat behind (Stirling and McEwan, 1975). In marked contrast to these feeding habits of land carnivores, pinnipeds do not cache food, nor do they scavenge, although the walrus may be an exception to this rule. Pinnipeds consume most of their prey entire and discard only the heads of large fish, particularly rockfish.

One drawback that pinnipeds experience in their marine habitat to which the larger land carnivores are relatively immune is predation. In carving their niche in the sea, pinnipeds became exposed to large predators who were also adapted to aquatic life and more formidable than themselves. At sea, the main predators on pinnipeds are large sharks, particularly the great white shark, *Carcharodon carcharias*, and the killer whale, *Orcinus orca*. All pinniped species living in the Pacific are preyed on by these animals. The degree of predation is unknown. When pinnipeds return to land or ice to give birth and nurse their young, they are vulnerable to predation by large land carnivores such as polar bears and grizzly bears, perhaps wolves, and, of course, man. Small carnivores, such as foxes, and skuas, gulls, and hawks, may prey on their young. Being adapted primarily for locomotion in water, they are no match defending themselves against large land predators. Thus, it would appear that predator pressure was important in causing pinnipeds to breed in remote sanctuaries free from these predators; that is, offshore islands or rocks, sandbars and ice floes, and offshore breeding areas are limited. This is particularly true of the food-rich waters of the temperate north Pacific, the north Atlantic, and the circumpolar Antarctic.

4 SOCIAL BEHAVIOR AND REPRODUCTION

Given this set of circumstances, it is likely that pinnipeds were forced to share limited breeding areas, and this led to the high degree of sociality and the large social gatherings that we find in pinnipeds today. In terms of the sheer number of animals that congregate together, the pinnipeds are much more social than any land carnivore. As many as 2 million Alaska fur seals can be found every summer on two tiny Pribilof Islands in the Bering Sea. Three thousand northern elephant seals may be found packed together tightly on one beach on Isla de Guadalupe, Mexico, during the peak of the breeding season (Fig. 9.2). Two thousand California sea lions may be found sleeping together in close contact ½ km inland on San Miguel Island, California, during the nonbreeding season (Fig. 9.3). The largest wolf or wild dog packs are miniscule in comparison.

Pinnipeds are among the most polygynous mammals. Apparently, this mode of life developed very early in their history, and it was closely tied to their amphibious habits (Bartholomew, 1970). When females began clustering in time and space, the conditions became ideal for promoting male-male competition, polygyny, and sexual dimorphism (see Trivers, 1972). Males must have competed to mate with as many females as possible. Those who kept other males away from areas containing females sired more pups. In their short breeding seasons on traditional rookeries, fur seals and sea lions developed a social structure characterized by territoriality among males (Fig. 9.4 and 9.5). Males without territories do not copulate, or they copulate only rarely; those who secure the most well-placed territories—territories containing the most estrous females—do most of the breeding (Bartholomew, 1953; Gentry, 1970). Another system that developed was for males to dominate other males and thus gain access to more estrous females wherever they were situated. This was the strategy adopted by northern elephant

FIGURE 9.2 Approximately 2000 northern elephant seal males, females, and newborn pups gathered on Pilot Rock Beach, Isla de Guadalupe, Mexico on 5 February 1973, a week after the peak of the breeding season. An observer is located in the extreme foreground.

FIGURE 9.3 A large aggregation of California sea lions about 1/2 km inland from the water's edge on San Miguel Island, California, during the nonbreeding season. Normally the sea lions would be sleeping in close contact with each other, but shortly before the picture was taken they were startled and rose up on their foreflippers.

FIGURE 9.4 Both California sea lion males and Alaska fur seal males are territorial during the breeding season, and on San Miguel Island they breed at the same time, and there is often interspecific competition over territories. The fur seal territories (circled in the foreground) are well defined spatially, and males actively herd females. California sea lions' territories are plastic and change with fluctuations in several variables. The sea lions are all other animals except those circled and those indicated by arrows; the latter are sleeping subadult male elephant seals.

FIGURE 9.5   Two Steller sea lion males engaged in a mutual threat at the boundary between their respective territories.

seal males. They fight for social status in a dominance hierarchy. The highest ranking male or males—depending on the number of females present—locate themselves nearest the females and keep all others away. One or a few of the highest-ranking males do most of the breeding in a harem; most males in a colony do not breed at all. One male may dominate a harem for several years and inseminate more than 200 females (Le Boeuf, 1974). Grey seal society is similar to that of elephant seals.

Thus, in most of the well-studied pinnipeds, males are polygynous and are either territorial or exhibit a dominance hierarchy during the breeding season. This is a reflection of the manner in which the largest and strongest males go about monopolizing a large number of females. Since size and physical aggression convey such a great reproductive advantage to males, these traits have become increasingly elaborated in time. Sexual dimorphism is greater in some seals and sea lions than in other mammals. For example, the Alaska fur seal male is five times larger than the female (Fig. 9.6).

FIGURE 9.6   Northern fur seal harem on Kitovi Rookery, Pribilof Islands, Alaska, during the breeding season. The male in the foreground has eight females in his territory; the male immediately behind him has none. Note the extreme sexual dimorphism. Photographed by R. S. Peterson in June, 1963.

Canids are "social" in quite a different way from pinnipeds. Social organization is characterized by seasonal or permanent pair bonds in foxes (Storm, 1965; MacPherson, 1969) and jackals (e.g., van Lawick-Goodall and van Lawick-Goodall, 1971; Eisenberg and Lockhard, 1972) and by cooperative hunting and group life in the wolf, dhole, and wild dog (Kleiman and Eisenberg, 1973; Mech, 1975). Black bears are essentially solitary, but female-cub associations are long lasting, and strong and female cubs inherit their mother's feeding territories (Rogers, 1974). Wolf packs are organized into separate male and female social hierarchies. Although the female hierarchy is more ambiguous, it is clearly more pronounced than the size-related dominance observed in female elephant seals. Hunting dog packs have similar hierarchies, particularly during the breeding season, but it is the female hierarchy that is most evident (van Lawick-Goodall and van Lawick-Goodall, 1971). In wolves and wild dogs, the dominant breeding female may prevent subordinate females from breeding or may drive them out of the pack and kill their pups. Dominant females may also enlist the help of males, and they may prevent other adults from feeding the subordinate female or her young.

Although many canids and ursids are territorial in the sense that they defend a feeding or home range against other individuals or groups of individuals, this behavior is quite different from the defense of rigid individual territories by fur seal males and Steller sea lion males against conspecific males during the breeding season.

When it comes to reproductive behavior and parental care, pinnipeds and terrestrial carnivores differ in many ways. Most canids and ursids, like pinnipeds, have one estrus per year (Asdell, 1964; Kleiman, 1968). However, male-female sexual interactions in the land carnivores can be prolonged and complex. Canids exhibit extensive precopulatory court-ship, frequent olfactory examination of the partners, and frequent urine and faecal marking (Kleiman, 1968). In some domestic canids, females actively solicit males (Le Boeuf, 1967). Canid copulation is characterized by a genital lock or tie. After intromission is achieved, the pair remains joined together by the genitalia and face in opposite directions for sev-eral minutes or as long as an hour. Females may be in estrus for several days and may copulate several times with different males. Usually, only the alpha female in a wolf pack breeds (Kleiman and Eisenberg, 1973; Rabb, Woolpy, and Ginsburg, 1967; Zimen, 1975, 1976).

In contrast, there is little or no courtship in pinniped sexual behavior (Le Boeuf, 1972). Male northern elephant seals pounce on females and attempt to force copulation at any time during the breeding season, regardless of the female's reproductive condition (Cox and Le Boeuf, 1977). Sea lions and fur seals may investigate the female's genitalia be-fore mounting, but there is little parallel to the direct solicitation of males by females seen in the domestic dog (Beach and Le Boeuf, 1967; Beach, 1976). Male seals do not mark with urine or feces, and they do not exhibit a copulatory lock. Copulation duration is equally long in both animal groups, lasting 3 to 7 min in elephant seals and 15 to 20 min in Steller sea lions. Some phocid females are in estrus for several days; most otariid females (in which the males are territorial) copulate only once during the estrous period (Le Boeuf, 1972). Copulation is *more canem* except in elephant seals, where the male mounts from the rear and to one side, perhaps a necessity because of the large bulk of the animals. Elephant seal males, like male wolves, prevent or interrupt each other's copula-tions; female seals, unlike wolf bitches, do not prevent other females from mating, but they threaten, attack, and on occasion kill pups of neighboring females (Le Boeuf and Briggs, 1977).

Canids have a short gestation period of about 2 months and a litter size that ranges from 2 to 15, with 5 being the mode (Asdell, 1964; Kleiman, 1968). The gestation period of bears is 6 to 7½ months, and the litter size is usually 2 to 4 (Asdell, 1964). Wild canid pups are born in dens or burrows. Weaning from mother's milk is at about 40 days in the domestic dog. But during the transition to solid food in most canids, the altricial young are provisioned by regurgitation feeding of partially masticated food. This is done by the parent male as well as by the mother in the smaller pair-bonding canids. In wolves and wild dogs, all adults in the pack, male and female, regurgitate to young pups as well as to the nursing mother not involved in the hunt. It is not clear how long this type of provisioning of the young goes on, but apparently it lasts until the young are able to obtain food on their own (see Mech, 1970; several reviews in Fox, 1975).

Females of all pinniped species give birth to a single pup once a year. They do not eat the placenta as the carnivores do. Within a few days or weeks after parturition, copulation takes place. Gestation, including delayed implantation, lasts 1 year. Thus, females give birth at about the same time each year and usually in the same place (except for seals that breed on ice). Most species give birth in the open, whether it is on sand, rock or ice; the ringed seal is an exception and gives birth in subnivean lairs in the pressure ridges of sea ice (Stirling and McEwan, 1975). Newborns of all species are physically well developed at birth. Pups are nursed for a minimum of 3 weeks (southern elephant seal, Laws, 1956) to more than a year (Steller sea lion, Gentry, 1970; walrus, Brookes, 1954). The northern elephant seal female is a mammalian phenomenon in that she doesn't feed during the entire 4 week nursing period! Weaning is abrupt in species like the elephant seal and gradual in others like the Pacific sea lions. Apparently, mothers feed their pups exclusively by nursing; they have not been observed carrying food to the young or regurgitating to them. Females of several species that breed colonially will not nurse pups other than their own. Northern elephant seal females bite and sometimes kill orphaned pups that attempt to suckle them. Adoption of orphaned pups by females who have lost their own pups may occur in elephant seals, grey seals, and, rarely, in Steller sea lions. Unlike the canids, male pinnipeds that breed in colonies do not help in rearing or feeding the young. So far as I know, no male seal helps the female in any way. Quite the contrary, males are inadvertently responsible for a sizeable portion of pup mortality in elephant seals and grey seals (Le Boeuf, Whiting, and Gantt, 1972; Le Boeuf and Briggs, 1977; Coulson and Hickling, 1964).

Evidently, there are fundamental differences in the social and reproductive behavior of these two related groups of animals. Two basic differences having to do with the origin of sociality and the rate of reproductive behavior stand out.

Social behavior seems to have quite a different origin in these two animal groups; that is, they must have been exposed to quite different selection pressures. In the carnivores, there developed a premium on grouping together, cooperating in the hunt, and feeding other pack members, because these behaviors increased the efficiency of predation (Wilson, 1975). Being social enhanced survival through the process of kin selection (Maynard Smith, 1964; Hamilton, 1964). On the other hand, pinniped sociality seems to have developed first because of a paucity of breeding sites free of predators; later, this trend became elaborated through the operation of sexual selection. It is unique to pinnipeds that feeding and breeding have always been spatially separated and have occurred in different habitats (Bartholomew, 1970). Unlike the typical terrestrial carnivore with an extensive home range in which mating also takes place, pinnipeds opted to travel great distances to breed on traditional sanctuaries. Since such sanctuaries were limited, females were forced to clump together; this situation predisposed males to maximize their reproductive success by attempting to inseminate as many females as possible (see Trivers, 1972). Successful males were belligerent and big. Unbridled male-male competition led quickly to extreme polygyny, sexual dimorphism, lack of parental behavior on the part of the male, sex differences in behavior, and continued gathering of a large number of animals for breeding. Once this system was started, the inertia of sexual selection kept it moving in the same direction. For example, females that move from the main aggregation of females are apt to be fertilized by a male who is unsuccessful in competing with other males—that is, a "marginal" male. If he is subordinate because of genetic factors, his progeny will be less successful in the next generation. Thus, any tendency of females to become less gregarious would be selected against and would be self-limiting (McLaren, 1967). Gregariousness in females should be positively reinforced as long as competition among males—whether for territories or for social status—results in the exclusion of some males (Bartholomew, 1970).

The second fundamental difference between pinnipeds and terrestrial carnivores has to do with reproductive turnover. In general, natural selection has favored two contrasting responses to the problems of population replacement and the colonization of new habitats. According to MacArthur and Wilson (1967), in environments where there is little crowding and food is abundant, r-selection will favor animals that utilize the most food and rear the larger families—that is, those with a high population growth rate. On the other hand, when there is crowding and intense competition for food, K-selection will favor animals that can replace themselves with the lowest possible intake of food. The first is a strategy of productivity, and the second is one of efficiency of reproduction.

In general, pinnipeds appear to have been K-selected and terrestrial carnivores r-selected—Pianka's (1970) admonition that all organisms represent a compromise on this continuum is certainly applicable here. One of the most interesting correlates of r- and K-selection is the pair of complexes that Martin (1975) calls, respectively, the altricial and precocial complex. Pinnipeds conform to many of the attributes of the precocial complex. Only one pup is born per year (one every 2 years in the walrus, according to Brooks, 1954) and the young exhibit advanced physical development at birth. Alaska fur seals can locomote and vocalize within a moment of birth, and they are as advanced at birth as domestic dogs about 3 weeks old (Bartholomew, 1959). Northern elephant seal pups open their eyes and may exhibit the characteristic sand-flipping movements of the foreflippers before completely expelled from the birth canal. Harbor seal pups are able to swim and dive at birth (Bishop, 1967). Lactation is of long duration, lasting more than a year in some sea lions and the walrus. Even in seals having a relatively short nursing period, energy investment in the offspring may be enormous. Elephant seal milk is approximately 55% fat, and although pups are weaned at 4 weeks of age, they are left with a tremendous fat store (Fig. 9.7). These pups weigh more at weaning than they do a year later! Other attributes of the precocial complex are late sexual maturity and a long life. Most pinniped females ovulate for the first time at about 2 to 5 years of age; males reach sexual maturity at about 3 to 6 years of age (e.g., harbor seals, Bigg, 1969; Alaska fur seals, Bartholomew and Hoel, 1953; anonymous, 1975; northern elephant seals, Le Boeuf, unpublished data). In the colonial species, males do not complete successfully for females until much later in life, until approximately 10+ years of age in the northern elephant seal (Le Boeuf, 1974). Pinnipeds may live a long time. Harbor seals live for 20 to 29 years (Biggs, 1969). Alaska fur seals for up to 26 years (Niggol, Fiscus, and Wilke, 1959), and the life span of the northern elephant seal is typically about 14 years (Le Boeuf and Briggs, unpublished data). Like that in primates and other long-lived mammals,

FIGURE 9.7 A suckling northern elephant seal pup appears almost as large as its mother shortly before it is weaned. At this time, it is four or five times larger than it was at birth, and heavier than it will be a year later. Its sole nurturance has come from mother's milk. The mother has provided this enormous fat store to her offspring during a four-week period in which she did not feed.

the trend in pinniped reproduction has been toward quality rather than quantity.

Terrestrial carnivores, especially the smaller canids, exhibit the altricial complex. Most canids give birth in a shelter to a large litter of pups that are poorly developed and incapable of coordinated behavior except suckling. Gestation is short and lactation brief compared to most pinnipeds. Sexual maturity occurs at an early age, at the end of the second year in wild wolves (Mech, 1970), and at the end of the first year is some captive wolves (Medjo and Mech, 1976) and in the Arctic fox (Chesemore, 1975). Life spans are short compared to those of pinnipeds. Although wolves have lived 10 to 16 years in captivity (Young, 1944), 10 is considered very old (Mech, 1970). Seven is considered old age in large dogs (Fuller and DuBuis, 1962). The life span of foxes is considerably less, 6 years of age in the gray fox, *Urocyon littoralis* (Laughlin, 1973). Apparently, canids and ursids have been selected for quantity in reproduction. The paradoxically low fecundity rate in wolf and wild dog packs, where only one female may give birth, may be related to low availability of food. It is interesting to note that if only one female gives birth in a pack, it is usually the most dominant one. One might expect the fecundity rate to go up when food was abundant. Whether this happens or not, the point is that the potential for a high reproductive rate is there.

Unlike land carnivores, pinnipeds must deal with problems that arise from making a living to two quite different habitats. The high metabolic rate and thick layer of blubber that are so adaptive in cold water create difficulties in thermoregulation on land, particularly when the ambient temperature is high, or after sustained activity has taken place. Numerous behavioral adjustments are important in preventing overheating (White and Odell, 1971; Gentry, 1973; Odell, 1974; Whittow, 1974). In addition, one negative consequence of the large social gatherings on land is that the animals are more vulnerable to disease and parasite transmission. The colonial breeding sea lions contain a wide variety of internal and external parasites (Dailey and Brownell, 1972). For example, seven species of trematodes, eight species of nematodes, one cestode, and various species of Acanthocephala, Acarina, and Anoplura have been identified in the California sea lion. Lungworm infestation is particularly heavy in this species and may be an important cause of juvenile mortality. Land carnivores do not seem to harbor the variety or the same high levels of parasite infestation as do these marine mammals. However, this comparison needs to be investigated more systematically.

5 SUMMARY

In summary, these two groups of animals have obvious similarities, some of which can be attributed to having a common ancestor. Pinnipeds bear the stamp of their canine, ursine, and lutrine relatives, especially in the structure of the head and the pronounced canine teeth. Most species in both orders are flesh eaters; they eat great quantities at a time, and they eat a wide variety of prey. However, subsistence in different habitats and exposure to differential selection for at least 20 million years have produced some even more obvious and interesting differences in social behavior. The larger canids evidently were selected to join social groups, in which there is a high degree of cooperation, because this allowed them to exploit large prey. Canids that prey on animals smaller than themselves are far less social, and kin-network welfare is reduced. Pinnipeds are social for a different reason. The most gregarious of them congregate in immense gatherings that may include thousands of individuals. These aggregations are located on offshore areas that are free from predators. Since these locations are restricted in number and size, it appears that pinnipeds were forced to group together in order to avoid predators. Once this step was taken, sexual selection put a premium on continued social living; for example, males who dominated other males in the large social gatherings probably bore more offspring than those who pair-bonded with single females away from the group. The few pinniped species that are solitary live in a habitat where there are few or no predators and where hauling-out areas, such as pack ice, are virtually unlimited. Finally, strategies of reproduction seem to differ in the two groups of animals. In general, the terrestrial carnivores appear to have been selected to produce a great quantity of offspring quickly, a strategy that works best in a varying environment, while pinnipeds appear to have been selected to produce fewer progeny of high quality, a strategy that is most characteristic of stable environments.

REFERENCES

Anderson, S. S., W. N. Bonner, J. R. Baker, and R. Richards. 1974. Grey seals, *Halichoerus grypus*, of the Dee Estuary and observations on a characteristic skin lesion in British seals. J. Zool. (Lond.) **174:** 429–440.

Asdell, S. A. 1964. *Patterns of Mammalian Reproduction.* 2nd ed. Cornell University Press, New York. 670 p.

Bartholomew, G. A. 1953. Behavioral factors affecting social structure in the Alaska fur seal. Trans. 18th No. Amer. Wildl. Conf. 481–502.

Bartholomew, G. A. 1959. Mother-young relations and the maturation of pup behavior in the Alaska fur seal. Anim. Behav. **7:** 163–171.

Bartholomew, G. A. 1970. A model for the evolution of pinniped polygyny. Evolution **24:** 546–559.

Bartholomew, G. A. and P. G. Hoel. 1953. Reproductive behaviour of the Alaska fur seal, *Callorhinus ursinus*. J. Mamm. **34:** 417–436.

Beach, F. A. 1976. Sexual attractivity, proceptivity, and receptivity in female mammals. Horm. and Behav. **7:** 105–138.

Beach, F. A. and B. J. Le Boeuf. 1967. Coital behavior in dogs: I. Preferential mating in the bitch. Anim. Behav. **15:** 546–558.

Bekoff, M. 1975. Social behavior and ecology of the African Canidae: A review. *In:* M. W. Fox, Ed. *The Wild Canids.* Van Nostrand Reinhold, New York. P. 120–142.

Bigg, M. A. 1969. The harbour seal in British Columbia. Fisheries Research Board of Canada Bulletin, Ottawa. 33 p.

Bishop, R. H. 1967. Reproduction, age determination, and behavior of the harbor seal, *Phoca vitulina* L., in the Gulf of Alaska. Unpublished M. S. thesis, University of Alaska, 121 p.

Bonnell, M. L. and R. K. Selander. 1974. Elephant seals: genetic variation and near extinction. Science **184:** 908–909.

Brooks, J. W. 1954. A contribution to the life history and ecology of the Pacific walrus. Unpublished M. S. thesis, University of Alaska. 103 p.

Bruce, W. S. 1915. Measurements and weights of antarctic seals, Part II. *In: Report on the Scientific Results of the Voyage of S.Y. 'Scotia' during the years 1902, 1903, and 1904.* Scottish Oceanographic Laboratory, Edinburgh. P. 149–174.

Chesemore, D. L. 1975. Ecology of the Arctic fox (*Alopex lagopus*) in North America: a review. *In:* M. W. Fox, Ed. *The Wild Canids.* Van Nostrand Reinhold, New York. P. 143–163.

Coulson, J. C. and G. Hickling. 1964. The breeding biology of the grey seal, *Halichoerus grypus* (Fab.) on the Farne Islands, Northumberland. J. Anim. Ecol. **33:** 485–512.

Cox, C. R. and B. J. Le Boeuf. 1977. Female incitation of male competition: A mechanism in sexual selection. Am. Nat. **111:** 317–335.

Dailey, M. D. and R. L. Brownell, Jr. 1972. A checklist of marine mammal parasites. *In:* S. H. Ridgeway, Ed. *Mammals of the Sea: Biology and Medicine.* Charles C. Thomas, Springfield, Ill. P. 528–576.

Davidar, E. R. C. 1975. Ecology and behavior of the Dhole or Indian wild dog, *Cuon alpinus* (Pallas). *In:* M. W. Fox, Ed. *The Wild Canids.* Van Nostrand Reinhold, New York. P. 109–119.

Davies, J. L. 1958a. The Pinnipedia: an essay in zoogeography. Geogr. Rev. **48:** 474–493.

Davies, J. L. 1958b. Pleistocene geography and the distribution of northern pinnipeds. Ecology **39:** 97–113.

Downs, T. 1956. A new pinniped from the Miocene of southern California: with remarks on the Otariidae. J. Paleontol. **30:** 115–131.

Eisenberg, J. F. and M. Lockhart. 1972. An ecological reconnaissance of Wilpattu National Park. Smithson. Contrib. Knowl. (Zool.). **101:** 1–118.

Erdbrink, D. P. 1953. *A Review of Fossil and Recent Bears of the Old World.* 2 parts. Deventer, De Lange. 597 p.

Estes, R. D. and J. Goddard. 1967. Prey selection and hunting behavior of the African wild dog. J. Wildlife Manag. **31:** 52–70.

Fiscus, C. H. and G. A. Baines. 1966. Food and feeding behavior of Steller and California sea lions. J. Mamm. **47:** 195–200.

Fiscus, C. H., K. Niggol, and F. Wilke. 1961. Pelagic Fur Seal Investigations: California to British Columbia. U.S. Fish and Wildlife Service, Seattle, Washington. 87 p.

Fox, M. W., Ed. 1975. *The Wild Canids.* Van Nostrand Reinhold, New York. 508 p.

Fuller, J. L. and E. M. DuBuis. 1962. The behavior of dogs. *In:* E. Hafez, Ed. *The Behavior of Domestic Animals.* Bailliére, Tindall, and Cox, London. P. 415–452.

Gentry, R. L. 1970. Social behavior of the Steller sea lion. Unpublished doctoral dissertation, University of California, Santa Cruz. 113 p.

Gentry, R. L. 1973. Thermoregulatory behavior of earred seals. Behaviour **46:** 73–93.

Hamilton, W. D. 1964. The genetical theory of social behaviour. I, II. J. Theor. Biol. **7:** 1–52.

Hendley, Q. B. 1972. The evolution and dispersal of the Monochinae (Mammalia: Pinnipedia). Ann. S. Afr. Mus. **59:** 99–113.

Huey, L. M. 1930. Capture of an elephant seal off San Diego, California, with notes on stomach contents. J. Mamm. **11:** 229–231.

Illiger, C. 1811. *Prodromus Systematis Mammalium et Avium.* Salfeld, Berlin.

Kelsall, J. P. 1968. *The Migratory Barren Ground Caribou of Canada.* Can. Wildl. Serv., Queen's Printer, Ottawa. 340 p.

Kenyon, K. W. 1965. Food of harbor seals at Amchitka Island, Alaska. J. Mamm. **46:** 103–104.

Kenyon, K. W. and D. W. Rice. 1961. Abundance and distribution of the Steller sea lion. J. Mamm. **42:** 233–234.

King, J. E. 1964. *Seals of the World.* British Museum (Natural History), London. 154 p.

Kleiman, D. G. 1968. Reproduction in the Canidae. Int. Zool. Yearb. **8:** 3–8.

Kleiman, D. G. and J. F. Eisenberg. 1973. Comparisons of canid and felid social systems from an evolutionary perspective. Anim. Behav. **21:** 637–659.

Laughrin, L. L. 1973. California Island fox survey. Wildl. Manag. Branch Adm. Rept. No. 73-3. 17 p.

Laws, R. M. 1953. The elephant seal (*Mirounga leonina*, Linn.). I. Growth and age. Falkland Isl. Depend. Surv. Sci. Repts. No. 8: 1–62.

Laws, R. M. 1956. The elephant seal (*Mirounga leonina*, Linn.). II. General social and reproductive behavior. Falkland Isl. Depend. Surv. Sci. Repts. **13:** 1–88.

Le Boeuf, B. J. 1967. Interindividual associations in dogs. Behaviour **29:** 268–295.

Le Boeuf, B. J. 1972. Sexual behavior in the northern elephant seal, *Mirounga angustirostris.* Behaviour **41:** 1–26.

Le Boeuf, B. J. 1974. Male-male competition and reproductive success in elephant seals. Am. Zool. **14:** 163–176.

Le Boeuf, B. J. 1977. Back from extation? Pacific Discovery **30:** 1–9.

Le Boeuf, B. J. and K. T. Briggs. 1977. The cost of living in a seal harem. Mammalia. **41:** 167–195.

Le Boeuf, B. J. and R. S. Peterson. 1969. Social status and mating activity in elephant seals. Science **163:** 91–93.

Le Boeuf, B. J., R. J. Whiting, and R. F. Gantt. 1972. Perinatal behavior of northern elephant seal females and their young. Behaviour **43:** 121–156.

MacArthur, R. H. and E. O. Wilson. 1967. *The Theory of Island Biogeography.* Princeton University Press, Princeton. 203 p.

MacPherson, A. H. 1969. The dynamics of Canadian Arctic fox populations. Can. Wildl. Serv. Rept. Ser. 8, Queen's Printer, Ottawa.

Martin, R. D. 1975. Strategies of reproduction. Nat. Hist. **84:** 48–57.

Matthew, W. D. 1939. *Climate and Evolution.* 2nd ed. Special Publications. New York Academy of Science. Vol 1. 223 p.

Maynard Smith, J. 1964. Kin selection and group selection. Nature **201:** 1145–1147.

McKenna, M. 1969. The origin and early differentiation of therian mammals. Ann. N.Y. Acad. Sci. **167:** 217–240.

McLaren, I. A. 1960. Are the Pinnipedia biphyletic? Syst. Zool. **9:** 18–28.

McLaren, I. A. 1967. Seals and group selection. Ecology **48:** 104–110.

Mech, L. D. 1970. *The Wolf: The Ecology and Behavior of an Endangered Species.* Natural History Press, Garden City, New York. 384 p.

Mech, L. D. 1975. Hunting behavior in two similar species of social canids. *In:* M. W. Fox, Ed. *The Wild Canids.* Van Nostrand Reinhold, New York. P. 363–368.

Medjo, D. C. and L. D. Mech. 1976. Reproductive activity in nine- and ten-month-old wolves. J. Mamm. **57:** 406–408.

Mitchell, E. and R. H. Tedford. 1973. The Enaliarctinae, a new group of extinct aquatic Carnivora and a consideration of the origin of the Otaridae. Bull. Am. Mus. Nat. Hist. **151:** 201–284.

Mivart, G. 1885. Notes on the Pinnipedia. Proc. Zool. Soc. London: 484–500.

Montagna, W. and R. J. Harrison. 1957. Specializations in the skin of the seal (*Phoca vitulina*). Am. J. Anat. **100:** 81–114.

Morejohn, G. V. and D. M. Baltz. 1970. Contents of the stomach of an elephant seal. J. Mamm. **51:** 173–174.

Niggol, K., C. H. Fiscus, and F. Wilke. 1959. *Pelagic Fur Seal Investigations: California-Oregon and Washington.* U.S. Fish and Wildlife Service, Seattle, Washington. 92 p.

Odell, D. K. 1974. Behavioral thermoregulation in the California Sea Lion. Behav. Biol. **10:** 231–237.

Pianka, E. R. 1970. On r- and K-selection. Am. Nat. **104:** 592–597.

Rabb, G. B., J. H. Woolpy, and B. E. Ginsberg. 1967. Social relationships in a group of captive wolves. Am. Zool. **7:** 305–311.

Repenning, C. A. 1970. Pinniped evolution: the fossil record. Talk given at a symposium on marine biology. 21 November 1970. University of California, Santa Cruz.

Ridgeway, S. H. 1972. Homeostasis in the aquatic environment. *In:* S. H. Ridgeway, Ed. *Mammals of the Sea.* Charles C. Thomas, Springfield, Ill. P. 590–747.

Rogers, L. L. 1974. Movement patterns and social organization of black bears in Minnesota. Unpublished doctoral dissertation, University of Minnesota, Minneapolis.

Russell, R. H. 1975. The food habits of polar bears of James Bay and southwestern Hudson Bay in summer and autumn. Arctic **28:** 117–129.

Sarich, V. M. 1969. Pinniped origins and the rate of evolution of carnivore albumins. Syst. Zool. **18:** 286–295.

Scheffer, V. B. 1958. *Seals, Sea Lions and Walruses.* Stanford University Press, Stanford, Cal. 179 p.

Schusterman, R. J. 1972. Visual acuity in pinnipeds. *In:* H. E. Winn and B. L. Olla, Eds. *Behavior of Marine Mammals.* Vol. 2. Plenum Publishing, New York. P. 469–492.

Simpson, G. G. 1945. The principles of classification and a classification of mammals. Bull. Am. Mus. Nat. Hist. 85. 350 p.

Spaulding, D. J. 1964. *Comparative Feeding Habits of the Fur Seal, Sea Lion, and Harbour Seal on the British Columbia Coast.* Fisheries Research Board of Canada, Ottawa. 52 p.

Stirling, I. and E. H. McEwan. 1975. The caloric value of whole ringed seals (*Phoca hispida*) in relation to polar bear (*Ursus maritimus*) ecology and hunting behavior. Can. J. Zool. **53:** 1021–1027.

Storm, G. L. 1965. Movements and activities of foxes as determined by radio-tracking. J. Wildl. Manag. **29:** 1–13.

Trivers, R. L. 1972. Parental investment and sexual selection. *In:* B. Campbell, Ed. *Sexual Selection and the Descent of Man, 1871–1971.* Aldine, Chicago. P. 136–179.

van Lawick-Goodall, H. and J. van Lawick-Goodall. 1971. *Innocent Killers.* Houghton Mifflin, Boston. 222 p.

White, F. N. and D. K. Odell. 1971. Thermoregulatory behavior of the northern elephant seal, *Mirounga angustirostris.* J. Mamm. **52:** 758–774.

Whittow, G. C. 1974. Sun, sand, and sea lions. Nat. Hist. **1974.** 56–63.

Wilson, E. O. 1975. *Sociobiology: The New Synthesis.* Belknap Press, Harvard University Press, Cambridge, Mass. 697 p.

Wyman, J. 1967. The jackals of the Serengeti. Animals **10:** 79–83.

Young, S. P. 1944. *The Wolves of North America,* Part I. American Wildlife Institute, Washington, D. C. 385 p.

Zimen, E. 1975. Social dynamics of the wolf pack. *In:* M. W. Fox, Ed. *The Wild Canids.* Van Nostrand Reinhold, New York. P. 336–362.

Zimen, E. 1976. On the regulation of pack size in wolves. Z. Tierpsychol. **40:** 300–341.

10

AGONISTIC BEHAVIOR IN FISHES AND TERRESTRIAL VERTEBRATES

RUDOLPH J. MILLER

School of Biological Sciences
Oklahoma State University, Stillwater

1 INTRODUCTION

In comparing agonistic behavior in fishes with that of terrestrial vertebrates, I recognized the problem of culling from the enormous literature on the subject a set of statements that might provide some useful insights to biologists who are not specialists in the field, without simply paraphrasing the ideas and generalizations of other scholars. After reviewing the several score volumes and many of the hundreds of papers dealing with the ecology, behavior, and physiology of agonistic activities in vertebrates, I have become more acutely aware of the difficulty of such a task. This paper must, therefore, be recognized as a highly selective overview and critique of the subject, emphasizing material from the fish behavior literature that can be related to the generally better-known bird and mammal literature.

The two principal areas of research on the subject (adaptiveness of agonistic behavior; causation of agonistic behavior) are briefly reviewed, and I attempt to explore some ways in which evolutionary trajectories (i.e., phylogenetic trends) may affect proximate and ultimate causes of behavior in vertebrates. Finally, I try to determine whether appreciable evidence exists to support the concept of a causal continuum underlying agonistic behavior in vertebrates. The nature and significance of such a continuum seems to me to be at the heart of much of the controversy surrounding the study of agonistic behavior in man and other vertebrates. Just how far can biologists extend data derived from studies on "lower vertebrates" to gain insight into the behavior of *Homo sapiens*? Where and how do we draw the lines delimiting distinct (or intergrading?) conceptual models for agonistic behavior?

The issue seems to be a simple one for ecologist E. O. Wilson, who considers aggression and related phenomena primarily from an ecological and evolutionary viewpoint and classifies these behaviors entirely on a functional basis in his monumental treatise *Sociobiology* (1975). In his view, aggressive acts serve as "competitive techniques" that lead to the acquisition of resources that are actually or potentially limiting. Although Wilson points out that aggressive behavior serves diverse functions among different species, and that different control centers in the brain may be involved in the performance of different "functional categories," the question of proximate causality enters his discussion largely to the extent that it relates to the personal genetic fitness of individuals exhibiting the behavior. Such a perspective is in keeping with current views recognizing the primacy of the roles of selection and genetic fitness in determining which structures, behaviors, or social orders will be present in a given population or species.

This approach may suffice if one is seeking to construct models linking generalized operations with social strategies or functions and adaptiveness of behaviors, but it may be of little help to those seeking to understand better human behavior that is sometimes interpretable as being pathological and that no longer operates under the strict constraints imposed by natural selection. We have not yet reached the point in science where the social psychologist and evolutionary ecologist ask the same kinds of questions or even speak the same language. I hope that the brief review that follows will point out ways in which we may hope to explore some common ground and understand better that evolutionary concepts and causal concepts are part of a multidimensional whole, none of whose parts alone can provide us with an unbiased perception of the nature of agonism.

2 THE NATURE OF AGONISTIC ACTIVITIES

Behaviors usually lumped as agonistic are among the most frequently studied of all animal and human activities because of their conspicuousness and evident significance in the lives of social animals. A brief, generally accepted, definition of this class of activities can be obtained from Hinde (1970), who suggested that "attacking, threat, submissive, and fleeing behavior form a complex, often referred to as 'agonistic behavior' (Scott and Frederickson, 1951)." My usage of the term will follow this basic definition. Hinde points out that such a concept is often useful because of the presence of simultaneous tendencies to attack and to flee and the associated occurrence of threat behavior. Examination of Hinde's and other authors' uses of the term "agonistic" suggests that the temporal, functional, and possibly causal association of several diverse movement patterns is not the only reason for lumping them in a single category. Although part of the usefulness of the term lies in its inclusiveness, part also is due to the difficulty encountered in dealing with the concept of aggression. In an excellent review of the topic, Johnson (1972) cites dozens of different examples of behaviors that could be said to have something to do with aggression. After pointing out that "There is no single kind of behavior which can be called 'aggression,' " he suggests that

Where only modest levels of precision are necessary, it may be useful to adopt the term *agonistic behavior* as a desirable alternative to "aggressive behavior." . . It refers simply to fighting and competitive behavior, usually in animals, and includes threats and offensive attacks as well as defensive fighting.

The social learning theorist Bandura (1973) also acknowledges the difficulty of defining the term "aggression." His working definition, "behavior that results in personal injury and in destruction of property," is qualified to the extent that he wishes to make it clear that "aversive effects cannot serve as the sole defining characteristics of aggression"; otherwise, the pain-producing activities of dentists or surgeons would be defined as aggressive.

Wilson (1975) argues that views of aggression regarding it as the denial of rights or resources by the commission of acts or threats provide a reasonably accurate definition of the concept, given that any "loss" by the victim is real only if genetic fitness is lowered by the act. The term "agonistic" is essentially dismissed because it cannot be defined any more precisely than aggression. He asserts that most aggressive acts serve as competitive techniques used in various ways to enhance success in sexual or resource competition in species exhibiting "contest" competition (Nicholson, 1957). Wilson's identification of the type of competition associated with aggressive activity is useful in helping to avoid confounding some of the many kinds of "competition" constructs with some of the more subtle types of "aggression" recognized by theorists.

It seems fairly clear that while many scientists are largely interested in "aggressive behavior," however defined, they find it useful to have a seemingly nonsubjective, largely operationally defined label to encompass many acts that occur during fighting or in hostile or competitive situations, especially when animal rather than human behavior is considered. I think it is worth noting that Bandura's inclusion of psychological as well as physical injury would make it difficult for many ethologists to use his aggression concept in their studies on animal behavior. I suggest that the paradigms most often utilized by psychologists (e.g., Berkowitz, 1962; Kaufmann, 1970; Bandura, 1973) in studying human aggression or agonism are so distinctive from those used in animal behavior studies that a single definition encompassing the viable concepts in both fields is impossible to achieve. Thus, while some aspects of the operations, functions, and causes involved can be identified at all phylogenetic levels, the quantum leap associated with self-consciousness and purposiveness that occurs *demonstrably* only in man (and perhaps some other primates) prevents us from perceiving the kind of smooth conceptual transition that would justify development of a more or less unified model and definition of the system.

3   SITUATIONS ASSOCIATED WITH AGONISTIC BEHAVIOR

King's (1973) definition—"Agonistic behavior includes all behavior associated with the contest or struggle between individuals"—is definitely animal-oriented and emphasizes the situational component of this activity. Since agonistic behaviors are largely tool behaviors, functioning mainly in association with other organic or psychological needs, it is useful to examine the major contexts in which they are found.

Agonistic behaviors tend to occur in situations involving conflict or competition for space, resources, mates, or status, or for protection of self or young. Although Wilson (1975) suggests that most intraspecific aggression occurs in contest competition, some of his categories (parental disciplinary aggression, weaning aggression, moralistic aggression, predatory aggression, and aggression) are difficult to view as contests in the ecological sense that he utilizes (the other categories are territorial aggression, dominance aggression, and sexual aggression). Even though some of these types of behavior occur mainly or exclusively in mammals, such a functional classification may be useful in identifying the adaptive circumstances associated with most agonistic activities. A strictly functional view of aggression has some drawbacks, however, because it cannot encompass certain types of activities occurring in man that are often considered to be classic examples of aggression. Johnson (1972) cites examples like racial hatred, mob violence, suicide, and other pathological human actions as difficult to categorize consistently. The reason for this, of course, is that structures, physiological mechanisms, and behaviors may evolve under one set of evolutionary constraints and then relatively suddenly become exposed to an entirely different selective regime. The next step is often the appearance of altered use of the structures or behaviors. The mechanisms controlling aggressive activities in man undoubtedly evolved in precultural situations. It seems highly unlikely that the same selective pressures remained operable in cultural man. The imposition of complex language, social, and economic systems must surely have altered the relationships between physiological causal mechanisms and environmentally linked overt behaviors. Because the issue of genetic programming of human behavior is so poorly understood at present, it would seem prudent to eliminate from a consideration of agonistic behavior, at least for the time being, situations that do not conform comfortably with a clearly defined conflict or competitive situation.

Scott (1971) has pointed out that intraspecific fighting occurs mainly in the arthropods and vertebrates, and he suggests that it is absent in species where it would have no survival value. In his view, lack of adaptive value occurs in species in which the motor capacity for inflicting pain or injury is absent, and in which individuals are unable to recognize each other as individuals. Thus "Indiscriminate attacks on all members of the same species, including males, females, and young, could have only negative survival value." He feels that "defensive fighting in reaction to painful stimulation is the most basic type of social fighting," and that "pain is the most basic primary eliciting stimulus ('releaser') for fighting." Pointing out that such fighting can be observed even in the lower invertebrates, he concludes that social fighting may have evolved independently in various species from defensive threat or defensive attack behaviors.

Whether or not we accept Scott's ideas on the origin of agonistic behaviors, it is clear that such activity is highly situation-dependent, and while individual recognition may be an important concomitant in tetrapods, it has not been clearly demonstrated in many fishes. Lack of evidence on this point need not impede the development of generalizations, however, inasmuch as fish are very clearly capable of discriminating among individuals exhibiting differences in sex, age, or other criteria that may identify a particular caste (in the sense that Barlow, 1974, uses it). Thus socially related agonistic behavior in fishes often can be highly ordered to produce distinctive social structures not necessarily dependent on recognition of all members of the group. Pair-bonding in some cichlid fishes is, of course, one example of individual recognition, but such examples are not common among fishes.

Most agonistic situations occur among conspecifics, and some scholars limit the concept to intraspecific encounters. Lorenz (1964), for example, has stated that

If we put together, in the same container, two sticklebacks, lizards, robins, rats, monkeys, or boys, who have not had any previous experience of each other, they will fight. If we do the same with two animals of different species, there will be peace—unless, of course, there is a prey-predator relationship between them.

Predator-prey relationships are considered to be distinctive by many scholars because, as Hinde (1974) puts it,

In any one species predatory behavior and intraspecific fighting are usually elicited by different external stimuli, depend on different internal states, usually involve some different movement patterns, and may involve different neural mechanisms (Hutchinson and Renfrew, 1966).

Although Hinde admits that there may exist relationships between the two types of behavior, many ethologists have supported a hard line for separating the two categories. It is interesting that Wilson (1975), utilizing functional criteria within an evolutionary framework, recognizes categories for predatory and antipredatory aggression in his classification scheme but does not discuss the motivational implications of this treatment. Given a strong evolutionary-ecological bias, some difficult questions related to proximate causation or motivation can be evaded.

3.1 The Importance of Context in Interpreting Causation

The motivational substrates of aggressive activities have been the subject of much debate among ethologists and have been discussed recently in some detail by Huntingford (1976), who uses the term "aggression" in a broad sense to cover behavior ranging from overt fighting to "supposed symptoms of boldness or confidence." Huntingford makes no simple distinction between "initiation of a fight, attack in the conventional human sense, and retaliation or defense," though she admits that they may be distinct in their causes and consequences. She follows Lorenz (1966) in viewing conflict between animals in terms of three main situations: between members of the same species ("social aggression"); hunting and stalking as shown by a predator towards its prey ("predatory aggression"); and attack on a potential predator by a prey species ("antipredator aggression"). Her subsequent discussion suggests that analysis of the form of aggressive patterns provides limited information on the causal organization of the behavior and that information on the context and patterning of aggressive actions is required before inferences on causation can be justified. She points out that covariance in the frequency of occurrence of two patterns of behavior in a constant environment over the same time span argues for the existence of common motivating or inhibiting factors, and she presents data showing that both overlapping and distinctive patterns of variation of aggressive behaviors may occur in a wide variety of carefully studied vertebrates. Thus, social aggression and predatory aggression (or antipredatory aggression) have been shown to increase (or decrease) together with variations in dominance, sex, isolation, and so on, in sticklebacks, mice, rats, canids, and primates, while the three types of aggression may also vary independently in rats, canids, and felids. After pointing out that various physiological manipulations, such as castration, brain stimulation, or lesioning and neurochemical manipulation, may produce either covariance or independent fluctuation among the various patterns of aggressive behavior, she argues that it is unrealistic to view the different kinds of aggressive behavior as either irrevocably wedded or distinctly unique in causation. She concludes that the evidence supports the view that "social, antipredator, and predatory aggression are neither invariably linked nor inevitably distinct motivationally" and then discusses in some detail the ecological factors that may result in covariance or divergence of aggressive systems.

Huntingford's paper is a significant milestone in the understanding of aggression because it seeks to link ideas based on "causal analyses," often experimental in nature and sometimes buttressed by physiological investigations, with ideas from the increasingly important literature (summarized in part by Wilson, 1975) that identifies relationships between social organization and selection pressures imposed by specific ecological conditions. She argues convincingly that we cannot make strong inferences about the causal organization of agonistic behaviors without examining the selective pressures operating on populations of organisms. Knowledge of the ecological relevance of these behaviors will provide meaningful insights into the realm of potential selective pressures producing convergent or divergent patterns of behavioral control. The validity of our inferences thus will depend to a considerable extent on the soundness of our examinations of the ecological relationships within which each set of social behaviors evolved.

This idea is not new. It is, perhaps, one of the cornerstones of ethological theory and is prominently displayed in the writings of the founders of modern ethology (Tinbergen, 1952; Lorenz, 1935, 1950). Nonetheless, the rigorous use of population biology methods in concert with evolutionary ecology theory has provided a sound basis for understanding the adaptiveness of certain social organizations and social behaviors, largely within the last 10 to 20 years. Classical early studies of this sort (Fraser-Darling, 1937, 1938; Lack, 1954, 1955, 1968; Cullen, 1957; Tinbergen, 1959; and many others) clearly provided the impetus for the current rush of interest in "sociobiology," but relatively few were able to provide the systematic, comparative *ecological* data needed to support broader generalizations linking social behaviors to environmental constraints, partly because of the limited availability of comparable cognate studies.

Huntingford provides a scheme for evaluating the ways in which "aggressive" behaviors may have been integrated into the overall fabric of an animal's biology and for testing alternative hypotheses about behavioral control. It is worth noting that most recent published comments on the intraspecific nature of agonism have taken an either-or stance on the issue. For example, King (1973) omits species-specificity from the concept of agonistic behavior "because the motor or action patterns in the predator-prey encounter or in interspecific competition are often the same as those patterns exhibited between conspecific rivals." It seems possible that one's position on species-specificity may be determined partly or largely by the examples selected or the species or group most intensively studied by the scientist. Each individual may thus be strongly influenced in his views by animals exhibiting either convergent or divergent mechanisms for control of "aggressive" patterns, and may thus be unlikely to perceive the ease with which an alternate mechanism might evolve in species operating under distinctly different selective regimes.

In attempting to assess the significance of similarities or differences in the situations eliciting agonistic behavior in fishes as against the tetrapods, we must first acknowledge the enormous constraints imposed on the form and movement patterns of vertebrates by the medium in which they live. Fishes, living in a dense yet buoyant medium, typically

utilize in locomotion a complex, powerful lateral musculature, controlled and toned by the action of paired and median fins. Spines and other
armaments can be used as defensive weapons in some groups, but most
fish can attack only by biting, butting, or ramming some part of the body
against the opponent. Conversely, most tetrapods have moved into a
medium 800 times less dense than water and have been forced to develop a supportive appendicular skeleton, a largely nonmetameric
parietal musculature, and a highly differentiated appendicular musculature in order to support the individual during locomotion or other activity. The addition of well-developed, operationally flexible appendages
permits many tetrapods to increase the variety of movements that can be
used in signaling, attacking, and defending themselves. Despite this
profound distinction, it appears that remarkable similarities exist in the
contexts associated with agonistic behaviors in the two vertebrate types,
and that analogous behaviors often occur in analogous situations. I believe that this is especially true where visual and perhaps acoustic
stimuli play a role in agonistic encounters, but less true where other
sensory modalities are involved.

For example, a wide variety of visual fishes and tetrapods (including
man) utilize autonomic responses as signals to convey rather precise
information about motivation in fighting contexts (i.e., color changes in
fish and reptiles, piloerection in birds and mammals). Hostile encounters in fish often contain various combinations of autonomic and
nonautonomic responses, such as fin-spreading, fin-flicking, opercle-
spreading, tail-beating, mouth-gaping, and pendulum movements that
seem to have analogs in behaviors like wing-raising, feather-flashing,
gaping, pecking, neck-stretching and pendulum movements in birds
and back-arching, rearing, tooth-baring, head-raising, tail-rattling, and
foot-thumping in mammals. These behaviors and the less equivocal
movements, such as biting, butting, slashing, grasping, kicking, pecking, wing-beating, chasing, fleeing, freezing, and others, all occur in
various combinations in situations in which individual priorities or
needs must be determined. Although most such situations involve conspecific interactions, the obvious occurrence in most vertebrate groups
of interspecific competition involving agonistic behavior argues against
the hypothesis that conspecificity is a requisite aspect of the agonistic
context, either causally or functionally.

Many of the behaviors found in territorial fights, dominance encounters, and other competitive situations seem to involve movements that
serve either to increase the apparent size of the actor or to expose spe-
cially colored structures or potentially dangerous weapons. Conversely,
behaviors occurring in submissive or subordinate individuals often tend

to decrease apparent size or obscure dangerous or strikingly colored structures. The widespread distribution of these behavioral phenomena among many vertebrate groups leads one to ask whether or not such operational similarity is due to similarities (or perhaps even homologies) in the sensory, central, and neuromotor mechanisms of vertebrates at different phyletic levels. This point will be discussed in the final section.

3.2   Interspecific Territoriality: A Case Study

To summarize thus far: agonistic behavior occurs widely among non-colonial social animals and is prominent in most vertebrate groups. Among vertebrates, excluding man, it occurs most commonly, but not exclusively, as a competitive technique used in acquiring actually or potentially limiting resources. Since different resource needs of a species may each require the use of some kind of competitive technique (i.e., aggressive act), the species may evolve agonistic systems in which the overt acts are quite distinct, with distinct causal factors operating in each situation; or systems in which the overt acts are similar, but causal organization is distinct for each context; or systems in which both overt acts and causal factors are quite similar, even in distinctly different contexts. Perhaps less commonly, similar causal mechanisms may be associated with overtly different acts in different functional contexts. Most agonistic activities occur in predatory or antipredatory situations, or in fighting, usually in association with territorial or dominance encounters. Hinde (1956, 1970), Esser (1971), Johnson (1972), King (1973), Stokes (1974), and Wilson (1975) provide recent reviews documenting the functions of these important social phenomena and the ways in which agonistic behaviors are organized in time and space to achieve adaptive social goals.

Rather than delve more deeply into this enormous literature, I would like to present some information and ideas dealing with a phenomenon that is little touched on by Huntingford (1976), but that I believe is not only important for understanding the behavior of a significant minority of vertebrate species, but also crucial for understanding the full range of competitive phenomena that may evolve under rather special adaptive circumstances. This phenomenon is interspecific territory defense—first dealt with in detail in bird studies, but now receiving much attention because of its prominence in a conspicuous group of marine fishes, the damselfishes (Pomacentridae). The following discussion focuses on this group, and a fairly complete set of references is provided in order to allow interested individuals access to the relevant literature. It also includes some previously unpublished information based on my studies at the Hawaii Institute of Marine Biology of the University of Hawaii during 1971–1972.

Although the concept of territoriality has been well known to vertebrate biologists since at least 1920, when Howard published his treatise on territoriality in bird life, the causes and functions of various types of space defense have been the subject of almost continuous debate among ecologists and ethologists attempting to develop a comprehensive model for the phenomenon. Noble (1938), Nice (1941), Armstrong (1947), Hinde (1956), Tinbergen (1957), Carpenter (1958), Lack (1966), Wynne-Edwards (1962), Crook (1965, 1967, 1968), and many others have attempted to examine the fundamental nature of territorial behavior and the ultimate causes (adaptiveness) associated with it. Despite the fact that interspecific territory defense was known as far back as Howard's (1920) original work, many scientists have maintained that the territory construct was intimately linked to conspecific aggression. Murray (1971) recently argued that the interspecific territorial aggression of red-winged blackbirds toward tricolored blackbirds is a case of misdirected intraspecific territoriality, and he attempted to show that such behavior, while selected against, could maintain itself under certain geographical and ecological conditions. However, others have suggested that interspecific attacks are normal and functional in the territorial activities of many birds (Orians and Willson, 1964; Cody, 1969).

One of the first known examples of a teleost fish that defended a year-round territory against a variety of intruders was described by Rasa (1969) in the Pacific damselfish *Pomacentrus jenkinsi*. The damselfishes (*Pomacentridae*) represent one of the most common groups of fishes found in tropical waters around the world (Limbaugh, 1964). They are generally small, some are brightly colored, and they inhabit a variety of niches from the open-water, schooling planktivores (*Azurina, Chromis* sp.) through close association with the bottom (*Hypsypops, Microspathodon*, and *Pomacentrus*) to commensalism with sea anemones (*Amphiprion*). Because of their interesting breeding habits and their occurrence in relatively shallow waters, they have been the subjects of more behavioral research than any other group of marine fishes (Reese, 1964). Most species studied have been shown to defend breeding territories during the reproductive season. Among the more important of these studies are those of Verwey (1930) on *Amphiprion percula*, Abel (1961) on *Chromis chromis*, Turner and Ebert (1962) on *Chromis punctipinnis*, Stevenson (1963) on *Dascyllus albisella*, Helfrich (1958) on *Abudefduf abdominalis*, Limbaugh (1964) on *Hypsipops rubicunda*, Sale (1971) on *Dascyllus aruanus*, Rasa (1971) on *Microspathodon chrysurus*, Low (1971) on *Pomacentrus flavicauda*, and Myrberg (1972) on *Eupomacentrus partitus*.

Of these species, only three, *H. rubicunda, P. flavicauda*, and *P. jenkinsi*

(Clarke, 1970; Low, 1971; Rasa, 1969), were known to defend their territories year-round when I initiated my studies on *P. jenkinsi,* and Low's paper was not published until I had already begun work in the field. I had undertaken the study to try to determine why this species defended permanent territories, whereas most pomacentrids were territorial only during the breeding season. Rasa (1969) had suggested that adults defended feeding territories against all fishes invading the territory space. However, Clark (1970) concluded that year-round territory defense in *H. rubicunda* was more closely associated with maintenance of an optimum spawning site, and thus its principal function was to increase reproductive success. If Rasa was correct about the nature of territoriality in *P. jenkinsi,* it appeared that a careful study of the proximate causes of agonistic acts would clarify the nature of the origin and functions of this unique behavior.

My initial observations showed that individual *P. jenkinsi* defended specific sites, for at least several months, on coral reefs in Kaneohe Bay, Oahu. Territorial boundaries were relatively easy to discern but sometimes shifted slightly with topographic changes (loose coral or algal clumps may shift as a result of wave action) or movements into or out of the vicinity by other conspecifics. Most territories on Kaneohe reef sites had at least one clump of algae growing in them, and all had some kind of shelter hole(s) into which the fish disappeared when frightened. Fish often were observed grazing on the algae and associated *Aufwuchs* that constituted most of their diet.

A reasonable hypothesis about the function of territorial behavior in this species might be that such behavior serves to protect a food source for the territory defender (as Rasa inferred). If this were true, fishes receiving the brunt of most attack behavior should be those that are also herbivores or those that resemble food competitors physically or behaviorally. The most intense aggression should also be directed toward ultimate competitors—conspecifics. Low (1971) actually found such a situation in interspecific aggression in an Australian pomacentrid, *P. flavicauda,* which defended its territory against 38 species in 12 families, but ignored 16 other species in 6 families. All of the fishes attacked were food competitors (herbivores), while those not attacked were all carnivores.

My early observations, made entirely in one area, Checker Reef, generally were in accord with the simple trophic competition hypothesis outlined above, with most attacks directed toward herbivores or omnivores. Upon moving to a different reef, however, I quickly found that a common carnivorous wrass (*Thallasoma duperreyi*) that had almost never been attacked on Checker Reef was one of the prime targets on the second reef. Although the reefs were only a few hundred yards apart, the density of fishes of the two species, and many others, was much greater on the second reef. A third set of observations were made on the reef face of Coconut Island with the aid of an underwater TV camera and videotape recorder, and this proved even more revealing. In the absence of an observer, many species rarely or never previously observed to enter *P. jenkinsi* territories were found to be common, though transient, visitors. A number of these, including some other pomacentrid species, were primarily carnivorous and yet were frequently attacked by *P. jenkinsi*. One of the most surprising observations I made was that very few conspecifics were attacked, even when they penetrated deep into a neighbor's territory. One might expect that a conspecific, being an ultimate competitor for both food and space, would elicit the greatest amount of threat and attack. Yet I often observed two *P. jenkinsi* grazing side by side on the same clump of algae without the slightest indication of overt threat or hostile motivation. I observed fewer than a dozen cases of conspecific chasing or threat, despite the fact that territories were mainly contiguous on Checker Reef and that hundreds of opportunities for such hostility had arisen.

This appears to be a good example of the "Dear Enemy" phenomenon discussed by Wilson (1975: 273). Because it is energetically wasteful for adjacent territory holders to fight constantly, they develop means for recognizing neighbors and reducing hostility toward them (through habituation or learning of individual traits). Most previously known examples of the phenomenon are birds or mammals, and *P. jenkinsi* appears to be fairly unique among fishes in exhibiting this trait.

By the time I had completed field work in the summer of 1972, it had become abundantly clear that the causation (both proximate and ultimate) of territorial behavior was highly complex in *P. jenkinsi,* apparently much more so than in *P. flavicauda,* at least as it was described by Low. My quantitiative data, analyzed subsequently, showed that there was a high correlation between general activity of the resident *P. jenkinsi,* as measured by the number of patrol movements per unit time, and the number of foreign fish occurring in the territory per unit time. Although the rate of contraspecific chases often tended to increase with an increased number of intruders, there was no clear positive correlation between these two parameters. Furthermore, some species were chased at one time and ignored at others, even by the same fish. These observations, coupled with some obvious differences in the kinds of species chased on different reefs and the absence of conspecific attacks, led me to believe that control of aggressive behavior was in part situation-specific.

Since my initial studies were conducted, a number of significant papers on the behavior and biology of damselfishes have been published, and they point quite clearly to the nature of some key theoretical issues that can be clarified by the execution of additional work on *P. jenkinsi*. Smith and Tyler (1972) noted that *Eupomacentrus planifrons* on a reef in the Virgin Islands defended discrete territories against conspecifics and some contraspecifics, and suggested that *E. partitus* was excluded from that portion of the reef containing *E. planifrons* territories. Emery (1973), working on Alligator Reef in the Florida Keys, described territory defense, often apparently based on defense of feeding or shelter sites, in *Chromis insolatus* adults, *Chromis scotti* adults, *Eupomacentrus leucostictus*, *E. partitus*, *E. planifrons*, and *E. variabilis* (in which territory defense is especially strong in juveniles); he suggested that the abundance of food and variable habitats on the reef permitted the damselfishes to develop fairly distinctive niches, with a consequent minimal competition for food or habitat. Unfortunately, he provided little information on the permanence of territorial behavior for most species and none on the kinds of fishes chased from territories. Keenleyside (1972) reported long-term territory defense in *Abudefduf zonatus* at Heron Island, Great Barrier Reef, and indicated that similar types of territorial patterns existed in *Pomacentrus flavicauda* and *P. tripunctatus*. He suggested that "*A. zonatus* is a predominantly substrate species in which social structure and breeding system may be seen as adaptations to permanent residence on the shallow, inner reef flat." In his view,

This system of long-term, loosely associated territories, with each resident fish remaining close to the coral and sand substrate, allows the members of a local population to maintain contact with each other and with their breeding habitat throughout the reproductive season. It also assures proximity to food and to shelter from predators.

He also pointed out that *A. zonatus* was less aggressive toward conspecifics than toward small labrids, which are egg predators of many Heron Island pomacentrids. Unfortunately, he presented no quantitative data on attack frequency or species attacked, other than the above brief statement.

Most recently, Myrberg and Thresher (1974) and Thresher (1976a) have described field observations and experiments on the territorial behavior of *Eupomacentrus planifrons*, a drab-colored Caribbean damselfish. Using videotape analysis and live fish in bottles placed near the residence of territorial males, they concluded that these fish are capable of discriminating among a wide variety of species and reacting differently to them. This differential reactivity was formalized on the concept of "serial territory," whereby a defending fish would swim out from its residence for greater or lesser distances, depending on the species approaching (or presented in a bottle) and the time of year. In general, conspecifics were attacked farthest from the residence, congenerics somewhat closer, food competitors closer yet, and noncompetitors closest. These species-specific boundaries expanded during the reproductive season and contracted after spawning was over. Data on the number of nips directed at fish introduced (in bottles) directly in front of the residence also showed differences in attack patterns, but congenerics were attacked at about the same levels as other species, and conspecifics were attacked less than any other congeneric. Myrberg and Thresher (1974) suggested that "the territory appeared as a series of areas surrounding the residence, each area apparently reflecting the amount of space that secures a limited resource(s) from members of a particular species," and that species eliciting more nips at the residence than conspecifics "—must have been considered as greater threats at the residence, while just the opposite was apparent for the areas surrounding the residence. This indicates that there is a difference in functional significance of these two features. [i.e., attack distance vs. number of nips at residence, RJM]." They go on to point out that protection of a food supply, maintenance of a nest site and protection of eggs, and maintenance of a residence may all be functions of territoriality in this species. Thresher (1976a) presented data on videotaped interactions of territorial males with other members of the fish biota and came to generally similar conclusions, though he took the argument a step further when he stated:

One would predict the occurrence of serial territoriality wherever there exist in a restricted area numerous species whose niches overlap and which, therefore, are at least partial competitors. The advantages of a serial territory in terms of even reduced energy expenditures alone are clear.

The discussion above illustrates the fact that understanding of the social behavior and social organization of the damselfishes as a group has increased greatly over the last few years. Prior to 1969, most species were believed to act territorially (primarily toward conspecifics) only during the breeding season, when breeding adults defended the spawning site. We know now that many species defend territories for considerable periods outside the breeding season, and that attacks on contraspecifics are not cases of "mistaken identity," as has been postulated by some scholars. Indeed, several studies (Low, 1971; Myrberg and Thresher, 1974; Thresher, 1976a) have clearly demonstrated that territory defense in some damselfishes is a highly structured phenomenon with considerable discrimination involved in the determination of who will be attacked and how vigorous the attack will be. Several authors have suggested that territoriality may function in defense of limited resources, such as food, spawning site, or shelter, or some combination of the three.

Most species defending reef sites over long periods of time are herbivores or omnivores feeding on algae and other sessile organisms, a phenomenon indicating a high probability that a primary ultimate cause for permanent territoriality is the need to protect a food source. Syrop (1974) found that *Pomacentrus jenkinsi* maintained a higher standing crop of algae within territories that occurred in adjacent nondefended areas. Furthermore, territory size varied both with the productivity of the area and the abundance of herbivorous intruders in the vicinity. Another ultimate cause (function) probably lies in the protection of a spawning site, since Myrberg and Thresher (1974) clearly showed enlargement of serial territory dimensions during the breeding season, and my observations on *P. jenkinsi* suggest enhanced aggressiveness at this time. Finally, since these species utilize shelter holes in the reef at night and during the day when threatened, maintenance of a specific shelter site could serve as another ultimate cause. Smith and Tyler (1972), Collette and Talbot (1972), and Hobson (1972) all present data demonstrating the importance of shelter areas to many reef-inhabiting fishes.

Although the studies of Myrberg and Thresher (1974) and Thresher (1976a) have added new dimensions to our knowledge of operational aspects of the territorial behavior of pomacentrids, their speculations on causation must be critically examined. For example, the former (1974: 92) state that

If the entire area of defense is based upon a single limiting resource (eg., a specific type of food, such as benthic algae), the important variable across species lines, should in most cases be the amount each threatens that resource. If, in contrast, the different sized territories reflect the fact that various resources are being secured by the resident, then certain boundaries secure specific levels of one resource, while other boundaries secure specific levels of others. This is perhaps the more likely possibility.

Likewise, Thresher (1976a: 275) states that

Territoriality by *E. planifrons*, therefore, is probably multifunctional. The data suggest that it serves to protect a food supply, the spawn, and the residence. Additional functions, especially those related strictly to intraspecific defense, can only be speculated upon. The size of the territory maintained against any given intruder is a function of the degree with which it threatens any or all of these resources vital to the threespot.

Although these authors are probably correct about the functions of territoriality in *E. planifrons*, the relationship between function (ultimate cause) and (proximate) causation becomes so intimate in the discussion that the two appear to be inseparable. Thus, one gets the impression that a certain species is attacked farther from the residence because it is a greater food competitor than others in the community. This apparent confounding of levels of organization may be misleading, because attack behavior patterns could depend upon patterns of proximate causality quite unrelated to the degree of competition or threat to a resource offered by a given species. This is almost a truism in the behavior of lower vertebrates, where elaborate systems of releasers or other control and communication mechanisms typically serve to integrate limited sets of motor patterns that combine in various ways in different functional contexts. Mechanisms controlling responses to external cues (body shape, size, activity patterns) or regulating internal thresholds (habituation, diel activity rhythms, arousal processes) have been programmed to provide the animal with a motivational and motor capacity serving the ultimate cause (resource protection) without necessarily precluding use of some of the motor components in other contexts having other functions. To hypothesize a mechanism whereby proximate and ultimate causes are nearly identical is to require either a cognitive capacity for these animals far greater than is known to exist in fishes, or else a programmed behavioral template so complex that it is difficult to envision.

Thresher's most recent (1976b) publication suggests that some of the above statements may not have been intended to convey the unity of proximate and ultimate causality that can be read into them. He tested reactions of *E. planifrons* to *Holacanthus tricolor* by presenting the latter in bottles that could eliminate visual, olfactory, or acoustic cues. He also studied attack distances in relation to normal movements of four intruding (in bottles) species, including conspecifics, and tested for the effects of form and color by introducing to territorial males seven species of hamlets (*Hypoplectrus*), three of which are color mimics of three damselfish species also used in the experiment. He concluded that interspecific attack is mediated by form recognition, while conspecific attack depends on response to both form and color. He discarded the idea that interspecific attacks were based on "mistaken identity" and suggested that there were distinct differences between the displays directed to conspecifics and closely related congeners and those directed to nonrelatives.

The combination of distinctive perceptual and motor elements in this complex of territory defense activities recalls Huntingford's ideas on the variety of possible control systems for social, predatory, and antipredatory aggression. The threat to limiting resources represented by a conspecific may well be different from that represented by a different species; thus distinct competitive techniques (and/or control mechanisms) could evolve independently.

In the case of *P. jenkinsi,* where many territory defenders are packed into a limited area, and large numbers of a wide variety of species are almost constantly moving over the face of the reef, a rather different motivational organization may have evolved. I believe it is most parsimonious to hypothesize a limited number of proximate causal agents that interact in various ways to produce a state of overall adaptiveness serving to maintain the behaviors and social structure through time. This social organization would guarantee, in terms of population, the protection of critical resource(s) and thereby the maintenance of adaptive genomes without necessarily fixing agonistic behaviors along rigid stimulus-specific lines. For example, if the species is programmed to respond with increased patrolling and chasing activity to higher densities of fish in the vicinity, noncompetitors (while not providing many cues associated with competitors) could be attacked when a defender's attack threshold was lowered greatly by large numbers of fish in the vicinity (perhaps a general arousal phenomenon). In an overall sense, this could be adaptive if the (food) energy saved by attacking competitors at high rates when fish density is high (but still below the level producing attack of noncompetitors) was greater than that expended in attacking noncompetitors at extremely high densities. By cuing the threshold of attack to a nonspecific sensory input, some difficult problems of behavioral control might be solved. Precise measurements of the energetics of this situation would be extremely difficult to obtain, but experimental verification and quantification of these phenomena would provide at least circumstantial evidence that a density-dependent factor is involved in the control of attack behavior.

With the information presently available, the differences in agonistic patterns found among various pomacentrid species appear to be related to functional correlates of territory defense and the specific ecological variables occurring at the different study sites. I suspect that as more work is done, we will be able to identify the ways in which species diversity and individual density, niche overlap, diversity and quantity of food resources, amount of cover, pattern of movement of species within the habitat, and other variables interact to produce the range of social phenomena exhibited by territorial pomacentrids. The proximate causal mechanisms, however, may well prove to be quite distinct among species and may not show a high degree of correspondence with ultimate factors.

Although this discussion provides only a brief excursion into the complex world of causality as it relates to interspecific territoriality in damselfishes, it may be instructive to compare some of these embryonic visions with some ideas derived from the study of interspecific territoriality in birds and mammals. Earlier, I cited the views of Murray (1971), which conflicted with those of Orians and Willson (1964) and other students of bird societies with respect to the nature of the phenomenon of territoriality in birds. Grant (1972) pointed out that less work has been done on interspecific competition and territoriality in mammals than in birds, but he predicts it should be more widespread among rodents than among birds, because rodents have not been able to achieve niche separation in the vertical plane (as is so common in birds), and their predominant utilization of the structurally simpler horizontal dimensions of the environment should lead to more contact and increased possibility for competition. Wilson (1975) provided a brief but comprehensive review of the subject in which he utilized elements of both Orians and Willson's (1964) and Murray's (1972) ideas to create an interesting model for social evolution. Although his theory is too lengthy to pursue in detail here, a major conclusion that he presents is that interspecific territoriality is most likely to occur in cases where two cognate forms have recently evolved from a common ancestor and have just come into contact with one another. This argument leans somewhat toward Murray's ideas but shares an important feature with most of the published papers on the topic: interspecific territoriality is largely a mutual phenomenon, with two species actively competing with each other and both forms exhibiting territorial behavior.

None of the pomacentrids discussed above fit this pattern, though related species and genera are often among the species driven from damselfish territories. I believe there are some fairly simple reasons for this difference. Most of the avian work has been conducted on passerine species exhibiting reproductive territoriality. Although food and other resources are undoubtedly critical factors in the evolution of territorial behavior in birds, the entire system is in a different stage of development than that found in benthic damselfishes. The tropical reef ecosystem is an ancient one, and the fish assemblage is staggeringly diverse. Fish are notoriously opportunistic feeders, and though one can find considerable niche separation within a family, the sheer numbers of different families and genera occurring on the reef are certain to produce numerous instances of niche overlap—even among fairly distantly related species. Thus, for food-based territoriality to be adaptive on the reef, it simply can not be limited to close relatives or the rare convergent nonrelative, as seems to be the case in many birds and mammals. The combination of temporal and community differences seems to have brought about territorial systems based on rather different functional principles involving distinctly different causal systems. Within the damselfish themselves, however, I have argued that there exist fairly distinct differences in causation associated with community differences. I hope that future work will clarify the nature of proximate and ultimate factors influencing these activities in a wider range of vertebrate species.

4   CAUSATION: CONVERGENCE, DIVERGENCE, AND THE INTERPRETATION OF OVERT PHENOMENA

As Wilson (1975) has recently pointed out, social organization (and, I believe, the behavioral repertoire used to establish and define that organization) results from the competitive action of two broad classes of phenomena: phylogenetic inertia (factors tending to limit evolutionary change) and ecological pressure (factors promoting change via natural selection). Although many recent authors have attempted to examine social activities (including agonistic behavior) within the framework of such an evolutionary model, the great bulk of the literature does not yet reflect the importance of acknowledging and identifying the contributions of these two classes of competing pressures in the development and maintenance of specific social patterns among vertebrate groups. Wilson (1975) himself tends to slide over the specific phenomena responsible for producing particular social patterns when, in his desire to develop a methodology leading to a "unified science of sociobiology" he states that he has become "increasingly impressed with the functional similarities between invertebrate and vertebrate societies and less so with the structural differences that seem, at first glance, to constitute such an immense gulf between them."

The specific parameters and quantitative models that would serve in the development of the kind of overview that he seeks must necessarily depend upon a considerable degree of simplification, generalization, and abstraction that would eliminate precise definition of the details of the evolutionary process as reflected by the specific structures and behaviors exhibited in each distinctive phyletic line. However, I feel that it is as important to identify Wilson's "immense gulfs" and the processes that led to their development as it is to trace the "functional similarities" among animals. Any attempt to deal with diverse behavioral phenomena without examining *both* proximate and ultimate factors as they are reflected in the integrity of the organism can only provide us with a biased picture of the multidimensional nature of agonistic systems and other social phenomena.

The preceding discussion of interspecific territoriality illustrates the difficulty of interpreting the behaviors involved without having some insights into both their function and the nature of the stimulus-response mechanisms utilized. Since our knowledge is still imperfect, an integrated approach to the study of these phenomena offers a real opportunity to understand better how they are controlled and why they exist in somewhat different forms among different species and groups. I believe that much of the difficulty we have experienced in interpreting the nature of agonistic activities stems from the fact that we have often undertaken our studies as fairly narrow disciplinary approaches. The scholar competent to produce field study, comparative analysis, experimental study, and physiological investigation is still quite rare, so our direct experiences tend to be canalized, and our conceptual maps often have difficulty encompassing unfamiliar terrain. Thus, the psychologist concerned with reducing violent behavior in children may be less than completely receptive to theoretical arguments about the genetic incorporation of traits promoting "aggressiveness" in early hominid populations, and the evolutionary ecologist is baffled by the assertion that human behavior is essentially independent of genetic control. It is no solution to suggest that the answer lies somewhere in between, or to argue, as Lehrman (1970) has so eloquently argued, that much of the problem of interpretation lies in perception, conception, and semantics. This has been done and we still hear the echoes of earlier conflict on the nature-nurture, and so on, and so forth, dichotomies reverberating through the contemporary literature. Causation can most accurately be viewed (to borrow a metaphor from Hutchinson) as an n-dimensional hypervolume, with dimensions ranging from specific physiological events through contextual symmetries through phylogenetic adaptiveness. Though, practically speaking, we may be limited to conducting work at one level (using a limited number of dimensions), we must recognize that explanation of phenomena as widespread and complex as agonistic activities requires examination of as many of the dimensions as are accessible. At the very least, we must try to interpret the data on proximate phenomena within the framework of an evolutionary model that seeks to identify the nature of the balance between phylogenetic inertia and ecological pressure that has produced the specific mechanisms of behavior control.

Many people feel that the key to understanding the causation of agonistic behavior lies in understanding the nature of physiological mechanisms associated with aggressive acts. This area has become one of the fastest-growing and most productive fields of ethological-neurological-endocrine research, and it offers great promise for clarifying some of the more complex behavioral puzzles that ethologists have faced over the last 30 years (Clemente and Lindsley, 1967; Garattini & Sigg, 1969; Eleftheriou & Scott, 1971; Whalen, 1974; Moyer, 1976).

Despite the enormous literature on physiological correlates of agonistic behavior, it is difficult to formulate well-founded generalizations, partly because most of the work has been done on mammals (see citations above; and Huntingford, 1976), but also partly because of the high degree of specialization and differentiation found among vertebrate species. One of the best-known examples of vertebrate sensory specialization (though it is related to feeding rather than fighting) occurs in the frog, where the need to detect and capture mobile insects has led to the development of a unique "bug-detecting" system in the afferent visual apparatus (Lettvin, et al., 1959). The absence of similar specializations in other vertebrates that have been studied may be due to changes in the extent of peripheral processing of visual stimuli that occur in concert with the shift from small-brained to large-brained vertebrates. It appears that the highly complex synaptic interconnections found in the retina of lower vertebrates are necessary to accommodate considerable peripheral data processing in groups with poorly developed central mechanisms. The highly sophisticated visual cortical mechanisms of mammals, however, permit a simplification of peripheral synaptic organization (Dowling, 1968). Although I know of no definitive studies of similar types of perceptual organization that are related to agonistic activities in vertebrates, I would be surprised if the general principle were not operative in some social (including agonistic) behaviors as well. Capranica (1965) and Frishkopf et. al. (1968) demonstrated a correlation between threshold sensitivity of auditory nerve neurons and spectral characteristics of bullfrog calls, but some central processing appears necessary in the elicitation of appropriate responses. The fact that most birds and mammals appear capable of using visual, acoustic and/or olfactory signals for recognizing individuals in social groups suggests that much more central processing of sensory data occurs in amniotes.

On the motor side, we can use as an example of specialization the large Mauthner cells in the medulla of many fishes. These cells have the ability to initiate speedy locomotion (tail-flip) by linking acoustico-lateralis, optic, and cerebellar systems with motor neurons in the lateral musculature via collaterals from giant axons in the spinal cord, providing a reflex escape mechanism invaluable to the teleosts and tailed amphibians that possess it (Diamond, 1971). Why should the Mauthner system be present in most teleosts and tailed amphibians, yet absent in sharks and terrestrial vertebrates? Its absence in sharks is mainly an issue for speculation at this time, but the picture appears to be clearer for the tetrapods. The most parsimonious way to modify a primitive central nervous system (CNS) to activate rapidly a metameric locomotory musculature is to develop a reflex system utilizing giant axons carrying stimuli quickly to the muscle masses. In an evolutionary sense, it would be impossible to evolve or utilize a Mauthner-type apparatus in tetrapods simply because of the loss of metamerization and the development of a more highly differentiated neuromuscular coordination system. Furthermore, the increased complexity and organization of the CNS of higher vertebrates permits development of a wider diversity of neurobehavioral mechanisms for coping with novel or threatening stimuli. One kind of reflexive mechanism that can produce quick response of the whole organism in higher vertebrates is the orienting response studied by Sokolov (1960) and others. It is associated with orientation and alertness rather than with the startle response. Subsequent responses to the stimuli eliciting orientation depend upon the consequences of initial reactions to the stimuli, but are suggested by Sokolov to be dependent on cortical processes.

Clearly, then, one can find examples of both sensory and neuromotor mechanisms that are organized in fundamentally distinctive ways at different ends of (or perhaps more accurately, at various points on) the vertebrate phylogenetic spectrum. From the perspective I wish to establish here, the development of adaptive structural and functional complexes must be viewed as a mosaic of evolutionary trajectories, each represented by species or groups moving into new niches of varying breadth. Once initiated, these trajectories operate to constrain each viable phylogenetic unit, though the nature of these constraints would vary with time and the maturity of the ecosystem within which any unit is evolving. In some cases, once a particular trajectory had passed a given threshold (determined by genotypic modifications), further change in structure or function would be appreciably circumscribed, and the system would assume a determinate nature.

Many of the specializations we are concerned with, therefore, must be considered to be consequences of the phylogenetic process, dependent upon changes dictated by the needs of animals penetrating different worlds and developing new modes of structure, function, and behavior that permit them to cope with novel problems. Although each new major adaptive mode has produced a spectrum of characteristically unique structures and behaviors, these modifications were all based on the general vertebrate plan, and each represented new ways of organizing available materials. Quantum jumps to distinctly different levels of organization occurred rarely, as they may have in the case of the evolution of the human brain and culture, where certain emergent properties may exist.

The *apparently progressive* nature of many of these changes perhaps can be illustrated by a few brief examples. The visual projection area in fishes lies in the optic tectum, consisting of two bilateral dorsal mesencephalic hemispheres. The tectum contains at least six layers (A-riens Kappers *et al.*, 1960) and serves as the major integration center for visual and other sensory inputs and for information ascending or descending from other neural centers (Bernstein, 1970). However, while the tectum serves as the highest information and integration center for fishes, the forebrain and tectum share these functions about equally in reptiles, the basal ganglia take over most such functions in birds, and the neopallium is the major integrative structure in mammals (Hoar, 1975). The tectum (superior colliculus) of mammals serves mainly as a visual reflex center and as a relay and transducing gateway to the temporal cortex, which is the site of the visual projection.

Similarly, the endocrine systems of vertebrates exhibit a strong morphological tendency to form distinct vascularized organs in higher groups, whereas fishes still retain diffuse, often scattered, endocrine cells (i.e., adrenal cortex and medulla, and thyroid tissues) not far advanced structurally from their presumed ancestral homologues (Hoar, 1975). Presumably this shift reflects an evolutionary trajectory influenced by two major forces, according to Hoar: "The need for the seasonal regulation of reproduction, and the abandonment of non-selective filter feeding for the life of a selective, and often predaceous, feeder with major problems of regulating digestive and metabolic functions."

In examining the results of studies on agonistic systems at the physiological level, one can cite the work of Demski and Knigge (1971) who showed that stimulation of the region surrounding the lateral recess of the third ventricle of the inferior lobe of the hypothalamus of the bluegill elicited feeding and aggressive behavior, a pattern not unlike that found in numerous studies of hypothalamic stimulation in mammals. The mammal studies (citations above) have been much more comprehensive, however, pointing to the operation of an extensive system of interconnected telencephalic and diencephalic structures (limbic system) that contribute to elicitation of agonistic activities in a complex, nonunitary manner. Moyer (1968, 1969, 1976) has attempted to incorporate many of the often diverse observations on neural and endocrine substrates of aggression into a scheme recognizing eight different functional categories. Each category is based on some complex of neural, endocrine, and contextual characterisics that serve to identify the distinctive types of aggression. Though both Wilson (1975) and Huntingford (1976) criticize Moyer's classification because the categories are "introspective" and are not based on any consistent criteria, his contribution has been valuable in pointing out the diversity of control mechanisms underlying "aggression" in mammals. It has become more difficult to view "aggression" as a unitary construct in recent years.

Thus, while neural and endocrine substrates for the control and development of structure and behavior show a degree of continuity throughout the vertebrate line, shifts in the localization of functional elements and changes in the magnitude of influence that a particular neural or endocrine mechanism exerts on behavior may be quite prominent.

The point I wish to make here is that one can find numerous examples of distinctive physiological mechanisms underlying the sensory, neural, and motor functions involved in many behaviors, including agonistic activities, occurring in different vertebrate groups. Yet similar stimulus properties often elicit similar kinds of behaviors, considering the morphological equipment available. I believe that this similarity is due to the fact that there is a relatively restricted number of social problems that must be dealt with in any species, and that there are a limited number of ways in which any vertebrate kind can cope with them.

The immense power that selection has for producing convergent structures among distantly related animals is well known. To borrow another well-documented example from morphology, consider the tapetum lucidum, a reflective tissue found in the retinae of many nocturnal animals. According to Walls (1942) and others (in Hoar, 1975) the tapetum may be composed of guanine (fish and many other vertebrates), shiny tracheal tubes (insects), tryglyceride spheres (some fishes), white collagenous fibers (musk-ox), or riboflavin crystals (bush baby, *Galago*, and garpike). Quite obviously, the adoption of nocturnal habits increased the probability of development of a structure facilitating dim-light vision, and the specific chemical or physical mode utilized is almost irrelevant, in terms of adaptiveness. Examples, such as the preceding, of groups or species acquiring morphological or behavioral adaptations for a mode of existence strikingly different from that of other members of the same phyletic line are readily identified and require no further discussion here. However, subtle changes in fairly closely related groups may not be recognized at all as representing convergence; thus assumptions about the uniformity of causal mechanisms producing similar overt behaviors in different groups may not be justified where the entire chain of causality has not been studied. When studies on the causation of social activities are conducted on species primarily because of the ease with which they can be raised and manipulated in laboratories or observed in the field (as has often been the case in the past), the general practice of extrapolating these observations and conclusions to other similar organisms of possible distinctive ancestry seem to be particularly hazardous.

Because many basic coordinating and integrating mechanisms persist throughout the vertebrate line, we are essentially viewing a constellation of variations on a theme when we study the ways in which different species and groups operate to regulate the division of, or competition for, limited or limiting resources—that is, food, space, cover, mates, young, and so on. Thus, some response patterns, such as withdrawal from larger or approaching stimuli, may reflect the operation of homologous sensory and/or central mechanisms that are evolutionarily conservative in that they have maintained an association with adaptive responses throughout vertebrate phylogeny. Other reactions, similar in apparent function and context, may depend on quite distinctive physiological causal mechanisms that evolve in response to novel adaptive necessities. I suggest that a mosaic of conservative (homologous) and specialized (often convergent) mechanisms are available to most vertebrates for the elicitation and control of agonistic and other social activities. The relative contributions of these mechanisms are probably determined largely by the nature of the species and the adaptive context in which the interaction occurs, and analysis of the causal organization of behaviors must be carried out in each group or species with comprehension of the fact that parallel contexts and behavior need not imply parallel causality in its fullest sense.

Although it is tempting to focus attention on the adaptiveness and survival value of agonistic behaviors because of the breadth of variation extant in causal mechanisms subserving overt activity, I cannot help but believe that in striving to develop universal models, there has been too much confounding of functional, operational, and causal constructs. In this, of all areas of behavioral study, we must be most cautious of overextending data or raising tentative hypotheses to the level of dogma.

These conclusions may seem self-evident, but I believe that much of the controversy about the nature of aggressive motivation (especially in man) may be due to the fact that this duality of motivational origins, and the multidimensionality of species-typical agonistic causality, have seldom been examined in light of a truly broad evolutionary perspective.

Finally, to return briefly to a question I asked early in this paper. To what extent can we use information on the behavior of lower vertebrates to gain insight into the behavior of *Homo sapiens*? I have argued that structural, functional, and behavioral attributes in any animal species in any phyletic line represent a composite, or mosaic, of features derived from ancestral types and developed in response to specific selective pressures of the environment and life-mode (niche) of that particular population or species. The degree of singularity or novelty in the overall organization of the animal kind depends largely on the uniqueness of the specific niche occupied by that animal. Two factors tend to operate to preserve archaic or conservative features of an organism's design: (1) drastic, rapid changes often tend to be maladaptive; and (2) adaptations that successfully deal with major problems faced by a species may be retained by descendant forms as long as the same types of selective pressures are exerted on successive evolutionary types. For example, the development of a diencephalic-telencephalic neural axis to deal with classes of behavior involved in contest competition was a major achievement in vertebrate evolution. The fact that all vertebrates have not developed identical ways of utilizing this basic substrate to organize their competitive activities simply reflects the extent of adaptive radiation in the phylum. Depending on one's scientific goals, one can emphasize the similarity found among adaptive strategies that deal with similar evolutionary problems, or one can focus on the specific differences among related species that make them seem so unique. It is no more difficult to accept the view that the organic world is merely a reflection of the "strategy of the genes" than it is to agree with Geertz (1965) when he asserts that "there is no such thing as a human nature independent of culture." In my view neither approach has primacy. Comparative studies of social behavior can instruct us about the nature of selective pressures that produce certain kinds of functional wholes, while motivational studies and causal analyses show us how each unique animal kind developed its "functional whole." Without both types of insight we see only part of the reality accessible to us.

5 ACKNOWLEDGMENTS

I gratefully acknowlege the support of the National Science Foundation (BMS 74-24197) and the National Institute of Mental Health (MH 18 565-05) during the preparation of this paper and for the support of research leading to the development of some of the ideas expressed herein. I also wish to thank Dr. James Shaw, John Thornton, and Helen C. Miller for reading and criticizing the manuscript. Finally, I am most grateful to Drs. John Bardach, George Losey, and Ernst Reese for their hospitality and for the many kindnesses extended to me during my stay at the Hawaii Institute of Marine Biology.

REFERENCES

Abel, E. F. 1961. Freiwasserstudien über das Fortpflanzungsverhalten des Monchfishes *Chromis chromis* Linne, einem Vertveter der Pomacentriden in Mittlemeer. Z. Tierpsychol. **18:** 441–449.

Ariens Kappers, C. U., G. C. Huber, and E. C. Crosby. 1960. *The Comparative Anatomy of the Nervous System of Vertebrates, including Man.* Hafner, New York. 1845 p.

Bandura, A. 1973. *Aggression: a Social Learning Analysis.* Prentice-Hall, Englewood Cliffs. 390 p.

Barlow, G. W. 1974. Contrasts in social behavior between Central American cichlid fishes and coral reef surgeon fishes. Am. Zool. **14:** 9–34.

Berkowitz, L. 1962. *Aggression: A Social Psychological Analysis.* McGraw-Hill, New York.

Bernstein, J. J. 1970. Anatomy and physiology of the central nervous system. *In:* W. S. Hoar and D. J. Randall, Eds. *Fish Physiology.* Vol. IV. Academic Press, New York. P. 2–90.

Capranica, R. R. 1968. The vocal repertoire of the bullfrog (*Rana catesbeiana*). Behaviour **31:** 302–325.

Carpenter, C. R. 1958. Territoriality: A review of concepts and problems. *In:* M. A. Roe and G. G. Simpson, Eds. *Behavior and Evolution.* Yale University Press, New Haven. P. 224–250.

Clark, T. A. 1970. Territory boundaries, courtship, and social behavior in the garibaldi, *Hypsipops rubicunda* (Pomacentridae). Copeia **1970:** 295–299.

Clemente, C. D., and D. B. Lindsley, Eds. 1967. *Aggression and Defense.* University of California Press, Berkeley. 361 p.

Cody, M. L. 1969. Convergent characteristics in sympatric species: a possible relation to interspecific competition and aggression. Condor **71:** 223–239.

Collette, B. B. and F. H. Talbot. 1972. Activity patterns of coral reef fishes with emphasis on nocturnal-diurnal changeover. *In:* B. B. Collette and S. A. Earle, Eds. *Results of the Tektite Program: Ecology of Coral Fishes.* Natural History Museum of Los Angeles, Cal., Scientific Bulletin 14. P. 98–124.

Crook, J. H. 1965. The adaptive significance of avian social organizations. Symp. Zool. Soc. Lond. **14:** 181–218.

Crook, J. H. 1967. Evolutionary change in primate societies. Sci. J. **3.6:** 66–72.

Crook, J. H. 1968. The nature and function of territorial aggression. *In:* M. F. Montagu, Ed. *Man and Aggression.* Oxford University Press, New York. P. 141–178.

Cullen, E. 1957. Adaptations in the kittiwake to cliff nesting. Ibis **99:** 275–302.

Darling, F. F. 1937. *A Herd of Red Deer.* Oxford University Press, London. 215 p.

Darling, F. F. 1938. *Bird Flocks and the Breeding Cycle: a Contribution to the Study of Avian Sociality.* Cambridge University Press, Cambridge. 124 p.

Delgado, J. M. R. 1967. Aggression and defense under cerebral radio control. *In:* C. D. Clemente and D. B. Lindsley, Eds. *Aggression and Defense.* Univ. of California Press, Los Angeles. P. 171–194.

Demski, L. S. and K. M. Knigge. 1971. The telencephalon and hypothalamus of the bluegill (*Lepomis macrochirus*): evoked feeding, aggression, and reproductive behavior, with representative frontal sections. J. Comp. Neurol. **143:** 1–16.

Diamond, J. 1971. The Mauthner cell. *In:* W. S. Hoar and D. J. Randall, Eds. *Fish Physiology.* Vol V. Academic Press, New York. P. 265–346.

Dowling, J. E. 1968. Synaptic organization of the frog retina: an electron microscopic analysis comparing the retinas of frogs and primates. Proc. R. Soc. Lond. B. **170:** 205–228.

Eleftheriou, B. E. and J. P. Scott, Eds. 1971. *The Physiology of Aggression and Defeat.* Plenum Press, New York. 312 p.

Emery, A. R. 1973. Comparative ecology and functional osteology of 14 species of damselfish (Pisces: Pomacenridae) at Alligator Reef, Florida Keys. Bull. Mar. Sci. 23. No. 3: 649–770.

Esser, A. H., Ed. 1971. *Behavior and Environment.* Plenum Press, New York. 411 p.

Frishkopf, L. S., R. R. Capranica, and M. H. Goldstein, Jr. 1968. Neural coding in the bullfrog's auditory system—a teleological approach. Proc. IEEE, **56:** 969–980.

Garattini, S. and E. B. Sigg, Eds. 1969. *Aggressive Behavior.* John Wiley and Sons, New York. 387 p.

Geertz, C. 1965. The impact of the concept of culture on the concept of man. *In:* J. R. Platt, Ed. *New Views of the Nature of Man.* University of Chicago Press, Chicago. P. 93–118.

Grant, P. R. 1972. Interspecific competition among rodents. Ann. Rev. Ecol. and Syst. **3:** 79–106.

Helfrich, P. 1958. The early life history and reproductive behavior of the maomao, *Abudefduf abdominalis* (Quoy and Gaimard). Unpublished doctoral dissertation, University of Hawaii, Honolulu. 228 p.

Hinde, R. A. 1956. Ethological models and the concept of 'drive.' Br. J. Philos. Sci. **6:** 321–331.

Hinde, R. A. 1970. *Animal Behaviour.* McGraw-Hill, New York. 876 p.

Hinde, R. A. 1974. *Biological Bases of Human Social Behaviour.* McGraw-Hill, New York. 462 p.

Hoar, W. S. 1975. *General and Comparative Physiology.* Prentice-Hall, Englewood Cliffs. 848 p.

Hobson, E. S. 1972. Activity of Hawaiian reef fishes during the evening and morning transitions between daylight and darkness. Fish. Bull. **70:** 715–740.

Hogan, J. A. 1965. An experimental study of conflict and fear; an analysis of behavior of young chicks toward a mealworm. I. The behavior of chicks which do not eat the mealworm. Behaviour **24:** 45–97.

Howard, H. E. 1920. *Territory in Bird Life.* John Murray, London, 308 p.

Huntingford, F. A. 1976. The relationship between inter- and intra-specific aggression. Anim. Behav. **24:** 485–497.

Johnson, R. N. 1972. *Aggression in Man and Animals.* Saunders, Philadelphia. 269 p.

Kaada, B. 1967. Brain mechanisms related to aggressive behavior. *In:* C. D. Clemente and D. B. Lindsley, Eds. *Aggression and Defense,* University of California Press, Los Angeles. P. 95–134.

Kaufmann, H. 1970. *Aggression and Altruism.* Holt, Rinehart, and Winston, New York. 165 p.

Keenleyside, M. H. A. 1972. The behaviour of *Abudefduf zonatus* (Pisces, Pomacentridae). Anim. Behav. **20:** 763–774.

King, J. A. 1973. The ecology of aggressive behavior. *In:* R. F. Johnson, P. W. Frank, and C. D. Michener, Eds. *Annual Review of Ecology and Systematics.* Annual Reviews, Palo Alto. P. 117–138.

Lack, D. 1954. *The Natural Regulation of Animal Numbers.* Oxford University Press, Oxford. 343 p.

Lack, D. 1966. *Population Studies of Birds.* Oxford University Press, Oxford. 341 p.

Lack, D. 1968. *Ecological Adaptations for Breeding in Birds.* Methuen, London. 409 p.

Lehrman, D. S. 1970. Semantic and conceptual issues in the nature-nurture problem. *In:* L. R. Aronson, E. Tobach, D. S. Lehrman, and J. S. Rosenblatt, Eds. *Development and Evolution of Behavior.* Freeman, San Francisco. P. 17–52.

Lettvin, J. Y., H. R. Maturana, W. S. McCulloch, and W. H. Pitts. 1959. What the frog's eye tells the frog's brain. Proc. I.R.E. **47:** 1940–1951.

Limbaugh, C. 1964. Notes on the life history of two California pomacentrids: garibaldis, *Hypsipops rubicunda* (Girard), and blacksmiths, *Chromis punctipinnis* (Cooper). Pac. Sci. **18:** 41–50.

Lorenz, K. 1935. Der Kumpan in der Unwelt des Vogels. J. Ornithol. **83:** 137–215, 289–413.

Lorenz, K. 1950. The comparative method in studying innate behavior patterns. Symp. Soc. Exp. Biol. **4:** 221–268.

Lorenz, K. 1964. Ritualized fighting. *In:* J. D. Carthy and F. J. Ebling, Eds. *The Natural History of Aggression.* Academic Press, London. P. 39–50.

Lorenz, K. 1966. *On Aggression.* Methuen, London. 306 p.

Low, R. M. 1971. Interspecific territoriality in a pomacentrid reef fish, *Pomacentrus flavicauda* Whitley. Ecology **52:** 648–654.

Moyer, K. E. 1968. Kinds of aggression and their physiological basis. Comm. Behav. Biol. **2:** 65–87.

Moyer, K. E. 1969. Internal impulses to aggression. N.Y. Acad. Sci. **31:** 104–114.

Moyer, K. E. 1976. *The Psychobiology of Aggression.* Harper and Row, New York. 402 p.

Myrberg, A. A., Jr. 1972. Social dominance and territoriality in the bicolor damselfish *Eupomacentrus partitus* (poey) (Pisces: Pomacentridae). Behaviour **41:** 207–231.

Myrberg, A. A. and R. E. Thresher. 1974. Interspecific aggression and its relevance to the concept of territoriality in reef fishes. Am. Zool. **14:** 81–96.

Nice, M. M. 1941. The role of territory in bird life. Am. Midl. Nat. **26:** 441–487.

Orians, G. H. and M. F. Willson. 1964. Interspecific territories of birds. Ecology **45:** 736–745.

Rasa, O. Anne E. 1969. Territoriality and the establishment of dominance by means of visual cues in *Pomacentrus jenkinsi* (pisces: Pomacentridae). Z. Tierpsychol. **26:** 825–845.

Rasa, O. Anne E. 1971. Appetence for aggression in juvenile damselfish. Z. Tierpsychol. Suppl. 7. 70 p.

Reese, E. S. 1964. Ethology and marine zoology. Oceanogr. Mar. Biol. Ann. Rev. **2:** 445–488.

Sale, D. F. 1971. Extremely limited home range in a coral reef fish, *Dascyllus aruanus* (Pisces, Pomacentridae). Copeia **1971:** 324–327.

Scott, J. P. 1971. Theoretical issues concerning the origin and causes of fighting. *In:* B. E.

Eleftheriou and J. P. Scott, Eds. *The Physiology of Aggression and Defeat*. Plenum Press, New York. P. 11–42.

Smith, C. L. and J. C. Tyler. 1972. Space resource sharing in a coral reef fish community. *In:* B. B. Collette and S. A. Earle, Eds. *Results of the Tektite Program: Ecology of Coral Reef Fishes*. Natural History Museum, Los Angeles, Cal., Scientific Bulletin 14. P. 125–170.

Sokolov, E. N. 1960. Neuronal models and the orienting reflex. *In:* M. Brazier, Ed. The central nervous system and behavior. Macy Foundation, New York. P. 187–276.

Stevenson, R. A. 1963. Life history and behavior of *Dascyllus albisella* Gill, a pomacentrid reef fish. Unpublished doctoral dissertation, University of Hawaii, Honolulu. 221 p.

Stokes, A. W. 1974. *Territory*. Dowden, Hutchinson, and Ross, Stroudsburg. 398 p.

Syrop, S. B. 1974. Three selected aspects of the territorial behavior of a pomacentrid fish, *Pomacentrus jenkinsi*. Unpublished M. S. thesis, Univ. of Hawaii. 48 p.

Thresher, R. E. 1976a. Field analysis of the territoriality of the threespot damselfish, *Eupomacentrus planifrons* (Pomacentridae) Copeia **1976**: 266–276.

Thresher, R. E. 1976b. Field experiments on species recognition by the threespot damselfish, *Eupomacentrus planifrons*, (Pisces: Pomacentridae). Anim. Behav. **24**: 362–569.

Tinbergen, N. 1952. "Derived" activities, their causation, biological significance and emancipation during evolution. Q. Rev. Biol. **27**: 1–32.

Tinbergen, N. 1957. The functions of territory. Bird Study (British Trust for Ornithology) **4**: 14–27.

Tinbergen, N. 1959. Comparative studies of the behaviour of gulls (Laridae): a progress report. Behaviour **15**: 1–70.

Turner, C. H. and E. E. Ebert. 1962. The nesting of *Chromis punctipinnis* (Cooper) and a description of their eggs and larvae. Calif. Fish Game **43**: 243–248.

Verwey, J. 1930. Coral reef studies. 1. The symbiosis between damselfish and sea anemones in Batavia Bay. Treubia **12**: 305–366.

Whalen, R. E., Ed. 1974. *The Neuropsychology of Aggression*. Plenum Press, New York. 214 p.

Wilson, E. O. 1975. *Sociobiology*. Harvard University Press, Cambridge, Mass. 697 p.

Wynne-Edwards, V. C. 1962. *Animal Dispersion in Relation to Social Behavior*. Hafner, New York. 653 p.

11

REEF FISHES
AND OTHER VERTEBRATES:
A COMPARISON OF SOCIAL
STRUCTURES

PETER F. SALE

School of Biological Sciences
The University of Sydney
Sydney, N.S.W., Australia

1   INTRODUCTION

Over the past 15 years, many scientists interested in the behavior of fish have taken advantage of the availability of SCUBA equipment to carry out field observations. Coral reef fishes have received more than their share of this attention, and there are now sufficient data to warrant developing an overall picture of social organization among them. Such a depiction is one aim of this chapter.

It is now widely accepted among students of mammals and birds that social organization can vary considerably among species, and among different populations of a single species. These differences have often been successfully accounted for by a consideration of the different ecological constraints under which the different species or populations lived. For example, Kummer (1968) related the divergent social systems of *Papio hamadryas* and *P. cyanocephalus* to the more arid, less productive environment of the former, and Anderson (1961) discussed differences in the social organization of mice in dense and in sparse populations. This interdependence of ecology and social behavior has been explored successfully in a large number of specific instances among mammals (Archer, 1970; Devore and Hall, 1965; Crook, 1970; Crook, *et al*, 1976) and birds (Crook, 1964; McBride *et al.*, 1969; Orians, 1971).

I want to consider this question in a broader context—one, perhaps, that will turn out to be too broad. I consider the social structures maintained by reef fishes in relation to what is already known about social structures of higher vertebrates and other fishes.

Reef fishes are subjected to a different set of ecological constraints than are other vertebrates. They also show a different emphasis in the types of social structure they adopt. I believe that a comparison of the social structures of reef fishes and other vertebrates will tell us something of the ecological control of the development of sociality in vertebrates.

Taxonomic revisions are a continuing problem for anyone dealing with the behavior or ecology of reef fishes, particularly in the South Pacific. In this paper I have tried to use the most current names, but have included in parentheses the name used by the author being cited. This paper is an overview rather than a review of the extensive literature on reef fishes. I have omitted far more papers than I have included, but hope that the most important ones are among the latter.

2 ASPECTS OF ECOLOGY OF CORAL REEF FISHES

2.1 What Is a Reef Fish?

Numerous species of fish have been recorded from coral reef waters. They can be divided into two distinct groups. One of these (the smaller in number of species) consists of truly high-seas fishes—Scombridae, Myctophidae, and so on—that are only accidental associates of reefs. They are animals of the water column, and they do not make use of the structure of a reef in any special way. They are not considered here.

The other, and far larger, group consists of fishes that depend upon the substratum for food, shelter, or both. These are reef fishes, although many of them are not restricted to occurrence on living corals alone. For convenience, reef fishes can be divided into the behaviorally "visible" and "invisible" species. "Visible" reef fishes are the conspicuous, active, and usually diurnal species that one sees when diving. They have received most attention from behavioral ecologists, and belong chiefly, though not exclusively, to the Acanthuridae, Chaetodontidae, Labridae, Lutjanidae, Pomadasyidae, Pomacentridae, Scaridae, Serranidae, and Siganidae. The "invisible" species may be large, active, but nocturnal forms, such as Holocentridae or Apogonidae, or they may be cryptic forms that spend their lives deep among the interstices of a reef. They may be seen only when collections of fish are created through the use of rotenone or some other chemical. Some, like the Muraenidae, can be large, but most are fish less than 5 cm long.

It is important to recognize the existence of these two groups of reef fishes, because some of the conclusions drawn from studies of "visible" species may not apply when considering "invisible" forms. In the following I deal of necessity primarily with "visible" coral reef fishes.

2.2   Diversity of Coral Reef Fishes

It is a truism that coral reefs support a large number of species of fish (Ehrlich, 1975; Goldman and Talbot, 1976; Smith and Tyler, 1972). For example, numbers of species on the Great Barrier Reef range from about 1500 at the north to 900 at One Tree Reef, close to the southern limit of reef development.

Part of this high diversity is of a between-habitat type, since reef fishes tend to be sedentary, and, to a limited extent, habitat specialists. Nevertheless, there remains a high diversity within habitats. For example, Smith and Tyler (1972) reported 53 resident species and a total of 75 species of fish on a single Caribbean patch reef approximately 3 m in diameter and 1.6 m high. Smith (1973) collected up to 67 species in single small rotenone collections in the Bahamas, and Goldman and Talbot (1976) cite single collections containing 150 species (One Tree Reef) and 200 species (Palau) of fishes. That such large numbers of species coexist means, inevitably, that each individual has the opportunity to interact with fishes belonging to a wide range of species other than its own. These interactions are often social.

2.3   Site Attachment

The typical reef fish is a sedentary, strongly site-attached animal (Erhlich, 1975). Bardach (1958), Reese (1973), and Springer and McErlean (1962) have provided data on the range of movements of many species. Smith and Tyler (1972) have given estimates of the area used (none greater than 7 m radius) by individuals of 63 species, although 12 other species ranged more widely. Russell *et al.* (1974) have listed 58 of 85 species that colonized their artificial reefs as residents—that is, as restricting their movements over weeks or months to the immediate vicinity of a reef 1.6 × 0.5 × 0.6 m in size. Ogden and Buckman (1973) demonstrated that the apparently wide-ranging schools of *Scarus croicensis* restricted their movements to about 0.5 ha of reef. The membership of feeding schools included fish that successively joined and then left the school; the schools retained members only while they passed through their own home ranges of about 50 m².

Most observations of movements have been made on "visible" species. Among the "invisible" ones, the small cryptic gobiids, blenniids and others probably have even more restricted ranges of movement. The holocentrids and apogonids are active, and appear to range extensively when feeding at night, although little is known of their movements. Smith and Tyler (1972) recorded all 7 apogonids and 3 of 4 holocentrids present on their reef as residents with home ranges approximately 7 m in radius. Among pomadasyids, *Haemulon carbonarium* feeds at night in the immediate vicinity of its daytime resting site, but *H. flavoliniatum* may move each night as far as 1.6 km from its resting site to feed away from the reef (Hobson, 1973).

2.4   Reproduction and Dispersal

Reef fishes reproduce in a way quite different from that of any terrestrial vertebrate. Their reproductive patterns put important constraints upon the kinds of social systems that they develop. The typical reef fish breeds frequently during an extended, and even year-round, breeding season. It produces numerous clutches of pelagic eggs and larvae. Few reef fishes that have been studied appear atypical in this regard. Munro *et al.* (1973) have documented the times of occurrence of reproductively ripe fish for 83 species off Jamaica. In most of these, there was a pronounced peak of activity in February and March; but extended seasons were usual, and in some cases (e.g., Pomadasyidae, Lutjanidae, some Pomacentridae), ripe fish were present throughout the year. Their data do not permit determining the frequency of spawning by individuals. *Labroides dimidiatus*, which spawns daily just after high tide for seven months (Robertson, 1974), represents an extreme for repeated spawnings, but data on a number of other species are listed in Table 11.1. Multiple spawnings by each individual are likely to be the rule for reef fishes.

The Pomacentridae are an important family, and one that diverges somewhat from most other reef fishes in reproductive behavior. As documented in numerous studies (Allen, 1972; Fishelson, 1970a; Keenleyside, 1972; Myrberg, 1972; Reese, 1964; Sale, 1971a; Wickler, 1967), all

TABLE 11.1 Duration of season and frequency of spawning by individuals for a representative sample of reef fishes

Species	Duration of Season	Frequency of Spawning by Individuals	Source
Amphiprion chrysopterus	9 months	Monthly	Allen, 1972
Chromis caeruleus	8 months	Maximum twice per week	Sale, 1971a
Glyphidodontops biocellatus (= *Abudefduf zonatus*)	+2 months	Every two weeks	Keenleyside, 1972
Abudefduf saxatilis	5 months	Multiple	Fishelson, 1970a
Eupomacentrus partitus	All year	Multiple	Myrberg, 1972
Microspathodon chrysurus	12 months	Every 3–4 days	C. D. MacDonald, pers. comm.
Centropyge potteri	6 months	Multiple during 1 week each month	P. S. Lobel, pers. comm.
Crenilabrus (8 spp)	?	Weekly	Fiedler, 1964
Thalassoma bifasciatum	All year	Multiple	Feddern, 1965
Labridae (24 spp)	6 months	Multiple	Choat, 1969
Labroides dimidiatus	7 months	Daily	Robertson, 1974
Scarus (15 spp)	6 months	Multiple	Choat, 1969
Sparisoma rubripinne	All year	?	Randall & Randall, 1963
Acanthurus triostegus	8–12 months	Multiple	Randall, 1961
Gobiosoma oceanops	5 months	2–3 times	Valenti, 1972
Dendrochirus brachypterus	8 months	Weekly or more often	Fishelson, 1975

known pomacentrids produce demersal eggs cared for by the male (and in some cases the female) parent. With one known exception (below), their eggs hatch into minute larvae that are swept by currents to a pelagic existence of unknown duration.

The Apogonidae, though less well studied, also show egg care. So far, as is known, mouth-brooding of eggs, but not of young, occurs in all species (Breder and Rosen, 1966; Smith *et al.*, 1971).

Reef-dwelling Acanthuridae, Chaetodontidae, Labridae, Pomacanthidae, and Scaridae invariably produce pelagic eggs, and no brood care exists. Spawning (where observed) takes place in midwater on a falling tide (Choat, 1969; Feddern, 1965; Lobel, personal communication; Randall, 1961; Randall and Randall, 1963). This enhances the chance of gametes being swept away from the reef.

One species of reef fishes is known to exhibit more extensive parental care. The pomacentrid, *Acanthochromis polyacanthus*, pairs, and it shows complex reproductive and parental behavior for at least 1 month following hatching of the clutch (Robertson, 1973). During this time both parents are in continuous attendance with the brood of 100 to 150 young. The young may obtain nutriment by glancing off the parents' bodies in a manner analogous to that in some Cichlidae (Barlow, 1974; Noakes and Barlow, 1973).

Dispersal in *Acanthochromis polyacanthus* must be less extensive than in other reef fishes. The young do not leave the parents until they are 25 to 30 mm long, and at this size they remain in the vicinity of coral. Among the more typical species, the pelagic larval stage permits extensive dispersal. Information is sparse, but Randall (1961) established, for example, that larval life was approximately 2½ months in duration in *Acanthurus triostegus*. In Hawaii, Leis and Miller (1976) have demonstrated that larvae of acanthurid, chaetodontid, labrid, and other fish with pelagic eggs are most common 10 to 12 km from shore. Those of apogonid, pomacentrid, and other fish with demersal or brooded eggs and shorter larval life are most abundant less than 1 km from shore. The latter are presumably less dispersive larvae.

That even these less dispersive reef fishes do achieve a wide dispersal of their larvae is suggested by Soule's electrophoretic studies (reported in Ehrlich, 1975). He showed minimal variation in isozyme frequency between widely separated populations of a number of pomacentrids. For example, *Dascyllus aruanus* has virtually identical allele frequencies (more than 20 loci tested) along a 3000 km transect from the southern Great Barrier Reef to New Guinea. Populations of *Abudefduf saxatilis* in Bermuda and Panama are virtually identical in all but 1 or 2 of 28 loci.

On the other hand, the effective distance of dispersal of the larvae of any reef fish is not known yet. Despite long pelagic lives, gyrals and seasonally varying currents probably act to trap most larvae in the reef system if not on the particular reef where they were produced (Leis and Miller, 1976; Sale, 1970).

2.5   Consequences of Ecology

Reef fishes are animals that spend their juvenile and adult lives in a localized site on a coral reef. Despite their sedentary habits, individuals are likely to come into contact with a large number of other species. Reef fishes reproduce frequently, producing numerous clutches of pelagic larvae (and, in most families, pelagic eggs). These offspring are swept away to other sites. Meanwhile, offspring produced elsewhere occasionally colonize the region. The individual thus has the opportunity to interact with a number of known individuals, many of different species. Those of its own species will almost certainly be genetically unrelated to it. It is particularly unlikely that adult and juvenile fishes present on one site will be a family group.

3   ECOLOGICAL COMPARISONS

3.1   Other Fishes

There is a paucity of data on the behavioral ecology of demersal, rocky shore fishes. What there is suggests that they are similar in many ways to fish of coral reefs. *Hypsypops rubicunda* on the California coast (Clarke, 1970) and *Parma microlepis* on the New South Wales, Australia, coast (Moran and Sale, 1977) both appear to be typical pomacentrids, although the more seasonal climates to which they are exposed curtail their reproductive seasons. Studies of blennies by Gibson (1969) and Stephens *et al.* (1970) indicate a pattern of life in terms of site-attachment and reproductive patterns quite similar to that of coral reef blennies. Hobson's extensive studies of feeding patterns and diurnal movements of rocky shore fishes in the Gulf of California (Hobson, 1965, 1968, 1971), paint a picture very comparable to the ones he has produced for reef fishes (Hobson, 1973, 1974).

Reef fishes differ considerably from oceanic fishes in being site-attached and demersal. They differ most markedly from freshwater fishes in their lack of elaboration of parental behavior. While the majority of reef fishes produce pelagic eggs, the majority of freshwater fishes produce demersal eggs, and in families like Cichlidae and Centrarchidae, complex parental care of eggs and fry has developed. In lakes and streams there is evidence of considerable site-attachment (Gerking, 1959; Northcote, 1967), but in these places, juveniles and adults living nearby may often be closely related. Nowhere except on the coral reef are individuals exposed to such a diverse array of cohabiting species.

3.2 Differences between Reef Fishes and Terrestrial Vertebrates

Birds and mammals show several pronounced differences in ecology from reef fishes. Both groups exhibit elaborate parental care, and the production of large numbers of scattered young does not occur. Most young terrestrial vertebrates grow up near their parents, and social groups consist of related individuals. The diversity of cohabiting species is smaller.

In addition, terrestrial vertebrates can be shown to be more mobile than are reef fishes. In them, territoriality is a phenomenon closely associated with reproductive activity and is usually a transient condition lasting the breeding season (McBride *et al.*, 1969; Stokes, 1974). In reef fishes, permanently territorial species are common (Sec. 4.3). Furthermore, whether or not territorial, reef fishes appear to use space more rigidly, occupying areas an order of magnitude smaller than those used by terrestrial vertebrates of similar size.

McNab (1963) and Schoener (1968) have independently derived relationships between area used and body weight for mammals and birds respectively. Both authors considered the species examined to fall into two groups showing slightly different relations between body size and area of territory or home range.

In Fig. 11.1, I have reproduced the lines they obtained and have plotted points representing a number of reef fishes for which suitable data exist. In all cases, they obtained the information on area used by following individuals of a given species about, while disturbing them as little as possible. The species considered are all "visible" species. "Invisible" species would generally use still less space than these.

It is apparent that in most cases there is at least an order of magnitude difference between the amount of space used by a reef fish and that used by a mammal or bird of given size. (Note, too, that the lines for mammals and birds fall close to one another.)

This difference between reef fishes and terrestrial vertebrates is not simply a consequence of the need for less food (and thus less space in which to find it) by a poikilotherm than by a homeotherm of similar size.

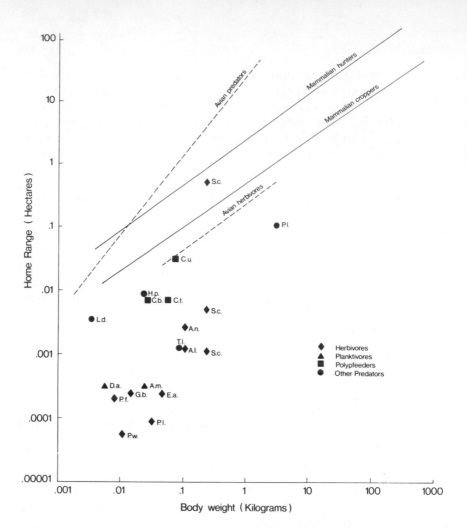

FIGURE 11.1 The relationship between body weight and area used for a number of reef fishes. The lines on the graph are obtained from studies of this relationship for mammals (McNab, 1963) and birds (Schoener, 1968). The species of fish shown, and the sources of information, are as follows:

A.l.: *Acanthurus lineatus* (Nursall, 1974b)

A.n: *Acanthurus nigrofuscus* (Barlow, 1974)

A.m.: *Amphiprion melanopterus* (Allen, 1972)

C.b.: *Chaetodon baronessa* (Reese, pers. comm.)

C.t.: *Chaetodon trifascialis* (Reese, pers. comm.)

C.u.: *Chaetodon unimaculatus* (Reese, 1973)

D.a.: *Dascyllus aruanus* (Sale, 1971b)

E.a.: *Eupomacentrus apicalis* (Sale, 1974)

G.b.: *Glyphidodontops biocellatus* (Keenleyside, 1972)

H.p.: *Hypoplectrus puella* (Barlow, 1975a)

L.d.: *Labroides dimidiatus* (Robertson, 1974)

P.f.: *Pomacentrus flavicauda* (Low, 1971)

P.l. (herbivore): *Plectroglyphidodon lacrymatus* (Sale, 1974).

P.l. (predator): *Plectropomus leopardus* (Goeden, 1974)

P.w.: *Pomacentrus wardi* (Sale, 1974)

S.c.: *Scarus croicensis* (Ogden and Buckman, 1973)

T.l.: *Thalassoma lunare* (Robertson and Choat, 1974)

Turner *et al.* (1969) provide data on space use by a variety of lizards. These data fall in the same region of Fig. 11.1 as the lines for birds and mammals. Of course, it remains possible that there is simply more food available per unit area on a reef than in any terrestrial habitat. Regardless of the cause, however, reef fishes restrict their movements to a greater extent than do terrestrial vertebrates.

Some specific comments should be made about the points plotted in Fig. 11.1. Three separate points are plotted for *Scarus croicensis*. These represent the area used by a feeding school (the highest point in the figure), that covered by an individual with a home range, and that used by a territorial fish. The pomacentrids are overrepresented in the figure. This family has received more attention from behavioral ecologists than any other, and I have omitted numerous species for which good data on movements exist. Those included are typical representatives of the principal genera. The acanthurids included are both territorial species. Many acanthurids form feeding schools (Barlow, 1974) and probably range over areas similar to those used by *S. croicensis*.

By using different symbols in Fig. 11.1, I have indicated the feeding method used by each species. There are as yet insufficient data to warrant comment on whether fish that feed in different ways show different patterns of use of space.

4 SOCIAL STRUCTURES OF REEF FISHES

4.1 Classification of Social Structures

There are a variety of ways in which to categorize the social system of animals. McBride (1971), in a theoretical account, and more recently, Barlow (1974), in a comparison of the behavior of cichlid and acanthurid fishes, have emphasized that the social system results from the ways in which behavioral interactions between individuals are carried out.

Behavioral interactions are influenced by the patterns of spatial distribution of animals, as well as by temporal changes in activity, both seasonal phases and daily or hourly subphases, through which the population passes. In addition, interactions may depend upon the caste—age, sex, reproductive stage, and so on—and the role—rank or social position—of the interacting individuals. Finally, the composition by caste and role of the social group, and the degree to which the group is closed to new members, influence the patterns of behavioral interactions, and thus the form of social structure, maintained.

In the following discussion I emphasize spatial and hierarchical patterns of organization of groups. The importance of phase, caste, role, and group composition will become apparent in this discussion.

4.2   Aggregations

4.2.1   Feeding and Resting Aggregations

The feeding aggregation may be a stationary shoal occurring above the reef in a place favorable for feeding on plankton. Large shoals of planktivorous fishes are common on reefs, but little in the way of social interactions is apparent except for occasional agonistic encounters when two fishes pursue the same prey item. There has been little study of the behavior of such groups (Fishelson, 1970a).

Other feeding aggregations are mobile assemblages of herbivores that range over the reef feeding together. More attention has been applied to these foraging groups by behavioral ecologists (Barlow, 1974, 1975b; Choat, 1969; Ogden and Buckman, 1973; Vine, 1974). They occur commonly among the Acanthuridae, Scaridae, and Siganidae.

Resting aggregations occur among several types of nocturnally active reef fishes that come together to rest during the daytime. The most conspicuous of these, because they form in the open, contain species of Pomadasyidae. Similar groups of Holocentridae and Apogonidae are less conspicuous because they form under shelter.

Feeding and resting aggregations are commonly heterospecific (Ehrlich and Ehrlich, 1973), containing individuals of two or more species at one time. Itzkowitz (1974) has distinguished between the associates and the core species. The latter is numerically dominant, and in mobile groups it appears to lead. Hobson (1974) has documented the movements that take place, particularly at dawn and dusk as individuals move to join their feeding aggregations or to return to resting groups. These movements are often precisely timed and consistently follow particular routes.

4.2.2   Schools

The polarized, or second-order, school of Shaw (1970), in contrast to other aggregations, is rare in reef fishes. Perhaps this is so because they are strongly site-attached, and, when moving, maintain close visual and even tactile contact with a nearby, topographically structured substratum. This use of environmental references may not be compatible with rigid interindividual positioning and orientation. Even the few true schooling species on reefs may maintain constant reference to the physical environment. Hobson and Chess (1973) have described in some detail the diurnal migration of a schooling atherinid, *Pranesus pinguis*, at Majuro Atoll. The highly ordered school they observed was found resting just below the surface in shallow water at the same site each day. It followed a set path each evening, and the members moved apart to feed on plankton in the same open-water region each night. Species of *Chromis, Abudefduf, Zanclus,* or *Chaetodon* will be seen schooling frequently (Barlow, 1974; Fishelson, 1970a), but only rarely do these schools last more than 5 or 10 min before breaking down into unpolarized shoals. Mobile feeding aggregations may become polarized schools when traveling between feeding areas, and particularly when moving between feeding and resting sites (Ogden and Buckman, 1973; Hobson, 1974).

4.2.3 Migratory Spawning Aggregations

Large migratory spawning groups have been reported for some reef fishes (Smith, 1972), but they are a rare event. The strong site-attachment of most reef species makes migrations for spawning unlikely, although many species will move short distances to favorable sites for releasing gametes (Barlow, 1974, 1975b; Choat, 1969; Randall and Randall, 1963; Robertson, 1974; Robertson and Choat, 1974; Warner *et al.*, 1975).

4.3 Site-Related Groups

4.3.1 Home Ranges

The result of the strong site-attachment of most reef fishes is that they also maintain well defined home ranges as a minimum degree of social organization. Home ranges commonly overlap and neighboring fishes share the same space. For example, *Thalassoma lunare* maintains individual, but overlapping home ranges, although some males are territorial when breeding (Robertson and Choat, 1974). In *Scarus croicensis*, some individuals of the population maintain home ranges of up to 50 m². Other individuals are territorial, or members of mobile aggregations (Ogden and Buckman, 1973). Reese (1973, 1975) has indicated that pairs of *Chaetodon trifasciatus* share a common home range. Some other chaetodontids may also move as pairs, or as unpaired fish in undefended home ranges (Ehrlich *et al.*, 1977; Reese, 1975), but others are territorial. In the Acanthuridae, Barlow (1974) suggests a range of behavior from strict territoriality to the maintenance of a home range with defense of the immediate feeding area as the fish moves about, to membership of a foraging group, possibly without maintenance of any home range. Itzkowitz (1974) has suggested that in the Caribbean, genera such as *Hypoplectrus, Rhycticus, Aulostomus, Halichoeres, Diodon,* and *Acanthostracion* are fish seen only as isolated individuals, and apparently not defending the area they occupy. They appear therefore to be holding individual home ranges. Barlow (1975a) has subsequently stated that *Hypoplectrus* species are in fact territorial. While some authors (Barlow, 1974; Fishelson, 1970a; Fishelson *et al.,* 1974; Itzkowitz, 1974; Reese, 1975) speak of "wandering" species, further study is likely to demonstrate that all of these are fishes with large but well-defined home ranges. The results of tagging studies (Bardach, 1958; Reese, 1973; Springer and McErlean, 1962), and long-term observations (Russell *et al.,* 1974; Smith and Tyler, 1972) indicate that this is so.

4.3.2 Individual Territories

There are numerous well-documented examples of pomacentrid species in which individual territories are held throughout the year by all juveniles and adults (Keenleyside, 1972; Low, 1971; Myrberg, 1972; Myrberg and Thresher, 1974; Nursall, 1974a; Rasa, 1969; Sale, 1974, 1975; Thresher, 1976). In these species, the territory is maintained primarily as a feeding site (Low, 1971; Sale, 1974), though males prepare nests within their territories. In this family, the area defended is often quite small, and observations of territorial behavior are readily made. In all of these species, defense of the territory is carried out against a large number of species in addition to that to which the territory-holder belongs. This has been particularly well established for *Pomacentrus flavicauda* (Low, 1971), and the work of Myrberg and Thresher (1974) on *Eupomacentrus planifrons* has demonstrated that this interspecific defense is not a case of mistaken identity of other fishes. In fact, the degree to which the site is defended from other species is specific to each invading species. Low, and Myrberg and Thresher, have argued that the primary function of territoriality in these species is to keep out those fishes that would compete for, or which would disturb, the algal food resources present within the territory. However, Thresher (1976) emphasizes that territoriality serves a reproductive function as well.

Individually held territories are not restricted to the Pomacentridae. Nursall (1974b) has documented this for *Acanthurus lineatus* and Barlow (1974) has provided some evidence for several other acanthurids. Ogden and Buckman (1973) have indicated that some individuals of *Scarus croicensis* are territorial. In this case the territory is one maintained by a female fish, within which she tolerates the presence of a male, and occasionally some smaller females. Reese (1973) has demonstrated that *Chaetodon trifascialis* (= *Megaprotodon strigangulus*) maintains individual feeding territories stable over several months. The same may be true for some other species (Ehrlich *et al.*, 1977; Reese, 1975). Robertson and Choat (1974) maintain that many labrid fishes can be expected to be territorial. Robertson (1974) has provided data on the individual territories held by *Labroides dimidiatus;* however the territorial system exhibited by this fish is complex and will be discussed below (Sec. 4.5.1.).

4.3.3 Pair Territories

Pair territories are areas occupied exclusively by a breeding pair, within which they carry out all or most feeding. By contrast with individual territories they are rare, so far as presently known, among reef fishes. One reason for the rarity of pair territories may be that so few reef fishes show any parental care. Cooperation in territorial defense may have only slight advantages in the absence of parental activities. Nevertheless, some examples do exist. *Chaetodon baronessa* (= *triangulum*) maintains permanent pair territories (Reese, 1973, 1975), and this may be true for some other members of this family. Potts (1973) has described the maintenance of pair territories in *Labroides dimidiatus* in Aldabra, and this pattern may represent a distinct social structure from the more complex pattern of individual territories reported at Heron Reef (Robertson, 1974). The pomacentrid, *Acanthochromis polyacanthus,* defends a pair territory for at least 5 weeks while raising a brood of young (Robertson, 1973), and the commensal *Amphiprion* spp. all form permanent breeding pairs occupying single anemones (Allen, 1972), although they do not care for the hatched larvae.

A number of other species of reef fish may hold pair territories, but further observations are necessary. Among the "invisible" fishes, species of *Gobiodon* and *Paragobiodon* appear to occur so frequently as pairs in single colonies of coral that the maintenance of a pair territory is likely. Lassig (1976) has provided recent information on three species of *Paragobiodon*.

4.3.4 Nest-Site Territories

Defense of the nest and immediate proximity by one or both parents, but with most foraging carried on outside this area, constitutes nest-site territoriality. In the families of reef fishes that possess demersal eggs, the nests of eggs are invariably defended by at least one of the parents. All pomacentrids that are not permanently territorial in some way have nest-site territories defended by the male, and, rarely, also the female, parent (Breder and Rosen, 1966; Fishelson, 1970a; Sale, 1971a; Wickler, 1967). The same appears to be true for gobies (Breder and Rosen, 1966; Reese, 1964; Valenti, 1972), and blennies (Stephens *et al.*, 1970; Wickler, 1961). Again, the female may share defense of the territory in some species.

4.3.5 Group Territories

The group territory, in the sense of a relatively large area defended by a mobile group that carries out all activities within it, is not known among reef fishes. Some stationary groups, however, cooperate in defending the area that is occupied from intruders. *Dascyllus aruanus* usually occurs in small groups that occupy single colonies of coral. Individuals do not divide up the coral, all having access to all parts of the colony. Holzberg (1973) has indicated that *Dascyllus marginatus* subdivides its coral colony into a series of individual resting sites, but this observation has not been supported by other studies on the genus (Coates, personal communication; Sale, 1972a).

  Dascyllus aruanus reacts belligerently to any of a wide variety of fishes that attempt to intrude (Sale, 1972a). The same reaction appears true for several other pomacentrids (Fricke, 1973), and groups comprising two or more of these species all appear to act together defending the site from intruders (personal observation). Coates (personal communication) has demonstrated in three species of *Dascyllus* a much higher level of agonism directed at introduced strange fish than at resident fishes reintroduced after being removed for 1 hour. Twenty percent of the strangers were successfully ejected from the coral and taken by predators during the observation period. This never happened to reintroduced residents.

  Barlow (1974) has briefly described the social structure of *Ctenochaetus hawaiiensis*, which lives in groups of 3 to 20 fish gathered at refuges. Individuals or groups may leave and return from time to time. It remains to be determined whether these groups have exclusive use of their refuges.

4.3.6 Lek Territories

Lek territories are maintained by males during the breeding season as exclusive courtship and breeding sites, typically tightly clustered on an arena or lek. For several species of acanthurid, labrid, and scarid fishes, there are reports of males competing for spawning sites within which they court females (Barlow, 1974; Feddern, 1965). Robertson and Choat (1974) suggest that *Thalassoma lunare* maintains such territories but that they are "weakly defined." *Thalassoma bifasciatum* also shows this behavior (Feddern, 1965; Reinboth, 1972; Warner *et al.*, 1975). Among the acanthurids, males of *Naso brevirostris* appear to hold stations along cliff faces while courting (Barlow, 1974). Lek behavior is discussed more fully elsewhere in this volume. In general, few reef fishes appear to maintain such territories, and those that do, do not maintain territories in a highly structured arena or on sites with some tradition of use.

4.4 Hierarchically Organized Groups

Dominance hierarchies have been documented for many species of fish, and it is well known that species that are territorial when uncrowded can be made to form a hierarchy when crowded in an aquarium (Erickson, 1967; Greenberg, 1947; Keenleyside and Yamamoto, 1962). McBride (1971) has suggested that territoriality and dominance hierarchies are but two ends of a spectrum of social systems. Among reef fishes, dominance hierarchies based upon relative difference in size of interacting individuals occur in those species that live in stable groups. For example, groups of *Amphiprion* species in an anemone (Allen, 1972), or of *Dascyllus aruanus* occupying a single coral colony (Sale, 1972a), are hierarchically structured. Coates (personal communication) has demonstrated that hierarchical position determines where, with reference to the home coral and the direction of water movement, individual *D. aruanus* forage on plankton.

Dominance hierarchies do not appear to exist in mobile groups, such as foraging aggregations and feeding shoals, but there has not been sufficient study of the interindividual behavior in such aggregations. Those individuals of *Scarus croicensis* that occupy a female's territory exhibit hierarchical dominance relationships among themselves, while the same species, in a foraging group, does not do so (Ogden and Buckman, 1973).

4.5 Simultaneous Territorial and Hierarchical Structure

4.5.1 Nested Territories in *Labroides dimidiatus*

In *Labroides dimidiatus*, a protogynous hermaphrodite, adult males are territorial and defend their territories from each other. Within the male's territory, there may exist one or more females. The females are all submissive to the male, and the largest of them assists the male in defense of his territorial borders. Occasionally, two large females will exist within a single male's territory. When this happens, each assists in the defense of the part of the male's territory that she occupies, but she exlcudes the other female, who occupies the remainder of the male's territory. It is thus clear that there are no pair territories formed, only overlapping individual territories. Smaller females may also be present. Each of these is also territorial within a small part of the male's territory. Each female fish in the group is thus submissive to all larger fishes, territorial with respect to members of similar size, and dominant to smaller fishes whose territories may fall within hers (Robertson, 1972, 1974; Robertson and Choat, 1974).

4.5.2 Overlapping Territories among Pomacentrids

Pomacentrus wardi usually maintains nonoverlapping individual territories (Sale, 1974, 1975). However, during periods of high recruitment of juveniles, overlapping of these territories may occur. Unlike *Labroides dimidiatus,* in which larger fish are dominant to, but tolerate the presence of, smaller fish, larger *P. wardi* continue intermittent attacks on the small individuals present in their territories. The continued existence of the smaller fish is dependent upon their having access to small crevices that provide a refuge from the larger fish. They successfully maintain territories around these refuges, but retreat to them when approached by the larger fish. Figure 11.2 shows a typical example of overlapped territories in this species. The same phenomenon may also occur in other territorial pomacentrids when sufficient numbers are present. Figure 11.2 shows limited overlapping among *Pomacentrus flavicauda.* At Heron Reef, juvenile *P. wardi* sometimes establish territories within the areas held by other species such as *Eupomacentrus* (= *Pomacentrus*) *apicalis,* or *Plectroglyphidodon* (= *Abudefduf*) *lacrymatus* (Sale, 1974). The mechanisms permitting this pattern do not appear to differ from those permitting intraspecific nesting of territories.

Itzkowitz (1974) has demonstrated that in *Eupomacentrus dorsopunicans* and *E. leucostictus* (and to a smaller extent, *E. planifrons*), juvenile fish commonly occur within the territories held by conspecific adults. It appears likely that a phenomenon similar to that seen at Heron Reef may occur here too. That Itzkowitz records juveniles only within the territories of conspecifics, however, may indicate a situation more comparable to that in *L. dimidiatus.*

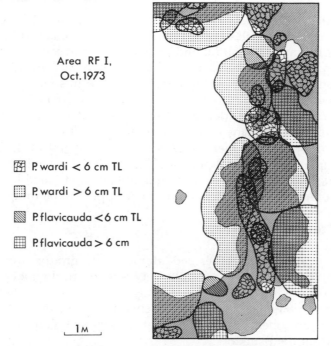

Area RF I,
Oct. 1973

P. wardi < 6 cm TL

P. wardi > 6 cm TL

P. flavicauda < 6 cm TL

P. flavicauda > 6 cm

1 M

FIGURE 11.2 A small area on the outer reef flat at Heron Reef, showing the locations of the territories held by a number of *Pomacentrus wardi* and *P. flavicauda* in October 1973. The darker substratum is rock, the rest sand. Note the frequent superimposition of territories.

4.6 Summary

4.6.1 Spatial and Hierarchical Patterns

From the survey above, it is apparent that many reef fishes show quite rigid patterns of physical spacing, and that territorial systems (usually interspecifically defended) are common. These rigid patterns of spacing mean that most relationships between individuals are site-determined. Some stable groups show hierarchical organization, and these hierarchies are invariably size-related. Feeding and resting aggregations appear to consist of equal, and perhaps indistinguishable, individuals.

4.6.2 Caste and Role

Caste is of some importance in most reef fishes, the commonest caste division being that between males and nonmales (females and juveniles). Among the labrids and scarids, a distinction between primary and secondary males is also often apparent. In many species (again particularly among the labrids and scarids), different color patterns identify the different castes (Barlow, 1974; Ogden and Buckman, 1973; Robertson and Choat, 1974; Warner *et al.*, 1975). In some pomacentrids (e.g., *Pomacentrus wardi*) juveniles are differently colored from adults, but there is as yet no evidence that they are treated as a distinct caste.

It is likely that in many instances, members of different castes will be found to be spatially or hierarchically organized in quite different ways. For example, Barlow (1974) points to the territorial behavior of juvenile *Acanthurus triostegus* and the feeding aggregations formed by adults.

Roles other than those defined by caste appear to be unimportant.

4.6.3 Group Structure

Among territorial and other sedentary forms, groups are generally closed, in that movements of adults between groups do not occur. Such movements are probably inhibited by agonistic encounters between residents and potential intruders. It seems, however, that all groups of reef fishes are open in the sense that all receive colonizing juveniles settling from the plankton.

Those species that aggregate may exist in still more open groups. This is something for which very few data currently exist. Indeed, the data of Smith and Tyler (1972) and Russell *et al.* (1974) suggest that even here, groups are closed and individuals rarely meet fishes they have not encountered before.

4.6.4 Phase

Phase may be relatively unimportant among reef fishes. This is not because the social behavior of reef fishes does not change during reproductive periods, but because the extended reproductive seasons (see Sec. 2.4.) mean that some individuals are breeding all the time. Instead of a population moving from nonreproductive to reproductive phase, the population at any given time contains some fish in reproductive and some in nonreproductive castes. Individuals in reproductive caste often show different patterns of social organization than those in nonreproductive castes. For example, males of the genera *Chromis* and *Abudefduf* are part of midwater feeding shoals when nonreproductive, but hold individual nest-site territories while reproductive (Fishelson, 1970a; Fishelson *et al.*, 1974; Reese, 1964; Sale, 1971a). Ogden and Buckman (1973) have demonstrated clearly the simultaneous occurrence of reproductive and nonreproductive castes in *Scarus croicensis,* and (partly a consequence) the simultaneous existence of territorial, home-ranging, and aggregating individuals. Among labrids, some males may be temporarily territorial in a lek system, while nonbreeding males continue to hold overlapping home ranges (Robertson and Choat, 1974; Warner *et al.*, 1975).

Some stable social groups exhibit synchronized reproduction, all members spawning every week or so (Holzberg, 1973; Keenleyside, 1972). In these, reproductive and nonreproductive phases can be considered to exist.

5 COMPLEX SOCIAL INTERACTIONS

5.1 General

Although cooperation within well-defined closed groups is not a conspicuous feature of social organizations of reef fishes, there now exist several well-documented complex patterns of behavior serving specifically to maintain group structure. It is likely that further study will produce additional examples of these types of behavior.

5.2 Regulation of Sexual Reversal

Robertson (1972, 1974), in his study of *Labroides dimidiatus,* pointed to the existence of a dominance display used only by males towards their females. Termed "flutter-running," it was directed toward the most dominant female of the group in 76% of observations. Robertson demonstrated experimentally that the death or removal of a male led, within 2 hours, to the adoption of male patterns of behavior, including "flutter-running," by the dominant female. Sex reversal was physiologically completed within 2 weeks. He concluded that male behavior, particularly "flutter-running," inhibited sex reversal by females and thus resulted in a social group in which all individuals contributed maximally to reproduction. A similar phenomenon has been documented in aquarium studies of *Anthias squamipinnis* (Fishelson, 1970b). Studies of sex ratio (Fricke and Holzberg, 1974) and experimental removal of males (Coates, personal communication) indicate that socially mediated sex reversal may also occur in *Dascyllus aruanus.* Robertson and Choat (1974) have predicted that similar patterns of behavioral regulation will be found in many hermaphroditic species.

5.3   Regulation of Maturation

Social behavior has been implicated in the regulation of growth in one pomacentrid fish. Allen (1972) demonstrated experimentally that a group of five juvenile *Amphiprion periderion* living in the field with two adults of the same species showed virtually no growth over six months, yet showed at least a 25% increase in length during the two months following removal of the adults. Regulation of growth of juveniles may serve to maintain group composition, but further work is needed to confirm Allen's result.

5.4   Maintenance of Social Contact

Among species maintaining permanent individual territories, it is presumably adaptive for fish to have nonagonistic contact with their neighbors, particularly those of the same species, since they will be the fish with which breeding occurs. It is now apparent that in many of the pomacentrids that have been studied, behavior patterns exist (that I term "visiting") that serve to achieve this contact. Similar behavior may also occur in territorial chaetodontids such as *Chaetodon trifascialis* (Reese, 1975).

In pomacentrids, "visiting" was first described in *Hypsypops rubicunda* (Clarke, 1970). On occasion, several territory holders were observed to rise 2 to 3 m above the substratum and to mill 20 to 30 cm apart in midwater. Aggregations formed throughout the year, but especially just prior to the breeding season. Clarke (1970) suggested that aggregations functioned as a communal courtship display, or to maintain nonterritorial contact among the members of a social group.

Subsequently, Keenleyside (1972) described "clustering" in *Glyphidodontops biocellatus* (= *Abudefduf zonatus*). His observations were restricted to midsummer, when breeding was at a peak. Clustering occurred as frequently as two to five times per hour, and each cluster lasted for 3 to 5 min. He described a cluster as the assembly, close to the substratum, of 8 to 10 fishes, both male and female. Rapid swimming, chasing, lateral and head-down displays all occurred, but only with a low intensity of agonism. Frequency of occurrence of clusters was not correlated with the 14 day cycle of breeding activity Keenleyside found. He suggested that clustering served 1) to distribute information about reproductive condition throughout the population, and 2) to facilitate, and perhaps synchronize, reproductive activity.

Moyer and Sawyers (1973) described visiting in an unusually extensive colony of *Amphiprion xanthurus*. Individuals milled about 2 to 3 m above the substratum as described for *Hypsypops rubicunda* (Clarke, 1970).

I have observed generally similar visiting in *Pomacentrus flavicauda, P. wardi, Eupomacentrus apicalis,* and *Plectroglyphidodon lacrymatus.* The behavior is quite conspicuous in *E. apicalis,* but in none of these species is visiting a frequent or a long-lasting phenomenon. Thus, it is difficult behavior to study, and the following discussion is based on a number of haphazard observations made over two years.

In *Eupomacentrus apicalis,* visiting can involve from 2 to 10 fishes. Bouts commence when one fish, always a male, invades the territories of one or more other fishes. In the most intense bouts, the visitor is joined by six to eight other neighbors who mill about close to the substratum, much as Keenleyside described in *Glyphidodontops biocellatus* (Keenleyside, 1972), and as it occurs in the other species I've observed. Agonistic behavior—particularly lateral display—occurs, but only at low intensity. Males may pale anteriorly into their reproductive coloration, and incipient courtship may occur. The mill may last up to 1 min. Then, either the fishes return to their own territories, or they engage in a rapid, single-file swim among the crevices and other shelters of one or more of the territories invaded. In this second phase, the territory of the initiating fish is always entered. Visiting occurs throughout the year (Table 11.2), but more frequently and at higher intensity during the summer months, when breeding occurs.

TABLE 11.2 Intensity of visiting behavior by *Eupomacentrus apicalis* at Heron Reef, on all occasions when observed

Date	Intensity [a]		
	Low	Moderate	High
24 May 1973	X		
25 May 1973	X		
27 May 1973	X		
31 May 1973			X
23 September 1973	X		
3 October 1972			X
4 October 1972			X
10 October 1973			X
3 November 1972		X	
7 November 1972			X
12 November 1972		X	
8 December 1973			X

[a] Low intensity—only one fish visits. Moderate—several fish visit, no color change. High—several fish, some adopt courtship coloration.

It is probable that in all of these species, visiting behavior in its various forms achieves nonagonistic contact. There is the possibility that through visiting, the identification of potential mates is achieved, and the topography of neighbors' territories is learned. The latter may be quite important during subsequent spawning bouts. In addition, as Keenleyside (1972) suggested, visiting may achieve facilitation and synchronization of reproductive development.

Visiting is not limited to those pomacentrids that maintain individual territories. I have observed visiting in *Dascyllus aruanus* during the summer months. When visiting, a number of individuals aggregate around and within the interstices of the home coral of an adult fish. Some individuals of this markedly sedentary species (Sale, 1971b) travel up to 10 m to join the milling group. As many as 10 fish, including older juveniles as well as adult males and females, form a mill. They weave rapidly in and out among the coral's branches, and males sometimes develop spawning coloration and perform incipient courtship. Low-intensity agonistic displays also occur. Visiting bouts rarely last more than one min, before all the fish return to their own colonies of coral.

5.5   Regulation of Group Size

In areas where *Dascyllus aruanus* is common, relative to the branching coral it uses as shelter, a correlation exists between the number of fish in a group and the size of the colony of coral being used (Sale, 1972b). Intragroup agonistic encounters are common, and a direct relationship exists between the amount of cover available and the level of this agonistic activity (Sale, 1972a). This relationship seems likely to be the basis of the mechanism that regulates group size. Individuals in crowded groups will be more aggressive, and thus more hostile to newly settling larvae, than those in uncrowded groups. This hypothesis has not been confirmed in the field.

For *Pomacentrus wardi*, the presence of resident adults of the same species or of *Eupomacentrus apicalis* reduces successful colonization of rubble patches by juveniles. Figure 11.3 illustrates the results of an experiment I carried out on four similar rubble patches (Sale, 1976). One was not disturbed, one had most of the adult residents removed by spearing, one had most adults removed and then had 25 juvenile *P. wardi* added, and the fourth had 25 juvenile *P. wardi* added, but the adults were allowed to remain. Juveniles added to patches had been collected elsewhere on the reef, and were introduced, as a small group, at sunset. Ten were added to each patch on one day, and 15 two days later.

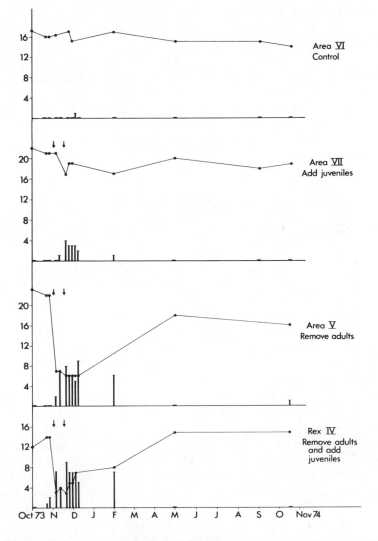

FIGURE 11.3 Number of resident adult pomacentrids (lines), and number of juvenile *Pomacentrus wardi* (histograms) on each of four small rubble patches during one year. Experimental manipulations were carried out on the dates indicated by arrows. Details are in text. (From Sale, 1976.)

The two patches from which adults were removed (Fig. 11.3) consistently supported the greatest numbers of juveniles, while juveniles added to the undisturbed patch did not survive well. In all four patches, the number of adults at the end of a year was similar to that at the start of the experiment. This was achieved in the patches from which adults were removed by (1) the growth of immigrant juveniles, and (2) the immigration of subadult fish from other areas. It appears likely, as previously suggested (Sale 1974, 1975), that under normal conditions, with adults present on rubble patches, many potential colonists are prevented from settling.

6   COMPARISONS OF SOCIAL STRUCTURES

6.1   Other Fishes

As already stated (see Sec. 3.1), demersal fishes of temperate rocky shores appear ecologically similar to those of coral reefs. From what is known, they are also very similar behaviorally (Clarke, 1970; Gibson, 1969; Moran and Sale, 1977; Phillips, 1974; Stephens et al., 1970). By contrast, some freshwater fishes—especially the Cichlidae—show a pronounced development of parental behavior compared to reef fishes. The social organization of *Acanthochromis polyacanthus* (Robertson, 1973), while unique among reef fishes, is a typical pattern of behavior among the cichlids (Baerends and Baerends-van Roon, 1950; Barlow, 1974). With the exception of this increased development of parental behavior, however, freshwater fish show many characteristics in common with reef fish. A tendency to be sedentary, and to maintain individual feeding territories in some cases, is well documented among stream fishes (Gerking, 1959; Northcote, 1967). Barlow (1974) suggests that nonbreeding groups of cichlids are open groups, as are aggregations of reef fishes. Where differences in emphasis occur—such as the prevalence of interspecific defense of territory, and the tendency for social interactions to be inter- as well as intraspecific among reef fishes—these may be an inevitable result of the more diverse community to which reef fishes belong. Similarly, the increased development of parental care among freshwater fishes may be a direct consequence of the greater opportunities that exist in freshwater habitats for individuals to develop in close proximity to their parents. A close comparison of social organization within the species-rich fish faunas of some African lakes and those of coral reefs would be valuable. A good basis already exists for a study of African cichlids (Fryer and Iles, 1972).

6.2 Terrestrial Vertebrates

6.2.1 General

Mammals and birds are more mobile animals than are reef fishes (see Sec. 3.2), and parental care is considerably more highly developed. These two factors appear to account for the principal differences between the social organization characteristic of mammals and birds and those of reef fishes. The increased mobility reduces the likelihood of social interactions being rigidly site determined. Simultaneously, the increased development of parental care both creates a greater variety of castes and roles in a group, and introduces the possibility of kin selection as an important evolutionary force (Wilson, 1975). As a consequence there develops a more complex social system based on the many complex and enduring relationships between individuals—between mates, siblings, parents and offspring, or simply members of the same group (Crook et al., 1976; Ewer, 1968; Wilson, 1975). In reef fishes, however, social organization is built upon a basis of precise relationships between individuals and their living sites and only secondarily on relationships between individuals. Here I consider three major differences that exist between the social organizations of reef fishes and those of mammals and birds.

6.2.2 Individual Recognition as Basis of Social Structure

The mobile, closed, and hierarchically structured group is found in many ungulates and primates (Crook, 1970; Crook et al., 1976; Devore and Hall, 1965; Ewer, 1968; Wilson, 1975) in particular. Mobile groups of reef fishes are open, with members joining and departing frequently (see Sec. 4.2). They are unstructured hierarchically, and it is possible that individuals are not distinguished. More sedentary but nonterritorial species of reef fishes may occur in hierarchically organized groups, but dominance relations seem based upon size differences. Coates' data (personal communication) indicate that *Dascyllus aruanus* can discriminate group members from introduced strangers; however, as Fricke (1975) points out, this discrimination does not take place if group members are introduced to one another away from their home coral. Recognition of individuals is thus not established. Territorial forms may recognize individual neighbors, but again this may be simply response to a fish in a particular site. Only in the few pair-forming species can individual recognition be assumed to occur (e.g., some chaetodontids, Reese, 1975).

In mammals and birds, there is considerable evidence of recognition of individuals and of social structures based upon such recognition. Goodall (1968) has documented the great importance of the family for an understanding of the social organization of chimpanzees, and familial relations are important elements in many other mammalian societies (Crook, 1970; Crook *et al.*, 1976; Ewer, 1968; Wilson, 1975).

6.2.3 Territoriality

Among territorial mammals and birds, the pair territory is the commonest type (Crook, 1964; Ewer, 1968; Hinde, 1956; Orians 1971; Stokes, 1974; Wilson, 1975). This type is rare among reef fishes, which overwhelmingly hold individual territories (see Sec. 4.3.2). Furthermore, reef fishes usually maintain territories as feeding areas held throughout the year, while birds, in particular, usually defend territories only during the breeding season. While interspecific defense of territory by birds is considered aberrant, and is usually attributed to cases of "mistaken identity" among morphologically similar species (Orians and Willson, 1964), this is demonstrably not true among reef fishes. They are predominantly interspecifically territorial, and Thresher (1976) has established for one species that the territorial response is specific to the species of intruder.

6.2.4 Interspecific Sociality

Territorial reef fishes are predominantly interspecifically territorial. Observations of the behavior of nonterritorial forms suggest that they also interact socially with members of other species. For example, heterotypic aggregations of many types are common (see Sec. 4.2). Indeed, a pronounced species distinction appears to be made only during courtship and spawning.

If such interspecific sociality (and I include the interactions of territorial forms) is frequent among mammals and birds, it has not been generally noted (Ewer, 1968; Orians and Willson, 1964; Wilson, 1975).

7   CONCLUSIONS

Reef fishes live in an environment that requires them to be sedentary and site-attached, because living space may often be in short supply. They achieve dispersal through the production of frequent clutches of pelagic larvae. The maintenance of a family group, even temporarily, is known for only one species (Robertson, 1973), although many species (a minority of the total) show care of eggs.

Nevertheless, reef fishes exhibit a wide range of patterns of social organization. All patterns of spatial organization shown by mammals and birds can be found, except for that of the mobile, closed, hierarchically structured group exemplified by many ungulates, primates, and other mammals (Ewer, 1968; Crook et al., 1976). But while possessing all but one of these patterns, reef fishes emphasize a different set. They are more likely than birds or mammals to operate as individuals occupying small home ranges or territories. When territorial, they usually defend the area against many species. Fish that form other than transitory breeding pairs are rare on reefs.

These differences in emphasis may be a reflection of a more limited ability of fishes to form lasting relationships based upon individual recognition (Wilson, 1975). More likely, however, is the suggestion that these differences are a direct result of the responses of reef fishes and terrestrial vertebrates to the very different environments in which they occur. The nature of the environment occupied by reef fishes both precludes the development of a family [and thus the evolution of complex social systems through kin selection (Wilson, 1975)], and imposes spatial constraints on social interactions.

8   ACKNOWLEDGMENTS

The original work reported here was carried out under the support of the Australian Research Grants Committee. I thank Mr. R. Dybdahl for his assistance and the Heron Island Research Station for the use of their facilities.

REFERENCES

Allen, G. R. 1972. The Anemonefishes. Their Classification and Biology. T. F. H. Publications, Neptune, N.J. 288 p.

Anderson, P. K. 1961. Density, social structure, and nonsocial environment in house-mouse populations and the implications for regulation of numbers. Trans. N.Y. Acad. Sci. 23: 447–451.

Archer, J. 1970. Effects of population density on behaviour in rodents. In: J. H. Crook, Ed. Social Behaviour in Birds and Mammals. Academic Press, London. P. 169–210.

Baerends, G. P. and J. M. Baerends-van Roon. 1950. An introduction to the study of the ethology of cichlid fishes. Behaviour Suppl. 1: 1–242.

Bardach, J. E. 1958. On the movements of certain Bermuda reef fishes. Ecology 39: 139–146.

Barlow, G. W. 1974. Contrasts in social behavior between central American cichlid fishes and coral reef surgeon fishes. Am. Zool. 14: 9–34.

Barlow, G. W. 1975a. On the sociobiology of some hermaphroditic serranid fishes, the hamlets, in Puerto Rico. Mar. Biol. 33: 295–300.

Barlow, G. W. 1975b. On the sociobiology of four Puerto Rican parrotfishes (Scaridae). Mar. Biol. 33: 281–294.

Breder, C. M. Jr., and D. E. Rosen. 1966. Modes of Reproduction in Fishes. American Museum of Natural History Press, New York. 941 p.

Choat, J. H. 1969. Studies on labroid fishes. Unpublished doctoral dissertation, University of Queensland. 433 p.

Clarke, T. A. 1970. Teritorial behavior and population dynamics of a pomacentrid fish, the garibaldi, Hypsypops rubicunda. Ecol. Monogr. 40: 189–212.

Crook, J. H. 1964. The evolution of social organisation and visual communication in the weaver birds (Ploceinae). Behaviour Suppl. 10: 1–178.

Crook, J. H. 1970. The socioecology of primates. In: J. H. Crook, Ed. Social Behaviour in Birds and Mammals. Academic Press, London. P. 103–166.

Crook, J. H., J. E. Ellis, and J. D. Goss-Custard. 1976. Mammalian social systems: structure and function. Anim. Behav. 24: 261–274.

Devore, I. and K.R.L. Hall. 1965. Baboon ecology. In: I. Devore, Ed. Primate Behavior. Field Studies of Monkeys and Apes. Holt, Rinehart, and Winston, New York. P. 20–52.

Ehrlich, P. R. 1975. The population biology of coral reef fishes. Ann. Rev. Ecol. Syst. 6: 211–247.

Ehrlich, P. R. and A. H. Ehrlich. 1973. Coevolution: heterotypic schooling in Caribbean reef fishes. Am. Nat. 107: 157–160.

Ehrlich, P. R., F. H. Talbot, B. C. Russell, and G. R. V. Anderson. 1977. The behaviour of chaetodontid fishes with special reference to Lorenz's "poster colouration" hypothesis. J. Zool. (Lond.): 183: 213–228.

Erickson, J. G. 1967. Social hierarchy, territoriality, and stress reaction in sunfish. Physiol. Zool. 40: 40–48.

Ewer, R. F. 1968. Ethology of Mammals. Lagos Press, London. 418 p.

Feddern, H. A. 1965. The spawning, growth, and general behavior of the bluehead wrasse, Thalassoma bifasciatum (Pisces: Labridae). Bull. Mar. Sci. 15: 896–941.

Fiedler, K. 1964. Verhaltensstudien an Lippfischen der Gattung Crenilabrus (Labridae; Perciformes). Z. Tierpsychol. 21: 521–591.

Fishelson, L. 1970a. Behaviour and ecology of a population of Abudefduf saxatilis (Pomacentridae, Teleostei) at Eilat (Red Sea). Anim. Behav. 18: 225–237.

Fishelson, L. 1970b. Protogynous sex reversal in the fish Anthias squamipinnis (Teleostei, Anthiidae) regulated by the presence or absence of a male fish. Nature 227: 90–91.

Fishelson, L. 1975. Ethology and reproduction of pteroid fishes found in the Gulf of Aqaba (Red Sea), especially Dendrochirus brachypterus (Cuvier), (Pteroidae, Teleostei). Pubbl. Sta. Zool. Napoli 39, Suppl.: 635–656.

Fishelson, L., D. Popper, and A. Avidor. 1974. Biosociology and ecology of pomacentrid fishes around the Sinai Peninsula, northern Red Sea. J. Fish Biol. 6: 119–133.

Fricke, H. W. 1973. Okologie und Sozialverhalten des Korallenbarsches Dascyllus trimaculatus (Pisces, Pomacentridae). Z. Tierpsychol. 32: 225–256.

Fricke, H. W. 1975. Evolution of social systems through site attachment in fish. Z. Tierpsychol. **39**: 206–210.

Fricke, H. W. and S. Holzberg. 1974. Social units and hermaphroditism in a pomacentrid fish. Naturwiss **61**: 367–368.

Fryer, G. and T. D. Iles. 1972. *The Cichlid Fishes of the Great Lakes of Africa. Their Biology and Evolution.* Oliver and Boyd, Edinburgh. 641 p.

Gerking, S. D. 1959. The restricted movements of fish populations. Biol. Rev. **34**: 221–237.

Gibson, R. N. 1969. The biology and behaviour of littoral fish. Oceanogr. Mar. Biol. Ann. Rev. **7**: 367–410.

Goeden, G. B. 1974. Aspects of the biology and ecology of the coral trout, *Plectropomus leopardus* (Lacepede) (Serranidae) at Heron Island, Great Barrier Reef. Unpublished doctoral dissertation, Univ. of Queensland. 352 p.

Goldman, B. and F. H. Talbot. 1976. Aspects of the ecology of coral reef fishes. *In:* O. A. Jones and R. Endean, Eds. *Biology and Geology of Coral Reefs.* Vol. 3: *Biology II.* Academic Press, New York. P. 125–154.

Goodall, J. van Lawick. 1968. The behaviour of free-living chimpanzees in the Gombe Stream Reserve. Anim. Behav. Monogr. **1**: 161–311.

Greenberg, B. 1947. Some relations between territory, social hierarchy, and leadership in the green sunfish (*Lepomis cyanellus*). Physiol. Zool. **20**: 267–299.

Hinde, R. A. 1956. The biological significance of the territories of birds. Ibis **98**: 340–369.

Hobson, E. S. 1965. Diurnal-nocturnal activity of some inshore fishes in the Gulf of California. Copeia **1965**: 291–302.

Hobson, E. S. 1968. Predatory behavior of some shore fishes in the Gulf of California. U.S. Dept. Inter. Fish, Wildl. Serv., Bur. Sport Fish. and Wildl. Res. Rept. **73**: 1–92.

Hobson, E. S. 1971. Cleaning symbiosis among California inshore fishes. Fish. Bull. **69**: 491–523.

Hobson, E. S. 1973. Diel feeding migrations in tropical reef fishes. Helgoländer Wiss. Meeresunters. **24**: 361–370.

Hobson, E. S. 1974. Feeding relationships of Teleostean fishes on coral reefs in Kona, Hawaii. Fish. Bull. **72**: 915–1031.

Hobson, E. S. and J. R. Chess. 1973. Feeding oriented movements of the atherinid fish, *Pranesus pinguis* at Majuro Atoll, Marshall Islands. Fish. Bull. **71**: 777–786.

Holzberg, S. 1973. Beobachtungen zur Okologie und zum Sozialverhalten des Korallen-barsches *Dascyllus marginatus* Ruppell (Pisces: Pomacentridae). Z. Tierpsychol. **33**: 492–513.

Itzkowitz, M. 1974. A behavioral reconnaissance of some Jamaican reef fishes. Zool. J. Linn. Soc. **55**: 87–118.

Keenleyside, M. H. A. 1972. The behaviour of *Abudefduf zonatus* (Pisces: Pomacentridae) at Heron Island,, Great Barrier Reef. Anim. Behav. **20**: 763–775.

Keenleyside, M. H. A. and F. T. Yamamoto. 1962. Territorial behaviour of juvenile Atlantic salmon (*Salmo salar,* L.). Behaviour **19**: 139–169.

Kummer, H. 1968. Two variations in the social organization of baboons. *In:* P. C. Jay, Ed. *Primates. Studies in Adaptation and Variability.* Holt, Rinehart, and Winston, New York. P. 293–312.

Lassig, B. 1976. Field observations on the reproductive behaviour of *Paragobiodon* spp. (Osteichthyes: Gobiidae) at Heron Island Great Barrier Reef. Mar. Behav. Physiol. **3**: 283–293.

Leis, J. M. and J. M. Miller. 1976. Offshore distributional patterns of Hawaiian fish larvae. Mar. Biol. **36**: 359–368.

Low, R. M. 1971. Interspecific territoriality in a pomacentrid reef fish, *Pomacentrus flavicauda* Whitley. Ecology **52**: 648–654.

McBride, G. 1971. Theories of animal spacing: the role of flight, fight, and social distance. *In*: A. H. Esser, Ed. *Behavior and Environment. the Use of Space by Animals and Men.* Plenum Press, New York. P. 53–68.

McBride, G., I. P. Parer, and F. Foenander. 1969. The social organisation and behaviour of the feral domestic fowl. Anim. Behav. Monogr. **2**: 127–181.

McNab, B. K. 1963. Bioenergetics and the determination of home range size. Am. Nat. **97**: 133–140.

Moran, M. J. and P. F. Sale, 1977. Seasonal variation in territorial response, and other aspects of ecology of Australian temperate pomacentrid fish, *Parma microlepis*. Mar. Biol. **39**: 121–128.

Moyer, J. T., and C. E. Sawyers. 1973. Territorial behavior of the anemonefish *Amphiprion xanthurus* with notes on the life history. Jap. J. Ichthyol. **20**: 85–93.

Munro, J. L., V. C. Grant, R. Thompson, and P. H. Reeson. 1973. The spawning seasons of Caribbean reef fishes. J. Fish Biol. **5**: 69–84.

Myrberg, A. A. 1972. Ethology of the bicolor damselfish, *Eupomacentrus partitus* (Pisces: Pomacentridae). A comparative analysis of laboratory and field behaviour. Anim. Behav. Monogr. **5**: 199–283.

Myrberg, A. A. and R. E. Thresher. 1974. Interspecific aggression and its relevance to the concept of territoriality in reef fishes. Am. Zool. **14**: 81–96.

Noakes, D. L. G. and G. W. Barlow. 1973. Cross-fostering and parent-offspring responses in *Cichlasoma citrinellum* (Pisces, Cichlidae). Z. Tierpsychol. **33**: 147–152.

Northcote, T. G. 1967. The relation of movements and migrations to production in freshwater fishes. *In*: S. D. Gerking, Ed. *The Biological Basis of Freshwater Fish Production.* Blackwell Scientific Publications, Oxford. P. 315–344.

Nursall J. R. 1974a. Character displacement and fish behavior, especially in coral reef communities. Am. Zool. **14**: 1099–1118.

Nursall, J. R. 1974b. Some territorial behavioral attributes of the surgeonfish *Acanthurus lineatus* at Heron Island, Queensland, Australia. Copeia **1974**: 950–959.

Ogden, J. C. and N. S. Buckman. 1973. Movements, foraging groups, and diurnal migrations of the striped parrotfish *Scarus croicensis* Bloch (Scaridae). Ecology **54**: 589–596.

Orians, G. H. 1971. Ecological aspects of behavior. *In*: D. S. Farner, J. R. King, and K. C. Parkes, Eds. *Avian Biology.* Vol. 1. Academic Press, New York. P. 513–546.

Orians, G. H. and M. F. Willson. 1964. Interspecific territories in birds. Ecology **45**: 736–745.

Phillips, R. R. 1974. The relationship between social behaviour and the use of space in the benthic fish *Chasmodes bosquianus* Lacepede (Teleostei, Blenniidae), III. The interaction between attraction/repulsion and prior social experience. Behaviour **49**: 205–226.

Potts, G. W. 1973. The ethology of *Labroides dimidiatus* (Cuv. & Val.) (Labridae, Pisces) on Aldabra. Anim. Behav. **21**: 250–291.

Randall, J. E. 1961. A contribution to the biology of the convict surgeonfish of the Hawaiian Islands, *Acanthurus triostegus sandvicensis*. Pac. Sci. **15**: 215–272.

Randall, J. E. and H. A. Randall. 1963. The spawning and early development of the

Atlantic parrotfish *Sparisoma rubripinne*, with notes on other scarid and labrid fishes. Zoologica (N.Y.) **48**: 49–60.

Rasa, O. A. E. 1969. Territoriality and the establishment of dominance by means of visual cues in *Pomacentrus jenkinsi* (Pisces: Pomacentridae). Z. Tierpsychol. **26**: 825–845.

Reese, E. S. 1964. Ethology and marine zoology. Oceanogr. Mar. Biol. Ann. Rev. **2**: 455–488.

Reese, E. S. 1973. Duration of residence by coral reef fishes on "home" reefs. Copeia **1973**: 145–149.

Reese, E. S. 1975. A comparative field study of the social behaviour and related ecology of reef fishes of the family Chaetodontidae. Z. Tierpsychol. **37**: 37–61.

Reinboth, R. 1972. Some remarks on secondary sex characters, sex, and sexual behavior in Teleosts. Gen. Comp. Endocrinol. Suppl. **3**: 565–570.

Robertson, D. R. 1972. Social control of sex reversal in a coral-reef fish. Science **177**: 1007–1009.

Robertson, D. R. 1973. Field observations on the reproductive behaviour of a pomacentrid fish, *Acanthochromis polyacanthus*. Z. Tierpsychol. **32**: 319–324.

Robertson, D. R. 1974. The ethology and reproductive biology of *Labroides dimidiatus*. Unpublished doctoral dissertation, University of Queensland, Brisbane. 295 p.

Robertson, D. R. and J. H. Choat. 1974. Protogynous hermaphroditism and social systems in labrid fish. *In: Second International Symposium on Coral Reefs, Proceedings*. Vol. 1. Great Barrier Reef Committee, Brisbane. P. 217–225.

Russell, B. C., F. H. Talbot, and S. Domm. 1974. Patterns of colonisation of artificial reefs by coral reef fishes. *In: Second International Symposium on Coral Reefs, Proceedings*. Vol. 1. Great Barrier Reef Committee, Brisbane. P. 207–215.

Sale, P. F. 1970. Distribution of larval Acanthuridae off Hawaii. Copeia **1970**: 765–766.

Sale, P. F. 1971a. The reproductive behaviour of the pomacentrid fish, *Chromis caeruleus*. Z. Tierpsychol. **29**: 156–164.

Sale, P. F. 1971b. Extremely limited home range in a coral reef fish, *Dascyllus aruanus* (Pisces: Pomacentridae). Copeia **1971**: 324–327.

Sale, P. F. 1972a. Effect of cover on agonistic behavior of a reef fish: a possible spacing mechanism. Ecology **53**: 753–758.

Sale, P. F. 1972b. Influence of corals in the dispersion of the pomacentrid fish, *Dascyllus aruanus*. Ecology **53**: 741–744.

Sale, P. F. 1974. Mechanisms of coexistence in a guild of territorial fishes at Heron Island. *In: Second International Symposium on Coral Reefs, Proceedings*. Vol. 1. Great Barrier Reef Committee, Brisbane. P. 193–206.

Sale, P. F. 1975. Patterns of use of space in a guild of territorial reef fishes. Mar. Biol. **29**: 89–97.

Sale, P. F. 1976. The effect of territorial adult pomacentrid fishes on the recruitment and survival of juveniles on patches of coral rubble. J. Exp. Mar. Biol. Ecol. **24**: 297–306.

Schoener, T. W. 1968. Sizes of feeding territories among birds. Ecology **49**: 123–141.

Shaw, E. 1970. Schooling in fishes: critique and review. *In*: L. R. Aronson, E. Tobach, D. S. Lehrman, and J. S. Rosenblatt, Eds. *Development and Evolution of Behavior: Essays in Memory of T. C. Schnierla*. W. H. Freeman, San Francisco. P. 542–580.

Smith, C. L. 1972. A spawning aggregation of Nassau grouper *Epinephalus striatus* (Bloch). Trans. Am. Fish Soc. **101**: 257–261.

Smith, C. L. 1973. Small rotenone stations: a tool for studying coral reef fish communities. Am. Mus. Novitates. **2512**: 1–21.

Smith, C. L., E. H. Atz, and J. C. Tyler. 1971. Aspects of oral brooding in the cardinalfish *Cheilodipterus affinis* (Apogonidae). Av. Mus. Novitates **2456**: 1–11.

Smith, C. L. and J. C. Tyler. 1972. Space resource sharing in a coral reef fish community. Nat. Hist. Mus. Los Ang. Cty. Bull. **14**: 125–170.

Springer, V. C. and A. J. McErlean. 1962. A study of the behavior of some tagged south Florida coral reef fishes. Am. Midl. Nat. **67**: 386–397.

Stephens, J. S. Jr., R. K. Johnson, G. S. Key, and J. E. McCosker. 1970. The comparative ecology of three sympatric species of California blennies of the genus *Hypsoblennius* Gill (Teleostomi, Blenniidae). Ecol. Monogr. **40**: 213–233.

Stokes, A. W. 1974. *Territory*. Dowden, Hutchinson and Ross, New York. 398 p.

Thresher, R. E. 1976. Field experiments on species recognition by the three spot damselfish *Eupomacentrus planifrons* (Pisces: Pomacentridae). Anim. Behav. **24**: 562–569.

Turner, F. B., R. I. Jennrich, and J. D. Weintraub. 1969. Home ranges and body size of lizards. Ecology **50**: 1076–1081.

Valenti, R. J. 1972. The embryology of the neon goby, *Gobiosoma oceanops*. Copeia **1972**: 477–482.

Vine, P. J. 1974. Effects of algal grazing and aggressive behaviour of the fishes *Pomacentrus lividus* and *Acanthurus sohal* on coral-reef ecology. Mar. Biol. **24**: 131–136.

Warner, R. R., D. R. Robertson, and E. G. Leigh, Jr. 1975. Sex change and sexual selection. Science **190**: 633–638.

Wickler, W. 1961. Uber das verhalten der Blenniidae *Runula* und *Aspidontus* (Pisces, Blenniidae). Z. Tierpsychol. **18**: 421–440.

Wickler, W. 1967. Vergleich des Ablaichverhaltens einiger paarbildender sowie nicht-paarbildender Pomacentriden und Cichliden (Pisces: Perciformes). Z. Tierpsychol. **24**: 457–470.

Wilson, E. O. 1975. *Sociobiology. The New Synthesis*. Belknap Press, Harvard University Press, Cambridge, Mass. 697 p.

12

THE STUDY OF
SPACE-RELATED BEHAVIOR
IN AQUATIC ANIMALS:
SPECIAL PROBLEMS
AND SELECTED EXAMPLES

ERNST S. REESE

Department of Zoology and The Hawaii
Institute of Marine Biology
University of Hawaii, Honolulu

1   INTRODUCTION

Behavior associated with the use of space, hereafter referred to as space-related behavior, is one of the most important determinants of social behavior in animals, including man. Dispersal is the phenomenon of spacing out or spreading into available habitats. It results from various kinds of behavior with different underlying motivations. For example, crowding causes an increase in agonistic behavior, and subordinate or defeated individuals disperse into adjacent habitats. These are frequently less optimal, and so the fitness of the animal forced to disperse is reduced. In such cases, dispersal and its attendant behaviors can be considered as "forced" in the proximate causal sense of the word. In other cases, dispersal is "voluntary" in the ultimate evolutionary sense. Animals disperse or migrate into habitats to feed, to reproduce, and to escape from predators. The time frame for dispersal is variable. It may be on a diel, lunar, or seasonal basis. In all cases, however, the resultant behavioral and ecological measure of dispersal is dispersion. Since dispersion is the static pattern of distribution of animals in space, it determines their proximity to one another and therefore affects the type, frequency, and intensity of social interactions. This is true for behavior both within and between species. Clearly, then, an appreciation of space-related behavior in animals is essential for an understanding of their social behavior. Recognition of the applicability of these ideas to the understanding of human behavior is evidenced by the emergence of what may be called biosocial anthropology and human ethology (Altman, 1975; Eibl-Eisbesfeldt, 1975; Eisenberg and Dillon, 1971; Esser, 1971; Fox, 1975; and Freedman, 1975).

Since the utilization of space affects important demographic parameters such as population density and distribution, it indirectly affects the breeding systems and hence the gene flow and age structure of populations. These are important determinants of social organization. Examples are available in Banks and Willson (1974), Ellis (1965), and Wilson (1975). Thus a thorough understanding of the sociobiology of any species must include a careful study of its space-related behavior.

The purpose of this chapter is to examine problems and solutions specific to the study of space-related behavior in aquatic animals, to explore the intuitive, pervasive ideas underlying the persuasive concept of territoriality, and to analyze selected examples of space-related behavior in fishes and compare them with the solution to similar problems by terrestrial animals, especially birds and mammals.

2 SPECIAL PROBLEMS AND METHODS OF STUDY

2.1 Special Problems

There are special problems associated with studying the space-related behavior of aquatic animals. They are due to the facts that instrumentation is more difficult to employ under water, and, perhaps most important, that the human observer—still the most sophisticated data collector—is severely limited in the time that he can spent underwater, for physiological reasons and, in the case of saturation diving, psychological reasons and the costs of operating an underwater habitat. Of course, certain studies can be done in aquaria, but even here the major restriction is space, which makes it doubly difficult to feel confident that the experiment is testing the variables under question—namely, the use of space. This isn't to say that excellent work on space-related behavior cannot be done in aquaria. It certainly can, and Van den Assem's (1967) experimental study of territoriality in the three-spined stickleback is an outstanding example. Other examples of laboratory aquarium studies of the social use of space and related behavioral phenomena, especially aggression in fishes, are Magnuson (1962), Phillips (1974), and Rasa (1971).

2.2 Electronic Tagging

Besides conventional tagging and recapture techniques that provide information on gross movements, ultrasonic and radio tags are also effective (see for example, Groot *et al.*, 1975; Monan *et al.*, 1975. Stasko, 1975; Tesch, 1975; and Warden and Lorio, 1975). They provide the possibility of obtaining details on movements during the time the tagged animal is monitored.

In addition to the gross movement patterns of large-mouth bass, Warden and Lorio (1975) measured eight movement and activity variables. Examples are number of home areas selected, average distance travelled to home areas, and average time spent at home areas. They defined home areas as any location in which bass remained for more than two days. The maximum distance moved from a central point within the home area was used as an indication of home range. Home-range size differed with seasonal water temperature. It rarely exceeded 30 m during summer months, but was larger, approximately 75 to 100 m during the spring and fall. The animals were inactive during winter. These data were obtained by the use of 16 tagged animals. Tags had an average life of 13.8 days. Tracking was continued daily for approximately 2.2 hours over a 6 week period, providing a total of 570 hours of tracking time.

However, electronic tagging and tracking methods provide very little information on details of social behavior. For example, even continuous tracking of an ultrasonically tagged animal does not provide information on other animals that are encountered (unless they are other tagged individuals) or the nature of the encounters. For example, was the encountered animal preyed on, attacked, fled from, courted, or simply ignored? Was it a conspecific? Was it larger or smaller, male or female? If not a conspecific, what species was it? Answers to questions such as these are essential if an understanding of the significance of the movement is desired. Only visual observations of the events can provide answers to these questions. Thus, if one wishes to carry out a thorough ethological study of an aquatic animal in the field, it is absolutely necessary to observe the animal's behavior for relatively long periods of time underwater. There are are simply no alternatives.

2.3   Underwater Television

Television provides a powerful tool for underwater observation (Barnes, 1963; Kumpf, 1964; Myrberg, 1973; Stevenson, 1967). It has been used successfully to study the behavior of two small, territorial pomacentrid fishes that remain in one place on the reef: *Eupomacentrus partitus*, by Myrberg (1972a, b) and Stevenson (1972), and *E. planifrons* by Thresher (1975a, b). They combined acoustical studies with their video observations. Given an elaborate and expensive television system, it is possible to keep individual fishes under continuous surveillance for many hours, and thereby to observe the details of their behavior. Myrberg *et al.*, (1969) have also used a video-acoustic system to study the behavior of sharks.

The major limitation to underwater television is that it is stationary, and even when the camera can be tilted and rotated by remote control, the area of underwater topography that is seen by the camera is relatively small.

In situations where the daily or seasonal migrations are well known, it is possible for the observer to predict a location from which certain kinds of behaviors can be observed. Under these conditions, underwater television can be used to great advantage.

2.4 SCUBA Techniques

Many species, however, move over larger areas of the reef in the course of their daily activities. A rough rule of thumb is that the larger the size of the fish, the larger is its area of activity. This is especially true for large predators. Ambush predators are, of course, an exception. To observe effectively the behavior of these species, it is necessary to follow the animals underwater, using SCUBA at a discrete distance. Various data-recording devices, such as underwater tape and event recorders and cameras, may be used. Underwater observation time, however, is the most important limiting factor. It becomes severely limiting as depth increases, and, in fact, the traditional observational techniques of ethologists become increasingly impractical at depths below about 10 and are impossible below 20 m. Ethological studies of species living at depths below 20 m can be done only with saturation diving from an underwater habitat. The difficulties of cost and of diver-observer fatigue and psychology are mentioned above.

In my own studies of butterflyfishes (Reese, 1973, 1975, 1977), I have relied on three basic underwater observational techniques using SCUBA. The first is to observe one area of the reef for a predetermined period of time. This technique provides detailed information on the behavior of the species that are resident in the particular location. It is possible to learn individual fishes of certain species on the basis of variation in their marking patterns, old scars, and torn fins. If one is working at depths of 10 m or less, it is possible to carry out three hours of observation a day. It is exhausting, however, and the total time of observation is equal to about half a day's work for an ethologist studying a terrestrial species. Clearly, in many instances, underwater television would be a superior alternative. The second method is to swim transects over selected areas of reef topography for known distances and pre-determined time periods. This technique permits sampling of many different individuals but provides few details of their behavior. Fishes usually are not recognized as individuals. The data take the form of instantaneous or "point-in-time" observations of distribution, abundance, and behavior. There are no alternative techniques available.

The third technique, which I believe is the most productive for the underwater ethologist, is to select an individual, pair or group of fishes and to follow it at a discreet distance, observing and recording the details of behavior. The use of an underwater tape recorder, used either with voice or with a touch-tone type of event recorder, provides a real-time frame for observations. Again, there are no alternatives available.

Although in my opinion this is the most fruitful technique, it is also the most difficult and potentially the most dangerous. Dangerous because the fish may lead the observer into deeper water, down current, and at a considerable distance from the boat. The swim back on the surface, without air and with the burden of equipment, can be exhausting. Difficult because the observer must learn what the discreet distance is for the particular species being studied. This takes experience and a gradually acquired intuitive feeling for when the observer's presence affects the behavior of the fish. In areas where there is much spear fishing, none of these techniques, especially the last one, are effective.

2.5 Methods of Mapping

Given the effective use of the third technique, it becomes possible to map the areas over which the fish forage. Mapping is easily achieved with the use of brightly painted and numbered lead weights, which are dropped at the points of greatest excursion. Distances between lead weights are easily measured after the observation period has elapsed. Preliminary studies, ascertaining that the weights do not affect the animal's behavior, must be made. For example, if the weights are inspected repeatedly or nipped at, then they should not be used. I have used this method successfully for mapping the home ranges and territories of coral-feeding chaetodontids. The species I have worked with ignore the bright orange weights.

Since there are limitations on the amount of time that an observer can spend underwater, it is difficult to apply G. K. Noble's classical criterion of defense of an area as the distinction between home range and territory. With only a few hours of observation daily, it is unreasonable to assume that defense of an area has in fact occurred, or, conversely, not occurred. The problem is confounded further if one considers the nuances and subtleties of threat behavior that, taken alone, may suffice as active defense of an area. Furthermore, since fishes as a group undoubtedly are able to learn each other as individuals (see Reese, 1975, for substantiating arguments), brief bouts of agonistic behavior, perhaps days apart, may serve the purpose of area defense. The chances of observing such bouts increase directly with total observation time.

For these reasons, the terminology and methodology developed by Weeden (1965) in her study of territorial behavior of the tree sparrow are especially appropriate to the study of space-related behavior of aquatic animals. Weeden argues that it is possible to measure accurately the space used by an animal in a defined time interval, and this measure is more useful to the behavioral ecologist than is an inaccurately measured defended area. The method is best applied with intensive and repeated observations of a few animals in a relatively small area. *Daily activity space* and *total activity space* are geographical units combining all kinds of observed behaviors in an arbitrarily defined time interval and time of day. *Daily activity space* in Weeden's study was based on daily 4 hour observation periods. At depths of 10 m or less and in warm tropical waters, 3 hours of observations, in two or three consecutive dives with short rest periods in between, are not unreasonable for an underwater ethologist. *Total activity space* is a composite of *daily activity space.* The technique developed by Odum and Kuenzler (1955) is used for determining when enough observations have been made for a particular animal. Since data on behavioral activity are recorded on a prepared grid sheet representing the study area, grids with different amounts of activity can be identified, and in this way the *total activity space* can be represented as a series of concentric circles representing a core area of intense utilization, an area of moderate behavioral activity, and an outer "doughnut" of space of lowest use but with its outer boundry including the entire *total activity space.*

A somewhat similar method for investigating area utilization within the home range was developed by Tester and Siniff (1965) in their study of raccoons. It was used successfully by Ables (1969) in his study of the home range of red foxes. An interesting comparison of techniques used to measure the area of activity of terrestrial animals is given by Mohr and Stumpf (1966).

To my knowledge, these techniques have not been applied to the study of the space-related behavior of aquatic animals, but I believe they will prove to be a fruitful approach. The basic idea in fact has been used in studying home ranges and territories of fishes. See, for example, the studies on the territoriality of pomacentrids (Clarke, 1971; Keenleyside, 1972; Low, 1971; MacDonald, 1973; Myrberg, 1972a, b; Myrberg and Thresher, 1974; Rasa, 1969; Thresher, 1976a, b) (see Fig. 12.1), of surgeonfishes and parrotfishes (Buckman and Ogden, 1973; Nursall, 1974), and of the social use of space by other species (Itzkowitz, 1974; Sale, 1975; Smith and Tyler, 1972).

3   TERRITORIALITY

Territoriality is only one point on the behavioral scale of space-related behavior, but it has received more attention than all the other categories combined. The subject has been repeatedly reviewed, and recent gen-

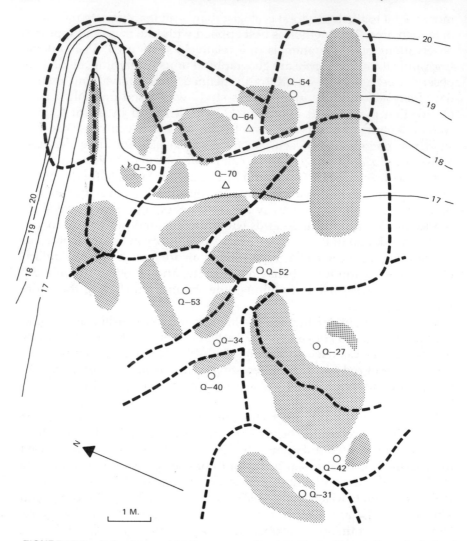

FIGURE 12.1   A. Territories of 11 *Hypsypops rubicunda*. Dashed lines indicate the limits of movement during a 15 min observation period. Nest sites of nine nesting males are shown by circles; shelter holes of the remaining two individuals are shown by triangles. Contours are in meters. Large rocks are shaded. (From Clarke, 1971.)

eral treatments are to be found in Brown (1975), Brown and Orians (1970, Stokes (1974), and Wilson (1975). Interesting examples of territorial and home-range behavior in mammals are reported in Ewer (1969), Jewell and Loisos (1966), and Geist and Walther (1974). In birds, space-related

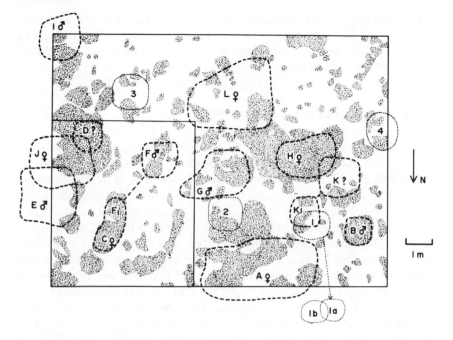

FIGURE 12.1 B. Territories of 16 *Abudefduf zonatus*. Dashed lines indicate territory boundaries of nonnesting fish. Dotted lines show the territories of breeding males. Coral is shaded. Clear areas are sand. (From Kennleyside, 1972.)

behavior, especially territoriality, has been the focus of much work. Besides the general reviews given above, Orians and Willson (1964) examine interspecific territoriality, Schoener (1968) extensively reviews sizes of feeding territories, and Cody (1974) views territory in the framework of community structure. Many of the ideas that follow have been gleaned from a perusal of these reviews.

Stokes' (1974) book entitled *Territory* deserves special mention. To read the collection of papers he presents is both an instructive as well as a humbling experience. Humbling because one learns that many of our current ideas about territoriality, including the concept of cost and benefit analysis, were recognized 100 years ago, in 1868, by Bernard Altum, and that critical questions regarding territorial behavior, such as the role of bird song, were recognized 75 years ago in 1903 by C. B. Moffat. And Maragaret M. Nice initiated careful quantitative studies on the movements and territories of song sparrows 40 years ago, in 1937. Since these pioneering studies, much has been written on the subject in both the primary and the secondary source literature, and much of this literature is reviewed in the selection of recent references given above. From a sampling of this vast literature there emerges what I will call the "intuitive concept" of territoriality.

3.1   The Intuitive Concept

The intuitive concept of territoriality includes the defense, if necessary, of a particular place and the prior, if not exclusive, use of the resources therein. The emphasis should be on use. On the face of it, this does not seem to be a particularly complex system, but when the time dimension is added and the nuances of complex social behavior, such as individual recognition, are superimposed, then ways in which territoriality may be expressed effectively become very complex and defy simple definition.

For example, let us examine the idea of the exclusive use of space. Multiple use of the same space may occur if the uses are separated in time, or if the resource is not space per se, and the two users are utilizing different resources in the same space. The observer would see two or more users in the space and conclude that it was multiple use when, in fact, each user would be utilizing the space exclusively for itself.

The situation is relatively simple if use is separated by time. The same refuge may be used by a nocturnal and diurnal species. For example, reef fishes generally sleep on the bottom, in holes or crevices on the reef. Although supportive data are needed, it is postulated that the same refuges on the reef are used by different species on a day and night basis.

The question of food is more difficult. The same type of food may be eaten by different individuals of the same or different species if eating periods are separated in time, and if different portions of the food resource are selected. Given sufficient food distributed in a relatively (i.e., relative to the foraging movements of the species in question) large area, it's possible to divide the food resource by using the territory exclusively at different points in time and by consuming different sizes of food. This system even works for large predators, such as leopards and tigers (Seidensticker, 1976), which differ in the size of prey killed, the use of vegetation types, and the time of activity. The same resource sharing can be expected to occur in large aquatic predators such as sharks and barracudas. However, if food becomes scarce, a condition necessitating extended foraging movements over greater distances and periods of time, then the probability of maintaining the "exclusiveness" of the use of the area decreases. Tension encounters and agonistic behavior may result, under the guise of territorial defense. The question then arises: Whose territory? The answer will be forthcoming when dispersal occurs. The situation can arise when food and space are shared by two different species, when they are both either nocturnal or diurnal; but if one of the species is diurnal and the other nocturnal, then the situation should not arise. However, food shortages may result in changes in the diel pattern of foraging.

Thus the concept of prior or exclusive use, at first relatively simple and straightforward, becomes increasingly complex. Nevertheless, territoriality is best thought of in terms of the benefits of resource use rather than the costs of territorial defense. The above considerations apply equally well to the concept of home range.

What is particularly challenging to the underwater ethologist is to ask how space-related behavior involving the prior or exclusive use of the resources within a particular space increases fitness. In this same regard, it is important to understand why one species is territorial while another is not, or why one species forages over the reef in male and female pairs, as do a number of omnivorous species of butterflyfishes (Reese, 1975), while other species do not. Through an understanding of how these differences in space-related behaviors between species affect fitness, we will gain insights into how differences and similarities in social organization are actually produced.

3.2 Effect of Topography

It is well known that animals, including man, center their activities on important topographical features. Pioneering trade settlements were built on rivers and fortresses on high ground. Baboon troops have sleeping trees in favored locations within their territories. The presence of a shrub or tree in which to build a nest is a prerequisite of many bird territories. Obviously, there is a close relationship between space-related social systems in animals and their environment, both physical as well as biotic. Since space-related behavior must be adapted to the habitat in which it is expressed, it is to be expected that the shape of territorities and home ranges will be influenced by topography.

An interesting parallel exists between the linear home ranges and territories of butterflyfishes and those of a number of species of mammals, including muskrats (Errington, 1963), otters (Erlinge, 1967, 1968; Liers, 1951), and wolves (Burkholder, 1959; Mech, 1970) along rivers, streams, and lake shores. The muskrat is a semiaquatic rodent, and it prefers to establish itself along shorelines with adequate vegetation and with little wave action or current. Tracts of stream edge, lake shore, or marsh that are recognizable as territories may be as far apart as 1000 m in sparsely occupied habitats, but at higher densities they are separated by only 20 to 40 m. Females, not males, are primarily involved with territorial defense, especially when they have young. Aggression is directed toward other species, such as mink and conspecific strangers. Local resident individuals are tolerated. Consequently, it is again difficult to characterize muskrats as either territorial or home ranging. They show both kinds of space-related behavior, depending on the situation. Erlinge (1967, 1968) found that family groups of fish otters consisting of a mother and her young cubs establish their home ranges along streams and occasionally the shoreline of lakes. The size of the home range, which may be as large as 7 km, is affected more by the growth of the cubs, topography, and access to open water in winter, than by food supply and population density. Adult male dog otters wander over greater distances and may have home ranges as large as 15 km. In winter, otters become territorial. Liers (1951) noted that families of the river otter range about 3 to 10 km in a season, and about three families occur in an area along 20 km of stream.

Wolves live in packs, and packs space themselves in the wild in areas of hundreds of square miles. According to Mech (1970), it is not clear whether packs live in true territories in the sense of a defended areas, because meetings between packs in the wild have rarely been seen. The few known cases are of large packs meeting single, or pairs of, strangers. Intolerance was shown by the large pack. They chased the strangers and if they caught them attacked them. Mech observed fleeing lone wolves run at top speed for as long as a mile *after* the pack had stopped chasing them. The evidence suggests that territorial spacing does occur, and packs probably avoid one another. There is relatively little overlap in the use of space by smaller packs, and, if it does occur, the packs use the space at different times. Movement of packs often, but not always, follows topographic features, such as rivers, ridges, and valleys. Burkholder (1959) found moose kills along rivers and creeks, whereas caribou kills were not so distributed.

The shapes of the home ranges of red foxes are influenced, but not determined entirely, by habitat features (Ables, 1969; Sargeant, 1972). The same is true of mice (Stumpf and Mohr, 1962). In arctic ground squirrels, territories are necessary for successful breeding and for hibernation, but again topography is of great importance. Subordinate, younger, less experienced animals establish territories in marginal areas and are subject to greater mortality from drowning and predation (Carl, 1971; Walton and Keenleyside, 1974). However, Kruuk (1972) found that natural obstacles or topography are not important in establishing boundaries for home ranges and territories of the spotted hyena. This finding supports the suggestion of Stumpf and Mohr (1962) that linearity of home ranges and territories, which they believe is a characteristic of many mammals, may be due to behavioral factors not associated with habitat terrain. The question deserves further study.

There are, however, interesting examples from the invertebrates that support the opposing view—namely, that habitat topography does play an important role in determining the shapes of activity areas of animals. Male ghost crabs defend the areas around their burrows, where they construct a display pyramid. The burrows are arranged linearly within the intertidal zone of sandy beaches (Lighter, 1974, 1977). Dragonfly males establish reproductive territories along the shorelines of rivers, streams, and lakes, and a prerequisite of the territory is that it contain a suitable perch, usually a shrub leaf or twig, where the male can settle and rest after courtship display (Furtado, 1970, 1975; Heymer, 1972; Johnson, 1964).

In many coral reef environments, a relatively flat shallow water area extends out from the shore to a variable distance where the bottom drops off at a steeper grade into deeper water. At Heron Island on Australia's Great Barrier Reef, the drop-off has an estimated grade of between 20° to 40°, and it is here that one finds the most luxurious growth of corals and the greatest concentration of coral reef fishes.

Pairs of a number of species of omnivorous butterflyfishes, including *Chaetodon ephippium, C. unimaculatus,* and *C. vagabundus,* maintain what appears to be extended, linear home ranges along the upper portion of the reef slope. The same is true for *C. auriga,* which may occur in pairs but more often is seen swimming alone or in small groups along the reef front (Fig. 12.2). Interestingly, it tends to swim in pairs at Enewetak Atoll in the Marshall Islands (Reese, 1975). Since individually recognized pairs often were not seen for a number of days, either in the study area or along the transect area, which extended 100m along the reef slope, the home ranges of these species are believed to exceed 100 m in linear dimension. Furthermore, the pairs were seen within a depth of 10 m and never more than perhaps 5 to 10 m from the surface of the reef. Thus, the home ranges are visualized as long, thin, narrow volumes along the reef slope. The distinction between home range and territory in these species is based on the single criterion of whether or not bouts of agonistic behavior occurred when the pairs met. Unfortunately, the sophisticated criterion of use, as discussed above, was not applied during the study. Fighting occurred only between pairs of *C. ephippium,* and hence their living space may be referred to as an intraspecific territory. In any case,

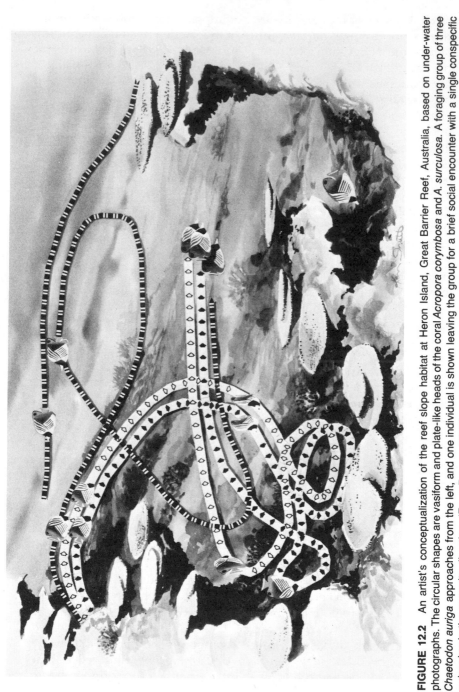

FIGURE 12.2 An artist's conceptualization of the reef slope habitat at Heron Island, Great Barrier Reef, Australia, based on under-water photographs. The circular shapes are vasiform and plate-like heads of the coral *Acropora corymbosa* and *A. surculosa*. A foraging group of three *Chaetodon auriga* approaches from the left, and one individual is shown leaving the group for a brief social encounter with a single conspecific swimming in the opposite direction. (From Reese, 1975.)

both within and between the species, living spaces overlapped as different pairs were observed at different times in the same area of the reef. Avoidance behavior, in the sense of "not paying any attention to one another" or just slightly altering swimming direction so as to avoid one another, seems to be the most common form of social interaction, both intra- as well as interspecifically. *Chaetodon ephippium* is the exception. Pairs do show aggressive behavior toward each other when they meet, both at Heron Island and on the reefs at Enewetak Atoll in the Marshall Islands. Recent observations by L. Boucher (personal communication) at Enewetak indicate that the social group of *C. unimaculatus* is larger than a pair and that subtle bouts of agonistic behavior occur between the groups. MacDonald (1973) observed a linear arrangement of male reproductive territories of the pomacentrid *Microspathodon chrysurus* along the reef drop-off in Puerto Rico.

It appears that habitat topography affects the shape of home ranges and territories of mammals, arthropods, and coral reef fishes. Further study of this relationship is called for, since it is clear that there is a similar response in the space-related behavior of these diverse animals to a particular dimension, linearity, of their habitat.

4   CENTRAL PLACE SYSTEMS AND TRADITION

4.1   Refuging

Refuging (Hamilton and Watt, 1970) is another form of behavior at a group, or perhaps deme, level related to the social use of space. Generally it should be looked for where food resources are distributed widely in an area surrounding a particular part of the environment in which the animals take shelter or find refuge when not feeding. Perhaps the best-known example is that of starlings returning to a central roosting location to spend the night after a day of foraging for food as individuals or in smaller social groups (Hamilton et al., 1967; Hamilton and Gilbert, 1969). The same phenomenon is well known for mynah birds in Hawaii, where the raucous noise they make in their roosting site, often a large banyan tree, can be annoying. Hamilton and Watt (1970) give other examples from birds, mammals, including man, and social insects, ants, and bees. Presumably there is a benefit to be accrued from the behavior of coming together in one central place. It may be related to defense from predators, and it may serve functions of social priming.

Refuging behavior is now becoming well documented for fishes as well. Many herbivorous and omnivorous species migrate along frequently well-established routes from nighttime sleeping refuges to day-time feeding grounds (Hobson, 1965, 1973; Ogden and Buckman, 1973; Winn *et al.*, 1964). Nocturnal species, for the most part predators, show a reverse migration, often moving considerable distances offshore to feed (Hobson, 1965, 1973). The grunt, *Haemulon flavolineatum*, spends the day hiding in holes on the reef, but at dusk it aggregates, and within 20 to 30 min after dusk it streams out, following well-defined routes, onto the surrounding seagrass flats where it feeds until dawn. At dawn the movement is reversed, and they return to their home reef for the day (Ogden and Zieman, 1977).

Large mixed schools of acanthurids swim from one area of the reef to another to feed and may be exhibiting refuging behavior (Barlow, 1974a, b; Jones, 1968). In all probability planktivorous species show refuging behavior as they move in groups from their shelters on the reef to feed in the water column above (Davis and Birdsong, 1973; Hobson, 1974; Hobson and Chess, 1976; Ralston, 1975; Stevenson, 1972; and Vivien, 1975). Sharks are known to form large aggregations during the daytime (D. R. Nelson, personal communication) that presumably disband at night for individual foraging. Barlow (1974c) suggests that these daytime aggregations are refuging groups.

So far, refuging is considered only as a central place system of space utilization on a diel rhythm for the procurement of food. However, the concept is applicable in a larger time frame to lunar and seasonal movements related to feeding and reproduction. The concept has little utility, however, when applied to single events in an animal's biology, such as the spawning migrations of salmon.

4.2 Radial Packs

A derivation of refuging as a central place system is the occurrence of radial packs (Hamilton and Watt, 1970). Instead of individuals dispersing from the central place refuge, larger social groups either roam throughout the peripheral area or move into specific home ranges or territories. A prerequisite here is some degree of integrity and organization over time of the dispersing social groups. To my knowledge, radial packs are not described for fishes.

Central place systems seem to have evolved in response to the coaction of increasing population size relative to the distribution pattern of resources, usually food, making the exclusive use of fixed space too costly for the benefits derived therefrom. In the aquatic environment, the food resources of plankton and algae are frequently widely distributed, and animals feeding on them may be expected to show refuging behavior. Whether or not radial packs occur in fishes is a challenging question for underwater ethologists.

4.3 Tradition

The predictable movements of groups of fishes along well-defined migration routes, often over considerable distances, either on a diel or a seasonal temporal basis, suggests the possibility of tradition. Tradition is well known in birds and mammals, especially primates, and numerous examples are reviewed by Wilson (1975).

The traditional learning of seasonal home ranges and the migratory access routes to them by mountain sheep (Geist, 1971) is an outstanding example of tradition and one that lends itself as a model to the study of tradition in fishes. Since fishes are capable of associative learning, all that is needed for the study of tradition is the occurrence of different age classes of individuals migrating together. The younger individuals could then learn the traditional route from the older, experienced individuals. Although Wilson (1975) examines this question on the basis of seasonal spawning migrations of fishes, he concludes that tradition may not exist in fishes. Again, I believe that the question is a challenging one for underwater ethologists. In other aquatic animals, tradition most certainly exists in the well-known migrations of marine mammals where the young accompany their mothers in small social groups that may in fact be extended family groups.

5 PLANKTON FEEDING

The feeding of fishes on plankton above a reef is a particularly interesting example of space-related behavior (Birdsong and Davis, 1973; Eggers, 1977; Hobson and Chess, 1976; Stevenson, 1972). There are a number of important differences between plankton feeding and other kinds of feeding behavior. In most cases, the predatory or grazing animal moves over a two-dimensional surface in search of food. In contrast, the planktonic food resource is distributed unevenly in patches in three-dimensional space. Furthermore, currents carry the food to the consumer, making it possible to remain stationary. Thus, the foraging strategy of certain plankivorous fishes is reduced to the maintaining of a particularly advantageous position in space. From this position, the fish makes visually directed darting movements at planktonic prey as the prey is swept in the current past the fish's feeding position. Stevenson (1972) called this characteristic feeding movement "deflection." It involves orienting oneself and moving toward the prey, visually inspecting it, and engulfing or rejecting the food item. Since the prey is coming "down stream," there exists the possibility of olfactory discrimination as well.

The strategy is most closely approximated by ambushing predators (Curio, 1976), but, even in these cases, rarely is the food presented in three-dimensional space. An exception is spiders, which construct their webs so as to intercept airborne prey. Bats and certain insectivorous birds demonstrate feeding behavior that in many ways is similar to plankton feeding, but the distinction to be made here is that the planktivorous predator feeding above a reef remains in one position, and the prey is transported to it.

There are also certain similarities to what Wilson (1975) refers to as Horn's Principle. The planktonic food resource is variable in space and time, but the group of planktivorous fishes, maintaining itself in space above the reef by swimming into the current, is behaving differently from a foraging flock of birds. The end result, the effective capture of food, is the same, but the behaviors involved are markedly different in their deployment. Unlike foraging flocks of birds, groups of planktivorous fishes feeding in the water column above a reef are stationary. What is crucial to an individual fish is the success with which it can maintain itself effectively in a particularly advantageous position from where its prey-catching success is greater than that of its neighbors. There may be further subdivision of space, with the group's feeding area based on competition and dominance. Myrberg (1972b) found this to occur in the pomacentrid, *Eupomacentrus partitus.* The same considerations are relevant to maintaining a particular position within a school of pelagic planktivorous or small piscivorous fishes. Such schools forage in the open sea for their prey, and there is greater similarity to foraging flocks of birds.

In his extensive review of predatory behavior, Curio (1976) does not address himself directly to the problem of plankton feeding. Nor does plankton feeding fit into any of the categories or strategies discussed by Krebs (1976). Rather, plankton feeding potentially has components characteristic of at least three of Krebs' strategies—hunting by expectation, area-restricted searching, and niche hunting—and may well also involve hunting by search image, although Krebs questions the usefulness of the search image hypothesis. Eggers (1977) presents a model for prey selection by planktivorous fish. The model seems overly simple from the behavioral point of view, since it ignores intraspecific social factors such as dominance relationships, the effects of predators, and possible evasive behaviors of zooplankters. Nevertheless, it is a testable model that should be applied to inshore reef fishes as well as pelagic planktivores. Motivational factors acting on the planktivore, such as the potential threat of a predator and its distance from shelter, may override the factors of prey density, patchiness, capture success, and so forth, on which the model is based. Similarly, as Eggers correctly recognizes, the energy expenditure to maximize prey capture may exceed the benefits in terms of net energy gain. Hobson and Chess (1976) point out that predation pressures from planktivores have influenced the evolution of shallow water plankters. Thus, avoidance behavior and other antipredator mechanisms must be considered as possibilities for zooplankters.

Of special interest, therefore, to the problem of plankton feeding is the analysis of the benefits and costs of occupying a particular feeding location. Presumably, certain locations are more advantageous than others. A feeding location where the current is sufficiently strong to carry in a continuous supply of food must be balanced against the current being so strong that the fish must expend a large amount of energy to swim against it. If the space above the shelter is viewed as a series of concentric hemispheres, then the further distant the feeding location is from shelter, the larger the potential feeding area can be, and, presumably, the fewer competitiors there will be. However, these benefits are offset by the increasing potential risk from predators. Submarine light and underwater visibility (Schumacher, 1973; Weinberg, 1976) are confounding variables, because the detection of both prey and predators is visually mediated. Studies of the escape response in the damselfish *Chromis cyanea* to a crude model that simulated a predator showed that speed of approach of the model and its shape were unimportant, but larger, darker models elicited escape behavior at greater distances (Hurley and Hartline, 1974). Cues in addition to these visual stimuli are suspected. It is exceedingly interesting to note that habituation did not occur at intertrial intervals of 0.5 to 4 min. The adaptive significance of this result is obvious if one visualizes the repeated attention a predator may give to a group of prey until it is successful in capturing one or a few prey. Eibl-Eibesfeldt (1962) noted that C. *cyanea* always escapes to the same refuge in a predictable way that suggests familiarity with the landmarks in its immediate spatial environment.

Dill (1974a, b) analyzed the visually mediated escape response of a small cyprinid fish. He found that the reactive distance for flight to occur from both real and artificial predators could be predicted from three parameters: predator approach velocity, predator size in terms of front diameter, and the rate of change of visual angle. It is interesting that escape velocity, although higher in response to real predators than to artificial ones, is not correlated with reactive distance. Furthermore, the reactive field is circular, indicating that the escape response is not dependent on binocular vision. Seeing the predator approach with one eye is sufficient. Naive fish show the response. Reactive or flight distance and escape velocity increase with experience, but the angle of escape is not affected. There is no decrement in the learned change in reactive distance, even after 10 days without reinforcement. It is clear from the studies by Hurley and Hartline (1974) and Dill (1974a, b) that the escape response is a highly adaptive behavioral mechanism that is the result of strong selection pressure for antipredator behavior in the two species of fish. There is every reason to believe that selection pressure for an escape response is just as strong in other planktivorous fishes (Chromis cyanea is a planktivore) that leave the shelter of the reef to feed in the water column above it. Therefore, the potential presence of a predator and the distance from shelter are important parameters that must be included in any analysis of plankton-feeding strategies.

The success of individuals at different feeding locations could be measured by collecting them after extended bouts of feeding and examining their stomach contents both in terms of quality and quantity of food ingested. Long-term observational data may provide evidence of the costs, in terms of predation, of occupying peripheral, more distant, feeding locations as opposed to locations closer to shelter. The size of the feeding area necessary to maintain a fish of a certain size will be directly proportional to the abundance and distribution of plankton, its nutritional value, and the rate at which the plankton is carried into the feeding area by the current.

Where plankton is scarce and distributed in widely scattered patches, and where current velocity is low, the planktivorous fish must have a large feeding area and must make large deflections in order to get enough to eat. Under these conditions, feeding location is of great importance. Where food is abundant, patches are close together, and the current is flowing rapidly, the planktivore may be able to obtain enough food with only minor deflections or movements from its feeding location. The position of the feeding location in the water column is less important under these conditions.

The model becomes more complex when conspecific or heterospecific food competitors are added, and, of course, when predators are added. Intraspecific competition would tend to result in individuals feeding further and further away from their shelter, and in the feeding area getting larger, in much the same way as, in theory, the area under the niche exploitation curve increases with intraspecific competition (Root,

1967). However, larger feeding areas more remote from shelter increase the risk of predation. Presumably, then, subordinate individuals would be forced to occupy these more dangerous feeding locations. The extent to which the same argument holds for interspecific competitors depends on the narrowness of the feeding guild to which they both belong. Both types of competition may lead to separation of the feeding guild. Although, as Root suggests, this separation is expected to occur with interspecific competition, it also may occur within a species when different-size classes of individuals exploit different portions of the food resource.

In many ways, plankton feeding is a unique type of space-related behavior that deserves further study. It is becoming increasingly evident what the critical parameters are that must be measured in order to demonstrate how this interesting and specialized type of feeding behavior affects fitness, and it is a challenge to look for comparable situations in terrestrial animals. Detailed comparisons are called for, and they may provide new insights into predator-prey coevolution.

6 CONCLUSIONS

Ethological field study on the space-related behavior of aquatic animals requires many hours of underwater observation. Electronic tagging and tracking techniques are used for following the movements of individuals, but little behavioral information on social encounters is obtained with sonic tagging. Underwater television is useful in monitoring the behavior of animals for long periods of time in one area of the reef. The shortcoming of underwater TV is that the behavior of an animal under observation is lost when the animal moves out of the field of view of the television camera. The major advantages of underwater television are that it can record for long periods of time, and can be used at low light levels; in addition, of course, the replay capability of videotape permits detailed, quantitative analysis of behavioral events.

In situations where the activity space of the animal under observation is relatively large, and it is necessary to observe details of social behavior, the underwater ethologist must turn to the use of self-contained underwater breathing apparatus, or SCUBA. The major shortcoming of SCUBA is the relatively short duration of underwater observation time, imposed by depth, water temperature, and diver physiology. This constraint, however, can be overcome through the judicious choice of observational paradigms. In the study of space-related behavior, a technique for mapping activity and location of events must be devised that is appropriate to the time constraint imposed on underwater observation. Such methods are available and have been used successfully in the terrestrial environment. One method that appears to be particularly appropriate for application in the aquatic environment is described. It involves the daily mapping of the movements of the animal being studied on a grid system data format, a method by which the *daily activity space* is obtained. The number of observation periods is determined by notation of the point at which the number of new grid squares utilized each day reaches an asymptotic level. The *total activity space* is simply a combination of all the daily records. Quantitative differences in the use of preferred areas within the *total activity space* are graphically shown by a system of concentric circles based on the frequency of use of individual squares in the grid format data sheet for the habitat area. Although this particularly thorough method has not been used by underwater ethologists, the basic idea on which it is based, namely the frequency of use of an area, is used in studying the activity patterns of aquatic animals. The studies on space-related behavior of pomacentrid reef fishes are examples.

Territoriality is the most thought-about and talked-about, and the best-studied, type of space-related behavior in both the terrestrial and aquatic environments. Indeed, it stands out as a perhaps universal solution to problems of resource use by a wide variety of animals in many different habitats in which resources are distributed in space. Yet in spite of the great interest in territoriality, there is much uncertainty in how it is best defined and measured. Classically, defense of the area is the criterion that separates territory from home range; but because of the subtle forms in which defense may be expressed and the impossibility of observing all behavioral interactions, it is a criterion that is extremely difficult to apply precisely. Instead, the way in which resources are used in the activity area appears to be a more accurate and biologically meaningful criterion. Where prior or exclusive use of resources is observed, territoriality probably exists. Environmental factors, such as habitat terrain, influence the geographical boundaries and shapes of activity areas. For example, linearity characterizes the activity areas of mammals that establish home ranges and territories along streams, rivers, and shorelines of lakes; of dragonflies in similar habitats; of ghost crabs along beaches; and of coral reef fishes that swim in home ranges and territories along the slope of the reef front.

Refuging occurs when it is advantageous for animals to aggregate during certain times, usually for resting, but when at other times they must disperse into adjacent areas to find food. The selection pressure for aggregating may be related to predation during vulnerable resting times, while that for dispersal is related to obtaining food. The larger the population of animals, the further they must disperse from their central place to insure an adequate food supply, especially when the food is widely scattered in the surrounding habitat space. There are many examples from a wide variety of animals in both the aquatic and terrestrial environments. Although refuging is not as widespread as territoriality, it appears to be an example of space-related behavior that has evolved independently in different animals in different environments in response to similar selection pressures—namely, to derive the benefits of group living while, at the same time, obtaining enough to eat when the food resource is widely dispersed.

Since the patterns of movement during the dispersal and aggregating phases of refuging frequently take the form of migrations and occur repeatedly over the same routes, they offer good research possibilities to look for the interesting behavioral phenomenon of tradition. Indeed, this is the case in a number of terrestrial animals and in all probability marine mammals as well, but tradition remains to be adequately demonstrated in fishes and other aquatic animals.

Finally, plankton feeding by fishes was discussed. It is particularly interesting because it is a successful and widespread strategy of food procurement in aquatic animals, especially fishes; but it is poorly represented in terrestrial animals. Bats and birds that forage while in flight bear certain resemblances to open-water plankton-feeding species of fishes such as familiar herring and tuna. Many species of reef fishes, however, do not swim in search of their prey. Instead, they maintain themselves off the bottom in a particular position and wait for the current to bring them their planktonic food. There are similarities to certain terrestrial ambush predators, but it appears not to be a widespread and successful strategy in terrestrial environments. Plankton feeding and its terrestrial counterparts are examples of space-related behavior that is very successful in the aquatic environment, but that seems only marginally successful in the terrestrial one. The single factor that determines this important distinction is the high density of water, relative to that of air, which permits the existence of the floating community of planktonic organisms. Planktivorous fishes, especially, have exploited plankton as a food resource; a result has been the evolution of a highly successful and widespread type of space-related behavior that is characteristic of the aquatic environment but is relatively poorly represented in terrestrial animals.

REFERENCES

Ables, E. D. 1969. Home-range studies of red foxes (*Vulpes vulpes*). J. Mamm. **50**: 108–120.

Altman, I. 1975. *The Environment and Social Behavior*. Brooks/Cole Publishing Co., Monterey. 256 p.

Banks, E. M. and M. F. Willson, Eds. 1974. Ecology and evolution of social organization. Am. Zool. **14**: 1–264.

Barlow, G. W. 1974a. Extraspecific imposition of social grouping among surgeonfishes (Pisces: Acanthuridae). J. Zool. Lond. **174**: 333–340.

Barlow, G. W. 1974b. Contrasts in social behavior between Central American cichlid fishes and coral-reef surgeon fishes. Am. Zool. **14**: 9–34.

Barlow, G. W. 1974c. Derivation of threat display in the gray reef shark. Mar. Behav. Physiol. **3**: 71–81.

Barnes, H. 1963. Underwater television. Oceanogr. Mar. Biol. Ann. Rev. **1**: 115–128.

Brown, J. L. 1975. *The Evolution of Behavior*. W. W. Norton, New York. 761 p.

Brown, J. L. and G. H. Orians. 1970. Spacing patterns in mobile animals. Ann. Rev. Ecol. Syst. **1**: 239–262.

Buckman, N. S. and J. C. Ogden. 1973. Territorial behavior of the striped parrotfish *Scarus croicensis* Bloch (Scaridae). Ecology **54**: 1377–1382.

Burkholder, B. L. 1959. Movements and behavior of a wolf pack in Alaska. J. Wildl. Manag. **23**: 1–11.

Carl, E. A. 1971. Population control in arctic ground squirrels. Ecology **52**: 395–413.

Clarke, T. A. 1971. Territory boundaries, courtship, and social behavior in the garibaldi, *Hypsypops rubicunda* (Pomacentridae). Copeia **1971**: 295–299.

Cody, M. L. 1974. *Bird Communities*. Princeton University Press, Princeton. 318 p.

Curio, E. 1976. *The Ethology of Predation*. Springer Verlag, Berlin. 250 p.

Davis, W. P. and R. S. Birdsong. 1973. Coral reef fishes which forage in the water column. Helgoländer Wiss. Meeresunters. **24**: 292–306.

Dill, L. M. 1974a. The escape response of the zebra danio (*Brachydanio rerio*) I. The stimulus for escape. Anim. Behav. **22**: 711–722.

Dill, L. M. 1974b. The escape response of the zebra danio (*Brachydanio rerio*) II. The effect of experience. Anim. Behav. **22**: 723–730.

Eggers, D. M. 1977. The nature of prey selection by planktivorous fish. Ecology **58**: 46–59.

Eibl-Eibesfeldt, I. 1962. Freiwasserbeobachtungen zur Deutung des Schwarmverhaltens verschiedener Fische. Z. Tierpsychol. **19**: 165–182.

Eibl-Eibesfeldt, I. 1975. *Ethology*. 2nd ed. Holt, Rinehart, and Winston, New York. 625 p.

Eisenberg, J. F. and W. S. Dillon, Eds. 1971. *Man and Beast: Comparative Social Behavior*. Smithsonian Institution Press, Washington. 401 p.

Ellis, P. E., Ed. 1965. Social organization of animal communities. Zool. Soc. Lond. Symp. 14. 314 p.

Erlinge, S. 1967. Home range of the otter *Lutra lutra* L. in southern Sweden. Oikos **18**: 186–209.

Erlinge, S. 1968. Territoriality of the otter *Lutra lutra* L. Oikos **19**: 81–98.

Errington, P. L. 1963. *Muskrat Populations*. Iowa State University Press, Ames. 665 p.

Esser, A. H., Ed. 1971. *Behavior and Environment.* Plenum Press, New York. 411 p.

Ewer, R. F. 1969. Ethology of Mammals. Plenum Press, New York. 416 p.

Fox, R., Ed. 1975. *Biosocial Anthropology.* John Wiley and Sons, New York. 169 p.

Freedman, J. L. 1975. *Crowding and Behavior.* W. H. Freeman, San Francisco. 177 p.

Furtado, J. I. 1970. The territorial behavior of *Devadatta a. argyoides* (Selys) (Odonata, Amphipterygidae). Tombo **13:** 12–16.

Furtado, J. I. 1975. The reproductive behavior of *Prodasineura collaris* (Selys) and *P. verticalis* (Selys) (Odonata, Protoneuridae). Malaysian J. Sci. **3:** 61–67.

Geist, V. 1971. *Mountain Sheep.* University of Chicago Press, Chicago. 383 p.

Geist, V. and F. Walther, Eds.1974. *The Behaviour of Ungulates and Its Relation to Management.* Inter. Union Conservation Nature Publications. New series, No. 24, 2 vols. 942 p.

Groot, C. 1965. On the orientation of young sockeye salmon (*Oncorhynchus nerka*) during their seaward migration out of lakes. Behaviour Suppl. 14. 198 p.

Groot, C., K. Simpson, I. Todd, P. D. Murray, and G. A. Buxton. 1975. Movements of sockeye salmon (*Oncorhynchus nerka*) in the Skeena River estuary as revealed by ultrasonic tracking. J. Fish. Res. Board Can. **32:** 233–242.

Hamilton, W. J. III, W. M. Gilbert, F. H. Heppner, and R. J. Planck. 1967. Starling roost dispersal and a hypothetical mechanism regulating rhythmical animal movement to and from dispersal centers. Ecology **48:** 825–833.

Hamilton, W. J. III and W. M. Gilbert. 1969. Starling dispersal from a winter roost. Ecology **50:** 886–898.

Hamilton, W. J. III and K. E. F. Watt. 1970. Refuging. Ann. Rev. Ecol. Syst. **1:** 263–286.

Heymer, A. 1972. Verhaltensstudien an Prachtlibellen. Z. Tierpsychol. Suppl. 11. 94 p.

Hobson, E. S. 1965. Diurnal-nocturnal activity of some inshore fishes in the Gulf of California. Copeia **1965:** 291–302.

Hobson, E. S. 1973. Diel feeding migrations in tropical reef fishes. Helgoländer Wiss. Meeresunters. **24:** 361–370.

Hobson, E. S. 1974. Feeding relationships of teleostean fishes on coral reefs in Kona, Hawaii. Fish Bull. U.S. **72:** 915–1031.

Hobson, E. S. and J. R. Chess. 1976. Trophic interactions among fishes and zooplankters near shore at Santa Cataline Island, California. Fish. Bull. U.S. **74:** 567–598.

Hurley, A. C. and P. H. Hartline. 1974. Escape response in the damselfish *Chromis cyanea* (Pisces: Pomacentridae): A quantitative study. Anim. Behav. **22:** 430–437.

Itzkowitz, M. 1974. A behavioral reconnaissance of some Jamaican reef fishes. Zool. J. Linn. Soc. **55:** 87–118.

Jewell, P. A. and C. Loizos, Eds. 1966. Play, exploration, and territory in mammals. *Zool. Soc. Lond. Symp.* 18. 280 p.

Johnson, C. 1964. The evolution of territoriality in Odonata. Evolution **18:** 89–92.

Jones, R. S. 1968. Ecological relationships in Hawaiian and Johnston Island Acanthuridae (Surgeonfishes). Micronesica **4:** 309–361.

Keenleyside, M. H. A. 1972. The behaviour of *Abudefduf zonatus* (Pisces, Pomacentridae) at Heron Island, Great Barrier Reef. Anim. Behav. **20:** 763–774.

Krebs, J. R. 1973. Behavioral aspects of predation. *In:* P. P. G. Bateson and P. H. Klopfer, Eds. *Perspectives in Ethology.* Plenum Press, New York. P. 73–111.

Kruuk, H. 1972. *The Spotted Hyena.* University of Chicago Press, Chicago. 335 p.

Kumpf, H. E. 1964. Use of underwater television in bio-acoustic research. *In:* W. N. Tavolga, Ed. *Marine Bio-Acoustics.* Pergamon Press, New York. P. 47–57.

Liers, E. E. 1951. Notes on the river otter (*Lutra canadensis*). J. Mamm. **32:** 1–9.

Lighter, F. J. 1974. A note on a behavioral spacing mechanism of the ghost crab *Ocypode ceratophthalmus* (Pallas) (Decapoda, Family Ocypodidae). Crustaceana **27:** 312–314.

Lighter, F. J. 1977. The social use of space: aspects of ecology, ethology, and endocrinology of the ghost crab *Ocypode ceratophthalmus* (Pallas) and *Ocypode laevis* Dana. Unpublished doctoral dissertation, University of Hawaii. 149 p.

Low, R. M. 1971. Interspecific territoriality in a pomacentrid reef fish, *Pomacentrus flavicauda* Whitley. Ecology **52:** 648–654.

MacDonald, C. D. 1973. Reproductive behavior and social dynamics of the yellowtail damselfish, *Microspathodon chrysurus* (Perciformes: Pomacentridae). Unpublished M.S. thesis, University of Puerto Rico. 157 p.

Magnuson, J. J. 1962. An analysis of aggressive behavior, growth, and competition for food and space in medaka (*Oryzias latipes* (Pisces, Crypinodontidae)). Can. J. Zool. **40:** 313–363.

Mech, L. D. 1970. *The Wolf.* Natural History Press, Garden City, N.Y. 384 p.

Mohr, C. O. and W. A. Stumpf. 1966. Comparison of methods for calculating areas of animal activity. J. Wildl. Manag. **30:** 293–304.

Monan, G. E., J. H. Johnson, and G. F. Esterberg. 1975. Electronic tags and related tracking techniques aid in study of migrating salmon and steelhead trout in the Columbia River basin. Mar. Fish. Rev. **37:** 9–15.

Myrberg, A. A., Jr. 1972a. Ethology of the bicolor damselfish. *Eupomacentrus partitus* (Pisces: Pomacentridae): A comparative analysis of laboratory and field behavior. Anim. Behav. Monogr. **5:** 197–283.

Myrberg, A. A. Jr. 1972b. Social dominance and territoriality in the bicolor damselfish, *Eupomacentrus partitus* (Poey) (Pisces: Pomacentridae). Behaviour **41:** 207–231.

Myrberg, A. A., Jr. 1973. Underwater television—a tool for the marine biologist. Bull. Mar. Sci. **23:** 824–836.

Myrberg, A. A., Jr., A. Banner, and J. D. Richard. 1969. Shark attraction using a videoacoustic system. Mar. Biol. **2:** 264–276.

Myrberg, A. A., Jr. and R. E. Thresher. 1974. Interspecific aggression and its relevance to the concept of territoriality in reef fishes. Am. Zool. **14:** 81–96.

Nursall, J. R. 1974. Some territorial behavioral attributes of the surgeonfish *Acanthurus lineatus* at Heron Island, Queensland. Copeia **1974:** 950–959.

Odum, E. P. and E. J. Kuenzler. 1955. Measurement of territory and home range size in birds. Auk **72:** 128–137.

Ogden, J. C. 1976. Some aspects of herbivore-plant relationships on Caribbean reefs and seagrass beds. Aquatic Bot. **2:** 103–116.

Ogden, J. C. and N. S. Buckman. 1973. Movements, foraging groups, and diurnal migrations of the striped parrotfish *Scarus croicensis* Bloch (Scaridae). Ecology **54:** 589–596.

Ogden, J. C. and J. C. Zieman. 1977. Ecological aspects of coral reef-seagrass bed contacts in the Caribbean. Proc. Third Inter. Coral Reef Symposium, Miami, Florida, **1:** 377–382.

Orians, G. H. and M. F. Willson. 1964. Interspecific territories of birds. Ecology **45:** 736–745.

Phillips, R. R. 1974. The relationship between social behavior and the use of space in the benthic fish *Chasmodes bosquianus* Lacépède (Teleostei, Blenniidae). III. The interaction between attraction/repulsion and prior social experience. Behaviour **49**: 205–226.

Ralston, S. 1976. Anomalous growth and reproductive patterns in populations of *Chaetodon miliaris* (Pisces, Chaetodontidae) from Kaneohe Bay, Oahu, Hawaiian Islands. Pacific Sci. **30**: 395–403.

Rasa. O. A. E. 1969. Territoriality and the establishment of dominance by means of visual cues in *Pomacentrus jenkensi* (Pisces: Pomacentridae). Z. Tierpsychol. **26**: 825–845.

Rasa, O. A. E. 1971. Appetence for aggression in juvenile damselfish. Z. Tierpsychol. Suppl. 7. 70 p.

Reese, E. S. 1973. Duration of residence of coral reef fishes on "home" reefs. Copeia **1973**: 145–149.

Reese, E. S. 1975. A comparative field study of the social behavior and related ecology of reef fishes of the family Chaetodontidae. Z. Tierpsychol. **37**: 37–61.

Reese, E. S. 1977. Coevolution of corals and coral feeding fishes of the family Chaetodontidae. Proc. Third. Inter. Coral Reef Symposium, Miami, Florida, **1**: 267–274.

Root, R. B. 1967. The niche exploitation pattern of the blue-gray gnatcatcher. Ecol. Monogr. **37**: 317–350.

Sale, P. F. 1975. Patterns of use of space in a guild of territorial reef fishes. Mar. Biol. **29**: 89–97.

Sargeant, A. B. 1972. Red fox spatial characteristics in relation to waterfowl predation. J. Wildl. Manag. **36**: 225–236.

Schoener, T. W. 1968. Sizes of feeding territories among birds. Ecology **49**: 123–141.

Schuhmacher, H. 1973. Die lichtabhängige Besiedlung von Hafenstützpfeilern durch sessile Tiere und Algen aus dem Korallenriff bei Eilat (Rotes Meer). Helgoländer. Wiss. Meeresunters. **24**: 307–326.

Seidensticker, J. 1976. On the ecological separation between tigers and leopards. Biotropica **8**: 225–234.

Smith, C. L. and J. C. Tyler. 1972. Space resource sharing in a coral reef fish community. Sci. Bull. Los Angeles City Mus. Nat. Hist. **14**: 125–170.

Stasko, A. B. 1975. Progress of migrating Atlantic salmon (*Salmo salar*) along an estuary, observed by ultrasonic tracking. J. Fish. Biol. **7**: 329–338.

Stevenson, R. A., Jr. 1967. Underwater television. Oceanol. Int. **2**:30–35.

Stevenson, R. A., Jr. 1972. Regulation of feeding behavior of the bicolor damselfish (*Eupomacentrus partitus* Poey) by environmental factors. *In:* H. E. Winn and B. L. Olla, Eds. *Behavior of Marine Animals.* Vol. 2: *Vertebrates.* Plenum Press, New York. P. 278–302.

Stokes, A. W., Ed. 1974. *Territory.* Dowden, Hutchinson, and Ross, Stroudsburg, Pa. 398 p.

Stumpf, W. A. and C. O. Mohr. 1962. Linearity of home ranges of California mice and other animals. J. Wildl. Manag. **26**: 149–154.

Tesch, R.-W. 1975. Migratory behaviour of displaced homing yellow eels (*Anguilla anguilla*) in the North Sea. Helgoländer Wiss. Meeresunters. **27**: 190–198.

Tester, J. R. and D. B. Siniff. 1965. Aspects of animal movement and home range data obtained by telemetry. Trans. N. Am. Wildl. Nat. Resour. Conf. **30**: 379–392.

Thresher, R. E. 1976a. Field analysis of the territoriality of the threespot damselfish.

Eupomacentrus planifrons (Pomacentridae). Copeia **1976**: 266–276.

Thresher, R. E. 1976b. Field experiments on species recognition by the threespot damsel-fish, *Eupomacentrus planifrons* (Pisces: Pomacentridae). Anim. Behav. **24**: 562–569.

Van Den Assem, J. 1967. Territory in the three-spined stickleback *Gasterosteus aculeatus* L., an experimental study in intraspecific competition. Behaviour Suppl. 16. 164 p.

Vivien, M. L. 1975. Place of Apogonid fish in the food webs of a Malagasy coral reef. Micronesica **11**: 185–198.

Warden, R. L., Jr. and W. J. Lorio. 1975. Movements of largemouth bass (*Micropterus salmoides*) in impounded waters as determined by underwater telemetry. Trans. Am. Fish. Soc. **104**: 696–702.

Watton, D. G. and H. M. A. Keenleyside. 1974. Social behaviour of the arctic ground squirrel, *Spermophilus undulatus*. Behaviour **50**: 77–99.

Weeden, J. S. 1965. Territorial behavior of the tree sparrow. Condor **67**: 193–209.

Weinberg, S. 1976. Submarine daylight and ecology. Mar. Biol. **37**: 291–304.

Wilson, E. O. 1975. *Sociobiology*. Harvard University Press, Cambridge, Mass. 697 p.

Winn, H. E., M. Salmon, and N. Roberts. 1964. Sun-compass orientation by parrot fishes. Z. Tierpsychol. **21**: 798–812.

CONCLUDING REMARKS

The purpose of this volume, as stated in the preface, has been to demonstrate the usefulness of the comparative method for gaining insights into, and perspective on, problems of animal behavior. Each chapter, of course, speaks for itself, but we believe that, whether considered individually or as a whole, the contributions clearly serve the purpose. The decision to juxtapose the behavior of animals living in the two most extreme environments, the aquatic and the terrestrial, is justified by the stimulating comparisons found in each chapter. The question of whether or not the preparation and writing of the chapters proved stimulating, in the sense of producing new ideas in each contributor's own research, must be answered individually.

To what extent are reviews and other secondary literature sources helpful in developing broad and meaningful comparisons? The answer to this question is found in the individual contributions, and it is a qualified affirmative. We say "qualified" because the authors have relied on secondary literature sources to varying degrees. For the most part, reviews have helped to identify and locate the kinds and sources of comparative studies relevant to each author's own research area, but usually they do not provide sufficient details for quantitative comparisons of results. Where this quantitative detail is important, it is necessary to go to the primary literature. The point to be made is that reviews serve an extremely useful and time-saving function by enabling a researcher to range outside the familiar literature of his own research field. Without the aid of the secondary sources, it would become an exhaustive and time-consuming task. Furthermore, smaller libraries may not have a selection of journals available for casual perusal. At first glance, it appears that an easy solution is to urge reviewers to include representative data from original papers dealing with the subject under review. There are, however, two difficulties with this recommendation. First, it is difficult to know how many data to include, of what type, and in what format. Second, since it is important to know the conditions under which data were collected, it may be misleading to present even representative data out of the conditional context of their acquisition. If these two difficulties are met, then a review has enhanced usefulness with the thoughtful addition of representative original data.

The initial premise in applying the comparative method is that all animals share a common set of problems. Where these are behavioral problems and where the same solution is arrived at repeatedly and independently by different animals in different environments, then the convergence on a particular solution may be thought of as a criterion for establishing valid and meaningful principles of animal behavior. Of course, convergence on a common solution is only one criterion. More criteria should be sought before a category of behavior is classified as a principle; nevertheless, we believe that this concept is a step in the right direction. Too often the term "principle" is applied without the establishment of the criteria on which it is based.

Although it is somewhat presumptive, we will attempt to summarize in a few paragraphs to what extent we believe the chapters illustrate this concept. We ask that each reader, however, make a personal evaluation of each chapter along the lines we have suggested, and then decide to what degree the adaptive response, or solution, to a type of behavioral problem that has evolved in different animals in different environments is sufficiently similar for that similarity or convergence to be used as a criterion in support of the particular category of behavior being made a candidate for a principle of animal behavior.

Lekking behavior is really a highly specialized form of space-related behavior. It represents an example of convergent behavior that has evolved independently in taxonomically very different animals, insects, fishes, amphibians, birds, and mammals, in both the aquatic and the terrestrial environments. In spite of its specialized nature and the fact that it is not widespread in the groups of animals in which it occurs, lekking behavior is nevertheless a highly successful solution to the problem of reproduction under conditions in which natural selection favors a system of temporary aggregations of sexually active and displaying males for the purpose of facilitating female choice. The widespread, though not universal, convergence on lekking as a solution by diverse groups of animals is a criterion in favor of its establishment as a principle of behavior, given the constraints stated above.

In contrast, intensive and prolonged care of the young beyond the egg-guarding stage by one or both parents, a widespread and successful solution to the problem of insuring an individual's progeny are represented in the next generation, is a pattern that has evolved only in higher vertebrates, birds, and mammals. Although parental care occurs in lower poikilothermic vertebrates, both aquatic and terrestrial, it is not a characteristic or conspicuous adaptation. In vertebrates, the evolution of parental care beyond the egg-guarding stage appears to be related to homeothermy and, concomitantly, to rates of development. Parental care is widespread throughout the invertebrates. In most cases, it is simply the guarding of the eggs, but in insects, especially the social insects, it is extended into feeding of the young through nest provisioning and trophallaxis.

The evidence suggests that parental care, in the sense of simple egg guarding, is a widespread and successful solution that should be considered as a criterion in favor of establishing egg guarding as a principle of animal behavior; but the elaboration and extension of parental care into feeding, defending, and even teaching the neonates is a trend found well developed only in birds and mammals.

In the case of communicative behavior, lateral displays, a solution to the problem of an animal advertising or signaling its presence to another in a distinctive and characteristic manner, are a widespread phenomenon in both lower vertebrates, as discussed in Chapter 4, and higher vertebrates, in both the aquatic and terrestrial environments. Similarly, in the case of acoustical communication, data derived from studies on insects, fishes, amphibians, and birds indicate that temporal patterning or coding of pulsed sounds is distinctly important to the effective transfer of information. It is, however, unclear at present to what extent the similarity to the solution of the problem of signal specificity, as represented separately in lateral displays and temporally patterned acoustical signals, is due to convergent evolution in the groups of animals discussed. Nevertheless, the evidence suggests that they are candidates as principles of communicative behavior in animals in both the aquatic and terrestrial environments.

With respect to hermaphroditism and unisexuality and their related patterns of behavior, the differences between the aquatic and terrestrial environments appear to play a decisive role. Among the vertebrates, hermaphroditism is restricted to the fishes, although it would appear to be a beneficial strategy in many polygynous reptiles, birds, and mammals. Unisexuality is widespread only in the reptiles. The selective advantage of unisexuality as an adaptive reproductive strategy is unclear. Neither hermaphroditism nor unisexuality are candidates for principles of behavior. Both represent, rather, specialized solutions to problems associated with successful reproduction that in the vertebrates are restricted to fishes and reptiles.

Temperature regulation in poikilothermic animals is achieved through habitat selection. Behavior plays a major role in both fishes and reptiles. Although there are differences related to the heat capacities of water and air, clearly, behaviorally mediated thermal regulation is widespread in

fishes and reptiles and must be considered as a candidate for a principle
of animal behavior, given the condition of limitation to the lower vertebrates.

Territoriality is a type of space-related behavior that is almost universal as a solution to the problem of an individual's increasing its fitness
by having exclusive, preemptive, or prior use of the resources within a
particular area. It is well developed in many invertebrate and all vertebrate animals, with numerous examples in both the aquatic and terrestrial
environments. There can be no question that territoriality must be considered a candidate as a principle of spatial behavior in animals. Variations on the basic theme of resource use in a particular area, such as
home range behavior and group structure, are points along the scale of
space-related behaviors. Territoriality, which can be thought of as being
at one extreme of the scale, is perhaps the most striking example.

There is continuous warfare between predators and prey, with each
trying to outsmart the other. This drama occurs in the day-to-day life of
the individual, as well as in the evolutionary time frame of the species.
Aggregating behavior is widespread in the animal kingdom in both the
aquatic and the terrestrial environments. In vertebrates it appears to be a
solution arrived at independently by prey animals to decrease the
chances of an individual encountering a predator. Concomitantly, the
feeding behavior of most animals involves the need for locomotor activity, which increases the chances of detection by predators. A solution to
this problem in both fishes and mammals is to modulate behavior in
response to the photoperiod and, to a lesser degree, seasons. Thus,
there is evidence to suggest that aggregating and what we will call
photo-period specific activity, are candidates to be considered as principles of predator-prey feeding and avoidance behavior.

The effects of being carnivorous are reflected in the social behavior,
and especially the feeding and reproduction, of pinnipeds in the marine
environment and canids in the terrestrial environment. Although there
are similarities, these are overshadowed by differences in their social
organizations in terms of reproduction and hunting strategies, the size
of prey taken, and, in turn, the effects of predators on social groupings.
There does not appear to be any evidence for convergence on one set of
solutions, but, instead, divergence in response to differences in the
aquatic and terrestrial environments is the overall effect.

Aggressive, or more correctly, agonistic behavior is the most controversial and most widely reported of all the categories of behavior discussed in this book. Depending on definitions, its occurrence ranges from
the simplest to the most complex of animals. Its adaptiveness and causation are the subjects most often addressed, and these are reviewed for

fishes and terrestrial vertebrates in Chapter 10. Clearly, agonistic behavior is a solution to the problem of increasing individual fitness, achieved by the securing of necessary resources, either directly or indirectly. It has evolved repeatedly in the animal kingdom. As such, agonistic behavior should, we believe, be considered as a candidate for a principle of behavior. It is important to bear in mind, however, Rudolph Miller's cautionary statement (page 306), "In this, of all areas of behavioral study, we must be most cautious of overextending data or raising tentative hypotheses to the level of dogma." These words of caution should be voiced with respect to what we have written about principles of behavior in these concluding remarks. Nevertheless, it is an instructive exercise and seems productive in the achievement of a better understanding of the many fascinating contrasts in animal behavior.

SYSTEMATIC INDEX

AUTHOR INDEX

SUBJECT INDEX